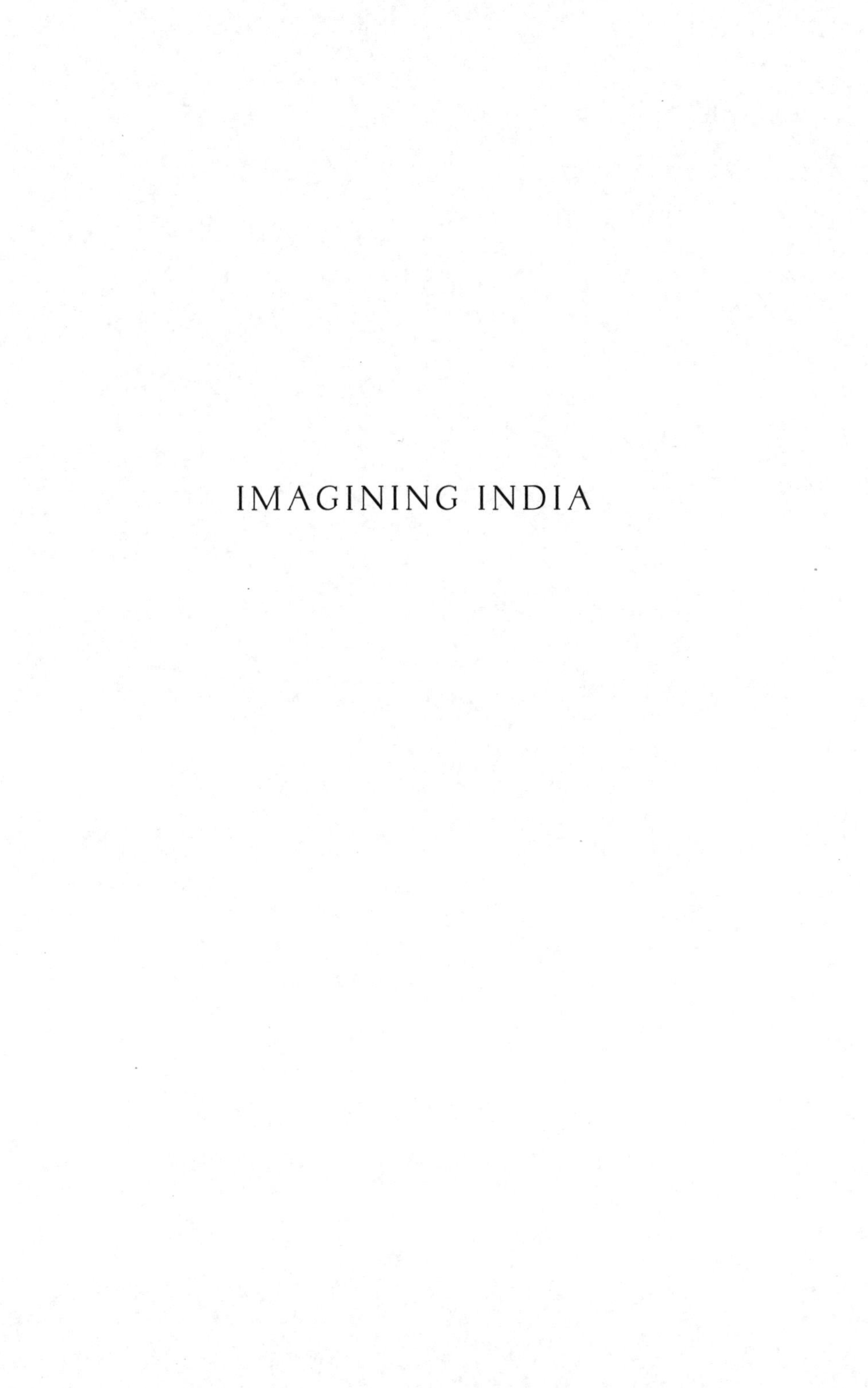

IMAGINING INDIA

IMAGINING INDIA

Ideas for the New Century

NANDAN NILEKANI

ALLEN LANE
an imprint of
PENGUIN BOOKS

ALLEN LANE

Published by the Penguin Group
Penguin Books Ltd, 80 Strand, London WC2R 0RL, England
Penguin Group (USA) Inc., 375 Hudson Street, New York, New York 10014, USA
Penguin Group (Canada), 90 Eglinton Avenue East, Suite 700, Toronto, Ontario, Canada M4P 2Y3
(a division of Pearson Penguin Canada Inc.)
Penguin Ireland, 25 St Stephen's Green, Dublin 2, Ireland (a division of Penguin Books Ltd)
Penguin Group (Australia), 250 Camberwell Road, Camberwell, Victoria 3124, Australia
(a division of Pearson Australia Group Pty Ltd)
Penguin Books India Pvt Ltd, 11 Community Centre, Panchsheel Park, New Delhi – 110 017, India
Penguin Group (NZ), 67 Apollo Drive, Rosedale, North Shore 0632, New Zealand
(a division of Pearson New Zealand Ltd)
Penguin Books (South Africa) (Pty) Ltd, 24 Sturdee Avenue, Rosebank, Johannesburg 2196, South Africa

Penguin Books Ltd, Registered Offices: 80 Strand, London WC2R 0RL, England

www.penguin.com

First published in the United States of America by the Penguin Press,
a member of Penguin Group (USA) Inc. 2009
First published in Great Britain by Allen Lane 2009
1

Printed in Great Britain by Clays Ltd, St Ives plc

A CIP catalogue record for this book is available from the British Library

978–1–846–14122–5

www.greenpenguin.co.uk

For

Nihar, Janhavi and Rohini,

who keep me grounded

CONTENTS

Part Three

FIGHTING WORDS

Part Four

CLOSER THAN THEY APPEAR

FOREWORD

EVERY TIME I go to India, people ask me about China. Every time I go to China, people ask me about India. Who's going to win between these two emerging giants?

I always give them the same answer: India and China are like two giant superhighways, and each has a big question mark hanging over its future. The Chinese superhighway is perfectly paved, with sidewalks everywhere and streetlights and white lines neatly down the middle of the road. There's just one problem. Off in the distance, there is a speed bump called "political reform." When 1.3 billion people going 80 miles an hour hit a speed bump, one of two things happens. One is that the car jumps into the air, slams down, and the drivers and passengers turn to each other and say, "You okay? You okay?" Everyone is okay, and so they drive on. The other thing that happens is that the car jumps up in the air, slams down, and all the wheels fall off. Which will it be with China? We don't know, but I am hoping for the best—the stability of the world depends upon it.

India is also a giant superhighway, only most of the road has potholes, some of the sidewalks haven't been finished, a lot of the streetlights are out, and there are no visible lane dividers. It's all a bit chaotic, yet the traffic always seems to move. But wait a minute. Off there in the distance it looks like the Indian road smoothes out into a perfect six-lane superhighway, with sidewalks, streetlights, and white lines. Is that perfect Indian superhighway a mirage or is that an oasis? Will India one day claim its future or will it always be chasing it, teasing us with its vast potential?

My teacher and friend Nandan Nilekani is bound and determined to make sure it is not a mirage. Like me, he remains an optimist, a sober optimist, but an optimist about his country's future. He knows that the shape of India's future, as the great environmentalist Dana Meadows once said about the future of our planet, "is a choice not a fate." And this book is a loud, engaging, noisy, spirited argument about how and why India and its friends need to go about making the right choices—and never resign themselves to fate.

I can think of no one better to make this argument. There are not a lot of executives around the world who are known simply by their first names. Silicon Valley has "Steve"—as in Jobs. Seattle has "Bill"—as in Gates. Omaha has "Warren"—as in Buffett. And Bangalore has "Nandan"—as in Nilekani.

Nandan helped to found Infosys Technologies Ltd., based in Bangalore—India's Silicon Valley. And Infosys, Wipro, and Tata Consultancy Services are the Microsoft, IBM, and Sun Microsystems of India. What makes Nandan unique? For me it comes down to one moniker: great explainer. Yes, he, the other cofounders, and N. R. Narayana Murthy, Infosys's legendary chairman, have built a great global company from scratch. But the reason Nandan is so sought out is that he has a unique ability not simply to program software but also to explain how that program fits into the emerging trends in computing, how those trends will transform the computing business, how that transformation will affect global politics and economics, and, ultimately, how it will all loop back and transform India. It was his insight that the global playing field was being "leveled" by technology that inspired me to write my own book *The World Is Flat.* And nowhere are his explanatory skills more on display than in this, his first book.

While this book is an enormously valuable explainer of where India has been and needs to go, it is much more than that. It is a prod to his fellow Indians, and India's American friends, to imagine and deliver on a different future by refusing to settle anymore for an Indian politics and governance that is so much less than the talents possessed and needed by the Indian people. Nandan knows what Indian entrepreneurs have accomplished without government or in the face of government obstruction and political dysfunction. He knows what sort of energy is exploding from India's youth bubble. And on every other page I can almost hear him saying: "If only our political system performed with the same energy and high aspirations. India would be unstoppable. *It would be unstoppable.* It would be that smooth six-lane superhighway." India, he rightly insists, despite its age and size, has barely scratched its potential.

In some ways Nandan's views are summed up in this one passage: "At the time of independence, India's leaders were clearly ahead of the people. The creation of a new, secular democracy with universal suffrage, anchored by the Indian Constitution, was a leap of faith the government took with an uncompromising, yet trusting country. Sixty years on, however, it seems that the roles have reversed. The people have gained more confidence and are reaching for the stars. India's leaders, however, seem timorous—our politics has become more tactical than visionary and, as Montek points out, what we now see among our politicians 'is a strong consensus for weak reforms.'"

Nandan repeatedly and usefully reminds us that India's economic revolution since 1990 has been a "people-driven transformation." It has actually been, in its own way, the biggest peaceful revolution in the last sixty years. It has never quite gotten its due because it happened peacefully and in slow motion—and the people did not topple a monarch or bring down a wall. But it did involve a society throwing off something huge—throwing off the shackles of a half-century of low aspirations and failed economic ideas imposed from above and replacing them with its own energy and boundless aspirations. And it wasn't just the famous software entrepreneurs like Nandan who were engaged. They started it. They showed what was possible. But they were soon followed by the farmers who demanded that schools teach their children more English and the mothers who saved for their kids to have that extra tutoring to get into a local technology college and by the call center kids, who worked the phones at night and hit the business school classrooms by day—sleeping God only knows when in between. It was the revolution of a post–Nehruvian youth bubble that refused to settle anymore for its assigned role or station in life. That is what makes this Indian people's revolution so powerful and that is what makes it, as Nandan tells us, "irreversible."

To be sure, this book does not ignore India's massive income inequalities and challenges in job creation. It simply says that to get there will "require the courage and optimism to embrace good ideas and not remain imprisoned by bad ones." It is all about execution. It is not enough, Nandan insists, to get the ideas right; they have to be adopted. And it is not enough to adopt them;

they have to be implemented correctly. And it is not enough to implement them correctly; they have to be constantly reviewed and adjusted over time as we see what works and what doesn't.

Nandan Nilekani's life and book are testament to the fact that the new India has truly arrived—in many ways and many places. Yes, the new India, he declares, is now present in the business community. It is now present on the college campuses. It is now present in many villages. It is now present in many schools. But will it achieve a critical mass—will it spread so far and wide, so up and down, that it will truly add up one day to that smooth, sleek superhighway? Or will that India always remain just off in the distance?

Nandan is optimistic but not naïve. He would tell you it all depends: It all depends on India having a government as aspiring as its people, politicians as optimistic as its youth, bureaucrats as innovative as its entrepreneurs, and state, local, and national leaders as impatient, creative, and energetic as their kids—and, in my view, as Nandan Nilekani.

Thomas L. Friedman
Washington, D.C.
November 2008

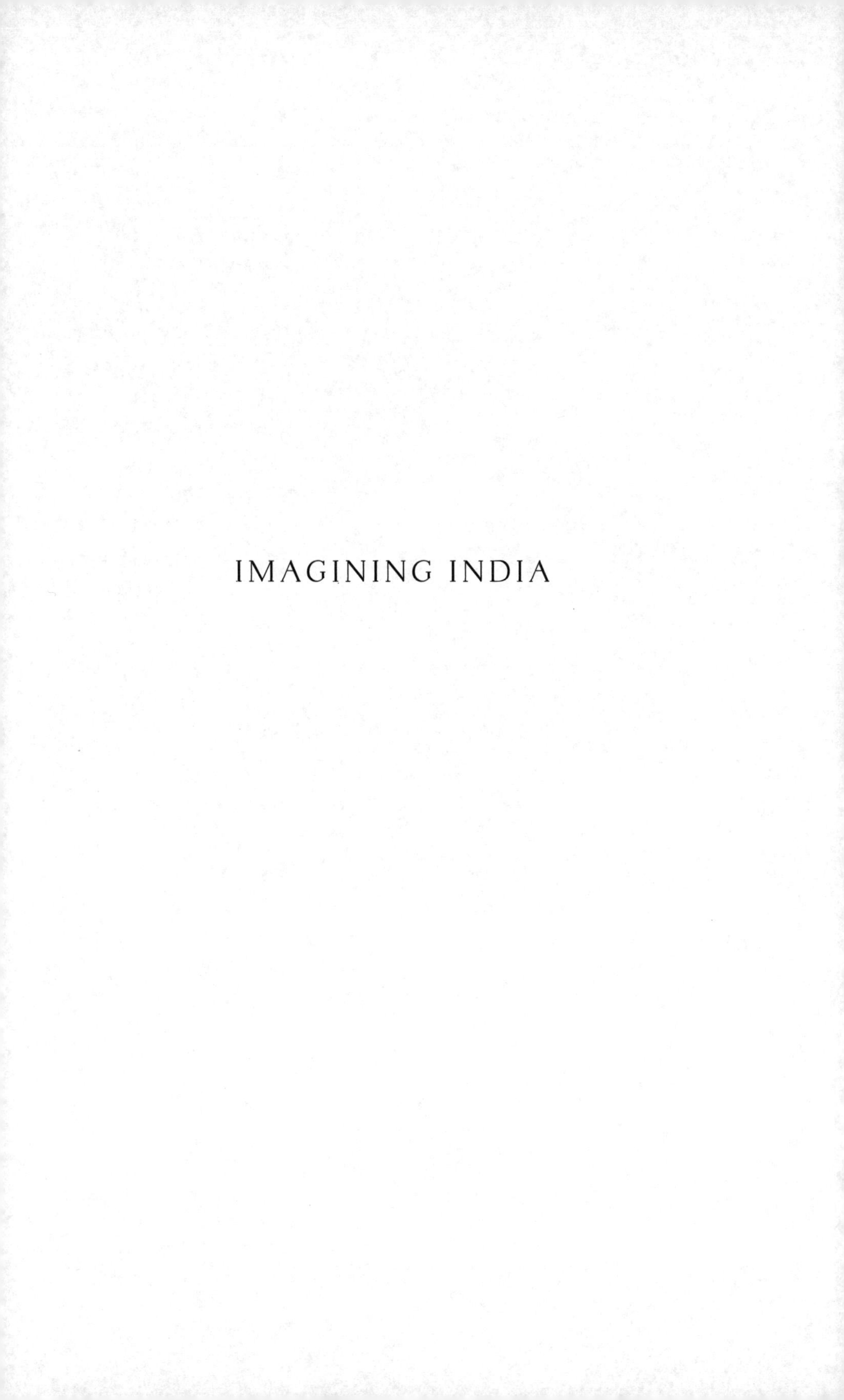

IMAGINING INDIA

NOTES FROM AN ACCIDENTAL ENTREPRENEUR

IF YOU CAN have such good roads in the Infosys campus, why are the roads outside so terrible?" demanded my visitor. I had just ended my pitch to him about why India was emerging as the world's next growth engine and how the country was rapidly catching up with the developed world. But my guest, who had flown in from New York, was openly skeptical, having spent two hours on Bangalore's chaotic, unforgiving Hosur highway to get to my office.

Although his question was one that I had heard several times, it always gave me pause. How could I respond without offering a long-winding explanation? I usually picked the short answer: "Politics," I mumbled. "Well," he persisted, "why don't people like *you* get into politics?" I told him this was not the United States, where a Michael Bloomberg could be the CEO of a large company one day and get elected as New York's mayor the next. Being an entrepreneur automatically made me a very long shot in Indian politics, and an easy target for populist rhetoric. I was, I said, quite unelectable.

But his questions got me thinking. The fact that the roads inside the Infosys campus were so good and so bad outside it was certainly not due to a lack of resources, technology or expertise. India has always seemed to be defined by such contradictions, to the point that our contrasts are clichés:

Asia's second-largest slum is here, in the world's fastest-growing democracy. A nation that is a burgeoning knowledge power also has the largest number of school dropouts in the world. Our biggest businesses are building international brands, yet red tape continues to throttle the new entrepreneur and frustrate the small business owner.

My years as an entrepreneur have especially brought home to me how much India, despite its recent tremendous growth, is straining against the challenges that hold it back. Today, we are a nation that has barely scratched its potential. Almost two decades after economic liberalization, the absence of critical reforms means that for a majority of Indians daily life continues to be a struggle—for the millions of marginal farmers unable to find alternatives to bare, hard livelihoods; for people living in slums for want of cheaper housing; for families cobbling together their savings to send their children to private schools because our government schools are a mess.

A big reason for our struggle lies in our inability to push through and implement critical ideas. Once in a while, at a committee consultation in Delhi or in a state-level advisory role, I have had the chance to have candid conversations with our ministers. Admittedly, an Indian politician for all his faults faces a complicated balancing act in our government, where the socialist ethos is still dominant. Being a legislator in this system means negotiating for money from both the central and the state governments; getting work out of an often reluctant bureaucracy; navigating an agenda through the various, often unconnected, state organizations; and of course meeting the demands of one's constituents and somehow retaining power through our unpredictable election cycles. These various pulls and pressures mean that when it comes to policy the urgent wins over the important, tactic triumphs over strategy and patronage over public good. The result is a certain cynicism, evident in what a prominent politician said to me when I buttonholed him with some policy ideas: "I don't see much upside in talking to you—you're neither good for notes [money] nor votes."

During such conversations I have felt very far away from India's new optimism and its bustling markets. It is not easy to find common ground—between governments, entrepreneurs, the middle class and the poor—when people's priorities and incentives are set so wide apart. In fact our ideas for the Indian economy have in recent years become more ghettoized than ever.

A different view

I have been fortunate to have had a unique perch from where to witness these divisions. I am of course an outsider in India's politics, but the label also applies to me when it comes to Indian business. Having cofounded and worked in Infosys for twenty-six years, I can call myself an Indian entrepreneur. But as an information technology (IT) company, Infosys always faced challenges different from the rest of the Indian industry. Shortages in infrastructure did not affect us, as our markets were international, and all we needed to do business was a wire and some computers. We experienced little of the labor problems and strikes that plagued India's traditional industries. Since the government did not recognize us as a "conventional" business for a long time, their regulations did not hamper us, and we worked outside the controls that stifled companies in manufacturing and agriculture. We did not need the raw material—iron or coal, for instance—that required Indian firms to interface with the state-run companies that controlled these resources. And we did not have to build relationships with bureaucrats or make periodic visits to Delhi, so we were not drawn into the charmed circle of Indian companies whose relationships with governments both benefited and constrained them.

Culturally as well, we stuck out. We were seven skinny (alas, no longer!) engineers, first-generation entrepreneurs who were untested in business. This was quite an anomaly at a time when family-owned firms dominated Indian industry. These were companies whose owners wielded tremendous operational and financial control, and while some of them remained competent despite the perverse incentives that came from such power, quite a few were run haphazardly and rarely made profits for the small shareholder. Their operations were often opaque and misleading—for instance, they would report inflated prices while purchasing raw material or importing capital goods, and underreport sales. A common joke in those days was that the owners of these companies had returns that were "RBI"—"returns before investment." Industry observers would note wryly, "These firms are going bankrupt, but their owners are not."

Infosys was among the first companies to change this perception of Indian business through an ethos of transparency and strong internal governance. We quickly built a reputation for creating widespread shareholder wealth. People began to call us India's "new economy" company. Fifteen years later, they still call us that.

Infosys came with none of Indian industry's typical history, family ties and regulatory baggage. Consequently I have been more of an observer than a participant in the trials of Indian industry. I am hopeful enough to believe that this combination of proximity and objectivity gives me a rare and valuable perspective. And although I have spent my entire career in the private sector, I have been lucky in the chances I have had to foray into public policy, both at the state and the national level, and to directly experience the challenges in the government since the reforms of the early 1990s.

But while I have been privy to many interesting conversations and views on India, writing a book on the country required a leap of a different order. I have never considered myself a writer, and there was no long-hibernating desire within me to pen down something in the hope that a book would eventually emerge. However, one reason to write this book came to me when I met Vijay Kelkar early in 2006. Dr. Kelkar is one of India's most respected economists and a passionate reformer. I have been a long-time admirer of his, especially after I saw a remarkable presentation he gave in 2002, titled "India: On the Growth Turnpike," which predicted—with what would turn out to be unusual accuracy—India's growth trends over the next few years. Dr. Kelkar looks very much the serious academician, but he has a wicked sense of humor and a reputation for straight talk, which has sometimes created a few problems in his interactions with the government. "What I discovered, however," he told me, "is that just putting my ideas out there—regardless of how unwelcome they were to our legislators at the time—mattered. Doing this seeds new ideas among people, and sometimes they catch on. This kind of legacy is, I think, the most enduring one you can have."

Dr. Kelkar's remark got me thinking. Perhaps I could write a worthwhile book if I could distill my experiences—and those of the policy makers, entrepreneurs, academicians, social activists and politicians I knew—into ideas that not only explained the peculiar animal that the Indian economy was shaping up to be, but also helped chart a way forward for the country (even if this meant courting controversy).

As both an entrepreneur and a citizen, I have been heartened by our economic progress in the last twenty-five years. India's annual growth of more than 6 percent since the early 1990s is surpassed in history by only one other country, China. And we have made incredible strides in other areas—

in the rise of our domestic market, our average incomes and a powerful middle class. But our successes are bittersweet. The immense challenges India faces more than two decades after reform trigger a range of emotions in me, as they do among many of my fellow citizens—puzzlement and frustration at the modest pace at which we are bringing about change, and sadness at the persistent inequity that is visible across India. There is a growing sense that these problems are now coming to a head—that our inequalities are making people angry and also limiting our ability to take advantage of the huge opportunities India has today.

The fact that India has a great opportunity before it seems more apparent when I travel—in people's minds across the world, India has unique promise. The country has enormous advantages in its young population and its entrepreneurs, a growing IT capability, an English-speaking workforce and strength as a democracy. It seems poised to grow into a strong economic power.

But what optimism I encounter about India is more often among people far from our shores—these are opinions shaped by our economic numbers, distant from and untouched by the tumult of our domestic politics and debates. At home, this opportunity feels much more fragile. Here, it is clear that there are many things holding us back—our pessimism around what we have accomplished so far, and a resistance to the ideas we need to implement in order to solve our remaining challenges.

India's weaknesses are all within, in the ongoing struggle to define the direction of our future ideas and policies for the country. This book is my small attempt to make sense of this struggle and the possible ways we can resolve it.

Beyond business

When I told people that I was working on a book, they assumed it was a memoir of my business career, or my take on management strategy. They looked quizzical (and were probably alarmed) when I said that I was writing a book on India. Businessmen, after all, do not usually make good public intellectuals. I console myself that I am but an accidental entrepreneur, who if he had not walked into the office of the charismatic N. R. Narayana Murthy in late 1978 in search of a job would probably have at best languished in a regular nine-to-fiver while living in a New Jersey suburb, taking the daily train to Manhattan.

The way I see it, the fact that I am not a specialist of any particular stripe, whether in history, sociology, economics or politics, may actually give me a broader viewpoint on our most significant issues. At a time when our arguments are so polarized, what we need might indeed be an avid amateur, and someone who can avoid the extreme ends of the debate.

While this is a book on India, this is not a book for people fascinated with Indian cinema and cricket—I would not be able to add very much to either topic, colorful as they are. Instead, I have attempted to understand India through the evolution of its ideas. I think that no matter how complicated, every country is governed through some overarching themes and ideas—an intricate web of shared, core beliefs among a country's people is, after all, what unites them. The ideals of French nationalism, for instance, the notion of the United States as the land of opportunity and the emphasis on "harmony" in Singapore were all dominant ideas that shaped the economic and social policies of these countries.

India in particular, for all its complexity, is a country that is as much an idea as it is a nation. The years of colonialism have meant that India has not evolved through a natural arc; disparate regions were brought together by the ideas, good and bad, of British administrators and Indian leaders. My first glimmer of the power of these ideas came when I was five years old. I understand this in hindsight, of course. One day my father bundled all of us into his Austin motorcar and drove us to a rally. It was 1960, the Congress session was being held in Bangalore, and we were there to see the charismatic Jawaharlal Nehru. As a towering leader of our independence struggle and the country's first prime minister, his stature both within the country and outside was immense—to a whole generation, he was synonymous with India. My memory of standing on the sidelines, caught up in the large crowd and waving at this thin, intense man is an unforgettable one.

Growing up in those days, it was very easy to believe in the idea of a nurturing government and public sector. A paternal, socialist state would own companies that would create wealth and the wealth would be used for the betterment of society. Why allow wealth to be created in private hands where it would probably be used for nefarious purposes? It all made perfect sense. The logic of it, especially coming from the benevolent patriarch Nehru, appeared unimpeachable. My father, an ardent Nehruvian, would constantly rail against the evils of big business, and how the Indian approach was the ideal approach. Many Indians believed in these ideas then; few of us believe them now.

The structure of my book is based on this ebb and flow of ideas, and how this has shaped the changes in our economy and politics. For example, through the early days of independent India, many saw English as a language of the imperialists and did everything possible to marginalize the tongue. This included attempts to make Hindi the sole national language, and restricting or banning outright the teaching of English in state schools. But once outsourcing made English the entry ticket to a global economy and higher incomes, the language rapidly became a popular aspiration, a ladder to upward mobility for both the middle class and India's poor. As a result state governments across the country are now reversing historically anti-English policies, even in places where Hindi-language nationalism was trenchant. Such is the power of changing ideas.

I have divided the book into four parts, depending on where we stand on a variety of ideas. Part One discusses issues where our attitudes have changed radically over the years, and I believe it is the shifts here that are at the heart of India's dynamism today. For instance, many of us now see India's huge population—once regarded as a drag on growth—as potential for "human capital" and a tremendous asset. Apart from our new, widespread acceptance of the Indian entrepreneur, we also hold a more sanguine view on globalization than we used to. In the postreform years, we saw plenty of protests against multinationals in India; Coca-Cola put up billboards announcing "We're back!" on which activists wrote, "Till we throw you out again"; KFC faced visits from local inspectors suspicious of their chicken and Hindu activists protested in front of McDonald's in Bombay, evoking pre–Independence era slogans with their demand that the restaurant "Quit India." Now, however, the entry of new international companies into India goes unremarked—and Indians take particular pride in domestic firms acquiring companies abroad.

The second part of the book examines those issues that are still in the ether: they are now widely accepted but have yet to see results on the ground. For instance, the idea of full literacy has gained popular appeal over the last two decades, but we are still framing strategies to implement universal education and address the discontent around the state of our schools.

Similarly, the India of our imagination has for long been a country that "lives in its villages." Our early governments went so far as to assert that rural–urban migration was an evil trend that had to be controlled and even reversed. Now, after decades of hostility toward urbanization, we are coming to terms with the fact that cities are both inevitable and necessary for our economic health. We have also accepted that we need to overhaul our woeful infrastructure, and do it fast. And we are finally beginning to abandon a system that created a hodgepodge of regulations restricting interstate trade—there is now widespread consensus that our laws have to be less provincial and must aim to create a common domestic market.

Part Three of the book deals with our biggest arguments. These are the issues where partisanship has peaked and where the lack of any consensus has stonewalled progress on urgent policies. For example, there is a furious ongoing debate around higher education, in terms of how we regulate our colleges and what the role of the state should be vis-à-vis private universities. Labor is another breathing-fire debate, and even as there is an unprecedented demand for workers as every aspect of the Indian economy goes into overdrive, the government remains deeply polarized on the need to ease up our labor regulations. These issues have created a charged battleground—the divide here is a chasm between people who see reforms as empowering and those who see them as exclusionary.

The last part of the book goes into our forgotten nooks of policy, taking up those ideas that have been largely missing from our public discourse, even though they are growing critical to our future. This final set of ideas presents us with a challenge we are not as adept at meeting as we once used to be. Before the eighteenth century, our region was a dominant player in the world economy: at their peak, India and China together accounted for close to 50 percent of world GDP. Ideas from the subcontinent helped shape the culture, law, philosophy and science of the time. However, postcolonial India has tended to follow the example of the countries that preceded it in development. We imported many of our existing structures—our parliamentary system and constitutional model, above all—from the British, and our early socialist ideas from Europe and the Soviet Union. Even our reforms, while courageously carried out, have followed economic templates that have proved successful across the world, and our corporations have modeled themselves on global best practices and standards.

But India's rapid economic growth is demanding much more innovative ideas from us as existing solutions for issues like health, energy and the environment have proved ineffective around the world. India cannot, for instance, have an energy policy that is based entirely on the heavy use of hydrocarbons. We should worry about the environment right now, rather than try like other developed countries to salvage it after industrialization has ripped through our natural resources. We also have to put in place a sustainable, realistic social security system and ensure that our public health challenges do not swing, as they have in the developed world, from one end of the health spectrum—starvation—to the other—excess. And finally, we must incorporate modern technology and innovation more fully into the economy.

The challenge we have faced across our ideas is in uniting our people and policy makers toward urgent and necessary solutions. Our coalition governments at the center often give themselves labels that reiterate unity and a common purpose—the United Front, the United Progressive Alliance (UPA), the National Democratic Alliance (NDA). But in reality they represent fiercely sparring ideals and reflect an India that is intensely fractured, its divisions sharply defined not so much by ideology as by religion, caste, class and region.

But the reason I am optimistic is that we have achieved consensus before. Through our history, our divisions and debates have been in constant flux, as the ideas that define and animate us as a people changed and evolved.

What Nehru remembered, and all that he forgot

In India, people live among looming reminders of the past. We find ancient temples, most of them still in use, in the heart of our cities, with hawkers selling glossy prints and sandalwood replicas of gods and goddesses outside their steps; Mughal-era palaces and tombs stand in the middle of busy, crowded localities; and we are all deeply familiar with our rituals and ancient epics like the *Mahabharata,* which is nine times longer than the *Iliad,* and far better remembered. Yet the writer Ved Mehta wrote that in India we have propped up our country "with a dead history."[1]

The problem was that the curve of India's history and its ideas had been an extremely discontinuous one—a foreign occupation had long divorced the region from its pre-British ideas and economic and social structures. It is true that many of those ideas were horribly primitive and ones that we can be glad to be rid of—sati, child marriage and a highly repressive caste system were only the more egregious sins of a very feudal people. Our medieval past was, as Rabindranath Tagore once said, "a place from which we were glad to be rescued." But British rule also created a deep disconnect among educated Indians from the best of India's early literature, philosophy, history and identity.[2]

What we saw in its place instead was a strange grafting of the Indian identity with an entirely new culture. The British brought with them the English language and Western education, and with such education came the ideas of modern nationalism, self-determination and democracy. However, these ideas only reached a small elite—the British consensus was that, on the whole, Indians and their customs were best left alone.* The large majority of Indians were left unmoored, disconnected from both their foreign government and their English-educated Indian leaders, and untouched by the rise of the modern economy and liberal ideas around the world. Colonial India as a result stagnated in terms of income growth, urbanization and education. In fact the British often collaborated with India's traditional elites and the lumpen aristocracy, deliberately strengthening feudal systems. For instance, they protected landlords from land transfers to an emerging urban capitalist class, and encouraged the martial, patriarchal systems of the Jats, Bhumihars, Rajputs and Sikhs since these "warrior castes" were a significant source of manpower for the British army.[3]

This divide gave rise to a strange, two-tiered cultural hierarchy in India, with such a vast space in between that the Indian identity seemed a split personality. Many of the elite, upper-middle-class Indians who were educated in British schools embraced the Renaissance ideas of democracy, self-determination and nationalism, and several among them became leaders of the national freedom movement. On the other side of the chasm was India's vast majority, defined by the subcontinent's common culture, dominated by the iron rules of caste, religion and social custom.

There was little in common in ideas across this divide, and India's reformers stood at one bank and stared across, appalled at what they saw. The

*This attitude caught on after the 1857 army rebellions. The insecurity among the British following the revolt meant that they barricaded themselves from the natives and lost interest in their role as reformers. Christopher Hitchens has suggested that this distancing grew even stronger once British officers moved into India with their families. The presence of their wives and children in an alien land made many of these officers nervous, and they drew further inward into their cantonments and English-only clubs.

reformer Bipin Chandra Pal wrote, "We loved the abstraction we called India but . . . hated the thing it actually was."

No one exemplified the divide between India's leaders and the rest of the country more strongly than Jawaharlal Nehru. Understanding him is, I think, key to understanding the role ideas have had in shaping and uniting the country. In retrospect, Nehru was an odd man to have prevailed in shaping the Indian identity. He had described himself as "the last Englishman to rule India"—he had grown up under the eye of a Westernized father, a successful lawyer and a late convert to the cause of India's independence from the British. Motilal Nehru insisted on knives and forks at the dining table, spoke in English at home (although his wife did not know the language) and employed British tutors for his children. Nehru was sent to England when he was a teenager, to study in Harrow, then Cambridge and the Inns of Court.

Nehru was thus very much a child of the Western Enlightenment. Even while he admired Gandhi's mass appeal and determination—he called him "as clear-cut as a diamond"—he also disagreed with his more traditional beliefs, once writing, "Ideologically, he [is] sometimes amazingly backward." He was not religious in the least and responded to questions about his faith with a shrug and a quote from Voltaire: "If God did not exist, it would be necessary to invent him." And he was wary of the political pulls in India, especially after he became the country's first prime minister. While his allegiances to India were clear, he was uncomfortable with its deeply rooted social, regional and caste divisions. The distance between Nehru's personal beliefs and what he experienced in the heart of India was sometimes stark: during a visit to Uttar Pradesh, the local Congress leader Kalka Prasad introduced Nehru as the "new king," and the peasants gathered echoed, "The king, the king has arrived," to Nehru's great astonishment and anger.

But Nehru eventually proved to be the only statesman who could navigate India's intense divides and unite the country under a core political and economic idea. Ironically, this may have been precisely because of his distance from the country, rather than in spite of it. His greatest strength was that even as the rest of India doubted its own capacity as a nation, Nehru never did. These romantic notions of his were backed up by an iron will and a remarkable ability to bridge disagreements. There was also the great gift of his charisma: he could talk persuasively and build towering visions. He helped construct a national consciousness—by giving people the universal right to vote and a secular government—during the most tempestuous years after independence. When India's divisions—religious and regional—did assert themselves despite his leadership and Gandhi's influence, they took him by surprise. The brutality and violence of Partition, which left more than a million people dead, was especially devastating for him.

Nehru had other early advantages in pushing through ideas of secularism and rationality in a country so deeply divided. The independence movement had helped shunt aside all other loyalties in favor of a singular national identity. This early unity helped the champions of secular government to drown out other, more divisive voices—the ideologies of Hindu chauvinists, whose idea of pluralism was that India would be "a country of Hindus, Hindu Muslims, Hindu Christians and Hindu Sikhs"; and Muslim leaders who demanded to be the sole representatives of the country's Muslim population.

But even as Nehru and his colleagues in government managed to quiet India's fissiparous tendencies for a while, they also did not address them head on. There was no attempt to bridge the distances between the many countries within the country.* The government instead ignored the vast space that existed between the educated leaders who put in place India's Constitution and the masses, most of whom could not read the Constitution and who, even if they could, would have failed to understand its appeal. The policies that would have narrowed this distance and made the theories of secularism and liberty popular—such as a mass education system and urbanization—were ones that the state failed to implement. And the government's hostility to business meant that entrepreneurship, so critical in strengthening the foundation of a modern civil society, was constrained.

The lack of a large middle class in India only deepened this division. There was some movement in the 1970s toward the creation of an Indian bourgeoisie when the high noon of the public sector and bank nationalization by Indira Gandhi created a sizable middle class comprising government and public sector employees. But this was still a tiny percentage of the country's population. The great gap between the old India and the India of the

*In fact, the government, having made a united India a priority above all else, suppressed any dissension that threatened this ideal—a costly move in the long term. This happened with Jammu and Kashmir—when the state's highly popular chief minister (and Nehru's friend) Sheikh Abdullah shifted from his early, pro-India stance toward the idea of a "free Kashmir," the Indian government put him in jail and replaced him with more sympathetic ministers. He stayed in prison for eleven years, much to the anger and disillusionment of the Kashmiris.

leaders and the elite remained, and we are still caught between the different tempers of these two nations—between "the feudal and the secular, the rational and the traditional."[4] India in the first twenty or twenty-five years after independence was united mainly by residual popular feelings for the independence movement and the Congress party that had led it. Later, the wars with Pakistan and China did bring Indians together for brief periods—during these times, people turned up at railway stations to cheer army *jawans* on their way to do battle, and playback singers traveled to border posts to sing of the motherland and the valor of her sons. Nevertheless, it was a tenuous unity.

The first fissures

V. S. Naipaul once said, "The politics of a country can only be an extension of its human relationships." As the years progressed and the Congress party's hold on India's voters started to unravel, Indian politics began to mirror back to us the many challenges of our social and cultural relationships.

Salman Rushdie has called India "carnivalesque" in its differences—intricate divisions set communities apart in terms of caste, region and religion. These parts of the Indian identity are embedded even in Indian names—Indian surnames indicate the region you are from and the caste you belong to. In some parts of the country, surnames are so elaborate as to include the title of the family home as well. And as our unity narrative fractured, these divides in the Indian identity asserted themselves in our politics—new caste and regional parties mushroomed, and a rapid fragmentation of voters began along our familiar fault lines.

When Nehru's daughter, Indira Gandhi, became prime minister, she held to the belief that she could command just the sort of unity that Nehru had. She was almost smug in her assumption of how the people regarded her, apparently telling the author and journalist Bruce Chatwin, "You have no idea how tiring it is to be a goddess."* But instead, Indira ended up presiding over the rise of new regional political parties and surging dissent across the country. She tried to stem the tide by first resorting to populism—bank

---

*It is only fair to reproduce her remark in full. As she sat on a balcony, with more than 250,000 people showing up "to pay their respects" to her, what she told Chatwin was, "Do get me some more of those cashew nuts. You have no idea how tiring it is to be a goddess."

nationalization is only one example—and then, for a disastrous period of eighteen months, she tried dictatorship, imposing a state of emergency in the country. When she lifted the Emergency and allowed elections, she and her party were routed. Voted back into office in 1980, she was never as much in control as in her early years as prime minister. Insurgencies flared up across the country, the most serious in Punjab, and she was assassinated by her Sikh bodyguards in 1984.

Her son Rajiv Gandhi, who came to power "to help Mummy out,"[5] also took a shot at bringing the country together. His route was to create a common cultural platform through televising Hindu epics on state-owned television and searching out Congress candidates who could unite, such as popular movie stars Amitabh Bachchan and Sunil Dutt. But none of this achieved the kind of political cohesion India had seen immediately after independence, which had enabled our leaders to implement the ideas of a planned economy, democracy and secularism.

India's fragmentation has grown only more complicated with economic reforms. The new policies transferred economic power from the center to the states, giving more strength to regional parties. Since then, we have seen our divisions come into high relief. In the 1990s, the right-wing Bharatiya Janata Party (BJP) formed strategic alliances with smaller, state-based political parties and rode to power with Hindu-nationalist rhetoric that was openly hostile to the Muslim and Christian minorities. The governments that the Congress and the BJP have led at the center since have been coalitions propped up by regional parties.

The leaders of these smaller parties have a very different political and social vision from that of India's founders and align themselves to the interests of not just the state they represent but also of particular caste and religious communities within it. India's first leaders had wanted to put an end to "categorizing, separating, classifying, enumerating and granting of special concessions."[6] But with the rise of powerful community-based parties, such concessions have become central. For instance, in Uttar Pradesh, Mayawati's Bahujan Samaj Party (BSP) has brought specific benefits to voters from her caste, the state's oppressed Dalit communities, in government appointments and jobs. In Bihar, some complained that "the department heads and heads of electricity and water boards Laloo Prasad Yadav appointed were all Yadavs."[7]

India now experiences its biggest questions of identity every election day. Our politics is broadly organized along the lines of caste, religion, region and class. These form the basis of our loyalties and, often, of our development policies.

A cautious hope

It would be a mistake to be entirely fatalistic about India's multiple divides. Our divisions were overcome once, in the heady days after independence, and this may happen again. After all, the Kerala communist leader E.M.S. Namboodiripad once told the sociologist André Béteille that caste was irrelevant and was "an obsession of American sociologists who come to study India."

Some people might consider me a hopeless optimist here, but I think it is likely that we Indians are finally becoming more than what is defined by caste, religion, region and family, and are linking ourselves more closely with the notion of Indianness. I had recognized this faith in my father as he followed Nehru's career and his soaring, unifying rhetoric with hope and a deep sense of possibility. I had to discard my father's beliefs in Nehruvian socialism when I began working at Infosys, but his optimism for India's politics has persisted in me.

It is true that this vision of an Indian identity—one that moves beyond feudal ideas—seems very distant at times. Only as recently as 1998, Laloo Yadav was successful in convincing many of his voters in Bihar that one of his candidates, Shakuni Chaudhry, was a reincarnation of Kush—the son of Lord Vishnu. We have watched our politics degenerate constantly into appalling spectacle—with the throwing of punches in parliament as our politicians duke it out over the narrow interests of religion, region or caste, and as jobs and college seats are parceled out on the basis of caste identities. But there have been some changes in recent years that give me hope. The rising number of entrepreneurs among the backward castes, demands for English-language education and the mushrooming of private schools even in villages, the surge in civil activism through NGOs and legislation such as the Right to Information Act—these are all signs of positive change, even if slow and tentative.

As economic development and income mobility erode the day-to-day authority of the caste system, it is possible that this identity will no longer be the sole reason for voters to elect our leaders. In recent elections, people have been voting out populist politicians who fail to deliver results, regardless of their caste. This is true even in the most feudal states, Bihar and Uttar Pradesh. In Bihar, Laloo Yadav's rule of fifteen years ended in 2005 with his party finishing in third place. In Uttar Pradesh, Mayawati engineered an improbable coalition of Dalits and Brahmins to win the state in 2007 and since then has emphasized (as rhetoric, at least) a mantra of *sarvajan samaj*—a party for all people.

Over the last two decades, the dissatisfactions of voters have also become more pronounced, as they have systemically voted out governments at the state level and also at the center. India's voters are clearly shifting back and forth between the available options in search of someone who will offer them an alternative to economic and social neglect, someone who can provide real opportunities—economic choices and a chance to better their lives. I believe it is the force of new ideas that is catalyzing this shift.

I call the divides we have faced in caste, religion and region the "vertical" issues in Indian society. These issues do dominate our electoral space, but there is a chance today that they will become much less central. And the reason for this is that over time a set of "horizontal themes"—ideas related to development, education, health, employment and other issues—has been gaining momentum. Outlining these vertical and horizontal themes is a useful way of looking at our future. It allows us a perspective on our elections beyond the immediacy of which caste and political combination is likely to win in the next polls, and to take a bird's-eye view of our political concerns. What this view tells us is that certain ideas often overwhelm our divides, they become widespread demands among the electorate and they can sway the outcome of an election.

At first glance such a notion seems optimistic, especially if we look at our most dysfunctional states—Bihar, Uttar Pradesh and Rajasthan. The political scientist Kanchan Chandra has made a fascinating study of how caste allegiances during elections in these states have made even the most basic public goods tradable for votes. This means that the day-to-day security of a particular caste of voters and their access to identity certificates and ration cards for subsidized food and essential commodities depend on their chosen party winning at the polls. "Voters here need their own caste group in power if they want access to the most minimum of services," Kanchan tells me. Else the government is indifferent to them at best and antagonistic at worst. Voters, especially the poorest ones, see their votes in these states as a trade for safeguarding their basic rights.

In slightly more developed states such as Andhra Pradesh—and this is now the most prevalent dynamic across India—basic public services and protections are widely available. Here, the aim of caste- and religion-based combinations in the government is to ensure specific benefits for their own group and community. These are usually in the form of reserved jobs or reserved seats in colleges or the state legislature.

A third scenario, however, can serve as a kind of gradual tipping point. A few Indian states—such as Maharashtra, Karnataka and Tamil Nadu—are economically fairly advanced, and citizens do not have to resort to caste-based bargaining for public services. Elections here may still be fought along caste lines, but the primary aspirations of the people are more broad based—such as in their demands for better infrastructure and more effective schools. This is becoming especially evident with the rise of the swing voters, who vote more on material development issues than along caste lines. In Karnataka's state elections in 2008, these voters became the kingmakers by engineering a swing of more than 5 percent toward the BJP.

The undeniable fact is that in each of these three scenarios caste plays an important role in electoral choice. But based on the levels of governance and prosperity, the needs and demands of citizens in these states vary a great deal. In the real world, this means that in Bangalore, people across all castes may demand access to private education in English; in rural Bihar, however, the most widespread concern among voters may be access to land certificates. Caste barriers still exist, but certain common issues unite people nevertheless.

This is why I think that a "safety net" of ideas becomes critical in shifting our dialogues from feudal, chauvinist issues to secular ones. Once a core set of ideas and issues catches on across the population, it becomes difficult to limit party platforms solely to whipping up anger and resentment against the "other," the outsiders to one's caste, religion, region or class.

Such an idea-based approach could transform how we address our various challenges. Successive governments have often tended to view the problems across our education, health, industry and infrastructure policies in isolation from one another, where each problem is separately "an aching tooth that can be taken out."[8] Our top-down technocratic attitude here has meant, for instance, that even after we passed industry reforms, we allowed infrastructure to languish. So our recent industrial growth has badly strained our weak roads and failing ports and has created massive bottlenecks and crises.

Looking at our problems through the prism of ideas helps us see clearly how these intermingling, flawed policies limit our growth. This is especially true when it comes to our agricultural crisis—the most tragic failure of our isolated, aching-tooth approach. The deepening crisis in agriculture is partly due to the lack of labor-market flexibility, which has prevented the shift of farm workers into manufacturing and consequently kept productivity across our farms low and unemployment high. In part the crisis has also come from the lack of infrastructure, which has limited farmers' access to markets, even as a variety of regulations tie them down to local buyers and low profits. At the same time, our growing environmental problems have degraded the soil and diminished water resources, placing our farmers at the mercy of a fickle monsoon. The lack of an organized retail chain and supply network has also increased spoilage and losses for agri-produce. And the absence of any effective financial coverage for the bulk of our rural households has limited their ability to innovate, experiment and take meaningful risks.

Our approach to these problems has to be upgraded into a far more wide-ranging mix of new policy ideas. Only then will we be in a position to address the gritty, real-life concerns of our billion-plus citizens.

Cards on the table

My own position on the way forward is unequivocal. I believe that the most important driver for growth lies in expanding access to resources and opportunity. People everywhere, regardless of their income levels, should have access to health facilities, clean water, basic infrastructure, jobs and capital, a reliable social security system and good schools where their children can be educated in the English language.

While this kind of access seems obvious as a goal, most countries are not designed to provide it. This dawned on me fully only when I heard the Nobel Prize–winning economist-historian Douglass North speak on how economies limit such opportunities for citizens. I was in the audience at a conference board meeting in Ireland in June 2005 when Dr. North delivered his compelling speech. He spoke animatedly and with passion on the immense importance of promoting what he called "open access societies." "The limited access order is what we now see in most countries," Dr. North told me later. "It promotes policies that cut off easy entry into markets and institutions for everyone." These limitations include difficult access to capital that people need to start businesses and education systems where quality is directly linked to affordability. As a result we see existing elites consolidate their hold on power and wealth, and it becomes very difficult for people to break out of the income class they are born into.

Listening to him, I could relate his example of a closed access economy to the India of my childhood, where employment was scarce, businesses were difficult to start and capitalize, and the quality of education systems varied widely. My parents were never wealthy—but my father, a manager in a textile mill, was plum in the Indian middle class and prized education above all else. It was at his insistence that I attended a private English-medium school and was later fortunate enough to get admission into the Indian Institute of Technology (IIT) Bombay. This education, and the ability to speak English, helped me enter the software industry. But the majority of Indians lacked—as they still do—these chances. Most parents could only afford to send their children to state schools that had weak standards and taught only in the regional languages. This alone meant that in India if you were born poor it was very likely that you would remain poor for the rest of your life, and it was likely too that your children would not fare much better.

For an economy to shift into an open access we need competition and markets, because as Dr. North notes, this "ensures that neither political nor economic power is permanent or inherited, as people innovate and unleash their creativity." Such an environment also encourages social stability, as it creates a sense of fairness and a belief that everyone has a chance to change their income and status. From this perspective India is now, nearly twenty years after its economic reforms, still in the throes of becoming an open access order. A free democracy in 1947 laid the ground for political competition, but it took until the 1980s for Indian elections to become genuinely competitive. We have had some measure of economic freedom since 1991, but our social programs remain subsidy driven and weak. The low standards of our state-run schools and our weak infrastructure have especially hurt the poor in terms of access: those of us who can afford alternatives merely opt out, turning to private schools, private electricity and gated communities—or we emigrate, leaving behind rickety, nonfunctioning systems for the less fortunate to endure.

There is great resistance to an open access order, and it comes from both business and government. Interest groups and elites are leery about relinquishing power. There are good reasons why they prefer the status quo: labor reforms threaten not only businesses employing cheap contract labor but also protected trade unions. Better empowered parents and students in schools challenge the sway of teachers' unions and administrators. Greater economic and social rights for women threaten the relative bargaining power of male citizens and relatives.

Reforms that expand access are thus most crucial for the disempowered. They are critical in bringing income mobility to the weakest and poorest groups. And this mobility is at the heart of the successes of free markets: we tend to forget that a prerequisite to productivity and efficiency is a large pool of educated people, which requires in turn easy and widespread access to good schools and colleges. When more people get a shot at better jobs and good education, chances of innovation and "productivity leaps" for the economy only increase.

Consequently, when it comes to our development goals, I strongly believe that our greatest advances "come not in our discoveries, but in how we apply [them] to reduce inequality and create access."[9] Ignoring this is not just bad policy—it carries high political risks. Across countries, we have seen a populist backlash against markets when they have failed to address crises around access—such as in Europe during the 1920s and 1930s, and more recently in large parts of Latin America. Even the United States, a country that supposedly holds the values of the free market close to its heart, saw anticapitalist sentiment soar during the New Deal years with rising poverty and unemployment, when Franklin Roosevelt condemned businesses as "fascist" and seeking "the enslavement for the public." The United States is seeing a return to such rhetoric and anger against big business as income inequalities and unemployment rise across the country, and as lax regulation allows the financial sector to run amok. It shows how easily a country's economic mood can change—since the U.S. financial crisis reached a head in September 2008 and near $1 trillion of taxpayer money has been set aside to bail out failing banks, even the staunchest free-market believers are expressing hostility against Wall Street. American commentators have called the bailout "socialism for the rich," and as one angry taxpayer wrote, "I can either afford to bail out irresponsible lenders and borrowers . . . or I can buy myself a house. I don't think there is room in my budget for both."[10]

Governments ignore such challenges in fairness and equality at their peril, and if these discontents are left to fester, they trigger enormous backlash against open market policies.

In this context, I see the current forces of globalization as working largely in India's favor. Globalization is right now a pretty incendiary issue. For some it is a metaphor for free trade and an increasingly interdependent world. For others it is a sinister force that homogenizes cultures, adds to threats of hegemony, hurts global diversity as consumer trends expand across borders and destroys the earth's environment. But I think that all things considered, India's changing position in the world combined with current global factors means that India has far more to gain than lose by embracing globalization more fully. India has unique advantages at the moment—the biggest pool of English speakers in the world and ambitious young entrepreneurs who are experimenting with low-cost models of doing business. Our large domestic consumer markets, besides the opportunity they offer also provide some insulation from the ups and downs of global trade.

The politics of the present also favor India. In the 1950s India's interaction with the West, thanks to our barriers to international trade, was limited to realpolitik and complicated by the Cold War and the Non-Aligned Movement. Not surprisingly, the relationships with the West of Indian statesmen like Nehru and V. K. Krishna Menon, India's defense minister and ambassador to the UN, were fraught. They only grew more so as India began to depend on international aid from the International Monetary Fund (IMF) and the World Bank, and Indira Gandhi, even as she went socialist with a vengeance, had to turn to the United States time and again for food-aid supplies in the late 1960s. Today, however, Indian businesses are playing a powerful role in shaping India's image as they diversify internationally, establish partnerships and make acquisitions. Our political leaders too are playing a more prominent role at multilateral organizations and building relationships with the United States and Europe. As the world's fastest-growing democracy, we also have the potential to emerge both as a balancing power in an era of authoritarian regimes and as an Asian nation that is among the closest culturally to the West.

Development and information technology

I also believe that technology in general and information technology in particular has a huge role to play—not just in providing better public services, but also in enabling an open, inclusive and less corrupt society. When I first became involved in the public sphere, taking on the role of chairman of the Bangalore Agenda Task Force (BATF) to improve the city's governance systems, I consciously avoided pitching IT as a means of solving public problems. I was wary of being labeled a "computer boy" who saw every problem as something that could be solved by writing a piece of code. After all, what do computers and software have to do with clearing garbage or providing safe drinking water? But after a decade of work on public issues, I am convinced that the strategic use of IT is key to addressing a wide range of challenges. In fact I do not see how things can be improved in the public sector without a massive dose of IT.

During those chaotic years at BATF when I attempted to juggle two very different goals—of being at Infosys during the week and working with the task force over the weekend—I saw at close quarters the differences between the private and public sectors. The most significant differences are in efficiency, accountability and initiative. In the private sector, productivity is paramount, and enterprise and intelligent risk-taking are encouraged. Investment and policy decisions are made and closely monitored by a team of people who have similar values and the same goals. In the public space, given the differences between and within the various departments, unpredictability about whom one will report to and the absence of tangible personal reward, there is a deep culture of risk aversion. The bureaucrats I encountered had learned that protecting their turf and not rocking the boat were key to thriving in government. I have seen enough enterprising bureaucrats in Karnataka who, when they tried to implement bold reforms in areas such as infrastructure or government transparency, found themselves transferred overnight to minor departments as punishment.

Even when benign and well-meaning, the public service culture prizes process and precedent over progress and results. As a result new projects fail to keep up with broader changes in technology and business innovation. The public sector also faces insurmountable challenges in the huge scale of the projects it has to manage.

Perhaps the most important difference to me was in how the public and private sectors looked at their goals. In the private sector, the focus is on efficiency and effectiveness—the aim, thanks to competition, is to increase revenues and profits by doing things faster, better and cheaper, and by meeting client needs. In the public space, on the other hand, it is equity that rules.

This is apparent across government policies—reservations in education, jobs and electoral seats is just one example.

What IT can do is bring all three—equity, efficiency and effectiveness—into the public sector. I call this the 3E effect. New IT infrastructure can bypass inefficient public systems and, by bringing in improved measurement of government objectives and outcomes, it can also enable greater effectiveness. And by improving allocation of resources as well as the transparency of such processes, the goal of equity, too, is achievable.

Information technology is also a key mechanism for addressing the knowledge asymmetry between the government and the governed. If the citizen has access to information about how decisions are made in government, how money is spent and to what end and who the beneficiaries are, it stands to reason that the quality of public decisions will improve considerably. Of course, IT cannot achieve this all by itself. But combined with laws that give people more access, such technology can bring dramatic changes into governance.

People power

Above all, it is democracy that is crucial for sustained development. Many people I meet complain about India's slow growth under democracy and suggest that a strong, authoritarian leader—who can be decisive when it comes to policy—would be more effective. Their angst is intensified by the quality of our public debate, the dismal record of some of our elected representatives and the corruption that seems to be ubiquitous.

It is true that India is a young democracy, saddled with the problems of inexperience, and that it has endured ineffective, populist governments. But the flag-carriers for authoritarian rule should remember that such power is always more dangerous than it is worth. An authoritarian system is always susceptible to tyranny and abuse—it is as likely to produce a Robert Mugabe as a Deng Xiaoping. It also creates errors that cannot be easily corrected, as we have seen in China's response to environmental issues and population growth. The democratic system, despite its flaws, is its own cure—in its guarantee of liberty for all people, irrespective of background and wealth, it offers the real drivers of change that can help overcome entrenched interests, inequalities and centuries-old divisions.

India's biggest weaknesses in fact may have come from too little democracy, rather than too much of it. Through our early decades, Congress-led governments, politically dominant and faced with little real opposition, could stick with pet policies long after they had proved ineffective. Theirs was an ideologically driven, top-down approach, largely undisturbed by the demands and reactions of its citizens. This only began to change as people started to speak out vociferously in the early 1970s, elect their own leaders and put up their own political parties in protest—pushback that came from the farmers, the Dalits and a growing middle class. India's reform process may have had the 1991 economic crisis as its immediate trigger, but more broadly it was also the result of the government trying to placate the anger of an electorate tired of crises, low growth and high unemployment.

Over the last two decades, such democratic forces have only grown stronger, as once marginal caste and regional groups have gained power in our political system and as a surging middle class has become more demanding and assertive. Indians are no longer waiting for the state to provide imperfect solutions. Instead, faced with stifling labor regulations, people have moved into a vast, unorganized labor market. Faced with high unemployment, they have set up their own small businesses and shops. They have responded to a broken-down public education system by sending their children to both legal and illegal private schools. People across India are taking charge, whether that means citizen organizations such as Apna Desh cleaning up garbage that the municipal bodies have neglected to collect, or villages and cities across India demanding more local representation and power, or people pushing for government transparency through the Right to Information Act. This can only be good for reforms, as policies that fail to work are quickly discarded, and governments are forced to frame agendas that will keep them popular with voters who have made growth and rising incomes a condition for granting political power.

The time is now

For a long period after independence, India's dream seemed to flicker. Our growth stagnated, and with Nehru's death the country's social divisions rapidly worsened; we seemed caught forever in the turmoil of spreading unrest and riots. It was a period when one commentator remarked fatalistically: "You always have floods . . . food is always a little short, and someone is always striking. India is a sleepy country, and things just go on."[11]

In the last quarter century, however, India has begun to move away from the roiling distress of those years. The early trigger for this change has been the growth of India's IT sector. This was among the first industries to see rapid growth following reforms—in this sense, the industry has been the flagship of India's new economy, instrumental in driving the growth of the 1990s and bringing India to the attention of the world. Most importantly, perhaps, the industry unlocked the aspirations of countless Indians as never before through the possibilities it offered for jobs and upward mobility.

This sense of possibility and the rising aspirations—that began with the IT sector and that have now intensified as India's growth has become broad based—are the new unifying themes across the country. These twin themes will largely determine where our politics and policies will be headed. We can see this aspiration across class and caste—in the slum schools that call themselves "Cambridge" and "Oxford"; in the surging growth of India's cities as people pour in looking for jobs; in the fact that India's new heroes are business leaders like Narayana Murthy and small-town stars like the cricketer Mahendra Singh Dhoni. New India is united not just by a respect for achievement and yearning for a better life, but also by an unprecedented belief that such a life is possible, regardless of one's social and economic status.

Open to our possibilities

We cannot forget the circumstances under which India abandoned the socialist model. Our government adopted reforms in the early 1990s only under duress and in the midst of crisis: P. V. Narasimha Rao, prime minister at the time, had said, "Decisions are easy when no options are left." Even when socialism had proved ineffective, the political class was reluctant to abandon what had come to be seen as the legacy of India's founders and part of independent India's bold counter to colonialism.

Today, however, reforms have built a strong, vibrant market and an expanding class of workers and consumers across India, and we are unlikely to retreat to our autarkic past. But to ensure a continued commitment to reform, we must create a wider consensus for it. This means focusing on rational, reasoned and genuinely egalitarian ideas to overcome special-interest politics and the temptations of populism.

Our policies must not be defined by the context of colonialism or capitalism. Instead, we should focus on results and rational outcomes—"not against any country or doctrine, but against hunger, poverty, desperation and chaos."[12] Our suspicion of private enterprise, globalization and the market has to do with our history, with the idealism we associate with our early leaders. But we need to remember that in some important ways India is still Nehru's India. Jairam Ramesh, who is the minister of state for commerce with the UPA government and also my former quiz partner at IIT Bombay, pointed out to me that despite the disadvantage of policies that encouraged monopoly businesses across Indian industries, "Our early trade protections created pockets of powerful domestic industry. We built 'scientific sultanates' in R&D, and created excellent higher education institutes." This legacy gave us certain advantages when we did liberalize, and it explains why India set off on a path of knowledge-intensive growth that was both unique and unusual for a developing economy. We were able to make effective use of the educated human capital pool we had built up over the years, and both our old and new industries have held their own as foreign trade and capital have flowed in. Our strength will always be reason and flexibility, not dogma and posturing. It is useful to remember what Nehru himself said shortly before he died: "If we do not ultimately solve the basic problems of our country . . . it will not matter if we call ourselves capitalists, socialists, communists or anything else."

At the end of the day, therefore, when it comes to our policies and ideas, I would rather be right than righteous and put aside emotion in favor of rational argument. I hope that I have done that in this book. And I hope that this book is read by my peers, by people in business, media and government—even if they only brandish it above their heads while loudly refuting my arguments. I would welcome the debate.

I see the divide between the India of old and India today as a generational one. "Age explains some of the biggest differences I've seen within our Parliament," Jay Panda, one of the country's youngest politicians, tells me. "The younger members are more open to new ideas, and more willing to try them out." Across the economy as well, the new, optimistic, aspirational India is clearly the India of the young. The entrepreneurs who are coming into prominence across industries, from telecommunications to banking to manufacturing, are remarkably youthful, their faces unlined; the private sector teems with young managers, analysts and engineers. At Infosys, the average age of employees is twenty-seven.

India is a country so young that 50 percent of the population is still not eligible to vote, and this means that the voice of an entire, large generation is now ignored in India's policy making and public debates. These are the children of liberalization who have an entirely different perspective on our traditions and policies compared with the majority of India's voters and policy makers today. They have their own take on urgent issues like our education policy, reservations and labor reforms, and on the more fundamental left–right divide.

It is the power and energy of our human capital, young and old, that has been central to the Indian transformation. And this force has not been limited to workers in the knowledge industry alone, or to India's educated class. The statesman Minocher Rustom Masani—or Minoo Masani, as everyone from his friends to his voters knew him—was among India's first truly liberal thinkers, and a deeply underrated statesman. As a Member of Parliament in the 1950s and 1960s, Minoo sat in the Opposition benches as a leader of India's sole pro–free market party, the Swatantra Party. His writings on India started out as optimistic, but later he despaired of the direction the country was headed both politically and economically. He wrote, "If India is to be saved, it will have to be saved by the small man."

This is exactly what is now taking place. It was not just the 1991 crisis that brought India's state-led economy down—by then, it was already being laid low by the thousand small cuts the people had dealt it through strikes, student protests, farmer riots, sandals hurled at ministers at election rallies and the electoral losses that had begun to pile up for incumbent governments. It is Minoo's "small man"—people demanding better solutions, people impatient and angry with ineffectual ideology—who is bringing new policies to the forefront, driving change and shaping a renewed idea of India.

Part One

INDIA REIMAGINED

Ideas That Have Arrived

IDEAS THAT HAVE ARRIVED

I LIKE TO THINK of my generation as the "bridging generation," the one that exists between the India of the old and the new, and which straddles the divides and the ideas that separate the two countries. We are the ones who were there in the crowds both in the 1950s and in the 1990s—as children, we accompanied our parents to cheer Nehru, a statesman an entire generation had found tremendously inspiring in his ideas for a "compassionate state" and his passion for the country. And we were also there, if weather-beaten by the years that had passed, to see Manmohan Singh release his reformist policy in 1991—a politician who could not be more different from Nehru in his quiet demeanor, economic beliefs and soft-spoken speech, but who was nevertheless as much a believer in the power of ideas. And in this shift, we have witnessed how much India has changed and how powerful a role ideas have played in overturning established beliefs.

It is interesting to see how an entire country changed its mind on core beliefs, in shifts that took decades. The Indian transformation was not one launched from the ramparts of the Red Fort in Delhi or from the corporate boardrooms of Nariman Point in Bombay.

Rather, these new ideas gained acceptance because a wide swathe of people across the country had experiences very different from what they had been told and taught to expect. People who had been steeped in Indian-language schools one day found their advancement thwarted as they encountered the English barrier. The construction worker who viewed technology and computers with suspicion found his mobile phone with its ten-rupee recharge indispensable in getting his next job. The Indian engineer who parlayed his education for a job in Silicon Valley experienced the promise of globalization. And the Dalit farm worker who had long been sidelined in economic opportunity began to discover that he too could use his growing political voice to bring about more inclusive policies.

Completely unintentionally, my career took place at the heart of this change in ideas. When the other founders and I contemplated the idea of Infosys in 1981, I had no shortage of friends and relatives trying to dissuade me from joining such a "foolhardy venture." "Don't be an idiot," an uncle told me. "A start-up will find it impossible to do business here." Two decades later, however, I was being fêted as a first-generation entrepreneur, and my socialist father was in attendance at each of Infosys's shareholder meetings.

In my time at the company, I saw many such transformations. One was how the perception of IT changed rapidly across Indian industry—fifteen years ago, the chairman of a leading bank, the Union Bank of India, criticized my efforts to promote the benefits of bank computerization to the industry. Recently, however, his successor called me up and told me with pride that they were running the entire bank on one central computer system.

India has gained dramatically from similar, massive changes in our attitudes toward our population, entrepreneurs, the English language, globalization and democracy. It has made India a country that right now has a unique cadence, where all our major strengths have come together and matured at the same time. There are countries around the world, for instance, that are at a demographic sweet spot but lack the democracy they need to exploit it. There are some nations that have huge natural resources but not the entrepreneurs and technologies to spread the wealth. And there are countries whose previous, unsuccessful experiences with globalization have scarred them so deeply that they shun it, and this limits how much they can gain from their domestic strength. In essence, I think no other country in the world right now has the combination that makes the Indian opportunity so significant.

We Indians have keenly felt both our humiliations and our successes. So the buzz surrounding our two and a half decades of growth has not been missed by any of us. Wherever I go, I find that Indians know our growth numbers backward and forward, and there is a strong, common feeling among us that our country has finally come of age. But it has not been an easy ride—the ideas that now bedrock India's economy took decades to be widely accepted and were often caught up in the storm of our politics and shifts in public opinion. In retrospect, each big part of the Indian miracle seems a little miraculous.

INDIA, BY ITS PEOPLE

IN DELHI this Monday morning, it is chaos. Despite its pristine new metro and expanding highways, the city can barely contain the morning hubbub, the swarm of people all trying to get somewhere. By the time I reach Kaushik Basu's home—set a little apart from the highway, on a quiet street that is empty except for a single, lazy cow who stops in front of the car, in no hurry to move—I am very late, a little grimy, but exhilarated.

Kaushik and I chat about how the crowds in the city look completely different compared with, say, two decades ago. Then, you would see people lounging near tea shops, reading the morning paper late into the afternoon, puffing languorously at their beedis* and generally shooting the breeze. But as India has changed—bursting forth as one of the world's fastest-growing countries—so has the scene on the street. And as Kaushik points out, it is this new restlessness, the hum and thrum of its people, that is the sound of India's economic engine today.

Kaushik is the author of a number of books on India and teaches economics at Cornell, and his take on India's growth—of a country driven by human capital—is now well accepted. India's position as the world's go-to destination for talent is hardly surprising; we may have been short on various

*These are thin, filterless cigarettes, usually made from leaves and tobacco.

things at various times, but we have always had plenty of people. The crowded tumult of our cities is something I experience every day as I navigate my way to our Bangalore office through a dense crowd that overflows from the footpaths and onto the road—of software engineers waiting at bus stops, groups of women in colorful saris, on their way to their jobs at the garment factories that line the road, men in construction hats heading toward the semi-completed highway. And then there are the people milling around the cars, hawking magazines and pirated versions of the latest bestsellers.* Looking around, I think that if people are the engine of India's growth, our economy has only just begun to rev up.

But to the demographic experts of the nineteenth and twentieth centuries, India's population made the country quite simply a disaster of epic proportions. Paul Ehrlich's visit to Delhi in 1966 forms the opening of his book *The Population Bomb*, and his shock as he describes India's crowds is palpable: "People eating, people washing, people sleeping . . . people visiting, arguing and screaming . . . people clinging to buses . . . people, people, people."

But in the last two decades, this depressing vision of India's population as an "overwhelming burden" has been turned on its head. With growth, our human capital has emerged as a vibrant source of workers and consumers not just for India, but also for the global economy. But this change in our attitudes has not come easily. Since independence, India struggled for decades with policies that tried to put the lid on its surging population. It is only recently that the country has been able to look its billion in the eye and consider its advantages.

"Millions on an anthill"

For most of the twentieth century, people both within and outside India viewed us through a lens that was distinctly Malthusian. As a poor and extremely crowded part of the world, we seemed to vindicate Thomas Malthus's uniquely despondent vision—that great population growth inevitably led to great famine and despair.

The time that Thomas Malthus, writer, amateur economist and clergy-

---

***The Alchemist, Liar's Poker* and (Tom Friedman would be delighted) *The World Is Flat* have been perennial favorites for Indian pirates.

man (the enduring term history gave him would be "the gloomy parson"), lived in may have greatly influenced his theory on population. Nineteenth-century England was seeing very high birth rates, with families having children by the baker's dozen. Malthus—who, as the second of eight children, was himself part of the population explosion he bemoaned—predicted in his *An Essay on the Principle of Population* that the unprecedented increases in population would lead to a cycle of famines, of "epidemics, and sickly seasons."

India in particular seemed to be speedily bearing down the path that Malthus predicted. On our shores, famine was a regular visitor. We endured thirty hunger famines* between 1770 and 1950—plagues during which entire provinces saw a third of their population disappear, and the countryside was covered "with the bleached bones of the millions dead."[1]

By the mid-twentieth century, neo-Malthusian prophets were sounding the alarm on the "disastrous" population growth in India and China, and predicted that the impact of such growth would be felt around the world. Their apocalyptic scenarios helped justify draconian approaches to birth control. Policies recommending "sterilization of the unfit and the disabled," and the killing of "defective" babies gained the air of respectable theory.[2] India's increasing dependence on food aid from the developed world due to domestic shortages also fueled the panic around its population growth—in 1960 India had consumed one eighth of the United States' total wheat production, and by 1966 this had grown to one fourth.

Consequently, if you were an adult in the 1950s and 1960s and followed the news, it was entirely plausible to believe that the endgame for humanity was just round the corner; you may also have believed that this catastrophe was the making of some overly fecund Indians. Nehru, observing the hand-wringing, remarked that the Western world was "getting frightened at the prospect of the masses of Asia becoming vaster and vaster, and swarming all over the place."

And it is true that Indians of this generation had a cultural affinity for big families, even among the middle class—every long holiday during my childhood was spent at my grandparents' house with my cousins, and a fam-

*Amartya Sen and others have pointed out, however, that while these famines may have seemed to be the consequence of a country that was both poor and overpopulated, they were in fact triggered partly by trade policies and the lack of infrastructure. Lord Lytton exported wheat from India at the height of the 1876–78 famine, and the lack of connectivity across the country affected transportation of grain to affected areas.

ily photo from that time has a hundred people crammed into the frame. Indian families were big enough to be your main social circle—most people did not mingle extensively outside family weddings, celebrations and visits to one another's homes.

The growing global worries around our population growth created immense pressure on India to impose some sort of control on our birth rates, and we became the first developing country to initiate a family planning program. But our early family planning policies had an unusual emphasis on "self-control."[3] In part this was influenced by leaders such as Gandhi, who preached abstinence; in an interesting departure from his usual policy of nonviolence, he had said, "Wives should fight off their husbands with force, if necessary."

This focus on abstinence and self-restraint continued with independent India's first health minister, Rajkumari Amrit Kaur, who was in the odd position of being at the helm of a family planning program while opposing family planning "in principle."[4] As a result Indian policy during this decade emphasized the rhythm method. Rural India was targeted for raising awareness of the method, and one villager remarked of its success, "They talked of the rhythm method to people who didn't know the calendar. Then they gave us rosaries of colored beads . . . at night, people couldn't tell the red bead for 'don't' from the green for 'go ahead.'"[5]

Not surprisingly, India's population continued to grow through the 1950s and 1960s, as fertility remained stubbornly high even while infant mortality and death rates fell rapidly. This was despite the massive awareness-building efforts around family planning that the government undertook. I still remember the "small family" songs on the radio, the walls of our cities and the sides of buses and trucks papered with posters that featured happy (and small) cartoon families, and slogans like "Us Two, Ours Two." And yet, each census release made it clear that our population numbers continued to relentlessly soar, and we despaired over a graph that was climbing too high, too fast.

Snip, snip

As the global panic around population growth surged, the Indian and Chinese governments began executing white-knuckle measures of family planning in the 1960s. "Our house is on fire," Dr. S. Chandrasekhar, minister of health and family planning, said in 1968. If we focus more on sterilization, he added, "We can get the blaze under control."[6]

By the 1970s, programs and targets for sterilization of citizens were set up for Indian states. There was even a vasectomy clinic set up at the Victoria Terminus rail station in Bombay, to cater to the passenger traffic flowing through.[7] But no matter how Indian governments tried to promote sterilization with incentives and sops, the number of people willing to undergo the procedure did not go up. India's poor wanted children—and especially sons—as economic security. State efforts to persuade citizens into sterilization backfired in unexpected ways—as when many people across rural India refused to have the anti-tuberculosis BCG (Bacillus Calmette-Guerin) injections because of a rumor that BCG stood for "birth control government."[8]

In 1975, however, Indira Gandhi announced the Emergency, which suspended democratic rights and elections and endowed her with new powers of persuasion, so to speak. The Indian government morphed into a frighteningly sycophantic group, there to do the bidding of the prime minister and her son Sanjay—the same hot-headed young man who had described the cabinet ministers as "ignorant buffoons," thought his mother a "ditherer" and regarded the Philippines dictator Ferdinand Marcos his role model.[9]

In the winter of 1976, I, along with some of my fellow IIT Bombay students, had arrived on the "festival circuit" in Delhi to participate in the student debates and quizzes (yes, I was an inveterate nerd). It meant going from college to college for competitions, from Hindu to St. Stephen's to Miranda House to IIT Delhi. Most of us from the sylvan, secluded campus of IIT Bombay were not as politically aware as the Delhi students—the only elections we followed were those for the IIT hostels and student body. But in the Delhi of the Emergency years, sitting around campfires, one heard the whispered tales of Emergency-era atrocities, and of one particular outrage—"nasbandi." Sanjay, who had discovered a taste and talent for authoritarianism with the Emergency, had made sterilization—specifically male sterilization or nasbandi—his pet project.

The sterilization measures that were introduced came to be known as the "Sanjay Effect"—a combination, as the demographer Ashish Bose put it to me, of "coercion, cruelty, corruption and cooked figures." Ashish notes that "incentives" to undergo the sterilization procedure included laws that required a sterilization certificate before government permits and rural credit could be granted. Children of parents with more than three children found that schools refused them admission, and prisoners did not get parole until they went under the knife. And some government departments "persuaded" their more reluctant employees to undergo the procedure by threatening them with charges of embezzlement.*

The steep sterilization targets for state governments meant that people were often rounded up like sheep and taken to "family planning" clinics. For instance, one journalist witnessed municipal police in the small town of Barsi, Maharashtra, "dragging several hundred peasants visiting Barsi on market day off the streets." They drove these men in two garbage trucks to the local family planning clinic, where beefy orderlies held them down while they were given vasectomies.[10] This scene repeated itself time and again across the country.

It was difficult to trust the sterlization figures the government released since there was so much pressure on the states for results. Nevertheless, the Emergency-era sterilization program, Ashish notes, may have achieved nearly two thirds of its target—eight million sterilizations. But democracy soon hit back with a stunning blow. When Indira Gandhi called for elections in 1977—ignoring Sanjay's protests, "much to his ire"[11]—the Congress was immediately tossed out of power.

The nasbandi program was the last gasp of coercive family planning in India on a large scale, and it became political suicide to implement similar policies. The Janata Party government that followed Indira even changed the label of the program to avoid the stigma it carried, and "family planning" became "family welfare." While sterilization programs have occasionally reappeared across states, they have been mostly voluntary, with the focus on incentives to undergo the procedure.†

---

*Asoka Bandarage describes the target fever in India's sterilization programs, which gave rise to "speed doctors" who competed against one another to perform the most operations every day, often under ghastly hygienic conditions. One celebrated figure was the Indian gynecologist P. V. Mehta, who entered the Guinness Book of World Records for sterilizing more than 350,000 people in a decade—he claimed that he could perform forty sterilizations in an hour.

†These sweeteners for the procedure have at times been very strange and a little suspect, such as Uttar Pradesh's "guns for sterilisation" policy in 2004, under which scheme Indians purchasing firearms or seeking gun licenses were told they would be fast-tracked if they could round up volunteers for sterilization. A district in Madhya Pradesh also made a similar "guns for vasectomies" offer to its residents in 2008.

Different demographic destinies

A common grouse we have in India is how slow we are—to reform, adapt and change, especially compared with our neighbor China. But my belief is that while democracies may be slow, they are also more cautious than autocracies, and this makes them less prone to committing truly egregious errors. Standing and ruminating over voter considerations after all is much more preferable to dashing straight into a gorge.

For instance, during the Malthusian hysteria of the 1960s, both India and China were pushed—at times shoved—by international organizations to control their population growth. What stood in its way were India's voters: they did not like the idea of family planning and no amount of pretty slogans was going to make them change their minds. After the government that had brought in the cutting implements for nasbandi got tossed out of power, no Indian government would touch forcible family planning with a beanpole.

China, however, was marching to a very different tune. At first, stemming the flood of babies was the last thing on their minds. It was during Malthus's lifetime that socialism and communism came into their own, and their leaders took a very anti-Malthus view on population.[12*] Marxist writers even argued, throwing caution to the winds, that socialism could "support any level of population"—the more the merrier.[13]

Echoing that ideological line, in the 1940s the Soviet Union had made abortion illegal and encouraged women to have several children; in China, Mao, in his enthusiasm to rev up the republic, championed larger families and talked up China's population growth. By 1970 China was averaging 5.8 births per woman. In fact when the president of Beijing University, Dr. Ma Yinchu, made a proposal for a family planning program in China in the 1950s, he was opposed quite strongly, publicly ridiculed and lost his university job.

But by the end of the 1970s, the Chinese government was also bitten by the population panic bug and began to emphasize population control to promote "social harmony" and optimum growth. The government first launched the "Later, Longer, Fewer" campaign, and then the one-child

---

*Marx dismissed Malthus with some contempt, writing, "If the reader reminds me of Malthus, whose essay on Population appeared in 1798, I remind him that this work . . . is nothing more than a schoolboyish, superficial plagiary . . . and does not contain a single sentence thought out by himself."

policy, which Deng Xiaoping implemented in 1981. Deng had a pretty unsparing approach to family planning and told his officials to " 'Just do it'—implement in any way and by any means possible."[14] What followed in China was the "technical policy on family planning," which required intrauterine devices for women in families with one child, and sterilization for couples with two children. "Illegal" children born in the provinces affected job evaluations of bureaucrats and ministers. In addition to the strong-arm tactics, the government advertised birth control reminders at movie theaters, billboards and in a multitude of leaflets. By the mid-1980s, birth-control surgeries peaked at "more than 30 million a year."[15]

Under the wisdom of the 1970s and 1980s, the family planning program in China was an enormous success. The argument in their defense is familiar dictator PR-speak—that it was "coercion for a good cause."[16] In 1983 Indira Gandhi and China's family planning minister, Qian Xinzhong, were jointly given the United Nations award for "the most outstanding contribution to the awareness of population questions."[17] However, even as these awards were being handed out, the view of population as a pestilence was beginning to shift.

From albatross to advantage

By the late 1970s, the Malthusian scientists had egg on their faces. They had predicted massive population-led catastrophes in India and China by the end of the 1970s; one scare-mongering book called *Famine1975!* by William and Paul Paddock had carried a list sorting which countries should be assisted during the imminent Great Famine. The list had read along the lines of "Pakistan: should receive food; India: can't be saved." These thinkers and writers had so much influence on popular culture that 1973 saw the release of the Hollywood movie *Soylent Green*, set in a future where an overpopulated earth struggles for food and resorts to cannibalism.

But the years passed—the doomsday year 1975 came and went, with much holding of breath, I am sure, by the Paddock brothers—and the moment of mass death failed to arrive. By the 1980s academics had begun to harrumph and shake their heads at the downer theorists and reexamine populations in terms of their impact on economic growth. The Indian economist (and later Nobel laureate) Amartya Sen pointed out that India had not seen a famine since it had become a democracy, even while its population had continued to grow. The economist Julian Simon argued that as population increased, so did the stock of creativity and innovation: "The ultimate resource is human imagination."[18]

Malthus's theory may appear in retrospect somewhat blinkered, but his ideas were a consequence of the times. He wrote his essay when the Industrial Revolution was just beginning to gain ground in Europe, and while he recognized the working capacity of more people, human capital did not possess the transformational role in the economy that it does now. The period was instead marked by the rise of a dark and somber landscape across England—its cities were populated by huge numbers of rural migrants in crowded housing, and Charles Dickens described these teeming places as "three families on the second [floor], starvation in the attics, Irishmen in the passage . . . a charwoman and five hungry children in the back room—filth everywhere."[19] People came cheap and were without civil and welfare rights, providing factory owners with a resource they could freely abuse; one factory owner, insisting on his relative kindness, said that "we beat only the younger . . . up to thirteen or fourteen, we use a strap."[20] The value of labor was at its lowest, and labor's share of Europe's national income kept falling until the world wars.

But while Malthus could be excused for his gloomy predictions, his later Lemming-like followers, obsessed with how much people were eating and consuming, failed to take the changing world economy into account. Since 1900 the world had witnessed a period of rapid growth in labor productivity which, with the rise of the industrial economy, contributed to remarkable increases in overall growth. This became especially pronounced as Europe's GDP began to double every thirty-five years after 1900. And as labor became a powerful economic force, a large working population became more valuable.

This idea of population as an asset rather than a burden has especially gained currency with the rise of knowledge-based industries such as IT, telecommunications and biotechnology in the 1970s. In fact the information economy is the culmination of what the Industrial Revolution started—it has placed human capital front and center as the main driver of productivity and growth.

I do shy away, however, from unbridled optimism—that would be almost as bad as the previous mood of relentless pessimism on population growth.

The pressures of India's vast population are indeed humungous—our natural resources are no bottomless pool. A billion people may offer us a deep base of human capital, but it also signals a potentially massive, detrimental burden on our environment, food production and resources, as millions of people join the middle class, ramp up their consumption, and per capita energy intake grows. We will have to find solutions for these concerns.

Nevertheless, the impact of human capital in India has so far had large payoffs for the economy, especially since the 1991 reforms. Our skilled workers have been the nerve stem of the IT, biotechnology, pharmaceuticals and telecommunications industries in India. Globally as well, human creativity and economic competitiveness are now closely linked, and competition among countries is competition between their human capital. As Tom Friedman notes, these days rather than tell his children to finish their dinner because people are going hungry, "I tell my daughters to finish their homework because people in China and India are starving for their jobs."*

For a better idea of what has happened to our attitudes toward population, I spoke to the Harvard demographer David Bloom.† I met David for the first time at Davos in 2006, a decade after his paper titled "Demographic Transitions and Economic Miracles in Emerging Asia" made him famous much beyond academic circles—he is now one of those enviable scientists who can have a cocktail party audience hang onto his every word.

David tells me that the key problem with early population theories was that "they were obsessed with overall population growth as an indicator, while ignoring the trends that lurked inside those figures." These trends, David notes, were uncovered when he and fellow demographer Jeffrey Williamson were puzzling over the growth in one particular region—East Asia.

Economists had found it difficult to explain what exactly had happened in East Asia between 1965 and 1990 to drive the region's impressive economic growth, which had clocked in at an average of almost 6 percent a year during those decades. Terminology-wise, David says, they had already begun to shrug it off, like fatalistic believers, as the East Asian growth "miracle."

But when David and Jeffrey looked inside East Asia's magic hat, they discovered a remarkable population trend that happened to coincide with its

*Ironically enough, tutors for homework are now part of a niche outsourcing service that Indian companies such as TutorVista offer U.S. parents.

†Bangalore has a personal claim on David—his father-in-law was the distinguished energy scientist Amulya K. N. Reddy.

rapid growth. Between 1950 and 2000, the chances that an infant would die in East Asia fell sharply from 181 per 1,000 births to just 34, and this caused fertility to fall from six children to two per woman.

"But there was a lag between these two drops," David says. "Infant deaths fell first while fertility remained high." To put it, well, a little bluntly, it took some time for people to realize that fewer babies were dying. Only then, David says, did people adjust toward lower fertility. "And the children who had unexpectedly survived formed a 'boom generation.'"

This generation created a large number of young, enterprising workers, who themselves had fewer children and therefore few dependants—in fact East Asia's working-age population at this time grew nearly four times faster than its dependent population. The economies in the region as a result had to spend a lower percentage of their incomes on the social costs of a dependent population. Lower costs meant that this generation could save more—we have seen this in India, where a larger working population has helped push the country's savings rate as a proportion of GDP to 34 percent in 2008, and it is set to rise even higher to 40 percent by 2015. Such savings create additional capital for investment across the economy.

This extra money is especially valuable during boom generations, when the cumulative energy and creativity of a young, unencumbered population frees people not just to spend and save, but also to invent and innovate. As Bloom and Williamson wrote, "When you have lots of babies, you also have to take care of them. The resources that are normally put into building up the economy—in infrastructure, capital and savings—are being diverted to raise children . . . you are not building as many bridges, digging as many harbors, or creating as many ports."

Additionally, as the number of children per woman in East Asia fell from six to two, women were able to join the workforce and contribute to GDP growth. This demographically rich generation drove East Asia's rise as a manufacturing and technology power—including the growth of Singapore in manufacturing and retail, of Hong Kong in finance and of Taiwan in electronics.

In all, Bloom and Williamson discovered, this wave of young workers contributed to as much as one third of East Asia's economic rise between 1965 and 1990.* "We showed," David tells me, "that particular kinds of

*Figuring out these contributions is not an exact science—Bloom and Williamson's numbers are estimates.

population growth could dramatically drive the country's growth, not impede it as economists used to believe."

David called this effect the "demographic dividend," a phrase that has quickly caught on. And with good reason. When demographers went back and looked at previous periods of sustained economic growth from Europe to the United States to Asia, they found that they coincided time and again with similar patterns of large numbers of young people, and fewer dependants.

Scientists have since been unearthing the hidden treasure of these dividends across history. The Industrial Revolution, for instance, had as its ballast a significant demographic boom—the boom Malthus had worried about. "The triggers for these dividends across countries have not been uniform," David tells me. "Different factors can cause shifts in mortality and fertility. Improved health care, for instance, caused the early dividends in Europe and Britain, since this resulted in significant drops in infant deaths. This is also true for developing countries—in India, health progress has triggered its dividend."*

In developed countries, with their already low mortality and fertility rates, a demographic dividend was rare and indicated an unusual event. That event was usually a war. The Second World War—which forced people to postpone having children, and then have them all together in one big wave—led to a baby boom and demographic dividend in the United States. Here, the postwar dividends enabled rapid growth, and it contributed to an estimated 20 percent of GDP growth between 1970 and 2000.

In Ireland it was the legalization of birth control that fueled its demographics—there were few infant deaths, but when this deeply Catholic country finally legalized contraceptives in 1979, Ireland's high fertility rate began to fall rapidly. David writes, "In 1970, the average Irishwoman had 3.9 children; by the mid-1990s, that number was less than two." As the number of dependants plunged and Irish women joined the workforce, Ireland's dividend became a springboard for its economy and its growth rates averaged 5.8 percent—higher than that of any other European country.

However, in all these examples, we are clearly talking of demographic bulges that are past—in David's words, "of the pigs that have already passed

---

*This also explains why sub-Saharan Africa has so far failed to experience a demographic dividend—the region has seen little gains in health and increased life expectancy; with HIV/AIDS, life expectancy is actually falling in some of these countries and infant mortality remains quite high.

through the python." The populations of the United States, Europe and East Asia are now graying, growing older. Which brings us to the question—where are the young now? In the 1970s, two very large economies were yet to experience a demographic dividend: India and China.

The dividends of an autocracy, versus a democracy

As early as 1938, India's National Planning Committee had made a statement on population that was an echo of the idea China championed in the 1970s: "The importance of deliberately controlled numbers [in population]," it said, "cannot be exaggerated in a planned economy."[21] As it turned out, this idea was unworkable in democratic India, even as it took off successfully in China. In terms of implementing policies that are good for you, whether you like it or not, autocratic regimes are far better than democracies. In the age of the demographic dividend, however, China's highly effective family planning policy has looked like a case of winning the battle, but perhaps losing the war.

In 1975 both India and China had similar shares of working-age people—in both countries, for every one person that did not work, there were around 1.3 people who did. The one thing that made the population story of India and China finally so different was India's slow-moving, frustrating, yet highly reactive politics.

A sharp decline in China's fertility that began in the 1970s—thanks in large part to the one-child policy—created an early demographics bumper crop for China. There was a rapid rise in the proportion of working-age to non-working-age people in the country from 1970, and by 2010 the number of working people will be two and a half times that of dependants.

China's birth control policies have thus created an especially fast-paced demographic shift in the country, a steep slope all the way down. A dividend that took a century to complete its arc in other countries has taken less than forty years here, and dependency is now set to explode. After 2010 China's working-age population will start falling. The country "is becoming gray before it has become rich"—by 2040, the world's second largest population after India will be Chinese pensioners, more than 400 million people![22]

Across the border in India, however, there was a far more languorous shift. India's politics ensured that its coercive family planning program failed spectacularly, and since the 1970s the demographic curves of these two once similar countries diverged rapidly. India's fertility rate fell slowly from 6.5 in the 1960s to 2.7 in 2006, brought down with rising literacy, improved health indicators and economic growth. Because of a more "natural" curve, India's dividend will last longer—we have started to experience a demographic dividend since 1980, and it will take until 2035 to peak. By this time India will have added more than 270 million people to the working population.

Democracy, in this context, has been a big payoff for India. Population scientists are universally fond of noting that "demographics is destiny," but in India's case, it is both demographics and democracy. Today, India's growth story is increasingly the story of its young population. Our economy is the most dynamic in terms of its human capital—India has one of the youngest populations in the world, with a median age of twenty-three, at a time when the rest of the globe is going gray.

China's young and unencumbered generation had come three decades earlier than India's, in the 1970s. It was the generation of the Great Leap, during which China shifted toward capitalism and rapid growth, and experienced massive social upheaval. China's one-child families also meant more focused investments in children, and this generation saw literacy and college completion rates explode. The one-child policy, however, has created the "4, 2, 1" population structure in China—four grandparents, two parents and one child, resulting in fewer young workers and below-replacement-level birth rates since the early 1990s.

These family structures in China have been far more disruptive than we immediately realize. The sociologist Dr. André Béteille makes an especially astute observation. "Almost none of the Chinese have siblings," he points out, "which means no aunts, uncles or cousins. An incredibly alien notion for the rest of the world is the Chinese reality." The single child family has also created the uniquely Chinese "little emperor" syndrome—an only child has the undivided attention of the adults in his or her family, which is creating a "me generation" of highly individualistic young.

Family planning has also intensified certain social challenges. Both China and India have a worrying but popular preference for sons—it is a feudal carryover, the consequence of a persistent, patriarchal mind-set. A recent court case in India for a missing girl underlined the worst of this attitude. The presiding judge in the case, astonished on hearing the name of the girl, turned to the parents and asked them, "Why did you name your daughter Nirasha [disappointment]?" Their lawyer responded, "My Lord, it was their fifth daughter."

Prosperity has not changed this preference completely—even as the status of women has improved and a rising emphasis on old-age security based on financial investments has dimmed the charms of the male child, factors such as ultrasound technology have made sex-selective births easier. Sex-selective abortions have dragged the sex ratio down to 925 girls for every 1,000 boys, and this has fallen below 750 in some north Indian districts. In China the one-child policy has intensified the girl deficit even more—nationally it stands at 855 girls for every 1,000 boys. This alarming "disappearance" of women will lead to an estimated forty million Chinese men between fifteen and thirty-nine by 2026 who will be "bare branches,"[23] unlikely to have families or children of their own. In retrospect, India may have gained some economic and social advantages simply due to its reluctance, or perhaps inability, to fiddle with its demographic curve.* This also means that our dividend is now right before us, both as a potential and as an enormous challenge.

Demographics and democracy: India's destiny

India is coming into its dividend as an unusually young country in an unusually aging market—a young, fresh-faced nation in a graying world. Globally, more people than ever before are entering retirement. In fact, even by the 1980s, the heads of European countries had begun to worry out loud about Europe's falling population. "Europe is vanishing . . . our countries will be empty,"[24] the French president Jacques Chirac had said—the continent was becoming a place of "old people, living in old houses, ruminating about old ideas."[25]

This trend of an aging, shrinking population now visible across much of the developed world, is coinciding with India's experience of a demographic

*Admittedly, India also faces the challenge of these "bare branches"—only not as severe as China.

dividend that will last until 2050. This opens up interesting new opportunities for the country, as the challenge of maintaining wealth in aging societies means that developed markets will have to increasingly outsource their labor requirements. In 2020 India is projected to have an additional 47 million workers, almost equal to the total world shortfall. The average Indian will be only twenty-nine years old, compared with the average age of thirty-seven in China and the United States, forty-five in Western Europe and forty-eight in Japan.

An early sign of the immense potential of our human capital has been the growth of India's IT/BPO sector and the rise of "transformational outsourcing" by multinational firms across industries. The country has seen its global profile rise rapidly on the strength of its human capital—its entrepreneurs, scientists, engineers and management graduates.

India already has the second largest reservoir of skilled labor in the world. It produces 2 million English-speaking graduates, 15,000 law graduates and about 9,000 PhDs every year. And the existing pool of 2.1 million engineering graduates increases by nearly 300,000 every year.

A talented pool of workers, along with abundant capital and investment, presents us with immense opportunities for creativity and innovation, which can in turn lead to rapid gains in productivity growth and GDP. This had once enabled Europe to emerge as a center for manufacturing innovation in the nineteenth century; similarly, at the peak of its dividend between 1970 and 1990, the United States saw the birth of new technology-based industries that determined the direction of the global economy over the past few decades. Such an opportunity—to emerge as the new creative power and a center for new knowledge and innovation—now lies with India.

India is also emerging as a rapidly growing consumer market for the world economy, with a middle class that is already larger than the population of the United States and two thirds the size of the European Union. Our demographic dividend is set to trigger a further explosion in middle-class consumers as the boom generation comes of age, and over the next two decades India's middle class will swell to more than 580 million people. At the same time, the lack of dependants will enable a new phase of guilt-free consumption. It is these multiple forces that are expected to drive a growth rate of 5 percent for India until 2050[26]—a trend, if it happens, that will be unique and unprecedented in economic history.

India's double hump: The camel in our demographics

"India's population growth is so different and disparate across its regions," Ashish tells me, "that looking at it as a single curve doesn't tell you very much." The two of us are sitting in a coffee shop, in midafternoon, with the light streaming in through glass walls. Around us, young people draw tables together and form cheerful, noisy groups. Ashish is sipping cautiously at his cappuccino—the coffee is steaming hot.

Ashish had come up with the phrase BIMARU (meaning "sick" in Hindi) back in the 1980s to describe the personality of India's poorest states—Bihar, Madhya Pradesh, Rajasthan and Uttar Pradesh. "I coined the phrase while on a project for Rajiv Gandhi," Ashish tells me. "It was an effective way to describe the economic and social condition of these particular states—they were deeply 'sick' in their poverty rates, education and health numbers." Ashish also found that these states had very different population structures from the south, and their numbers were growing much faster. The BIMARU states now have as much as 40 percent of India's population—in fact, as the economist Chris Wilson points out, if Uttar Pradesh were an independent country, it would be the world's fourth most populous one.

These northern states have been the major contributors to India's population growth. India's total fertility rate has dropped by just 40 percent over the past three decades, despite south India having already reached "replacement fertility" rates. As Ashish wrote, "What pushes the national fertility up is India's north, the BIMARU states. Fertility levels for the roughly half-billion population in the north are almost twice as high as for the quarter-billion people of the south."* As a result, as demographers such as Tim Dyson and P. N. Maribhat have shown, if we peel India's demographics like an onion, we end up with two very distinct areas within the country—a north that, thanks to its recent high fertility, stays remarkably young over the next two decades, and a south that faces rapid aging.[27] By 2025 north India's population will still be very young, with a median age of just twenty-six. But the median age in the south would be about thirty-four—similar to Europe's in the late 1980s.[28]

This means that India's demographic dividend is actually a double hump,

*At the extremes of this, Uttar Pradesh's fertility rate stands at 4.7, while for Kerala it is 1.8.

one of which is already nearly exhausted. The first hump of the dividend came from the south and has been "expensed" in the economic growth that the south and the west of India experienced as early as the 1970s, when their infant mortality began to fall. In the northern states, however, infant mortality has only just started to trend down.[29]*

As a result it is the second, larger hump in India's dividend which is yet to peak and which will come from the northern states—and primarily from the BIMARU regions. Ashish has estimated that the share of BIMARU states alone in our population growth between 2001 and 2026 will be around 50 percent, while the share of the south will be only 12.6 percent. As a result, over the next decade, the north should begin to ride the crest of its dividend, toward higher growth. We have to make sure, however, that this dividend does not turn out to be fool's gold.

Before sunset

Our double hump dividend is a particular challenge—India has to ensure a fall in infant mortality and a rise in the demographic dividend in the north that is rapid enough to coincide with the waning of the dividend in the south. A slow response could create a gap between these two humps, into which the Indian economy could fall.

India has to consequently move with some urgency to secure the blessings that the seasons have brought. In particular, we must equip India's extraordinarily young population in the northern states with the skills to participate in growth. But as Ashish notes, "These states are still in a terrible mess in their social indicators." In Madhya Pradesh, for instance, the malnutrition rate for children under three is 55 percent, more than double the rates in sub-Saharan Africa.

When it comes to dividends, what demographers say over and over until

*The reality of our double hump explains why India's debates on updating the share of elected seats in our parliament (according to the latest census data) was so convoluted. The earlier roadmap, as the Constitution defined it, would have updated the shares of seats in the parliament and state legislatures according to the 2001 population numbers. But southern states, ahead of the development and demographic curve and with low fertility rates, were reluctant to see states with burgeoning populations, such as Uttar Pradesh and Bihar, receive bigger seat shares at their expense. The final law—the Eighty-fourth Amendment in 2002—affected seat shares only *within* states, while the overall share of seats in the parliament remains frozen till 2026.

their voices go hoarse is: "The chance is not a certainty." Like people, countries are young once. The flip side of an enormous opportunity is the consequence of failing to take advantage of it. Demographic dividends bring with them the potential for rapid growth and innovation, but also, if we fail to take advantage of them, for dramatic social and cultural upheaval.

As David says, "So far, the success of the dividend in driving growth has not been uniform at all." He describes the countries that did not quite manage to cash in on their dividends—the window was open, but the sun did not come in. For instance, countries in Latin America including Brazil stumbled during the 1980s, despite possessing demographic trends that resembled East Asia's. For much of Latin America, this decade was a lost one, as a result of hyperinflation and weak economic policies. Similarly, Russia and Cuba have failed to gain from their demographic positives and a large supply of young workers.

The failure to meet the needs of a vast young population can lead to both instability and political rebellion against governments. The consequences of a failed dividend opportunity are clearly visible in large parts of Latin America, where a discontented population has turned to socialism and populist leaders, and is mired in stagnant growth.

The strength of a large pool of young workers can quickly turn into a weakness if India fails to implement effective policies in education and health, and create sufficient opportunities for work and income. Today, however, just 13 percent of our young population enrolls for higher education. As a result India is already experiencing constraints in its access to skilled labor, and companies have begun moving from B-class to C-class cities in search of lower employment costs.

India's challenges in creating enough jobs have also already begun—a large percentage of our labor force is now in the tenuous unorganized market, with its attendant frailties of seasonal employment and lack of social security. As more people join the workforce, the challenges of providing long-term employment will only grow. Our failure to create these opportunities can turn the dividend into a crisis. We have already experienced these problems through the 1970s and 1980s, when unemployment and the lack of income mobility for working-age Indians fed into criminality and extremist movements across India—such as the extreme-left Naxalite* and

*The Naxalite movement was named after the village Naxalbari, where in 1967 a peasant uprising broke out—one that represented, in the words of a Naxal leader, India's "first authentic Maoist phenomenon."

extreme-right Bajrang Dal (the Saffron People) movements—as well as the rise of the underworld in major cities. Key players in Bombay's underworld, for instance, were people belonging to discriminated groups and the impoverished underclass—Chhota Rajan was the son of a Dalit sweeper, Abu Salem's mother rolled beedis for a living, Chhota Shakeel grew up in a Bombay slum and Arun Gawli's father was a textile worker laid off during the mill strikes of the 1970s. While these circumstances do not exonerate their actions in the least, these are signs of how economic bitterness can create high social costs.

India will also need policies that address the balance of power for women in the workforce. The economist Abhijit Banerjee, who works at the Poverty Action Lab at the Massachusetts Institute of Technology, has emphasized that educating women is a very effective means of improving our social indicators, particularly those related to fertility and health. An educated woman, for instance, insists on educating her children, which is why, as Abhijit notes, "when you educate a woman, you typically educate a family." He points out how education would greatly empower women in participating in the workforce, boosting a group that has long been under-represented in the Indian economy. Participation among women right now still stands at a low 31 percent, and their education would "enable us to tap into our pool of workers much more effectively."

Once India's "double hump dividend" reaches its sunset years, social costs will soar. What we have right now is therefore a critical piggy-bank period for our economy; if we cannot increase incomes, education levels and output per capita for workers during the demographic window, any savings for our future aging will be low. This is our biggest, but also our last chance.

A young, turbulent people

"The difference between China and India," Dr. Béteille says, "is that China can maneuver into sharp policy shifts in order to manage its demographics, and quell violence." But India's coming demographic changes are complicated to control, thanks to its democracy. In addition, India has several demographically prominent religious and caste groups, who have been powerful in determining election outcomes. These groups can corner state resources and often demand policies that give them unique access to markets, in the form of reservations in jobs and colleges.

This makes demographics in India not just one factor in politics, but the central factor. This gives critical importance to India's ability to manage political and cultural tensions, and ensure that this competition for resources between groups does not turn into outright fights, as demographics change across regions, and as people migrate and push outward into the cities in search of opportunity.

India's tensions around its changing population are already evident in the strongly in-group rhetoric of parties in many Indian states. For instance, K. S. Sudarshan, the chief of the Hindu organization Rashtriya Swayamsevak Sangh (RSS), appeals to Hindu families to "have a dozen sons"—a windfall of infants meant to ensure that Hindus remain dominant in India's demographics and elections.* The double hump of India's demographics is also worsening regional rivalries, as labor shortages in the south enable migrants from the north to take advantage of jobs. And as different communities collide while competing for the same jobs and for seats in educational institutions, hostilities have soared—as in Maharashtra in the rhetoric against non-Marathi-speaking Indians, in Delhi in the debate over worker ID cards and in Karnataka in the efforts to make the local tongue, Kannada, the "sole language."

Governments can choose to either fan the flames for short-term votes or intelligently address the questions that are rising around hiring practices and admissions in educational institutions across states, the right to use one's language in the public sphere and cultural identity. Governments here will have to choose between reforms that improve access to jobs and education and short-term, divisive politics. This will be key to determining how much the country will gain from its emerging dividend.

The impact of our changing demographics will be a cycle in either effectiveness or disaster—harnessing it for growth will minimize our divides and dampen the demand for community-based benefits. But if we fail, our demographic curve will become a line to a powder keg.

---

*Sudarshan often celebrates the mata in his speeches, the prolific woman who produces large numbers of children; his blessing for women followers who meet him is the alarming "May you have a hundred sons."

"People, people, people": Our changing impressions

Looking back, the common man and woman have been bit players in our histories, their role determined by statistics and crowds. It is only recently, particularly since the 1970s, with the rise of labor productivity and the knowledge economy, that the political power of people has been accompanied with greater economic power.

This shift in power has been especially significant in India. For a long time, governments regarded the country's population as its great liability. Vastly poor and illiterate, India's people were "the great unwashed," a burden not just for the country but also a worry for the rest of the world. Today, however, India's growth is credited to its strength in human capital, and the rise of IT in India, for instance, is seen in terms of "Indian talent,"[30] as entrepreneurs and workers overcame the barriers that existed in the 1990s to drive growth.

Our human capital has thus transformed from an albatross into India's most significant advantage. There is a growing realization within our government that India's most critical reforms will be those that impact the quality of our upcoming demographic dividend—and it is consequently policies in education, health and labor laws that are receiving the closest attention.

We can trace the change in sentiment to the topmost levels of India's governments. Indira Gandhi, referring to the country's crowds, had once said, "We cannot afford to be a flabby nation." But Manmohan Singh says, "It is in India's superb human capital that our advantage lies." The change in this idea of population as a "burden" to population as an "asset" is central to what is driving India today.

But the role of people as "human capital" requires props that are still missing, or only half there. Our vast numbers of people can only participate in our growth story if we provide them "access"—to the roads that take them to work, to lights that allow them to study at night and the English skills that enable them to tap into the benefits of our growth.

In some ways, the rise of this boom generation is in itself paving the way toward the solutions it needs. The exuberance of this demographic, this pool of restless, ambitious, young workers not hamstrung by tradition and old habit, is a shot in the arm in terms of new ideas and opportunities. And democracy is ensuring that their voices are heard, and the state is beginning to respond.

For instance, the same day that the young Indian cricket captain Mahendra Singh Dhoni led his team of twenty-something players to victory in the Twenty/20 ICC World Cup, the Congress party announced Rajiv Gandhi's son, the thirty-eight-year-old Rahul, as the general secretary of the party. During the announcement, one party worker alluded to Rahul as Congress's Dhoni. This is not a token move—there has been a simultaneous push to induct other young leaders to senior positions in both the Congress and the Bharatiya Janata Party (BJP).

And at political rallies in even the most rural parts of India, there is a clear change in the tenor of the speeches. At one such rally in the small town of Bettiah in Bihar held in 2007, the air shimmered with heat and possibility. On a makeshift dais, the chief minister Nitish Kumar was promising more jobs and business investment for the state's young citizens. "Our young people leave the state and go for jobs elsewhere . . . we need to make such opportunities happen here. Only then will the young stay." His words were met with roars of approval. It is a sound that gives me hope.

FROM REJECTION TO OPEN ARMS

The Entrepreneur in India

THERE WERE TEN of us, all entrepreneurs, whom Montek Singh Ahluwalia, deputy chairman of India's Planning Commission, rang up in early 2005. "The prime minister is setting up a joint CEO forum along with the U.S. President, to advise us on trade issues,"* he said to me in his polite way, "and he would like you to be on the panel."

I can remember a time when the very idea of entrepreneurs being invited to provide policy inputs to the government was unthinkable—the prime minister would not have heard the end of it until the next election. The political attitude toward India's entrepreneurs used to be irredeemably hostile, especially through the 1960s and 1970s—the perception of businessmen was that of "devious capitalists"[1] and Indian industry was a favorite target for populist political rhetoric. With the exception of a few first families, business was not welcome into debates on economic or trade policy.

The reforms, however, brought new freedoms for Indian entrepreneurs, and as fast-growing firms across India's industries charted a new and impres-

*The eventual Indo-U.S. CEO Forum that Ratan Tata and William Harrison chaired consisted of ten CEOs from India and ten from the United States. As an advisory body to the prime minister and the U.S. president, our focus was on improving ties between India and the United States. We offered inputs on everything from FDI to trade relations and energy concerns.

sive path to growth, age-old grudges toward business began to finally dissipate. Since then, the story of India's rise has clearly been this story of the Indian entrepreneur, who after a long, painful period in shackles has been allowed to come out into the sun.

Our early moods: Capitalism as a nasty word

Ramachandra Guha's two very large, black Labradors eyeball me as I make my way to his home office but fortunately seem too sleepy to be really bothered by my presence. Ram, the historian and author of the epic and marvelous *India After Gandhi*, writes his books in his study, a tiny room with blue doors and green walls, its floors covered in a chaos of paper and books. If anyone can shed light on India's checkered relationship with its entrepreneurs, it is him.

Ram points out that India's tepid attitude toward business was inextricably intertwined with how our politics evolved. "At the time India became independent," Ram says, "the country was both deeply fragmented and extremely poor." Indian leaders consequently felt that this young, tenuous nation—this "infant state"—needed handholding by a paternal government, in both its politics and its economics. Such a vision left little room for a truly independent private sector.

The Indian leaders' views on capitalism were also being shaped by the events unfolding around them—and these were dismal times for business. In the 1940s and 1950s, the Great Depression was a fresh memory, and socialism seemed like a possible alternative to open markets. The Soviet Union's rapid rise as an economic powerhouse, despite what Nehru called its "defects, mistakes and ruthlessness,"* had given state-led growth a promising aura and captured the imagination of Indian leaders.[2]

The fact also remained that India's most significant experience with entrepreneurship was as a country captured by a business. The memory of a British company ransacking the Bengal treasury in 1757 haunted Indian leaders—India had experienced an extreme form of capitalism in the "negligence, profusion, and malversation"[3] of the monopolistic East India Com-

*The fact that official Soviet statistics greatly exaggerated levels of growth became clear only in the 1980s, when Mikhail Gorbachev's government reported growth rates that were "close to zero."

pany, and it made Indian leaders deeply suspicious of leaving business to its own devices.

In addition, there were many leaders within the first Indian government who had directly experienced the viciousness of imperial rule, its routine imprisonments and assaults, and emotions against the Empire were fresh and raw. Nehru's early disenchantment with the British had taken place in a railway carriage, where he overheard the toxic General Dyer bragging about his attack on Indian civilians at Jallianwala Bagh. Nehru described the incident in his diary with quiet outrage and disgust at the man's overweening sense of entitlement. "Dyer got off the train," he wrote, "in pajamas colored in bright pink stripes, and a dressing gown."[4] The incident was one among many that shaped his views on British imperialism—Nehru saw Britain as a hard, repressive state, and the market-friendly systems it had established got tarred with the same brush.

The antibusiness politics of our early years was thus shaped by two forces—the determination to take the country as far away as possible from the institutions that dominated colonial India and an enthusiasm to embrace the promise of a new, rising world order, socialism. It was both freedom and renunciation, an intoxicating blend.

Nehru was the biggest champion of socialist policy in these pre-independence years, and it was a real thorn in the side for India's business houses that the nation's most charming, popular politician regarded them at best with distaste and at worst with open hostility. In unguarded moments, Nehru described capitalism as "cut-throat" and was emphatic on wanting to "limit" the role of business.

In the early years, however, Indian industry did have some prominent leaders willing to defend their interests, particularly the probusiness leader and future home minister Vallabhbhai Patel. Patel was fearsome in both personality and the influence he wielded in the government—his critics called him "Herr Vallabhbhai"—and having him on the side of industry was reassuring. Through the first shaky years of independence, when Nehru shook them with his blunt, combative remarks, Patel would assure them, "Take it from me—if anyone talks of nationalisation, it is only for the sake of leadership."[5]

Nevertheless, Indian businessmen had an inkling which way popular opinion tilted—and it was not in their favor. The negativity did not stem from political rhetoric alone. The success of Indian business during the 1930s and 1940s, for one, had not been particularly pretty. It has been said that "the time to invest is when there is blood on the streets," and Indian businesses made their fortunes during the turbulent years of the First and Second World Wars in a country that had unwillingly sent its soldiers to fight on the British side. The demands of the imperial armies for sandbags, for instance, meant that the sales of Indian jute soared, as did the sale of Indian steel for weapons and railway expansion. In fact this surge in British demand was a big change in fortunes for Indian firms, which the British had dismissed as inferior in the prewar years. The Tata Iron and Steel Company (Tisco), for instance, had begun to produce steel in the early twentieth century, but the British chief commissioner of the Indian Railways, Sir Frederick Upcott, had sworn to "eat every pound of steel rail" they made, if it ever met British specifications. Post-1914, however, the British bought around 2,500 kilometers of rails from Tisco to build its network in Mesopotamia, and this prompted Dorab Tata to remark that Upcott would have suffered quite a bout of indigestion if he had kept his word.

For Indian businesses, the war was thus a chance to prove their mettle. But to the Indian public, money made by Indian industry on British trade during domestic war shortages carried the stench of betrayal. Indian companies did not help their own cause—for some firms, the war restrictions on imports into India presented an opportunity for profiteering, which they happily took up. This did not endear them to the public any further.

Worst of all perhaps was the impression that Indian businesses did not back India's fight against British rule wholeheartedly. The governor of the United Provinces pointed to Indian industry's penchant for fence-sitting, and commented on their "Vichy mentality"[6]—their hopes of appeasing everyone, annoying no one. Not surprisingly, antibusiness feeling during these years, and as India neared independence, became widespread. The Indian industrialist G. D. Birla, noticing this, worried about the "strong feelings among my workers that I have not seen before . . . they are even losing the great regard they had for my person."[7]

Moves and countermoves: The hopes of the Bombay Plan

So it was that by the 1940s, Indian business sensed that change was afoot and began to retreat in the face of their clear unpopularity and the rising threat of a state-dominated economy. The byword among them was "compromise, compromise, compromise,"* and in an attempt to make the best of things, a group of India's most prominent industrialists tried to meet Nehru halfway on policy with the Bombay Plan.†

But as the economist Vivek Chibber points out, Indian businesses had by then grown used to a paternal state that intervened on their behalf. In 1939, for instance, Patel had blocked a British firm from obtaining a license to set up an electrification project in Gujarat, and the Congress governments in the provinces championed Indian businesses over foreign ones.[8] The extended protections of the war years had also shielded them from competition since the 1930s,‡ and allowed the domestic prices of Indian commodities to soar substantially above world levels.

So Indian businesses wanted it both ways. The authors of the Bombay Plan endorsed centralized planning, but the document was less of a straight arrow in its notions of free markets. It was not business-friendly policies that the document lobbied for, but for policies friendly to *Indian* businesses. The Bombay Plan fondly envisaged a friendly state that would continue to shield them from the vagaries of foreign competition, and grandly stated, "The distinction between capitalism and socialism has lost much of its significance."[9]

But the search for such a happy medium in policy through the Bombay Plan was futile with someone like Nehru on the other side of the table. Nehru believed that capitalism was an unworkable system, one that left a "bloody and cruel mess," and was only biding his time, listening to their bluster and logic, impervious to their passionate lobbying.

It is not really surprising that Nehru and other leaders did not have much sympathy for the appeals of Indian businesses. Dr. André Béteille points out, "Most Indian businessmen during these years were uneducated, exclusively from the traditional business castes, and unconcerned about philanthropy or taking up a broader economic role. Nehru and the other politicians were, however, highly educated; most of them were lawyers and they possessed a

*Opinions differ on how much was compromise and how much of this was from industrialists who were true believers. Historians such as Baldev Raj Nayar have argued that the industrialists coauthoring the plan, including the Tatas, truly believed that state-led capitalism was "the only option" if India was to go from a desperately poor to a developed country.

†The Bombay Plan of 1944 was prepared by six Indian businessmen— G. D. Birla, J.R.D. Tata, Purushothamdas Thakurdas, John Mathai, Kasturbhai Lalbhai and Lala Sriram.

‡For instance, fifty-one "inquiries" (or requests) from businesses in India between 1929 and 1939 resulted in varying amounts of protectionism for textiles, iron and steel, sugar and paper, among others.

clear economic vision. I can see why they believed the government could manage the economy better."

The 1952 elections consolidated Nehru's power, even as Patel's death tilted the scales against business a little further, and Indian industry held its breath as it watched the government unfurl its economic policy. But the first five-year plan (1951–56) was an accommodating one, stating that in the light of the vast capital India needed for reconstruction, the "initiative and responsibility . . . of private enterprise" was indispensable.[10]

It was only in 1956 that the socialist agenda took on real life. In the second five-year plan, the Indian government pitched its economic strategy as a "mixed" approach that embraced the role of both the public and private sector. But the emphasis, as the Federation of India Chambers of Commerce and Industry (FICCI) pointed out, was on "suspicion and antipathy" to the private sector.[11]

With this plan, the government was on the offensive in the effort to take economic control away from businesses. Indian industry found itself out in the cold—across sectors, doors were shut in its face and labeled "government only," and new bureaucratic rules tracked their every move. The state took control of primary industries including steel, power and petrochemicals, and the production here was allocated to private sector firms according to their permits. Entry into industries kept aside for the private sector was regulated through a licensing system, and the government controlled the pricing of commodities such as sugar and textiles.

There was not much that business could do to break the wave. The industrialist and backer of the Bombay Plan Ardeshir Dalal pointed out, "The rank and file of political parties and the . . . mass of the country, however juvenile or unreasonable, are the most potent process to be reckoned with."[12] It was clear that socialism had become the only game in town. Public sentiment was on Nehru's side—popular films such as Mehboob Khan's *Mother India* and Ramesh Saigal's *Shaheed* (Martyr) extolled the nationalistic spirit, and the faith in the new state.[13]

It did not take very long, however, before it began to appear that India's "tryst with destiny" was becoming a tale of missed connections. The dominance of the state had created a decidedly unequal relationship between the business and the government. State-led planning helped the government justify a massive expansion in employment, creating a "welfare bureaucracy,"[14] and this began to clog up the industry with regulations, permissions and the slow transfer of paper from desk to desk. The licensing model for doing business also turned economic competition into a game with a crooked wheel, as bureaucrats who managed licenses became the gatekeepers to industry.*

These elite, educated bureaucrats were hardly industry allies, and the government's disdain for businessmen traveled down their ranks. The officers were especially risk-averse in awarding permits[15]—given the choice between a young upstart entrepreneur and an established business house, they awarded licenses to the latter, picking experience over innovation. Business procured multiple licenses to preempt competition in their industry; snap up enough, companies found out, and you could have your own little monopoly. By 1964 more than half of India's product industries had just one or two firms competing in them.

Ironically, in trying to eliminate the legacies of the East India Company, our leaders shaped Indian business into exactly the venal kind of capitalism they deplored. These firms picked their teeth while consumers complained. The licensing model created lazy monopolies, which held Indian consumers captive to products of terrible quality – yellow paper, refrigerators that didn't cool and cars that backfired on their way off the assembly line. The major drivers of GDP—capital investment and productivity growth—stagnated. It was as if the workers slept at the machines and the managers slept at their desks. The country's export earnings remained stagnant, and as our trade deficit grew from Rs 780 million to Rs 7.91 billion between 1950 and 1964, foreign aid grew from zero to Rs 8.19 billion.

Nehru had once said, "Standing on my head increases my good humor." One must wonder how often during this dark period of growth Nehru took to viewing the world upside down.

1964–80: "Then I, and you, and all of us fell down"

By the early 1960s India was acutely conscious of the darkening shadows over the economy, and its lack of capital caused Nehru to worry about the

*A clear sign of the prestige of Indian bureaucrats during this time was their immense preference as sons-in-law (we can trust the marriage market data since it was free of licensing, and demand and supply were unregulated). In the arranged-marriage market, IAS officers were the most preferred, followed by the IFS and the IPS. The competition for these officers started even before they graduated—in July and August, "placement season" would begin at the Lal Bahadur Shastri National Academy of IAS probationers in Mussoorie, as dozens of people with eligible daughters descended on the campus.

"crisis of our spirit, of being overwhelmed by fear." The country was forever in debt, wandering hat in hand from donor to donor for bailouts in food and cash. And yet, notwithstanding the disastrous results of India's growth strategy, the country did not move toward reform. India was like the friend who is always touching you for a loan but who also refuses to change his behavior in order to become solvent.

The challenge here was that India's economic policies have more often than not followed an unpredictable course, determined less by pragmatism than by a series of unfortunate accidents—of death or crisis. The first of these occurred in 1964, when Nehru, most inconveniently for the Congress party, died.

The death of the "village spellbinder" and beloved of the people turned the economic ideas he championed into gospel truth. Through the 1960s and 1970s, socialism thus became for the Congress a stand-in for the Nehruvian appeal, a prop for the actual leader.

To digress here a moment—in the longer term, the Congress party would pay dearly for this with their popularity. Many commentators have remarked on India's uniqueness as an enduring democracy among the young, free ex-colonial Asian nations. But like India, the rest of Asia's newly free economies had also become democracies after the Second World War. The difference between India and these countries was that by the late 1970s, as the writer Fareed Zakaria noted, many of them had become indifferent to real political competition and typically had a single dominant party, such as the People's Action Party in Singapore and the National Front in Malaysia.

The unique rise of India's multiparty democracy is, I believe, closely intertwined with the economic policies the Congress party persisted with. Between the 1940s and 1960s, India too was not a strong multiparty democracy. During these years the Indian Congress party was like East Asia's one-party systems today—a massive, sprawling organization that dominated political debate and easily won reelection, with its opposition squeezed into the margins. The Congress's intractable hold on the Parliament and the state assemblies was especially remarkable in a country that was so layered and diverse.

Given the chance, the Congress leadership probably could have consolidated political power in the same way some young Asian nations did in the 1970s. Indira Gandhi certainly attempted this in the 1960s and 1970s, when her government imposed presidential rule or toppled opposition parties in states such as Punjab, Haryana and West Bengal.

But the East Asian countries that were "one-party democracies" had consolidated their rule alongside the implementation of mercantile economic policies, keeping their currencies cheap, promoting exports and protecting businesses from external competition while encouraging entrepreneurship within the domestic economy. This ensured rapid economic growth—and people in these countries did not search for political alternatives for a fairly long period. (This began to change only in the 1990s, as education touched developed-country levels.) In India, however, the Congress saw its once powerful hold on the electorate disintegrate due to its inability to drive growth and increases in income.*

Of course, India is a larger, more disparate country, with divisions across caste, religion and region. Nevertheless, the gradual atomization in political power that followed could have been far less powerful had the decades under Congress governments enabled the kind of inclusive economic growth that dissolves feudal structures and relationships. Prosperity, after all, is the most unifying religion there is.

INSTEAD, THROUGH THE 1960s and 1970s, as policies suppressed entrepreneurship and joblessness soared, Indians found other ways to be, well, enterprising. Most of India's most violent movements and mobocracy trace their origins back to these decades. The hordes of unemployed degree holders fed the growth of an extreme left Naxalite movement. In Punjab and the northeast, militancy was on the rise, and Kashmir stayed on a constant simmer. The price controls of a socialist economy also fed the growth of a vibrant black market and powerful mafiosi such as Haji Mastan, Yusuf Patel and Vardhabhai.

This parallel black economy was—in its most profitable tier—dominated by an Indian obsession, gold. In fact, by the 1980s the amount Indians invested in gold and silver was double the money they put in the stock market. The ban on gold imports into India, along with the controlled rupee, meant

*I am by no means endorsing the concept of one-party rule. But now that we face no danger of it, it is interesting to wonder about the "might-have-beens."

that smuggling tola bars* of gold into the country from international markets was hugely profitable, especially with the massive demand for the metal during the wedding season. Smuggling dominated the Indian consciousness to such an extent that Bollywood movies featuring wealthy, cigar-chewing smugglers were widely popular. These characters—often played by the actor Ajit Khan—depicted villainous, handsome men, who like the smuggler Haji Mastan wore white designer suits, and whose passions revolved around their "Mona" and sona—their moll and their gold.

Unorganized violence was also at an all-time high. A tottering economy had turned India into an angry, seething nation—agricultural production was down by nearly a third by the mid-1960s, and prices hit new records as a series of droughts brought India to the brink of famine. Policemen held off mobs across the country, college campuses closed down and India's once-celebrated symbols became hubs of rioting—the shining steel towns of Bhilai and Rourkela were not spared, and Chandigarh, India's glittering showcase city, erupted with both communal and economic tensions.

There were a few fleeting moments, when it seemed that the widespread unhappiness would lead to policies opening up the economy to the private sector. The crunch of food shortages during this period, for instance, gave Lal Bahadur Shastri, Nehru's successor, an opportunity to pass some reforms in agriculture. He liberalized the fertilizer industry, opening it up to competition. The green revolution also took off thanks to new hybrid crops that Indian scientists created with the help of the Rockefeller Foundation and seeds the American agronomist Norman Borlaug sent to India.

But such concessions to entrepreneurs remained rare. In the midst of the food crunch, Shastri announced that he and his family would miss a meal every Wednesday, and the government placed ads in Indian newspapers telling readers, "Remember, today is a Dinnerless Day!" But articles on the same page would be carrying speeches by politicians chewing out Indian industry.

A passing opportunity for reforms did come along, when Indira Gandhi—a tough, hard-as-nails prime minister, whom one observer had called "the only man in a Cabinet full of old women"—was at the helm of

*The "tola" was an Indian weight measure, equal to 11.667 grams. The bars preferred by smugglers were, overwhelmingly, the rounded ones over the standard, sharp-cornered bars, since these could be wedged into body cavities. The experience was apparently still quite unpleasant, but of course we must look at this in relative terms.

the government. Indira initiated a series of economic reforms that the World Bank had made conditional for aid, which included devaluing the rupee by more than half to Rs 7.5 per dollar and relaxing some controls on the private sector. But this was spectacularly bad timing, since India was at the time still dependent on the conditional PL-480 food aid from the United States.[16] The Opposition decried the reforms, denouncing Indira as a sellout to "capitalist ideology" and a tool of the CIA.* This would eventually turn out to be very bad news for India's entrepreneurs. Faced with more enemies than friends both within and without her party, Indira veered leftward in defense, rolled back reforms and resorted to a full-throttle populist policy against Indian business. In a speech that followed, Indira came out full-throttle as a populist and referred to capitalism as one of the "dark and evil forces . . . which are intent on destroying the very base of our democratic and socialist objectives."[17] The government followed this through with a series of patently antibusiness acts.†

These were cold, dark years for Indian business—even as socialism tightened its grip on the economy, the defense of free enterprise in our politics dwindled. The Swatantra Party had declined with C. Rajagopalachari's death, selling its soul to a motley set of right-wing parties and—Rajagopalachari would have been spinning in his grave—socialists for political power.

Between 1970 and 1973, GDP per capita actually shrank by 5 percent and popular disenchantment with government policies had become intense. In Hyderabad, Indira faced a flurry of shoes, and she asked the crowd, "Has someone opened a new shoe shop here? He must be making a fortune."

Just as the movies during the 1950s had reflected the optimism of the early Nehru years, films during this time reflected the anger of people held hostage by an ineffective state. Films were revenge dramas whose heroes were either gangsters along the lines of Amitabh Bachchan in *Deewar* (The Wall) or ordinary men turned crusaders—Amitabh Bachchan in *Zanjeer* (Chains)—against an apathetic state and corruption. And the movie *Sholay* (Embers), a

*The latter accusation was the knee-jerk response to any move toward better relations with the West, and it is a charge that still has not disappeared. Rajiv Gandhi was the target of similar aspersions when he moved to establish better relations with the United States in the 1980s. Most recently, in 2008, left parties resorted once again to old anti-Americanisms in their opposition to the India–U.S. nuclear deal.

†Acts such as reservations for small-scale industries in expert sectors like leather and textiles and the Monopolies and Restrictive Trade Practices Act (MRTP) penalized business growth. Indira also announced the nationalization of banks through an ordinance, nationalized coal, iron and steel, and—when their imminent shutdown put seventy thousand jobs at stake—textile mills.

rebellious, violent, crooks-and-bandits story, became the biggest hit of the decade.

But we had to face one more crisis, which presented the biggest challenge yet to India's economy and its democracy, for policies toward entrepreneurs to change in a big way. The fuse was lit by the 1973 oil embargo. The economy was in no shape to cope with the fourfold increase in international oil prices, and India hung onto solvency by its fingernails. India's oil import bill surged to $1.3 billion—twice the amount of its foreign exchange reserves.

In 1969 Indira had responded to India's financial crisis with populism; this time, as strikes spread across the country, she tried dictatorship. On June 25, 1975, she declared the Emergency and the government initiated a probusiness economic policy, with the announcement of a twenty-point economic program. It prioritized growth and better capacity utilization, and put performance conditions on the public sector.

But even in the midst of the Emergency, the government believed that appearing probusiness was political hemlock (even worse, apparently, than appearing dictatorial). While releasing the new Emergency-era policy, Indira spoke of the need for a "socially conscious" private sector, and tried to soften the impact of liberal policy by carrying out public raids on the homes and offices of businessmen they suspected of evading taxes or working with the mafia.[18]

But soon enough, Indira Gandhi called elections and the government was tossed out; what followed was a period of uncertain policies and a weak coalition. By the end of this decade, the recurring crisis and macroeconomic shocks had exhausted the Indian state.

1980–91: Indian business comes in from the cold

"The 1980s marked quite a shift in attitudes toward business," the economist Arvind Subramanian says. Arvind is in my house, stretched out on my living room couch—he is tall, lanky, and completely dwarfs my sofa. He has brought with him a thick sheaf of papers, the manuscript of *India's Turn*, his most recent book, in which he discusses in part the government's changing vision in the 1980s toward businesses.

"There was a realization," Arvind says, "that the government by itself simply could not enable the kind of growth India needed." The 1982 and 1984 reforms that followed were primarily what Arvind calls a "pro-business" approach to reform rather than a "pro-market" one. The reforms delicensed twenty industries and introduced a "broadbanding" approach, where firms that had a presence in one industry could diversify into parallel ones. Price controls were also dismantled in industrial products such as cement and aluminum. Overall, however, while the reforms made doing business easier for existing firms, the government did not do very much to remove the license raj in its entirety. Industry licenses continued to be a bargaining chip, and the government used it, for instance, to discourage firms from investing in states with non-Congress governments. Many import controls also remained in place and this kept input costs for businesses high. Import tariff rates actually rose—in 1990 the highest tariff rate stood at 355 percent.

Montek suggests that while the 1980s saw some movement toward better policies, it took the 1991 reforms to bring about a real transformation in how the government viewed markets. Montek's reformist credentials are impeccable: he was the Finance Secretary during India's crucial 1991–96 years, and in his stint at the Planning Commission he has gained a reputation as a straight-talking champion for liberal policy.

When I visit Montek at his house, he sits across from me in his La-Z-Boy chair—the one sign of indulgence I spot in his otherwise spare home—and reclines, but never relaxes. When I bring up the 1980s reforms, he contends that these policies were never fundamental; they may have indicated an exhaustion with the planned economy but, "The changes they brought in weren't systemic. There wasn't a clear vision behind them, and there was quite a bit of negotiating and backtracking on these reforms." Nevertheless, the doors to the Indian economy had with these policies finally begun to creak open for the private sector, and a chink of light was shining through.

But as the state set about removing the props that had held the planning framework afloat, protests rose from Indian industry itself. Industry licensing and import quotas had created a group of Indian businesses that had grown fat, soft and mollycoddled in the closed economy. These businesses were fearful of promarket policies and also of that particular bugaboo, foreign competition. They angrily clamored against the new policies, shaking their chubby fists at the liberalization of some imports. The All-India Chemical Manufacturers' Association came out against the import of PVC resins, dyes and soda ash—which were being imported from Bulgaria at "throw away prices." At the same time, however, other Indian firms discovered the upside of these cheaper imports, and the All India Glass Manufacturers' Association pleaded for the continued import of the same soda ash, a critical input for their industry.[19]

But the sounds of an economy shaking itself awake were drowning out the tinny voices in favor of protectionism. Between 1985 and 1990, the rupee depreciated by about 30 percent, which helped Indian businesses surge in export competitiveness. GDP responded sharply to rising capital investment, and it averaged a growth of nearly 6 percent between 1980 and 1990.

The 1980s was also a period that marked the rise of software firms in India. Right out of college, I had joined Patni Computer Systems (PCS), a family firm, whose CEO Narendra Patni came from one of India's traditional business communities. I met Narayana Murthy here, and when Murthy's plan to set up a small, new software company inspired six of us to join him, we walked into a minefield of regulations. We did not need much from the government, but the rare times we did have to travel to Delhi to get permissions to import a piece of hardware, we would be trapped in bureaucratic paperwork for months. Once, when one of the cofounders, N. S. Raghavan, went to Delhi to change the "port of arrival" from Madras to Bangalore in an import permission letter, he had to hang around in the lobby outside a bureaucrat's office for eighteen days. The corridors of these government buildings felt like a maze you could not find a way out of.

Additionally, since India had huge shortages of foreign exchange through the 1980s, every trip that we made abroad required the approval and sanction of dollars from the authorities. One time I had to make two trips to the United States in quick succession, and the clerk at the Reserve Bank of India demanded to know why I was traveling abroad so often—he did not see the need of it and must have thought I was a hedonistic wastrel.

We also witnessed how much people favored working in the Indian public sector at the time. Soon after Infosys moved to Bangalore in the early 1980s, we had hired a few bright young engineers from IIT Madras. Within a few weeks, one of them came up to me and said he wanted to quit, to join a public-sector company in Bangalore—he told me that "a government company will never go under, and the job I have will be for life." The security of such employment was a very compelling argument in those years for an engineer from IIT.

It took one more crisis to change our small steps toward reform in the 1980s into a single leap to the other side. India's particular nemesis has been the oil price rise, which sent the economy reeling toward bankruptcy time after time. In 1991 yet another oil price rise triggered a crisis that I would call "third-time lucky." It was one that transformed our attitudes toward India's entrepreneurs.

India was staring into an abyss by the end of the 1990s—thanks to reckless government borrowings, our foreign debt had more than tripled since 1981 to $64.4 billion. Then came the Gulf War and high oil prices, which sucked out our foreign reserves to the extent that India had enough money for just ten days of imports and had to mortgage its gold for an emergency loan. With the Indian economy on the ropes, the finance minister Manmohan Singh introduced a reform agenda explicitly meant to bring the private sector fully into the economy. With this 1991 policy, the baton for growth passed from the government to "the human spirit of creativity, adventure and enterprise."

In entering its new age, India ended a long period of incomplete freedoms—a time of democratic rule but of severe economic shackles. The new policy released the private sector from industrial licensing and controls on capital. Financial reforms eased up access to credit for businesses by removing controls on interest rates.

Most dramatically for entrepreneurs, Manmohan Singh "rolled up the red tape and rolled out the red carpet" for foreign firms, bringing top import tariffs across sectors down from 355 percent in 1985 to 85 percent in 1993.* This was the most controversial change of all, and it was greeted with consternation by Indian businesses and politicians alike. P. Chidambaram, the Harvard-educated UPA finance minister who was also in the commerce ministry during the 1991 reforms (with a well-known penchant for quoting the Tamil poet Tiruvalluvar†), tells me, "When we abolished the licensing requirement for imports and liberalized our trade policies, many were convinced it would kill us." The misshapen head of protectionism reared up again—several Indian businesses demanded a slower opening to foreign in-

*Import tariffs were cut through a system that compressed the top tariff rate, while rationalizing the tariff structure through a reduction in the number of tariff bands. The top rate has continued to fall, to 12.5 percent in 2005–6.

†A few of the lines he has included in his budget speeches—on the need to drive agricultural growth: "If plowmen keep their hands folded/Even the sages claiming renunciation cannot find salvation." And on the government's goal with the budget: "Health, wealth, produce, the happiness that is the result, and security. These five the learned say are the ornaments of a polity."

vestment. This group of big businesses, which eventually came to be called the "Bombay Club," were strongly opposed to removing protections against foreign competition. The industrialist Rahul Bajaj, the most outspoken of these business leaders, appealed to the Indian government to consider our "national interests and national pride" and protect Indian industrialists "until there's a level playing field." But the policies passed, and Indian businesses for the first time since independence lost their guarantees and an assured market. But they were also offered, for the first time, the chance for something more.

A flurry of activity

In the 1970s and 1980s, nearly every Indian middle-class home had a cupboard made of wood or steel, with multiple locks and several small drawers. The favored brand was Godrej Storwel, with its hard-to-pick lock. Most Indian families kept their savings and jewelery here. People avoided putting money in stocks because of the "wealth tax" on such investments. When the "wealth tax" was eliminated, money came out of these cupboards and into India's stock markets. This combination of stock-market modernization and a vibrant market enabled an explosion of new entrepreneurs who could tap into market capital to compete across industries and turned many once-oligopolistic industry sectors, such as airlines and telecom, into highly competitive ones.

The businesses that emerged at the top of the heap after this struggle were different from the ones before—half of the top ten companies in market capitalization in 1991 had disappeared from the list by the decade's end. Some of the most prominent entrepreneurs who emerged post-1980, such as Sunil Mittal and Dhirubhai Ambani, had built their firms from scratch and were a breed far apart from the closed-circle, family entrepreneurs of the 1960s and 1970s.

For entrepreneurs, the reforms in our capital flows have not just brought in new efficiencies and competition, but have also created enormous consumer opportunity. Indian consumers now account for as much as 67 percent of the country's GDP, compared with less than half for China, and India is expected to become the world's fifth largest consumer market within the next fifteen years.

Arvind tells me that one of the most dramatic changes for Indian businessmen came from the tax reforms that started in 1985. "When the tax rates fell, it virtually unstoppered the tap in terms of cash on hand for entrepreneurs," he says. Instead of having to watch money disappear into the pockets of babus, Indian businesses were now able to rapidly reinvest their profits into expanding their businesses and investing in new technologies. The tax reforms triggered a rapid growth in tax revenues—it took India five decades to cross Rs 1,000 billion in tax revenue, but in the ten years that followed, the country's tax revenues have crossed Rs 6,000 billion.

Go west, young man: The Bombay House businesses

Our movies have as usual reflected the Indian transformation. The films of today are highly aspirational—*Chak de India* and *Munnabhai MBBS* are very different profiles of ordinary people passionate about success. And as India's human capital—its entrepreneurs, consumers and its millions of workers—has become the country's Atlas, holding the economy high up on its shoulders, films like *Rang de Basanti* and *Swades* channel a growing belief that ordinary Indians can bring about enormous change.

Over the last few years, these new ambitions have compelled many entrepreneurs to look outward. Many businesses immediately after reforms were cautious about the Indian ability to compete in international markets—we felt we would be easily bruised, that the competition would crush Indian firms. But the software industry had already oriented itself to global markets and the publicity we got through the 1990s, as our exports grew yearly at 50 percent, was a great source of confidence for a cautious nation and its entrepreneurs.

A focus on global competitiveness has now expanded across Indian industry and has enabled what I call the new Bombay House mind-set. Bombay House is the headquarters of the Tatas and sits in the heart of Bombay's business district. It is an enormous, beautiful building designed by the British architect George Wittet (who also designed Bombay's Victoria Terminus train station) and is not far from Dalal Street, the nerve center of India's capitalism, and from my favorite seafood restaurants.

The rise of Bombay House as a global headquarters is a symbol of Indian businesses shading its eyes, and looking far out, across our coasts—of companies wanting to compete where there is opportunity and invest where there is growth. The Tatas are a great instance of how some of India's oldest businesses have transformed themselves from conglomerates focused primarily on India's protected market to aggressive, international firms. Tata is now expanding across Europe, the United States and Asia, and recently made the biggest ever global acquisition by an Indian company with the purchase of the British steel firm Corus. Such deals are no longer rare. In 2007 Indian companies were involved in $70 billion worth of merger and acquisition (M&A) deals, with the number of acquisitions clocking in at more than 1,000 for the first time in Indian corporate history. In fact 2007 was also a year for truly bumper M&A announcements, which included the Tata-Corus, Hindalco-Novelis and the Vodafone–Hutchison Essar deals. Indian companies are becoming prominent, cash-rich buyers and financiers for American and European firms—with the Times Group buying Virgin Radio and Anil Ambani's ADA group financing Spielberg's Dreamworks SKG. And Rahul Bajaj, who had headed the Bombay Club of entrepreneurs protesting the fall of trade barriers, now has his eye firmly set on the international market, as his company expands its operations into Brazil and Indonesia.

In *Good Capitalism, Bad Capitalism,* the writers Baumol, Litan and Schramm argue that the best kind of markets are not state directed or oligarchic, but a blend of "big-firm" and "entrepreneurial" firms. India now has that blend—large companies that are state owned, family owned or foreign multinationals and thousands of smaller entrepreneurs from different backgrounds. There are now traditional business houses as well as first-generation businessmen whose fathers worked in farms, shops and offices. This entrepreneurial capital has been a critical ingredient in the cocktail of ideas propelling India forward.

I got a sense of the scale and ambition of some of India's entrepreneurs when I met with Mukesh Ambani, chairman of Reliance Industries, in 2005, just before he launched his retail businesses. We were both in Washington as part of the Indo-U.S. business forum accompanying Prime Minister Manmohan Singh. When we had a moment to spare, we hopped over to a nearby Starbucks, and there he explained to me in great detail his plans to revolutionize Indian retail. I added my bit by drawing some supply chain options on a paper napkin. I marveled at the scale of his ambition—to be present in every Indian city and town—and his meticulous attention to detail. Mukesh told me that his supply chains would go a long way in addressing the massive infrastructure gaps between India's farms and its markets—he called his initiative "from farm to fork." And as more such entrepreneurs focus on India's problems, a whole new force of change is becoming possible.

Yet, despite all this change, the blend of good capitalism that Baumol wrote about so convincingly is not yet fully present. In 2008 a local Delhi gang attacked the activist Madhu Kishwar—one among several assaults on Kishwar and her organization Manushi. These activists were being targeted for helping street hawkers and vegetable vendors in the city organize and file legal cases to avoid having to pay bribes to street gangs, the police and municipal offices. This is the big divide in India right now—the large and small entrepreneur in India face very different experiences with Indian regulations and bureaucracy. In Delhi, for instance, a stall owner needs a "tehbazari" license to set up a stall, which is difficult to get without contacts in the municipal office. As a result, the majority of Delhi stalls are illegal and have to, as Kishwar writes, "regularly placate the . . . deities of the license raj with cash offerings."[20]

When it comes to the full force of Indian regulation, India is still not a very business-friendly country, and we rank far below Pakistan and China in the ease of doing business. The regulations that remain hurt the small entrepreneur and the first-time businessman the hardest. Money in particular has been a touchy subject. While it is good to be on the conservative side in financial policy, the limitations India places on businesses in accessing credit and capital are severe—the government pulls the threads too tight and has had an unfortunate history of directing the bulk of the money in banks to itself. Even today, 30 percent of the assets sitting in bank vaults are long-term government bonds. This tendency of the state to hoard so much capital says a great deal about the ambivalence of Indian governments about how much freedom our businesses can have.

Unfortunately, ambivalence here hits the most vulnerable of India's self-employed. Without fully functioning commodity markets, the chances for farmers to diversify and make new investments are limited, and the lack of social security restricts their ability to take risks. Small entrepreneurs remain small and, without the information or funds to expand, stick with their carts and small one-room shops year after year. Difficulties in getting permits encourage their exploitation. Until the licensing system and bureaucracy change enough to affect even these small firms, India's potential remains only partially awakened.

From the Bombay Plan to the Bombay Club to Bombay House

When I think of India's entrepreneurial shift, I see it as a fundamental change in our attitudes toward competition, moving from the mind-set of the Bombay Plan, when companies clamored for state coddling and protectionism, to the Bombay Club, when they continued to demand trade barriers, to finally the tradition of Bombay House, where Indian businesses have become outward-looking, unafraid of competition and willing to take risks and enter new markets, targeting India's so-far untouched, rural country and the world beyond our borders.

In fact, the rise of the India Premier League (IPL)—which has combined India's two great passions, cricket and Bollywood—has become a fascinating instance of how fast the Indian attitude toward competition is changing. This Twenty/20* cricket tournament allowed franchises for the first time in Indian cricket, and teams formed and owned by India's biggest film stars and businesses competed for the tournament cup. Cricket stars were signed on in bidding wars, the more promising ones getting much higher contracts. Gone were the fixed salaries and the bias in selection toward entrenched and more senior players.

There was an old wag of a saying that "India has potential, and it will always have potential." It is as Indian attitudes toward entrepreneurs have transformed—from criticism and suspicion to a new appreciation of the "animal spirit"—that this potential is finally being realized. Nehru had once expressed contempt for what he called the "bania civilization," and Indira Gandhi had spoken of businessmen as "the dark and evil forces" that threatened to destroy the country. In the new era, however, Manmohan Singh lauds businessmen as "the source of India's confidence, and our optimism."

*Typical one-day cricket matches had fifty overs per team, which allowed a more leisurely pace of the game. The Twenty/20 version however has, as its name indicates, a shorter version of the game with twenty overs, which makes it faster paced, with players far more focused on scoring "big hits" to score runs.

THE PHOENIX TONGUE

The Rise, Fall and Rise of English

WHEN I TRAVEL outside India, my homesickness and sense of displacement are as aural as they are visual. In India it is impossible to miss the chatter and noise of a public space—which I find is often several decibels higher here than nearly anywhere else in the world. And not only do we love to talk, we do it in a thousand tongues—for there are as many documented languages and dialects in India.*

The crowds in our streets speak in a rich and varied tongue, a jostle of hybrid and home-grown languages. But across India's economy—especially in urban India—it is one language, India's "auntie tongue"[1] English, that seems ubiquitous. In bureaucrat-speak, it is our "associate official" language, and it is the predominant tongue in which business transactions, boardroom discussions and water-cooler gossip take place. In the early days of Infosys, when we were marketing our services outside India, many of our prospective customers were taken aback when they found that we spoke English. And they were even more surprised when we told them that the seven founders of Infosys between themselves spoke five different languages at home, and English was the only language we shared.

*The estimates of "total Indian languages" provided across our various censuses since 1921, however, vary anywhere from 150 languages to more than 1,500, depending on how they classified the dialects and the languages. We have the largest number of official languages in the world, at 22.

Yet, despite our apparent comfort, English is a *second* language for nearly all those Indians who speak it, and historically our attitude toward the tongue has been quite ambivalent. The language has been in some ways a reflection of India's relationship with Britain and the rest of the world, and has been a part of a young country's search for identity and unity. For Indians the language has consequently been, at various times over the last two hundred years, a symbol of oppression, resistance, compromise and, most recently, of an economy come of age.

A language of the ships and traders

English came to India with Europe's ships, and for much of the seventeenth and eighteenth centuries, it was seen mainly as a "port" language, a tongue spoken among merchants. In fact English was just one part of "Firangi,"[2] a pidgin tongue Indians used to communicate with foreign traders, which was a blend of Hindustani, Portuguese, French, Dutch and English. For a long time, few people used English exclusively, and even as the East India Company expanded its power across India, company officials kept Portuguese dictionaries and Persian translators by their side to help them communicate.[3]

One reason the Company did not force the English language in India was, as the historian Nicholas Ostler notes, Britain's recent loss of a major colony: the Americas. In India this loss felt especially close—Lord Cornwallis, governor general of Bengal from 1786 to 1793, had arrived in India after his defeat in the Americas, having handed over the British surrender to George Washington at Yorktown in 1781.[4] As Cornwallis's defeated army marched out, its band, as legend has it, played the tune "The World Turned Upside Down"—Britain was convinced that this loss in the Americas would result in the collapse of its Empire. It was therefore especially wary about bringing English to India, and one governor general remarked that educating Indians in English would result in the British getting kicked out in three months.[5]

But half a century later, with its finances in a mess and facing bankruptcy, the East India Company was forced to think out of the box. In 1828 the governor general William Bentinck was sent to India with the express mandate to cut the company's administrative costs.[6] One of his recommendations was to replace British workers in the company's judicial and administrative jobs with cheaper, Indian graduates.* To enable this, Bentinck added a clause in the Company's 1833 Charter Act opening up government posts to qualified persons "irrespective of religion, birth, descent or color."[7]

But to create enough qualified Indians conversant in English, an English-education policy was necessary, and for this Bentinck had to go through a committee of officials divided on the idea that they could simply transport their language into a foreign country. By the time Thomas Macaulay arrived in 1834 as the new president of the General Committee of Public Instruction (which framed the Company's education policies in India), there was growing support among the officials for an English-language policy. But Macaulay provided the policy with new, powerful ballast, bringing a righteous passion to the cause of English education in his famous Minute of February 2, 1835. Launching an outright attack on Indian learning, he said that if Indian education continued, "we shall [allow] at public expense, medical doctrines which would disgrace an English farrier, astronomy which would move laughter in girls at an English boarding school . . . and geography made of seas of treacle and seas of butter." Macaulay supported Bentinck in creating an elite group of English-educated Indians: "We must . . . form a class who may be interpreters between us and the millions whom we govern—a class of persons Indian in blood and color, but English in tastes, in opinions, in morals and in intellect."[8]

For good measure, Macaulay—his stiff upper lip, presumably, trembling for a moment—threatened the council with his resignation if the recommendations of his Minute were not taken up.[9] There was no risk of that, with Bentinck entirely supportive, and British India's education policies were soon transformed. English became the lingua franca of the administration, and the number of English government schools more than doubled within three years of the 1835 English Education Act. The Company announced in 1844 that English-educated Indians would receive preferential treatment in public-sector appointments, and in 1857 the first three English-language universities were set up.

The imposition of the English language, the historian and linguist Robert King notes, rankled among many Indians as a move against the native

*The whole argument for educating Indians in English was thus, in essence, to allow the British to offshore their governance jobs—replace British workers with Indian ones.

tongues, most of which were older than English—Tamil and Kannada, for instance, were centuries older. English was consequently viewed as a tool of imperialism, which the British were using to assert their authority over the country*—it symbolized "servility, meekness, bowed heads before the sahib and memsahib, and the topi."[10]

However, a small section of Indians did welcome English-language education, especially the social butterflies, who associated English with cultural prestige and considered it essential to life in the upper circles. The language became an additional accessory for the elite, a pretty bauble to be acquired in the same way upper-crust Indians adopted British dress, tea parties and socials.[11] Alongside this, English also rapidly took on the role of a career language. The Indian colony had been significantly deindustrialized under the British, and an administrative career was the major, and probably only, avenue for the educated Indian.[12] This made British education immensely popular, and by the 1900s India's education in the arts (the more favored stream) was dominated by 140 English colleges with more than 17,000 students, compared with five Indian colleges, which had a total of 503 students.

The policy also won the support of Indian social reformers such as Raja Ram Mohan Roy, who saw great advantages in English as a language for spreading literacy and education in India. Roy viewed English as a potentially universal second language, accessible to Indians across castes and communities, "a tongue that would exist outside the control of the native, caste- and religion-based elite—unlike the rarefied Sanskrit under the Brahmins and the courtly Persian of the Muslim elite." Roy went as far as to remark, "So long as the English language is universal, it will remain Indian." English was thus in the strange position of representing repression to some, and emancipation and social freedom to others.[13]

A tool for Indian nationalism

The learning curve for English in India was by no means smooth—English-educated Indians were sometimes unintentionally comic with the language, creating what the British called "babuisms," coined after the Indian "babu"

*Such "linguistic imperialism" during occupation has not been restricted to the British—the Japanese imposed their language on the Koreans and the Malays during the Second World War.

or civil servant who committed them. One incident that the viceroy Lord Lytton apparently liked to relate was of an English judge asking an Indian barrister why his female client was not at court. "I beg your pardon, Mr. Chandra Ram," the judge had asked, "but is your client an adult?" "No my Lord," the hapless lawyer replied, "she is an adulteress."[14]

But English did not remain an alien tongue for long. A unique characteristic of the English language has been its easy ability to absorb cultural influences, and English assimilated an Indian identity with astonishing speed. *The Oxford English Dictionary* first came out in 1884, and by 1886 the Hobson-Jobson dictionary of Indian English terms had been released, introducing words such as "veranda," "avatar," "cheroot" and "typhoon" into the language.

The goal of making Indians who were "English in tastes, in opinions, in morals and in intellect" also exposed Indians to the work of European writers and brought them closer to the Western ideas of nationalism, liberty and freedom. As the writer Surendranath Banerjea wrote in 1878, "English education has uplifted all who have come under its influence to a common platform of thoughts, feelings and aspirations." Uplift: this was an unexpected result for an "imperial" tongue.

The chain of events that the English-education policy had set off was clearly moving in unpredictable directions. Increasingly, English-educated Indians were getting angry: Indian graduates who were fluent in English and equipped with the skills of the bureaucrat found that they were denied power and responsibility beyond the lowest levels of administration by the British. And, as the number of English-speaking graduates expanded, the competition for the few junior administrative jobs grew increasingly severe. The shortage of jobs created what is probably the most combustible driver for social change—large numbers of people both educated and unemployed.

Around this time, the English language and the Indian English press were also quickly becoming common ground for a once-fractured Indian community to exchange ideas among themselves and agitate against British rule. An Indian lawyer had told the British government in its early years, "You cannot talk a person into slavery in the English language," and the British policy soon brought this truth home. During the Congress party's early demands for political representation, they employed the slogan of eighteenth-century British colonists: "No taxation without representation." The language did not make Indians more British; instead a shared tongue enabled people from across the kingdom states and British provinces to identify themselves as Indians and unite in resistance.[15] English had made them their own people.

Critically, English literacy also offered Indians the chance to access the English press. Indians, as a result, became increasingly aware of the struggles for independence in other countries—the rise of colonies across the world against imperialism, and the surge of European nationalism by the end of the nineteenth century.[16] The language was offering Indian leaders a window into movements like theirs, and with it, hope.

The fading favor for English: A "symbol of colonialism"

But as India neared independence, the English language found itself increasingly left out in the cold. For one, with the growing prospect of freedom, Indians had the opportunity to clearly consider the question of Indian identity after the end of colonial rule.

Indian leaders were pragmatic about adopting a constitution with a British heart* and enthusiastic about adopting European ideas of nationalism and democracy. And of course, no one wanted to rip out the railway tracks and lay new ones just because they had been put in place by British administrators.[17]

But when it came to the English language, they balked—it was one of the "colonial relics" that was unacceptable. Language was so intricately linked to blood and community that it was difficult to imagine that you could say "I am an Indian" in English, the colonial tongue, and still feel that was the case. Indian leaders such as Gandhi began to express strong views against the use and teaching of the language in Indian schools. Gandhi believed that "to give millions a knowledge of English is to enslave them." Gandhi wrote, "The foreign language has caused brain fag, put undue strain upon the nerves of our children, made them crammers and imitators, unfitted them for original work and thought."

The writer Aijaz Ahmad notes that this "either-or" chauvinism that erupted around independence was singularly alien to our attitudes on language. Many Indian leaders and intellectuals, from Nehru to Gandhi, Tagore,

*A large part of the Indian Constitution came from the 1935 Government of India Act that the British passed.

Rajagopalachari and Ambedkar, were at least bilingual;[18] Ram Mohan Roy had been fluent in five languages—English was his "fifth language," after Sanskrit, Bengali, Arabic and Persian. Indian leaders such as Rajagopalachari reflected this egalitarian sentiment, writing that English was "Saraswati's gift to India."[19] But in the political mood of the time, people like Rajagopalachari were in the minority and India's leaders were ready to toss English overboard, as a language that had outlived its welcome.

Strange bedfellows: English, the southern states and the Dalits

However, by 1950 English had become the lingua franca of India's central government and educational institutions. This sea change in our expectations of the colonial tongue had a lot to do with the early conflicts of the new nation-state.

India in 1947 was a young country whose boundaries were pristine and newly drawn. With no shared political history prior to British rule, it appeared to be a country that had more dividing than uniting it. Independent India was immediately embroiled in multiple arguments over language issues in the Constituent Assembly on the drawing of state boundaries according to language, on the official status for various regional languages and, critically, on the question of the national language.

India's first prime minister, Jawaharlal Nehru, was himself, as Robert King notes, a man "educated in English ideas but a nationalist when it came to language." Nehru had written in 1935, "Some people imagine that English is likely to become the lingua franca of India. That seems to me a fantastic conception." Nehru believed that "this status belonged to Hindi."[20] However, the proposal to adopt Hindi as the official language—favored by many of the Hindi-speaking ministers—met with strong resistance from the southern states, especially Tamil Nadu.

South Indian politicians quickly denounced this idea of making Hindi the national tongue as "language imperialism."[21] (Since independence, the charge of "imperialism" aimed at fellow Indians has had a sting with no substitute.) Hindi as a national language, they asserted, was being pushed down their throats by fiat, enforced by a majority who would have the advantages of their native tongue in the competition for education and job opportunities. The Tamil minister Ramalingam Chettiar complained, "The way north Indians are trying to dominate us and dictate to us is galling . . . I have been in Delhi for two years, and no north Indian has . . . invited me even once for social functions, just because I don't know Hindi."[22]

These ministers offered more than three hundred amendments to the language bill—one went as far as to suggest that Hindi be written in Roman letters instead of Devanagiri.

It was in the midst of this argument that English was brought back from once certain death—as a defense against the threat of Hindi. The southern states suggested that English—a tongue spoken by less than 3 percent of the Indian population and equally alien to the north and the south—be adopted as India's official language.

Meanwhile, the language was gaining support from the Dalit community. For the Dalits, English was a language exempt from the restrictive conventions of Indian literature, which was imbued with the traditions of caste and untouchability. Hindu texts were ambiguous at best on the question of education and literacy for the lower castes. At worst, they were outright discriminatory—the *Manusmrithi* (Laws of Manu), the authoritative Hindu text on India's caste system, said that "molten lead is to be poured into the ears of the 'low born' who dare to hear the recital of the written word." As a result, like many of the early Indian reformers, Dalit leaders viewed English as emancipatory, free of the smudgy fingerprints of Hindu discrimination and the stigma of "untouchable" traditions. The Dalits also came to support English as a language that enabled communication across linguistic regions, giving the low castes a "nationwide solidarity,"* and enabling their voices to be heard in the public sphere.

Nehru, watching the falling out and acrimony, got increasingly frustrated. He wrote in a letter to the Tamil minister Gopalaswami Ayyangar, "I am very tired of all this business."[23] Finally in 1950 Nehru declared a transition arrangement that would permit the official use of English for fifteen years, till 1965—and it would then be replaced with Hindi. He obviously hoped in the meantime tempers would cool and people might even settle into the language.

But by 1965 protests again erupted across the south against the imminent shift to Hindi as the official language. Rallies took place all over south India,

*In the Dalit movement for social rights, English is now playing a unifying role among these various castes spread across India, similar to the role it played in India's nationalist movement.

and south Indian cabinet ministers threatened to resign unless English was retained. Riots broke out in Tamil Nadu, people burned effigies of the "Hindu demoness" and students and members of the Dravida Munnetra Kazhagam* (DMK) immolated themselves across the state. Police opened fire on rioting crowds, killing three hundred people. In the Legislative Assembly, DMK members made fiery speeches threatening secession.[24] At the same time, as the journalist Swaminathan Aiyar notes, "pro-Hindi organizations such as the Jan Sangh launched a violent agitation in favor of abolishing English not only in official use but also in shop and street signs and on number plates."†

The government had thought Hindi would be "the great unifier," but it turned out that only English would do the job. The Language Act was finally amended in 1967, specifying both English and Hindi as official languages. English has since coexisted with Hindi as the official language and serves as a "linking language" for the north and the south.

In newly independent India, the English language had thus become a touchstone for neutrality and, given India's minorities—the southern states and the lower castes—some protection from what they saw as the tyranny of the majority. The DMK rode the anti-Hindi wave to election victory in 1967, taking Tamil Nadu out of Congress hands for the first time. Democracy had struck back against forcible language imposition in 1967, just as it would strike back in 1977 against forcible family planning.

There is a pretty good case to be made for not taking sides in a multilingual country, and the importance of English as a neutral player in India's language debate cannot be exaggerated. It was not rare for polyglot British colonies to address the challenge of the official language by opting for English, an outsider and consequently a language that could bypass the tug of war for political and economic power between linguistic communities. Singapore, for instance, chose English as the language of the government over other local languages such as Malay, Chinese and Tamil. Sri Lanka did the opposite, replacing English with Sinhalese, the majority tongue, a move that helped trigger sectarian war in the country—a powerful and disconcerting example of how the lack of neutrality and compromise in language policy can rapidly alienate minority communities.

---

*Federation for Dravidian Progress.

†One of the Jan Sangh agitators was Atal Bihari Vajpayee, future prime minister of India.

The invisible "career tongue"

In the late 1960s when I was growing up in Dharwad, I attended a convent school along with most of the neighborhood kids. The highlight for us was when the stern Father Soares, our principal, invited us to his home to listen to his records. There, he would pull out his treasured old spools of recordings of his favorite English plays and we would sit entranced, listening to Gielgud and Guinness perform Shakespeare. Even then, it was clear to us that knowing English was a high priority for our careers. English postindependence has emerged as India's main career language—the language of India's university and college education, central government institutions, as well as the working language of India's corporations.

In part, my parents' insistence that I study at English-medium schools was a result of our family background—our community, the Chitrapat Saraswats, were Brahmins who were educated and knew where the opportunities lay. Not many parents, however, knew the trade-offs that came from sending their children to a non-English school. This was because the role of English as a career language in independent India remained for a long time one of the unspoken truths in our politics, something that Indian legislators were reluctant to admit. Tamil students had once painted slogans saying, "Hindi never, English ever," but the early support for the English language in the south turned out to be half-hearted—it had been merely a way to protect their regional tongues.[25] English lost its champions in the south once the question of the national language was resolved, and the language became an orphaned tongue, never regaining the political support it had in the fifteen years after independence.

Instead, when India's education policy was being prepared, each Indian state in the north and the south clamored to prioritize and preserve its own language in state schools. The 1968 national policy resolution for education faced the bewildering challenge of accommodating the interests of Hindi and national pride, of English as the link language, and of the regional tongues. The education ministry proposed a "three-language" formula, where people from non-Hindi areas were to study their regional language, as well as Hindi and English. Hindi speakers could study Hindi, English and another language.

The three-language formula pitted Indian languages against one another, and states were embroiled in unruly political football. Tamil Nadu's hackles rose up again—its education minister, Thiru Thambidurai, declared that the formula was "an indirect attempt to impose Hindi as a language on the Tamil people." Both Tamil Nadu and Pondicherry refused to teach Hindi in state schools, and the northern states cheated on the third language requirement by teaching none of the regional languages, opting instead for Sanskrit. The southern states asserted that the regional language should take precedence over English, while to the Hindi-speaking states English was the pretender to the throne, slinking into a national, dominant role that had rightfully belonged to Hindi.

State education policies thus became a vehicle of either regional pride or Hindi nationalism, with each state out to demonstrate the superiority of its pet mother tongue. In the bargain, Hindi and English were sidelined in some southern states, and English was quite decisively marginalized everywhere. On average—with the exception of the northeastern states—less than 10 percent of state schools in India were English-medium schools, and many of the states passed policies that allowed the teaching of English only from the sixth standard. By the 1960s Gujarat had banned English from primary schools and the West Bengal CPI(M) government did the same in the 1970s. The Maharashtra government even mandated in 1956 that while Marathi would be the compulsory medium for state schools, only Indians whose mother tongue was English could attend English-medium schools. The order was blocked by the Supreme Court, which ruled that "Speaking constitutionally, English is more an Indian language than the other languages . . . it is the language India's Constitution is written in. It has entered into the blood and bones of India."

And when English was taught as a subject from the primary level, it was not taught effectively. In India's state-run vernacular schools students noted that "even the English teachers have trouble speaking in English."[26] While in reality English proficiency was the password for admission to the best careers—the top bureaucratic circles, or a career in the private sector—our state schools seemed oblivious of this fact.

State mandates to make the regional tongue the language of instruction across public schools led to the mushrooming of private, English-medium schools. But access to these schools was limited to the urban areas, and to the people who could afford them. The utopian notion of the three-language policy, of three languages taught equally well, has failed badly and left many students across state schools tongue-tied three ways and illiterate in English.

The Dalit writer and activist Chandrabhan Prasad—*The New York Times* recently did a profile of him, calling him a "chain-smoking, irrepressible didact," and I can attest to the fact that he is all three—does not mince words when he talks about the language policy. "We have an English language economy, but our education policy has denied people access to it. It is not an intelligent law, it's a political one," he says. "And it has only worsened divides across both castes and classes. Most of the lower castes are poor, and send their children to the free state schools, and eventually many of them struggle to put together a proper English sentence."

English: The language of upward mobility

The economist Omkar Goswami concurs with the Indian economists I know when he refuses to give in to unbridled optimism on how India is changing since reforms. He notes, however, that the shift in certain attitudes has been unmistakable. "We now rely less on knee-jerk hostility, when it comes to our feelings about foreign things," he says. This change is especially clear in our attitude toward English, which has undergone a transformation postreform. The change was largely driven by the rise of India's outsourcing industry. The 1990s had marked the rise of Indian IT companies including Infosys, and our key advantage in competing in the global services market—our purple poker chip—has been India's large numbers of affordable, educated and English-literate workers.

In the business process outsourcing (BPO) sector in particular, more than 65 percent of jobs are defined as voice-based jobs, and English-language proficiency is the main requirement for these companies. These firms were closely aligned with global corporations, and both productivity and wages were linked quite closely to global market averages. The result was that, through the 1990s, potential earnings for India's English-skilled graduates surged. In a sense, this Indian industry has carved out a route to the American dream for our workers.

The present number of English-literate, skilled graduates barely scratches the surface of what India is capable of. Even though the number of graduates and engineers in India has more than doubled over the last fifteen years, only 13 percent of India's youth actually opt for higher education, and English literacy in India remains below 30 percent. Companies in India's outsourcing industry are attempting to expand the number of English-proficient graduates through training courses for college students in English-language skills.

Not only can the talent pool get much deeper, this industry in India has the potential to absorb large numbers of English-skilled workers. Employment in the sector has crossed 1.6 million, and there remains immense room for more growth—the number of jobs created is set to cross three million by 2015.

This highly visible rise of the outsourcing sector has helped transform Indian attitudes toward the English language. English is emerging as the language of aspiration for the Indian population—as a passport to a lucrative job and entry into the country's growing middle class. A friend of mine is an entrepreneur who runs Corner House, a popular Bangalore ice cream and sundae parlor. He told me resignedly that he had taught his staff some English so that they would be able to take orders, and they left him to join a BPO company!

In fact, as demand has soared, Indian companies including Infosys now face severe shortages in finding enough English-speaking talent. We recruit engineers who are technically very talented but whose English education started only in their engineering colleges. Often this means a struggle with spoken English, which we have attempted to address with internal training programs. We also launched Project Genesis, a program that presently works with fifteen thousand students in more than 240 colleges to provide training in English and soft skills to make general degree college students "BPO-employable." The English training in Genesis has apparently become so popular that parents seeking admission in many colleges in the north now inquire if the college "is a Genesis one."

The rising payoffs of English-language skills across Indian industry are also creating a widespread demand to learn the language. The private sector has been quick in responding—English training in India has surged to a $100 million industry in annual revenues. Sriram Raghavan is an entrepreneur who runs Comat, a company dedicated to building rural IT kiosks across the country, and he says that one in three customers to the kiosks comes for

English lessons. "They have a sharp eye for the jobs that are available, and they are quite pragmatic," he tells me of his rural customers. "I have people coming to me asking for English lessons for their wives, since that can help them get jobs as receptionists and secretaries at government offices." The language is also popular among people migrating to the city. "They know," Sriram says, "that if they learn English before they move to the city, they will land much better paying jobs. It's the difference between working as a construction worker or being the manager of the construction team." The language is making a substantial difference across levels—people who work as janitors at offices, for instance, find that knowing English means better errands to run. "I run around bringing tea and snacks and cleaning up," one of them says. "There is another guy who knows to read and write English. He visits banks and clients and gets four times my salary."[27]

As a result this aspiration for English is now cutting across income classes—English-medium private schools have mushroomed across rural India and in the slums of the urban poor. Nearly one third of all rural schoolchildren are now enrolled in private schools, and close to 50 percent of these schools are English medium.* In the slums of Hyderabad, the number of private schools teaching in English now exceeds the number of government schools by two to one. In Bombay's Dharavi slum and the North Shahdara slum in Delhi, more than half of the schools are English medium. And standardized tests assessing the performance of these schools in English found that children in these mostly unrecognized private schools in slums did 246 percent better on an English test compared with government schools.[28]

Dalit leaders have also pushed for effective English instruction in schools. Organizations such as the Dalit Freedom Network are establishing English-medium schools to cater to the Dalit community. "I think that our leaders now recognize how important English is for Dalits to access both employment and economic opportunities," Chandrabhan tells me. In his own irreverent way, he has even initiated a campaign for English by celebrating the birthday of Lord Macaulay. "It helps raise awareness about the need to learn English," he grins, when I ask about the event. "We've now celebrated his birthday three years in a row."

---

*A major reason that parents cited for sending children to these schools was that even the non-English-medium private schools "teach English as a subject from kindergarten."

Rising from below

Increasingly, as English gains economic relevance across India, it has become very difficult to restrict access to the language on ideological grounds without seeming bull-headed. With globalization and the rise of IT/BPO, language policy across Indian states has had to respond to public pressure for English education. In a note on language, India's National Knowledge Commission* also underscored the advantage of English in Indian employment and higher education, and recommended that "English should be taught from Class I across the country."

Across states, pressure from the people is driving changes in our English-education policy—West Bengal and Gujarat have reversed anti-English policies and made the language compulsory from the first standard, and the Gujarat government has introduced an initiative called SCOPE, to teach English to Gujarati youth in the fifteen-to-thirty-five age group. Jammu and Kashmir also recently made all state schools English-medium institutions. Chauvinistic language policies have become largely ineffective as a political device—in September 2006 the Karnataka government ordered the closure of several elementary schools in the state that had been teaching in the English medium,† putting 270,000 students out of schools. The order met with severe public criticism and lost credibility when fifteen of the thirty Karnataka cabinet ministers supporting the policy admitted to sending their own children to English-medium schools.

From the beginning, it has been the force of the people that has compelled governments and policy makers to keep English in India. First it was the backlash and anger from the south against Hindi snootiness and hegemony; later it was the aspiration of people who protested against language policies that were limiting access to jobs for the poor. Rather than throwing the English language out, Indians have fought time and again to retain it. In itself, this may be a sign that the language has already become too Indian to get rid of.

---

*I was a member of the National Knowledge Commission, which was set up by Prime Minister Manmohan Singh in 2005 to "help promote excellence in the education system." Besides me, there were seven other initial members, and our motley group of academicians and entrepreneurs was headed by Sam Pitroda.

†The schools were charged with violating a 1994 order to teach in the local language, Kannada. Despite public resistance, the order was carried out and the schools were closed.

The global opportunity

For many years after independence, language policy had largely been held hostage by the perception of the English language as a "colonial relic." However, English is no longer a British tongue—it is more the language of international business and a powerful key in opening up geographical borders and gaining access to markets. It is the language of science and research, with 90 percent of papers across scientific journals written in English. It dominates the chatter of the Information Age—80 percent of the World Wide Web is in the English language. It has been estimated that within a decade half the world's population will have some skill in English. A commitment toward learning English was part of China's bid to host the Olympic Games, to the point that taxi drivers who failed an English test did not have their licenses renewed and hotlines were set up to report incorrect English use in public spaces. Most countries are fast recognizing English's role as a world language, and besides China, nations such as Japan, South Korea and Indonesia are including English as a compulsory language in their schools and setting up "English-immersion camps" for students.

India has an advantage in the global market in the depth and breadth of its English-language capability. Today Indians have embraced the idea of English as the language of the globalizing Indian economy. Most middle-class Indians speak in at least two tongues—besides their mother tongue, they have at least functional fluency in English for business purposes and to manage communication with different communities.

Over the last fifty years, English has grown deeper roots in the Indian community, beyond purely economic value. Its reach has spread—to print, film, television and ordinary conversation. English has rapidly become the language of creative discourse—and while Indian writers writing in English have remarked that they often face hecklers at their readings who demand to know why they do not write in their mother tongue, such criticism has become marginal in recent years. These Indian writers once called "dissenters" and "mavericks" now include Amitav Ghosh, who has attained a status in English literature that has moved far beyond the exotic value of an Indian writing in the language.

An Indian tongue

Certainly English's presence in India today can be attributed to a series of chance events in Indian history—Bentinck's parsimony, Macaulay's British condescension and a postindependence north–south squabble. This has contributed to the perception of English as an essentially alien language in independent India, and not "authentically Indian."[29]

This deep identification of language with culture and ethnicity is, I think, universal. Language is a natural fracture across communities, and it has, across history, formed a big part of arguments around identity and self-expression. Ireland's struggle to revive the Irish language during its fight for independence, the resurrection of the near-extinct Hebrew language in Israel and most recently the debates over government recognition of Spanish in the United States, all point to how closely people associate identity and community rights with language.[30]

English, a transplanted, Anglo-Saxon tongue, has survived as a language of power and upward mobility in postreform India. But there has been little sentimentality associated with the language—even among pro-English commentators and activists in India, the perception of English as a "foreign tongue" goes unchallenged. But should the association of English with our years as a colony mean that an Indian identity for the language is impossible? Sanskrit, after all, was also an "alien" tongue to the subcontinent and a language that entered the region with an invading army.[31] For that matter, linguists such as David Crystal note that the people after whom the language has been named no longer "own" English today. It is estimated that India has more than 300 million English users, which surpasses even the United States and makes us the country with the largest number of English speakers. The "English speaking world" today is certainly very different from what it was a century ago—to the point that the British, U.S. and Australian governments are hiring teachers from India to meet shortages of English-language teachers in their schools.

India has now "remade English in many voices"[32] with the rise of not just Standard Indian English but also of pidgins of English and regional languages such as Bengali English, Hindi English and Tamilian English—distinctive variants with a legitimacy of their own. One Kerala university permitted its students to write exams in a mix of English and the regional tongue, Malayalam, and when a syndicate member objected that "a sentence in Malayalam can be followed by a sentence in English, but they must not be mixed" he was dismissed by the others as being too uptight.

English in India has thus come full circle—the language gained a foothold in India as a result of the outsourcing of government jobs from Britain in 1844. Postindependence it was the tongue of exclusion and snobbery, the language of the boxwallahs* in their Calcutta clubs, speaking in clipped accents over their cigars and whiskey glasses. It was the password to the most rarefied social and corporate circles, a language connected with other rituals—candidates for job interviews at the most discerning private firms had to sport a flawless accent, and had to bring their wife along to a "lunch interview" so that they could ensure that she knew how to handle a fork and knife.

But after years of decline postindependence, the rise of English in the 1990s has, again, been enabled by outsourcing. And this time around, the rise of the language has been a groundswell.

The transformation of English and its blending with an explicitly Indian identity is something Macaulay did not want from his English-education policy. For instance, he was uncomfortable with the performance of Shakespeare in Indian schools, saying that, "I can conceive of nothing more grotesque than the scene from the *Merchant of Venice*, with Portia represented by a little black boy." Clearly we are no longer—to recall an old Indian slur against English-literate Indians—"Macaulay's children."

*A term that was used for Anglicized Indians, who usually worked for a British-owned firm or the Indian Civil Service (ICS).

FROM MANEATERS TO ENABLERS

"THEY'RE SO SELF-ABSORBED," one prominent MP said of Rajiv Gandhi's advisers in 1986. "They think everything is a management problem, whereas governing India takes an almost Tolstoyan compassion."[1]

Many have shared this sentiment about India's more technocrat leaders—they were regarded as members of a rarefied circle, distant from the country's daily, grinding challenges. Nehru and the group of scientists, economists and technologists he consulted were the "Nehruvians"; Rajiv Gandhi and his IT-savvy advisers were the "computer boys."

It is true that technology and its high-flying applications have often seemed of little relevance to a country where a majority of its people have no access to good roads and drinking water. When the economist Kenneth Keniston discussed the idea of computers in Indian villages with one of the premier sociologists on India, Myron Weiner, the latter's reaction was, "Are you insane? For the cost of a computer, you can have a school."[2]

But in recent years, our attitude toward technology in India has changed dramatically. Speaking to people in India's banks, stock exchanges and agriculture *mandis*, or markets, I have heard the same thing time and again, and almost word for word. "The way electronification is taking hold," they tell me, "has taken us by surprise."

This is a sentiment I can echo at a personal level. No one associated India with technology in the 1980s and, as a tiny software company in those days, Infosys astonished and even alarmed our potential customers when we said that we were an Indian company selling software solutions. Our company, and we—a gangly, bespectacled group of engineers—did not look all that promising, and no one would have imagined that firms like ours would help India emerge at the forefront of a technology revolution.

But post-1991 the information technology industry became the first star of India's emerging market economy, feeding the buzz and excitement around the country's rise. And since then the electronification story has taken hold across the country. PC and Internet penetration has yet to become significant in India, but even at the present levels, we are seeing astonishing new models that are giving people broader access to IT, from community IT centers to mobile-phone-linked services. These efforts are only fueling unprecedented demand, as villagers enroll for computer classes in Bihar and log onto commodity exchange kiosks in rural Orissa.

Much of the initial hostility toward IT was from unfamiliarity—when electronification finally came in touch with Indians across the economy, what was most surprising was why it had taken us so long to accept it into the fold.

The early years

"A nightmare of pulsing, twitching, flashing complexity," was how one intimidated journalist chose to describe a computer in 1954. He then went on to compare the sound it made to a swarm of insects.

The sheer strangeness that computers brought to technology made them in the early years a source of popular anxiety both in the West and in India. The computer became an easy target for every rabble-rouser, a symbol for whatever was his particular nemesis. The Luddites and conspiracy theorists in the West, for instance, feared that computers would widen the government's control—mainframes would increase the state's surveillance powers, and society would become Orwellian and devoted to propaganda. As a teenager, I also read plenty of science fiction stories by American writers that portrayed computers as evil, hyperintelligent misanthropes out to destroy the human race.

In socialist India, this fear was inverted. Here computers got demonized as tools of not the state but of the "capitalists," which would replace human labor in factories and offices. In 1966 there was an uproar against computers when the IBM chief supported India's short-lived currency reforms by arguing that rupee devaluation would make the manufacture of computers in India economical.[3] His remarks triggered a firestorm of criticism among India's political class, and Indian legislators opposed computers in no uncertain terms as "man-eating machines" that would "devour the jobs of working people."[4]

India's negativity was a marked deviation, by the way, from the pro-technology policy of other planned economies. The Soviet Union, for instance, placed a high priority on IT and robotics, and the government saw computers and robots as a viable alternative to a demoralized—and vodka-swilling—Soviet workforce. As Soviet policy makers explained, "Robots don't drink."[5]

But in India the arguments against computers as a threat to the working class persisted, and computer imports were severely restricted. Through the 1960s and 1970s, we saw little computerization across businesses, with the exception of the reconditioned 1401 computers that IBM sold in India. And after IBM exited India in 1978, people found it so difficult to get hold of a computer that the ones who did manage to import one made easy money by setting up a "computer service" bureau and leasing out computing time.[6]

A cautious shift: The 1980s

I have noticed that behind nearly every major shift in IT policy in India, there was an intelligent—and enterprisingly agile—bureaucrat. And when it came to the first tentative moves to open up the technology sector in the 1980s, I could spot one of the pioneers with ease.

Dr. N. Seshagiri lives in Bangalore and is now retired, and looks none the worse for wear, despite the cutthroat, volatile politics he had to deal with while working for the Rajiv Gandhi government. For Seshagiri and the other bureaucrats interested in nurturing India's IT industry, overcoming the prevailing animosity to computers was all about making the right converts. "I knew from the beginning that we had to inoculate some politicians from

IT opposition," he says. In this, Seshagiri and the other IT-savvy bureaucrats were lucky to meet Rajiv Gandhi, who was much younger than other political leaders and just forty years old when he became prime minister. Trained as a pilot for the Airbus A320, Rajiv was generally unafraid of technology. "He was a tinkerer," one bureaucrat who worked with him tells me. "He was always curious about how new technologies worked."

Rajiv's attitude to the role of computers in governance was shaped early on by the Asian Games, which India hosted in 1982. Rather typically, the ministry of sports dragged its feet on the project, and six months before the Games nothing had been done. Within the government, the panic was similar to when you opened your text for the first time the night before the exam. The project was handed over to Rajiv, and he and his team of bureaucrats got it running in the little time available, wiring it together with IT. "The system we put in place covered everything from managing costs to monitoring each game," Seshagiri says. "We also built a result information network, which was connected across Mumbai and Delhi." For Rajiv, the Games were a revelation of the possibilities of IT within the government, and when he came to power in 1984 the IT policy was one of the first initiatives he announced.

At the time, Infosys was already part of the fledgling IT industry that had come up in the early 1980s. Until the 1984 IT policy, we were not even really entrepreneurs in the eyes of the government—software did not qualify as a business. We were therefore ineligible for bank loans, and our start-up capital was a pile of crumpled bills that were our pooled savings. We struggled to get hold of a computer. We imported our first computer—which we installed in Bangalore—under the rule that allowed software exporters to import one if they had an active order from a client.

In 1982 Infosys applied for permission to import a 150 MB hard disk drive. (I know you are laughing, but 150 MB was a big deal in 1982.) But by the time we got the approval, enough months had gone by that the company manufacturing the drives had improved the capacity to 300 MB and reduced the price by 15 percent. This meant changing the import license—and that took another six to eight months, luckily coming through before the drive was upgraded again.

The 1984 policy, by easing some limits on IT exports, capital access and tax policies, was a step forward. But even with the policy in place, there were plenty of bumps in getting things done—as Montek Singh Ahluwalia noted before, the essential culture of government control was still pervasive, new incentives or not. Nevertheless, something had begun to stir—there were ripples of change in the telecom sector as well, thanks to one of the advisers in Rajiv's team of "computer boys," Sam Pitroda. Telecom in India at the time had grown stodgy and cobwebbed as a result of the state monopoly of the sector, and getting a phone line meant waiting for several years. "I saw my first phone," Sam tells me, "when I went to the U.S."

Sam, flamboyant and his hair already turning silver in 1984, set out to build a series of rural and urban telephone exchanges across the country in a colossal effort to bring phones to the masses. While few people had yet made the connection between telecom and computers, the parallel transformation of both was helping set the stage for a vibrant, connected economy.

The prime minister was an island of support for these efforts in a sea of opposition. Sam was accused by some in the left of being a CIA agent, and the 1984 IT policy ran into choppy waters almost immediately. Bank employees burned effigies of computers, and the Bharatiya Mazdoor Sangh, the BJP-affiliated trade union, observed Labor Day in 1984 as "anti-computer day." Rajiv's idea of electronification "as a tool for the removal of poverty" attracted wide disdain—the consensus was that these guys had their heads in the clouds and were out of touch with India's problems. "Rajiv was ahead of most people in the government when it came to technology," one bureaucrat tells me. "When he was PM, he had a meeting with the Railway Board where the officers presented him with data written out on several paper charts. He asked them, 'Why don't you just use a spreadsheet?' These officials had no idea what a spreadsheet was, and came back to him with an actual sheet, with their data marked all over it!"

The prevailing attitude drove key state IT initiatives off the rails—for instance, when the ministry of external affairs tried to computerize the passport department in 1986, the project got stuck in a quagmire of resistance from department officials. Across public sector offices, computers that arrived were often dumped in a corner and forgotten. The resistance to IT made state electronification efforts covert, backdoor operations, and the government implemented IT initiatives while taking great pains to avoid labeling them as such. The policy for the computerization of Indian banks, for instance, referred to computers as "ledger posting machines" (LPMs) and "advanced ledger posting machines" (ALPMs). The "computer boys" had to play hopscotch over the bureaucratic wires, and had to be quite artful to get departments to implement IT. "We'd meet the joint secretaries who were near a promotion," Seshagiri says, "and we'd tell them, if you adopt IT, it will make you look progressive. This helped us computerize twenty-five departments." And sometimes bureaucrats would agree because they had an eye on the air conditioner that came with the computers.

In those early years, our industry often got caught in bureaucratic crossfire. We would see IT policies take a bold step and then backtrack by a few years in progress. It took until 1990, when N. Vittal became the secretary of the department of electronics (DOE), for IT to get another big boost, with fewer restrictions on companies that came up within India's software technology parks (STPs).

Bureaucrats like Vittal often pushed hard against the wariness within the government toward technology and the new, liberal industry policies. Perhaps Seshagiri's remark says a lot for the resilience of these officers against the odds. "We'd learnt," and here Seshagiri has the demeanor of a cowboy in the Wild West, "that to get things done in the government, you have to occasionally break all the rules."

The 1990s: A new role for information technology

After the reforms in 1991, however, one thing changed dramatically—India's software industry turned superstar. Our growth through the decade made us the poster child for the success of reforms. It was an entirely new experience for us, an industry that had so far been either reviled or ignored, and it marked the beginning of a huge change in how India viewed electronification.

India's IT firms—Infosys, Wipro, Tata Consultancy Services (TCS)—propelled Indian industry and the economy into global view. We expanded faster than any other industry through the decade, growing from $150 million in 1991 to more than $5.7 billion in 2000. The rapid growth, the new technologies adopted and the expansion in both our competitors and value-chain partners made it an exhilarating time. In just a few years, we built the IT and operational infrastructure that had taken U.S. companies decades to put in place, and by the late 1990s we were competing in operational excellence and scale not just with one another, but also with Western firms.

The early predictions for Indian IT were rosy—the homegrown IT sector was expected to lead to technology and knowledge spillovers across the economy and trigger a widespread trend in electronification and IT-led surges in productivity. But in the early 1990s, our growth, though dramatic, was also quite isolated. There were continued restrictions on capital and labor that limited the ability of India's industries to invest in technology. Diffusion rates of such technology as a result stayed abysmally low, with the vast majority of Indian companies spending less than 1 percent of their turnover on IT.

Faced with a low-growth domestic market, our focus remained mostly on software exports. The way we grew reflected how little IT had penetrated outside our sector—government policies that carved out software parks situated on the edges of cities meant that we built our IT offices alongside other IT companies. We were small, walled-off islands of cutting-edge infrastructure in urban environments with bad connectivity, potholed roads and chickens on the streets.

Instead, the early spillover of our industry was mostly in transforming the culture of Indian business and entrepreneurship. By focusing on the export market, Indian IT firms absorbed global management practices and standards. Perhaps more importantly, it also enabled Indians to dream the dream of income growth and class mobility that had caught the imagination of the working class in the United States and Europe throughout the twentieth century. At Infosys we were taking in fresh-faced young graduates by the hundreds every month, people who within five years of employment could aspire to standards of living their parents had never experienced.

IT firms such as ours also had an enormous impact on attitudes toward entrepreneurship. We had grown up in an environment where Indian industry was monopolized by a dozen or so prominent business families—family enterprises where first, second and third cousins would dominate middle and senior levels of management. In contrast, firms such as Infosys were started by people without instantly recognizable surnames and who did not have a business background. My father had worked as a manager in a textile mill, and Narayana Murthy's had been a schoolteacher. Over the years, our unprecedented success motivated numerous new entrepreneurs—at conferences and industry events, we met young, ambitious, educated people setting up their own firms, who claimed they were inspired by us, and among whom we could sense a new energy and a seemingly unshakeable confidence.

The rise of information technology in Indian banking

The progress of electronification in India took place as a series of layers, an evolution of once seemingly disparate technologies and reforms, which are now connecting together to form the foundation of our expanding communications and technology network. First off was of course the growth of the IT industry, as well as the stirring of the telecom sector. The second layer was IT-enabled banking. It began to emerge in the 1990s, a major exception to the general, disappointing trend of low IT investment among businesses in that decade.

Banking in the 1980s and early 1990s was one of the most unionized industries in India—not surprisingly then, it was also the most hostile to IT. When I was visiting Indian banks in the 1990s with my presentation on future trends in the banking industry and the role of computerization, one organization that I made my earnest spiel to was the Indian Banks Association. After the presentation, the chairman of a bank came by and whispered to me that I should stop going around preaching such stuff, else "the unions will gherao your house!"

The anti-IT rhetoric was apparently a package deal, one that came with the union badge, and I encountered this personally time and again. Some time in the late 1990s a top banker in charge of technology at one of India's largest banks called me up with an unusual request. He had learned of the new "concept center" in the Infosys office, meant to demonstrate the evolution of banking and the impact of ATMs, "point of sale" and the Internet. He said, "I want to send over our union leaders to show them how technology will change banking in the future. Will you show them your concept center?"

I could not have been before a more hostile audience. I offered a passionate overview of the impact of technology on the future of banking, and the technologies Indian banks needed to embrace. They in turn made their point with equal fierceness and pooh-poohed my ideas. Later on, though, when we were having tea, one union leader came up to me, almost tiptoeing, and murmured, "I have two children, one is in Boston and the other in Seattle. Both are in software. I agree entirely with what you say, but how can I publicly support you? I have a constituency to protect." More than anything else, the opposition toward IT was one of fear of the changes it could bring.

Nevertheless, the banking sector's attitude transformed as the decade progressed. The turning point was the 1993 guidelines issued by India's central bank, the Reserve Bank of India (RBI), which allowed private banks to enter the country for the first time since 1969. The reform included a provision that such banks should upgrade the technology available in banking and use "modern infrastructure" across IT and telecommunications. The fate of IT was taken out of the unions' hands by this new policy environment and the entry of small, agile private banks such as ICICI, for whom the way to compete and catch up was to adopt automated processes and IT-enabled infrastructure.

And once India's new banks opened up to technology, there was no stopping this traditionally conservative industry. "The sector's dynamism in the 1990s was astonishing," says Pravir Vora, head of the retail technology group at ICICI bank. Pravir has a killer handshake and a booming voice, and he towers over me. He has been particularly well-placed to see the changes in the industry—he worked with the State Bank of India through the 1980s, before shifting to ICICI Bank.

Pravir notes that much of the dynamism and the risk taking was simply because new Indian banks had no set example to follow. "We had no precedent in terms of a competitive model," he says, "and that freed us to try out alternatives and experiment with new systems."

Postliberalization Indian banks had two options for growth. They could model themselves on old-style banks, build large, brick-and-mortar offices with five-meter-high ceilings, place stone lions at the entryway and emphasize face-to-face service. Or they could build lean, IT-enabled infrastructure that focused on an automated, networked business. Indian banks chose the latter, and banks such as ICICI adopted strategies with IT at the forefront, rapidly automating banking operations and building a network of ATMs across Indian cities.

Brick-and-mortar information technology: Building new systems

They say that everything from love to war is a matter of timing, and for India, IT was at the right place at the right time. The shift from a socialist to a market economy is not a painless one, and the 1990s was a decade of enormous turbulence for India. Market forces struck hard in an economy whose support institutions had been frayed by years of socialism.[7] This set off a series of scams, as people racked up huge profits from the chaos of our fledgling markets.

For the regulators in the trenches of the new economy, IT became a big part of the toolbox for fixing the glitches across our institutions. In 1992, less than a year after liberalization, India's stock exchange—the Bombay Sensex (BSE)—experienced a scam blowout running into more than fifty billion rupees. The scam was in some ways inevitable; the BSE was a tight, chummy network of brokers and investors, with highly suspect, weakly regulated trading and settlement processes. Ravi Narain, managing director of the National Stock Exchange (NSE) tells me, "Customers who made trades in the exchange had to take their brokers at their word when it came to the buying and selling price of their shares. Brokers could make far more money lying about price points than on their commissions." This skimming off had its own Indian term, the "gala."

After the 1992 scam, the regulator, Securities and Exchange Board of India (SEBI), first tried to get the exchange to modernize its systems, but that did not work—oversight was full of loopholes and there were too many entrenched interests opposing reform. SEBI's plan B was a new, rival stock exchange, the NSE, electronified from the word go.

Narain is a soft-spoken bureaucrat and gives the impression of a man with a quiet, geeky intelligence. I can see how the blustery traders of the BSE would have underestimated him when it came to the new exchange. "They told us that we were bound to fail in our attempt to electronify it," Narain says. "The brokers and management alike told us that exchanges were 'made of people, not technology.'" It was probably fortunate that no one expected them to succeed, since the brokers were a powerful group—they had often forced the government to withdraw income-tax raids by going on strike, and as Narain notes, "During the early days, they could have got us to roll back the new systems if they'd wanted to. But by the time they realized what IT could do, it was too big an animal to kill."

The new exchange allowed Internet trading and introduced an electronic order book system, eliminating the advantages Bombay's cozy broker networks had in terms of information on prices and trades. It also brought in massive new efficiencies. "In the old paper-based systems, brokers would complete just 30 percent of all orders and trade two hours a day," Narain tells me. "Then they'd spend six hours sifting through the paperwork. Now we can run the exchange for a full day."

Most importantly, electronic orders dramatically flattened trading costs for investors across the country. C. B. Bhave, former chairman of the National Securities Depository Ltd (NSDL), India's first IT-enabled depository, and now head of SEBI, tells me, "Before the NSE came up, 80 percent of the people trading on the stock market lived in Bombay. Three years after NSE, the proportion fell to 40 percent." The efficiency of the NSE also forced the lumbering BSE to modernize, install IT systems and bring transparency across its processes.

To ensure the success of these IT initiatives, bureaucrats such as Narain and Bhave also had to be IT evangelists who could not be intimidated by either wide-eyed appeals from corporations or bureaucratic pressure. As Bhave says, "You didn't have to be brilliant, but you had to be committed toward seeing the initiative through." But in choosing Bhave to build the NSDL, SEBI may have been fortunate in finding a combination of the two. Bhave calls himself a "career chameleon"—an engineer by education and with several years in the IAS, he came to the NSDL after a stint in finance, working with SEBI in secondary markets.

"My experience in the IAS did pay off," he tells me, when we met in the NSDL office in downtown Bombay. With the NSE in place, everyone had already become a little wary of IT, and electronifying the NSDL required all of Bhave's consensus-building skills, which he had honed in the administrative services. "Everyone—the government, the corporations, the share registries and the investors—had a 'good' reason to not have IT systems," Bhave says. "There were the paper absolutists, for instance, who told me that we were 'not an advanced country like the U.S.' and that Indians wouldn't trust electronic documents—we loved paper far too much."

But the biggest hurdle was in persuading traders. "The transparency IT systems would bring in was obviously a problem for traders," Bhave notes. The big unsaid issue was the amount of black money in the market. No one wanted a trail of crumbs that would lead back to the candy store. "We had to get the traders on our side, and to do that we couldn't think like bureaucrats, who want to know where the money is going, but like the investors, who would like to keep the loopholes. So we pointed out something to them that they had overlooked," Bhave says, grinning. "If they decided the best way to keep their money under wraps was to opt out of our depository, then all the government would have to do to corner the black money was demand a list of those investors who had not joined our system. They would only make it easier for them to be rounded up!"

The NSDL was eventually the fastest in the world to implement paperless trading. It now has more than 7.5 million investor accounts with an estimated $1 trillion worth of securities dematted. The information systems implemented at the NSE and NSDL have been especially good at picking up the trail of money across the economy, thanks to efficient real-time audit systems and the tracking of financial flows through banks and in and out of depositories and tax filings. This has made it remarkably effective in cleaning up and "whitening" our markets.

IT initiatives during this time were certainly isolated, but they targeted what were the economic disaster zones of India's equity markets. By cleaning up these snarls, IT has transformed these institutions into ones that rank among the most efficient in the world—NSE, for instance, rates in at "T+2" settlements, a global benchmark that indicates that the final settlements of any transactions done on a certain day (T) get settled within the next two days. Post these reforms, the number of transactions on India's stock exchanges has also exploded. Narain says, "In 1992 India would do maybe three hundred crore* rupees of business a day across all stock exchanges. In 2007 NSE alone did forty thousand to fifty thousand crore rupees a day."

This automation of the stock exchange and securities market paralleled the automation in Indian banking that was taking place. When these two trends came together, the effect was remarkable. Bringing IT into these two sectors had effectively digitized the country's money flows. This would have a powerful domino effect in the following years as Indian businesses invested in IT to combine their own capital flows with India's banks and stock markets.

India's regulators were, however, still lone rangers in a governing environment that was if not hostile, at least indifferent to IT systems. Beyond our capital markets, the 1990s saw countless instances of failed IT initiatives. We have struggled here with what Keniston called India's "Potemkin village" problem—we have plenty of showcase "pilot projects" that we have failed to

---

*One crore is 10 million, and one lakh is 100,000.

expand beyond a state or city level. More than 80 percent of state-led electronification projects in the 1990s failed. Innumerable pilot e-governance projects were launched with great fanfare and then forgotten. Our government departments remained, stubbornly, environments of paper pushers, filing cabinets and typewriters.

A touch of information technology for everyone: Elections and railways

However, there were a couple of successful electronification initiatives which, by demonstrating the capability of technology to millions of Indians across the country, were transforming popular opinion in its favor. One was the electronification of India's elections with the introduction of a colorful, pop-art style, easy-to-use voting machine, which became an enormous hit with Indian voters.

"It took us twenty-seven years to implement electronic voting from the time we conceived and built the machine," the chief election commissioner N. Gopalaswami tells me. "When we tried to use the machines in a 1981 Kerala by-election, one of the contenders challenged their validity but lost at the state's high court, so we went ahead." But in the election, the politician who had fought against the machines won, and the loser challenged the result at the Supreme Court. "The SC tossed out the results because the law required paper ballots."

Amending the law took six years, and then the machines went on the backburner. In 2001, after a long hiatus, the Election Commission again tried the machines out. In Tamil Nadu, the All India Anna Dravida Munnetru Kazhakam (AIADMK) leader Jayalalitha made a fuss, alleging that the machines were unreliable. "This time, the Supreme Court threw her case out," Gopalaswami says. "Good for her, because she won that election." Since then, it has been smooth sailing—in 2004 all elections across the country had electronic voting, with one million machines deployed across more than 700,000 polling booths.

India's elections have typically been corrupt and chaotic, with "ballot-box stuffing" part of the nuts and bolts of getting yourself elected, and voting fraud in some areas has been as high as 40 percent. The electronic voting machines (EVMs) considerably reduced the problem of ballot stuffing. As Gopalaswami says, "When one vote is cast, the machine takes twelve seconds to reactivate. So the 'productivity' of the fraudsters goes down, since you can't just stuff bunches of paper into a box." The time delay has also helped the commission figure out when "stuffing" has happened with a machine. "If we spot a series where votes were cast every twelve seconds, we simply cancel that result," he says.

Gopalaswami seems to take these challenges of our elections in his stride, and when he tells me of his technology-aided solutions to stop box-stuffing, I cannot miss the twinkle in his eye. Recently, the commission began to clean up the system by digitizing other parts of the process—such as using randomizing software to choose the presiding officers for election booths. "There are exclusion parameters that the software uses, which eliminate, for example, the guys whose home town is in the district." In addition, these presiding officers used to be selected a week before the election, which gave candidates enough time to ply him with his weakness of choice—alcohol or money. The new software, however, chooses the name of the presiding officer on the day of the election. It has, the commissioner tells me cheerfully, really annoyed some candidates.

And the sincere ballot-stuffers bring artistry and skill to their efforts. As Gopalaswami points out, "They can figure out elegant ways around regulation and anti-corruption measures. But IT helps us make it a lot harder for them."

Another major initiative that transformed the popular perception of IT and brought India's masses in direct contact with it was the electronification of the railways. The Indian Railways is a huge part of travel for most Indians; it crisscrosses the length and breadth of the country and transports fourteen million passengers a day. The computerized reservation system could not have been a better introduction to the value of IT systems—it was highly efficient and allowed the poor to bypass the long queues for tickets and the ineffectual, often exploitative bureaucracy.

At the railways ministry, I meet Sudhir Kumar, an IAS officer with a wide, infectious smile, one of the sharpest minds I have known, and a tendency to quote the management gurus Gary Hamel and C. K. Prahalad to get his point across. He is animated about how much computerizing reservation and ticketing has helped the rail traveler. "We transformed lives for a lot of people with computerized reservation systems," he says. "We freed up passengers from long queues, the mercy of touts and tickets being sold in the black. But there is so much more we can do with IT." One of his plans, he says, is "electronic dispersal of tickets through railway kiosks." He is hugely optimistic about the options technology offers in future services. "Software, intelligently applied, can help us mine a lot more information on customer behavior, and build dynamic pricing systems," he says. I get a sense that while people in India see the present transformation of the railways as dramatic, for Sudhir things have just started rolling.

The tipping point: 2000 and on

There is a point when a ripple turns into a tidal wave, a wind into a blizzard and a movement into a revolution. The tipping point that truly transformed IT attitudes across the country was the rise of the telecom sector.

Since the 1999 telecom policy, the industry has grown exponentially, and teledensity growth has surged from 0.7 percent in 1991 to 27 percent in 2008. India's mobile network is gaining more than eight million subscribers every month—its biggest problem right now is getting enough spectrum—and at the present rate the country is set to soon become the world's second largest telecom network.

This has been the transforming platform, which on top of our other layers of electronification is allowing us to try out multiple, mix-and-match IT-enabled infrastructure. It has, for example, enabled the banking network to integrate mobile and Internet networks with automated banking. Meanwhile, the NSDL-led national Tax Information Network (TIN) is tying in India's direct tax systems with the IT platform of stock exchanges, the depository market and banks. The network has helped the government dramatically expand the tax net and is a major factor for the rise in India's direct tax collections, which grew a record 40 percent in 2007–8.

The growing connections between the banking platform, the mobile phone platform and the railway reservation platform are paving the way for services that, among others, allow consumers to book and pay for train tickets on their mobile phones. One of the fastest growing of such transactions today is the payment for airline tickets purchased over the Internet with credit cards and mobile phones. And each time such a high-speed, telecom-enabled transaction replaces an "old-economy," slow, paper-based one, we are seeing a productivity pop that ripples through the economy.

The telecom revolution has also built the foundation for the rise of truly mass access to IT. In India the "two countries" rhetoric and the isolation of our villages has historically not been exaggerated. When Nehru was at the peak of his popularity—and no leader, it can safely be said, rivaled Nehru in this when he was at the top of his game—a researcher from Hyderabad traveled to a few somewhat inbound Indian villages and asked them who Nehru was. Many had not heard of him; a few said that he was a random Pandit, while others speculated that he was "some German." While access and information have improved since that low point, much of rural India still remains walled off from the rest of the country thanks to the terrible state of our infrastructure—one fourth of Indian villages do not have a road leading out of them.

The lack of the most basic connectivity has deeply limited rural India's growth, since it cuts off access to critical information such as market prices for crops and weather patterns. Transmitting information about a price shock around a certain crop from the central markets to the outlying rural areas can sometimes take months. As a result farmers in India find out about a price collapse too late, often after the planting season. For these farmers, IT is not just access to the information economy—it is their only access to it, and a critical, life-changing one.

The demand for IT has consequently grown dramatically across rural India, and rural IT-based services led by the private sector have soared in recent years. Sriram Raghavan's Internet community centers and kiosks, for instance, offer low-cost computing and networking services across villages, and ITC's 7000 e-Choupal centers allow farmers to check commodity prices and sell crops online.

"We have become the one-stop shop for literally everything," Sriram tells me. "From caste certificates to English language training, we are doing all kinds of things over a wire, and the demand we are seeing is astonishing." Sriram tells me of parents in villages who send their daughters in secondary school to the kiosk for online tuition classes. The IT kiosk in rural India has become a sort of supermarket for all kinds of services, from checking crop prices to accessing e-governance services, getting treated through telemedicine, and for education. "People often think that the Internet and computers are 'high technology' for villages," Sriram says. "But this is not true—for them, it is their passport to all kinds of opportunity, and they embrace it completely."

"The villages are taking to technology like fish to water," Ravi Kumar, former head of the National Commodity Index (NCDEX), concurs. An extension of the NSE, the NCDEX was started in 2002 and trades in agricultural commodities such as pulses and edible oils. It has already made waves in the short time it has been operational—in India's fragmented, dispersed rural markets, the index has behaved unlike any global exchange. Over the last four years, for instance, Ravi and his management team have installed a network of approximately twenty thousand commodity trading terminals in 750 locations across rural India. "We also have one commodity terminal present in each vegetable *mandi* across India," Ravi says, "and we update prices from the *mandis* to the exchange two or three times a day."

Ravi notes that the particular weaknesses of India's rural markets—such as the lack of roads and the weak distribution and supply chain networks—have compelled the NCDEX to innovate and build an IT-integrated network of crop procurement, financing of farmers, and selling and trading of crops that is unprecedented in the world. He says, "We have opened a network of warehouses which procure crops at exchange prices across the country." In addition, to combat the power of the moneylenders, the NCDEX is partnering with ICICI Bank to offer farmers microfinance loans, for procuring seeds and fertilizer. "We have had European commodity exchanges visiting us to see if they can replicate our systems," says Chandra Sekhar, head of IT systems at the exchange.

When we talk of the farmers who use the exchange, Ravi tells me of a farmer in rural Bihar, who typically earned less than Rs 6,000 every month. "His worry was that he had two daughters 'to marry off,' and no savings," Ravi says. "What wheat he grew, he sold to the local mills at a price that was well below the market rate. When the NCDEX warehouse set up thirty kilometers from his village, he began to take his crop there on his cycle, and better prices have brought him an income of close to fifteen thousand rupees." Ravi adds, "When we ask farmers how the exchange has affected their lives, what they say is that they've 'got their dignity back.'" The farmers are referring to the dignity that comes from choice—of no longer being beholden, virtually a serf, to a single-buyer market.

The response to the NCDEX has clearly been electric. "Farmers see the benefits instantly," Chandra Sekhar says. "We find it more difficult to persuade companies to participate in our networks." Accessing the exchange allows farmers to access prices of far-flung *mandis* with a single click. Purchasing crop futures on the exchange is also giving them some insight into the potential price volatility of their crops and helps them make their planting decisions accordingly.

From being virtually cut off, India's farmers are now moving, in a single leap, from third-world infrastructure into the information economy. The exchange is now expanding its efforts to reach farmers by putting up price tickers on rural bus stops. It has also tied up with Reliance Communications to transmit voice-enabled information on crop prices over the company's CDMA network, which now covers more than half of India's rural areas.

The other major commodity exchange in India, the Multi Commodity Exchange (MCX), is along with the NCDEX also tying in with the broader network, for example by bringing in more people within the Tax Information Network. Jignesh Shah, CEO and cofounder of the MCX, tells me, "More than three lakh Permanent Account Numbers (PANs)* have come to the government through our exchange." And the MCX is playing a complementary role to the NCDEX in expanding the reach of our markets. "We have twenty thousand terminals across the country," he tells me, "and we are now doing business worth ten thousand crore rupees in a day."

Across India's IT innovations in banking, retail, education, telecom or commodities, we are seeing the spread of such "high-volume, low-transaction-cost" models. In India's expanding mobile networks, 90 percent of all accounts are prepaid, and the cards are so ubiquitous that you can recharge the phone at a paanwalla's. Rural India's IT kiosks are a way for entire communities to access the Internet. Aravind Eye Hospital in Tamil Nadu and Narayana Hrudayalaya in Karnataka are building remote, low-cost health care networks that cover more than one million people in rural areas. In Andhra Pradesh an agro-advisory network allows villagers to take photographs of sick crops and send them to the university, where they are diagnosed by agricultural scientists who can then recommend treatments. Millions of such granular transactions are coming together in a torrent that involves people across the country, from its cities to its poorest, most backward regions.

*The income tax department requires tax-paying citizens to file taxes with their PANs to prevent multiple filings, ease reimbursements and track evasion.

Spreading power: The death of the gatekeeper

For Indian consumers, whether they are farmers, small traders or bank customers, IT has emerged as a tool that allows them to sidestep weak and crumbling systems. People are in essence realizing the "I" in IT, and as a result attitudes toward these technologies have undergone a sea change, from the hostility of the 1980s and the indifference of the 1990s to an overwhelming demand for electronification today.

Madhabi Buch, executive director of ICICI Bank, sits on the top floor of the bank's main office in Mumbai. Her glass-fronted cabin faces west, and it is, when I visit her in the afternoon, filled with light. Madhabi is astonished by, and takes hope from, what electronification has done for her banking customers. When she examines the impact of the bank's IT-enabled systems, what strikes her the most is the simple democracy of it.

"When you take the middleman out of services, you take away discrimination of the customer and differential service," she tells me. "This equal treatment of customers is fairest to the small account holder and the poor investor." Madhabi recalls meeting one of ICICI's online trading account holders, who turned out to be an elderly investor, "in a kurta and dhoti, who didn't speak English." He used the online service, he said, because it enabled him to buy and sell in multiple, small share transactions a day.

"No broker would take twenty calls a day from a small day trader like me," the investor told Madhabi. "I prefer the online account since it allows me to make as many market transactions as I like." IT-enabled systems thus not just lower costs, they also give the smallest customers more flexibility and authority, by allowing them to directly access our markets.

It is these communities that have the least power in our markets who are the quickest to recognize the value of information-rich IT systems. Economic power, after all, is built on the ability to access information and resources asymmetrically. For instance, investors in traditional stock exchanges must contact brokers to buy and sell shares; farmers in fragmented rural markets rely on middlemen to sell their wheat; people paying electricity bills or booking train tickets have to interact with government officials. The persistent corruption in these power structures made these interactions, as the writer Anish Bagchi puts it, very much like "predator–prey relationships."

IT has split such systems wide open, eliminating gatekeepers and linking investors, farmers and citizens directly to both information and resources, and rapidly democratizing access. The unprecedented access to information and resources is transforming both political and economic power structures. For example, Ravi notes that before the NCDEX brought in market-led prices, agricultural prices were set by a few major farming families in key states—pepper prices by a small circle of farmers in Cochin, and pulses and jeera by a few farmers in Delhi and Gujarat.

"It is never going to happen"

At its most dramatic, IT has been a stake in the heart of corrupt government. An example of this is Bhoomi (literally, "earth"), the initiative that digitized all of Karnataka's village land records. To understand how the deed was done, I met Rajiv Chawla. Chawla graduated from IIT Kanpur in 1984 before he joined the IAS, and as a bureaucrat, he is in the vein of Bhave and Sudhir, combining a passion for change and efficiency in government with a remarkable talent in getting things done. "In 1999 Karnataka's revenue minister thought I was making a joke when I told him that I wanted to digitize the land records system," Chawla says. "He told me that it was never going to happen." This sounded familiar—listening to Chawla, I thought that he, Ravi Narain and Bhave should frame the remark on their walls as a sign of what they have worked against.

Chawla believed that any change for the better in the land record system would be a dramatic improvement for the farmer, who has to update his land record with every crop season. The records system was managed by a coterie of twelve thousand accountants across Karnataka's villages and was quite simply a cesspool of corruption—bribes were mandatory to get land records updated. In addition, as Chawla notes, "Many of the villagers were illiterate, which allowed the accountants to make all kinds of changes to the records—even in ownership."

The task that Chawla faced in computerizing this system was indeed huge—it meant digitizing 20 million land records, with fifty fields each, across seventy thousand villages—and all filled by different accountants. "It was a mind-numbing job," he says. "We verified the records by involving the farmers themselves, and then we set about digitizing it." The Bhoomi network that was then formed had two hundred computerized centers connected to a centralized database where farmers could come and collect their records.

"From then on," Chawla says, "we digitized everything in the land system." Updating the digital records was itself a challenge, since changes to the lands alone amounted to 150,000 mutations a year. This was done by ten thousand people across the villages working with handhelds, which transmitted the data to the database. This has removed the role of the village accountant in editing the records, which has removed tampering from the system. Corruption has also been reduced to some extent, in an unusual way. "One day, we turned the database into a FIFO [first in, first out] system," Chawla tells me. "After this, accountants couldn't delay an order in the system if a farmer wouldn't pay a bribe." Here the general ignorance regarding IT served Chawla well. He implemented the system without resistance, and only when it began running did the accountants realize what had happened. "They had no idea then, but if you ask any of them now," he says, "they will all tell you what FIFO is."

Such transformations are heartening, and despite India's record of failed IT initiatives, they are now gathering steam. An effort that I fund is the eGovernments Foundation, which implements e-government systems across Indian cities. But Srikanth Nadhamuni, who leads the initiative, is its head and its heart—since he returned to India from a well-paying technology job in the United States two years ago, this part of his life accounts for sixteen-hour days and incessant traveling across the country. He estimates that to date, "Our e-systems have been implemented across 100 Indian cities." These systems have again empowered citizens by getting rid of the gatekeeper while paying utility bills and property taxes, filing complaints and applying for documents—people no longer have to negotiate, wait, pay a bribe or hope that they do not catch the officer on a bad day. "Given a choice," Srikanth says, "people overwhelmingly choose these systems over going to an office." In the office of the Municipal Corporation of Delhi, more than 20 percent of property tax transactions went through the online system in the first three weeks alone. And applications like the Public Grievance and Redressal system give citizens a keyhole view of how city governments work, by allowing them to file complaints and track their progress through the system. The media has also started paying attention and now publish the number of complaints filed and addressed. As a result, Srikanth says, the government has begun to seriously tackle complaints. "The officers are forced to sit up, and pay attention."

There is of course enormous resistance to IT within governments, but the groundswell of public support it has is forcing them to respond. A recent study done by professor Subhash Bhatnagar at the Indian Institute of Management Ahmedabad (IIMA) noted that computerized systems are now overwhelmingly preferred by citizens. Dr. Bhatnagar wrote that citizens vastly preferred IT-based systems "in service delivery, quality of governance, and waiting time." And people, over and over, "strongly supported the idea that more agencies needed to be computerized." Srikanth tells me that recently, when the printer went down at the Delhi revenue office and the officer in charge offered written bills to the people waiting, there was a near riot. "They told him to get the printer fixed—they would only take a 'bill from the computer,' not handwritten by an official."

IT has obviously come a long way—from something seen as a threat to people to something people are demanding as a way of protecting their rights. For Indians, it has become an enabler.

Leading the way

You know that electronification has truly arrived when you see it tacked onto populist slogans—"The common man's computer" and "Free broadband for all." Jaswant Singh, the same MP who in 1986 had criticized Rajiv Gandhi's technocrats and managers, described modern technology in a speech in 2000 as "the rivulets [that will] nourish the arid soil of poverty." The sentiment has caught on with India's left-led governments as well—West Bengal's IT policy exempts the state's IT/BPO sector from strikes, and the chief minister Buddhadeb Bhattacharjee has supported the sector as "essential for development, and more jobs."

It is also interesting how the Indian government has begun to leverage the strength of India's IT industry in its foreign relations with other countries, as IT companies have established offices and made acquisitions across the world. In the Middle East, for instance, India has pushed governments to locate and deport terrorists, while using investments by India's software firms there—and the threat of pullout—as leverage.[8] As the technology economy has expanded in India, IT companies have also shifted from software exports to addressing domestic opportunities. Infosys's software solutions, for instance, have enabled significant IT-led productivity growth in the banking sector in the last two decades. ICICI Bank has used our Finacle software suite to develop a cost-effective platform, and Pravir estimates that this helped the bank in expanding its transaction volume fivefold over five years.

Some of the domestic industries in India are even beginning to approach the outer edge of technology excellence. Banking, one of the early IT adopters, is leapfrogging developed-market banks thanks to the IT-enabled banking network.

Electronification has enabled Indian banks to discover new efficiencies—ATM banking in India is now half the cost in the United States; the cost of phone banking is one third. These systems are also highly labor efficient—it takes, Pravir says, just five people to manage the 250,000 transactions that go through ICICI Direct every day. "We are in uncharted territory," Pravir says. "We are on average five to ten years ahead of many countries in the West in our IT systems."

Information technology in the new Indian landscape

Increasingly, India's new identity has technology embedded in our fingerprints. IT in India has proved itself lithe and surprisingly agile, penetrating the nooks and corners of a country in ways we would have been unable to predict even a decade ago. IT-led business processes and supply chains are bringing in once marginal rural communities into the market, and also expanding access to scarce resources.

Electronification is reaching out across India's divides, whether they are geographical, cultural or economic. The technology is playing an emerging role in uniting communities under single national systems, which are quickly making geographical distances irrelevant. Early IT initiatives were often driven by ambitious state governments, such as Chandrababu Naidu's government in Andhra Pradesh and S. M. Krishna's in Karnataka. More recently, however, IT systems have been enabling tax payment and government services that function at a national level rather than a state level, and Indian citizens can access these regardless of where they live. In addition, IT-based institutions—whether it is the NSDL or NSE networks, the MCX and NCDEX trading centers or ICICI's e-banking systems—are bringing India's regional markets together. Bhave notes, for instance, that the rise of an accessible, electronified and national stock market has transformed regional economic issues into national ones. "A resident in Calcutta who owns shares in a Bangalore company is going to be concerned about Karnataka's economic policies."

This is the beginning of a transformation that is taking shape across India. "Before we knew it," Narain tells me, "seventy-year-old brokers were arguing the intricacies of our software with us, and recommending feature changes." Chawla concurs, "People see how the new systems change their lives, and the last thing they want to do is go back to how things were."

Even as technology itself has changed—from the grim and forbidding machines housed in secure complexes, which you programmed through punched cards, to user-friendly iPods where everything is a fingertip away—our view of IT too has been transformed. The idea of technology as something ominous and scary that is used by "Big Brother" to control our lives and eliminate jobs has given way to the idea that it empowers, liberates and gives us access to all the services that are due to us, as citizens and consumers. It provides the means for upward mobility and a tool for people to make their lives easier.

Our embrace of technology has been at the center of the ideas that are shaping India. The shift in sentiment here from hostility to hope has the potential to reshape our economy in unprecedented ways. We had once underestimated how welcome electronification would be here. It is now likely that even with all our optimism, we have once again underestimated the impact it will have on the country.

HOME AND THE WORLD

Our Changing Seasons

IN 1952, an Indian newsmagazine took it upon itself to suggest that the American soldiers fighting in the Korean War "were so effete, they had perfume [with them] in their trenches." The U.S. journalist E. J. Kahn, on reading this piece, objected and took pains to point out that when he himself had visited Korea, "I never saw or heard of any such refinement."[1]

The newsmagazine concerned was the over-the-top, outrageous *Blitz*, so a response was probably unnecessary. But the antagonistic stance it took was not unusual in India. Depending on the political leanings of the commentator, Indians across the political spectrum routinely made digs against the West or China and universally decried the slightest whiff of a "foreign hand" in the country's politics or economy. Our interactions with the world took place from a defensive crouch. This isolationism continued despite the heavy price we paid for it: our exports to the world were a blip—at 2.5 percent of our GDP—in the early 1970s. Tagore's vision of a "world not broken up into narrow . . . walls" was entirely forgotten—we had walled ourselves in, with the Arabian Sea as our moat.

We only need to look toward our media, gung-ho and optimistic about India's standing in the world today, to see how much things have changed. Despite our history as one of the world's biggest introverts, our transformation into a more globally oriented society and economy has been fast paced ever since the 1991 reforms forced us to integrate with world markets. Since then, India's experience with international trade has been transforming our perception of the role we can play in the world. And in our new openness to global debates on India's growth, our entrepreneurs are making up for the time lost looking inward.

Lost glories

"For much of its past," Nayan Chanda tells me, "India was one of the most globalized countries in the world."

First impressions when it comes to Nayan are pretty deceiving. He looks like the quintessential academic, frail and bespectacled, but he has had a remarkable career as a journalist present in dangerous places at dangerous times—he was in Vietnam when Saigon fell and sent the last wire out to Reuters before communications shut down. As a writer, he has in a way continued to indulge in his taste for danger, with a book on one of the most volatile topics of our time, globalization.

In his book *Bound Together,* Nayan points out that precolonization the Indian subcontinent was at the center of an intricate network of merchant ships from Europe and Asia. "The region was extremely hospitable to explorers and traders," Nayan says. "When Arab merchants landed in India with their produce, they were welcomed by the local rulers with the address 'mapilla'—which meant sons-in-law." India's openness to trade was in sharp contrast to other empires, which imposed a variety of trade restrictions from time to time, and often specifically on Indian imports. Nayan notes that Rome, for instance, banned the import of Indian silk on the pretext that it was being used for "flimsy, lascivious clothes worn by ladies." The Romans were clearly worried about the amount of Indian goods being imported, which by the time of Emperor Nero had almost fully depleted the Roman treasury.[2] Even as late as the eighteenth century, India was a dominant economy and the Western world was suspicious and fearful of it. In Britain the Calico Act in 1701 partially banned the import of Indian textiles.

Until the late eighteenth century, India together with China accounted for 40 percent of the global market. It was a time "when everything exquisite and admirable came from the East,"[3]* and the region was at the heart of trade for spices, textiles, hardwood and precious stones. There are interesting parallels between the Indian subcontinent of that time and the United States of today, as a promised land filled with riches that people were willing to take long, risky voyages to reach.

But war and colonialism sapped both India and China of their strength. Nevertheless, through the twentieth century India retained a sense of greatness and a historic cultural pride—pride that we sustained mainly through recollections of our past dominance. This often seemed absurd in the light of the poor economy that India became, but it persisted within us, tenacious and unrelenting. So when someone asked Gandhi what he thought about Western civilization, he replied thoughtfully, "It would be a good idea."

A free nation that turned its back on globalization

By the time of India's independence, our ancient connections—the legacy of openness and our centuries of trade—had been all but lost. It takes a certain amount of economic confidence for countries to embrace policies of trade openness, and the violence of colonization had not only sapped India's strength but also left it economically and politically insecure, battling the ghosts of its imperial years.

Nehru once wrote: "It is significant that one of the Hindustani words which has become part of the English language is 'loot.'" This bitterness was not without reason. Trade with international markets under British rule had been terribly damaging to Indian industry, and the movement of goods from India to Britain during this period had mainly been at prices low enough to suit British markets. And of course colonialism itself had arrived here, as the first vice president of India, Dr. S. Radhakrishnan, noted, through "merchants who came to trade but stayed to rule."[4]

Independent India, as a consequence, viewed trade as nothing more than Imperialism Lite, a system that would force us to remain under the British

*Europe at the time was considered so backward that exiles from the Mughal Empire were sent to that continent, "into the wilderness, among the barbarians," as punishment. The kings of the Eastern empires were disdainful about the wares Europe offered for trade—in the eighteenth century, China's Emperor Qianlong refused trade with England, writing to George III: "We possess all things . . . there is no need to import these manufactures of outside barbarians."

thumb; many believed that it would only mean continued colonial repression and economic exploitation for the country. India's economic policy thus became "anti-colonialism without colonialism"—a former world power and remarkably open economy now viewed global markets with deep suspicion, and the government, with the support of Indian businesses, walled up the country's markets with enormous trade restrictions.

This equating of trade with imperialism has meant that as a free nation our views on globalization have been intertwined with our insecurities. Successive governments saw globalization as a threat, something that would force the country to become both deeply dependent on and vulnerable to the outside world. This was aggravated by India's reliance on Western and multilateral organizations such as the World Bank and the International Monetary Fund (IMF) for food and monetary aid through the 1960s and 1970s. Such aid made us hyperaware of signs of foreign influence. For instance, Indira Gandhi had agreed to the U.S. president Lyndon Johnson's proposal that the millions of dollars that India owed the United States in PL 480 loan repayment should be plowed into Indian education instead; but she had to drop the plan when her advisers pointed out that implementing a suggestion from the United States would be politically disastrous.

This sensitivity blinkered us to the possibilities of globalization for economic growth and dictated the terms of India's engagement with the world at a time when growth was soaring across global markets. In fact India turned inward during an especially critical time: the 160 years between 1820 and 1980, when India suffered first under colonialism and then a closed economy, saw the rise of the modern, industrial market. Between 1820 and 2000, the Industrial Revolution and rising international trade drove worldwide growth at rates that were sustained and unprecedented. During this period, economic activity grew an astonishing forty-nine times, and at the centers of the Industrial Revolution—Europe and the United States—per capita income grew by fifteen and twenty-five times, respectively.*

India, however, experienced economic growth of just 0.2 percent per capita per year between 1870 and 1947. Between 1947 and 1980 it did not get much better, hovering at 1.2 percent. The rapid productivity growth enabled by the Industrial Revolution, the expansion of trade and the result-

*While studying these income shifts, the economist Angus Maddison also did a comparison of this period and the decades before—he noted that per capita income grew a mere 50 percent between CE 1000 and CE 1800.

ing boom in consumption and per capita income worldwide happened at a time when India stood outside, looking in.

After first light

When Infosys was set up in the 1980s, economic reforms were cautiously opening up India's domestic markets. We watched the government policies of the time closely for the signs of the liberal policies and transformation that Rajiv Gandhi had promised. He seemed committed to change, but the fact remained that every inch of access an Indian gained to global trade at the time was hard won and the result of tightly fought battles, since domestic businesses lobbied strongly against bringing down trade barriers and our politicians only favored opening up those areas where local alternatives were clearly unavailable.

Even the 1991 reforms did not immediately engender a change in our mind-set toward globalization, since for many the new policy was a bitter pill that had to be taken to avert a crisis. But the decisions we made in 1991, even if under duress and done half-heartedly, had immense implications. India, once it had liberalized its economy, had yielded to the rules of the international market and would find it extremely difficult to retreat back into socialism—we had no choice but to walk ahead as the path behind us disappeared.

India clearly entered the global market moody and uncertain about its new policies and disheartened by its recent crisis. But immediately post-reform, the country saw the takeoff of one particular sector, the software industry, and it saved us from a prolonged sulk.

Information technology firms like Infosys, small and initially uncertain, had set out to chart global opportunities in the 1980s, and we met with dramatic, early success, thanks to our cost advantages and our large pool of talent. Our success was particularly fortunate in its timing. Through the 1990s it helped smooth out early antiglobalization hostilities—when people had demonstrated in front of foreign banks and fast-food joints—and our economy began to wake up to the opportunities that had come with the new openness.

Information technology services served as the Trojan horse through which globalization entered the Indian economy and gained acceptance. Unconstrained by India's capital and infrastructure bottlenecks, the knockout growth of the sector in the years since reforms showed how well world markets could work to India's advantage.

The success of our domestic IT firms led to a dawning sense across Indian industry that we were in a position of almost unique strength in the international economy. While other countries were blowing either too hot or too cold, India was the "Goldilocks economy"—its economic factors across capital, labor and industry were becoming just right to compete in the world market.

In the 1960s and 1970s, when the Western press made references to India, certain adjectives were mandatory and leaped out of the text. Interactions with India during this period were largely limited to our bureaucrats and diplomats, and opinions on Indians were shaped accordingly. We were always "distant," "proud" and of course "bureaucratic." And beyond India's puzzling government representatives, Indians were "a faceless mass," the people of a vast, poor nation.[5] These perceptions started changing only when Indian entrepreneurs began to venture outside. Entrepreneurs from India's IT companies were among the first to do so—immediately after I joined Infosys in 1981, I had to leave for Tampa, Florida, to work with a client. In these years, as India's software entrepreneurs crossed the Atlantic to market their services, Western corporations began to encounter Indians who were educated, pro–free markets and positive about global trade, international standards and best practices.

Through the past two decades, these soft advantages have only intensified, as Indian firms across our manufacturing and, increasingly, agriculture sectors have been exporting and diversifying internationally. And I think these skills have massively aided our economic advantages as India reaches out to the world.

A constellation of opportunities: Our triple plays

"Our future capacity to produce goods and services is so high," Roopa Purushothaman tells me, "that the domestic economy is not enough to absorb it." And this capacity is especially valuable in the changing world market. In its strengths, India is a jigsaw piece that is falling perfectly into place in the landscape of the global economy.

The single biggest advantage in this context is India's demographic dividend, which is well-known thanks to the landmark Goldman Sachs BRICs report that came out in 2003. I discuss this demographic opportunity with Roopa Purushothaman, the brilliant and precocious economist—she was twenty-five at the time of the BRICs analysis—who coauthored the report. "We didn't realize at the time the impact these projections would have," Roopa tells me, "but the report created waves, and it drew a lot of attention to the potential effects of India's demographic dividend." It certainly did—I remember the somewhat premature blowing of trumpets across India when the report was released, and it formed the basis of the ill-fated "India Shining" campaign that the NDA government, up for reelection, launched.

The campaign might have collapsed, but the incessant drumbeat around the report made Indians aware of the huge, barreling potential in our labor market. India's overwhelmingly young population means that more than 270 million people are expected to join the workforce over the next two decades.

As Roopa points out, the demographic dividend will be the wave on which India rides to high and stable growth rates over the next four or five decades. This dividend also underlines what is at stake for us on the globalization front. With the rapid aging that is set to occur across the developed world and in China, the demographic advantage is giving India a potential "triple play" opportunity for growth—in the domestic market; in the world economy through migration; and through the rise of the outsourcing industry.

A country of entrepreneurs

Before the crosshatch of high tariffs began unraveling in the 1980s, a closed coterie of entrepreneurs dominated Indian industry—people who played rummy and celebrated birthdays and anniversaries together were hand in glove with government bureaucrats. They were provincial and happy with their domestic monopolies. The Indian entrepreneur Lala Charat Ram hit the nail on the head when he remarked of this period, "You cannot make a loss, unless you are an utter fool."[6]

Now, the Indian economy boasts a highly competitive, vibrant and broad entrepreneur base, which depends not on closed and exclusive networks, but on the wide open global market. In this environment, we have seen the old monopolies fade as a new wave of risk taking, ambitious and increasingly young businesses has emerged across industries. DCM, the family company led by Lala Charat Ram, split up into smaller companies a decade after reforms, as industries they once dominated saw scrappy, new competitors emerge. The rise of this new generation of Indian entrepreneurs has been timely for both India and the world. As their populations age, developed markets need higher returns on the investments of their older citizens to meet rising pension and social costs. India's entrepreneurial growth is the kind that the world's markets have been waiting for—even among the Asian sizzlers, Indian firms stand out in average growth rates and profit margins.

As a result, India has emerged primarily as a foreign institutional investment (FII) destination, with foreign inflows funding its growing domestic companies. The country has in fact attracted nearly 20 percent of net portfolio investments into developing countries. In comparison, China attracts more foreign direct investment (FDI) than FII* and is less entrepreneurial than India—two thirds of China's exports are by foreign multinationals or joint ventures, mainly owned by Taiwanese, Hong Kong, Japanese and U.S. companies.

The flush of foreign capital has enabled Indian entrepreneurs to target business opportunities all over the globe. This, combined with the disruptive models that young Indian companies with large cost advantages have adopted, has made the average profit margin of listed Indian firms an astounding 8 percent. This has given Indian companies the capital and stock market prowess to make major acquisitions. The acquisition targets of Indian firms have since exploded—the size of the average Indian foreign acquisition has grown ten times, to $315 million in recent years.

For Indian business, there is a promising shimmer in the air that underlines emerging opportunity here and abroad, a willingness to take risks and see whether they win or lose—and a belief that they are more likely to win.

"The luckiest country of the twenty-first century"

India's unique combination of IT skills, its labor advantages, capital flows and pool of ambitious, outward-looking companies is giving it a second,

*This has meant that China has more entrepreneurs entering the country than investors, unlike India, where foreign investment has been more focused on infusing capital into the local entrepreneurial base.

massive triple-play advantage across sectors—in manufacturing, services and agriculture.

Only recently have we begun to recognize the broader implications of the IT revolution—that it is nothing less than a seismic shift in how the world economy works and that India may be especially well-placed to take advantage of it. But then, economic power comes to countries in unexpected ways and at unexpected times, and it is usually enabled by new technologies. When Europe began invading eastern shores, the Asian empires were horrified—they had regarded them as little more than impoverished barbarians. Europe's growth in the sixteenth and seventeenth centuries was a result of technological advances in building large, multimasted ships that could sail in the rough, open seas. The rise of new navigation tools—better maps, sextants and chronometers—also allowed explorers to chart out better sea routes, giving Europe access to colonies, slaves, silks and gold.

The tiny island of Britain emerged as the major European power in the eighteenth century with innovations in public finance and an embryonic stock market. These institutions created richly funded, powerful companies that quickly dominated global trade—our old acquaintance the East India Company was in fact the very first "joint-stock" company of Britain. And of course, the technological prowess of the Industrial Revolution enabled Britain and Europe to dominate world economic growth for more than a hundred years.

In this context, India has been fortunate even in its barriers. In the 1970s and 1980s, IT was literally the only option for a start-up entrepreneur to begin a business without political access or capital. A slow-growing economy also ended up diverting much of its huge talent into a small but burgeoning IT sector, and these firms got by on very little—a leased computer, a data line—over which they sold Indian brainpower to the outside world. India thus literally stumbled onto services growth, one that happens to be the emerging story for the international economy.

Today, the exploding global, IT-led services economy is impacting more business processes than we thought possible, as technology transforms more and more processes across the value chain into work over wire—from research and development (R&D) to medical diagnostics and, in one rather unusual case, even on-scene news reporting when Indian "reporters" watched conferences by video and typed up news reports for a U.S. paper. As a result the world market for offshored IT services and business processes has nearly tripled since 2001—it is now estimated to be a $300 billion opportunity, of which service providers have so far captured just 10 percent. And as the dominant player in the sector, India is now uniquely placed to capture this market—compelling Tom Friedman to call us "the luckiest country of the twentieth century."

Indian companies are also emerging as the IT economy's nerve center. In 2001, after the capacity glut in bandwidth and the telecom bubble burst, fiber-optic companies were being sold for a song and a prayer, and Indian companies were there to buy them. Reliance ADAG bought the Bermuda-based Flag Telecom after it exited from bankruptcy protection in 2003, and Tata bought Tyco Global's networks and Canada's Teleglobe. These companies now have immense ambitions in wiring the continents of Asia and Africa, where they are building the information economy's equivalent of railroads and highways.

As India further liberalizes, we can also integrate much more strongly with the global services market across sectors such as manufacturing, finance, education and health. A new breed of entrepreneurs across India makes these once seemingly impossible opportunities look very realistic.

Jignesh Shah is a perfect example of this new breed, though he defies the stereotypes of both the old and the new entrepreneur—he is a seamless blend, with Evian bottles on his conference room table and a small idol of Lord Ganesha in one corner. Jignesh is an example of how the post-1991 decades have created new possibilities for young and talented Indians—he admits that if it had not been for the rise of India's financial markets post-reform, he would have done an MS in engineering in the United States and become an employee in an American IT firm. Instead, he says, "I saw the chance in 1995 to build something from scratch, a financial product company that would encompass commodities, equities, currencies and bonds." The result, MCX, is India's largest commodity exchange, which Jignesh got up and running in nine months after he received approval. Jignesh is India's newest kind of entrepreneur—young, brashly confident, an expert in both technology and the industry he works in and highly talented at using this cross-domain knowledge.

The British economist R. M. Grindley had written in 1837, "India can never again be a great manufacturing country." It may have taken us close to two centuries to prove him wrong, but today India is leveraging its software advantage in a manufacturing sector that is being rapidly integrated with IT.

A focus on operational excellence and technology among Indian companies such as Jindal Steel, Reliance Industries, Mahindra and Mahindra and Sundaram Clayton means that these companies are now rivaling—and even surpassing—global firms in manufacturing standards and efficiencies, and this has driven profits and high returns.

Indian firms are in fact raising the bar when it comes to quality standards. Seventy percent of the world's CMMI Level 5 firms—which rates software maturity—are Indian, and companies across our industries have rapidly adopted quality initiatives such as ISO 9000 certifications and Total Quality Management (TQM). Indian manufacturing companies have made great strides here in the last two decades—they rank second only to the Japanese in the number of Deming awards (given for quality management) won per country.

A big driver in the growth of these sectors has also been India's enormous talent in figuring out a way past obstacles, so perhaps our decades under an autarkic economy were not entirely wasted. For instance, a large segment of Indian manufacturing, thanks to high entry costs as well as labor limitations, is dominated by smaller, local firms that face problems such as communication barriers and a lack of awareness of international quality standards and processes. This has led to the establishment of buying houses that understand both the lingo and the standards of trading partners and whose sole function is to facilitate communication between global firms and Indian factories.

AS INDIA BUILDS UP its high-end manufacturing base, new opportunities are emerging in the large-scale manufacturing sector, and these will only grow over the next decade, as China's demographic dividend begins to wane. With our factory worker costs 80 percent lower than averages in developed markets, India can, with a deepening of reforms, become the next big source of manufacturing labor to the world.

India can also benefit from emerging opportunities within what has for the last decade been our economic underperformer, agriculture. Again, a unique confluence of global factors—including the rise of biofuel production in developed markets as well as the pressure on developed market subsidies due to Europe's straining budgets—is likely to push agricultural prices upward in the coming decades. Many countries, thanks to demographic shifts and rising costs of labor, are beginning to look outside their borders for cheaper agricultural imports, and India's labor-intensive agriculture, strengthened by emerging farm reforms, is in a unique position to utilize global markets as a launch pad for rapid growth. Exploiting these opportunities across sectors will, however, require a dramatic shift in policy—both in executing present policies better in infrastructure and single markets and in furthering reforms across our labor markets and education systems.

Quid pro quo

I have often heard the opinion—a popular one among diplomats and trade negotiators from the developing world—that developed economies are reacting extremely cautiously to the new trade dynamic in favor of emerging economies and choose to play hardball. These countries have been reluctant to expose their domestic industries to the highly cost-competitive products from countries such as India. Demands of protectionism in the West, for instance, have been on the rise even in committed free-market economies such as the United States, and Europe has held onto its subsidy-heavy agricultural policies against international pressure.

But global trade is a potluck system, and it helps if economies bring something to the party. India's white-knuckle rise has been unique in that its growth has not followed the Asian-style export-driven, mercantile model that is making China and East Asia rich. India's growth has instead been driven by its domestic market, which accounts for two thirds of its GDP and is powered by an already 300-million-strong middle class, a group larger than the population of the United States.

This surging consumer class holds great promise for global retailers, especially in the light of the slowing markets of the West. The 300 million plus who comprise our middle class may still have modest incomes, but their aspirational mood is compelling both domestic and multinational companies to cater to their demands in innovative ways—through single-serve FMCG products and cheaper cars and mobile phones. As my colleague on the Infosys board of directors and brand guru Rama Bijapurkar remarked, "The aspirations of an Indian consumer, whether rich or poor, have transformed upward, and people are no longer happy with owning just a television, or a radio." Rama tells me that she finds the rapid shifts in consumerism that are now taking place both compelling and unmistakable. "Indians want what they see others buying, they want to keep up. For global retailers, that is the dream customer."

Growth here will also have more direct benefits for international markets with the expansion of Indian tourism—Indian tourists are expected to grow 132 percent between 2006 and 2011 alone, rising to 16.3 million annually. The stereotype of the camera-happy, ubiquitous Japanese tourist is set to be replaced with another—that of bustling Indian families with a dozen suitcases.

The uniqueness of India's consumers—where vast numbers are still poor and have very limited purchasing power—has also meant that Indian companies who have cut their teeth on an extremely cost-competitive, domestic market are now taking their business models and products international. The Tata Nano, set to be the world's cheapest car, is I think only the beginning of what Indian businesses across industries can do in terms of low-cost innovation.

The way India has grown also makes it far less aggressive in policy when it comes to international markets. China, for instance, has both its politics and its economy holding its trade policies hostage—the country has built a delicate understanding between its people and its government, which restricts democratic rights but offers them economic prosperity in return. "To get rich is glorious" indeed, as a Chinese government slogan goes, but to ensure this China has had to maintain consistent, export-driven job growth for its population. In fact mass protests in China over the last ten years have all been triggered by economic factors, such as the lack of jobs for migrants, poor working conditions and the loss of agricultural land.

This means that China must remain as globally competitive as possible, leading it to adopt those "comparative advantage" currency policies that limit the appreciation of the yuan and keep Chinese exports dominant in world trade. This has invited glares and tariff threats from around the world. The Indian state, on the other hand, with its low share in international trade and exports has had to ensure certain *domestic* market conditions to stay in power. Inflation is a red-letter word for India's governments, guaranteed to get its opponents crying themselves hoarse over "social justice"; price rises in India have ignited student riots, nationwide demonstrations and government collapse. Track inflation and government approval in India, and you will see that the correlation is near perfect—inflation goes up, and government popularity goes down.*

The leeway that Indian citizens give governments on prices has also reduced over the years. While governments could survive double-digit inflation rates in the 1970s and 1980s—Indira Gandhi presided over rates of 26 percent and 20 percent in 1973–74 and 1980–81—such tolerance has dramatically reduced since reforms. Now, inflation touching 5 percent triggers fears of voter reprisal. As inflation crossed 12 percent in mid-2008, the Indian government began to openly panic, and coalition members criticized and distanced themselves from state policy. The inability of India's voters to tolerate inflation means that our governments have tended to favor an appreciating currency, the reverse of the Chinese approach. Such a policy makes it difficult to argue that India is not playing fair, and it has made its integration into global trade easier to stomach.

The biggest untapped resource?

In my view, it is not just the economic benefits the country has to offer that make India a force to reckon with across the world. It is the country's more intangible advantages, its identity as a diverse, democratic country, that may be its biggest strength.

As a former colony, we remain strongly linked to the West in history, language, trade and sheer familiarity. The writer Sunil Khilnani, when I run into him during one of his whirlwind trips to India, recalls for me his now famous phrase defining India's opportunity as a link between two parts of the world. "I would restate it even more strongly today—that India can become the 'bridging power,' the country that can position itself between developing and developed nations."

India is also by far the biggest democracy that has entered the world economy in recent years, bringing with it the kind of entrepreneurship that thrives in a democratic environment. India's acquisitions around the world as a result should be more successful on a global scale, thanks to a shared

*Indira Gandhi's shaky terms as prime minister were marked by high inflation, which she tried to smooth over with pro-poor rhetoric. Controlling inflation while retaining bad socialist-era policies has also been the cause of India's persistent and rising deficit, created by a deficit–money–inflation–deficit spiral.

emphasis with the West on transparency, independence from the government* and fair business practices. The capital Indian firms bring may consequently trigger less soul-searching among Western firms that need financing and support. India's young demographics also consist of people who share common values with Western firms and their customers, which means that foreign firms do not have to enter India with fears of censorship, repression or a playing field unfairly tilted toward domestic firms.

India's rise as a prominent provider of global services, especially in the IT and BPO sectors, is potentially strengthening its democratic institutions even further. An Indian BPO employee who provides train schedules to a user of the London Underground questions the absence of such systems in Indian infrastructure. As these workers directly interact with customers in the West, they encounter new standards of excellence and quality, which they apply to the Indian environment. This may explain why Bangalore, the hub of the IT/BPO industry, has also had the most vocal civil society organizations demanding better infrastructure and stronger local governments.

In fact, despite the many years of being a closed, high-tariff economy, we can argue that Indians have always been more open-minded than the economic models we have lived under. Bollywood movies were and continue to be filled with vistas of European cities, with songs shot in Switzerland and in front of Big Ben. A big reason for our openness has been our vibrant diaspora of nonresident Indians (NRIs), who provided us a window to the world even during the years that the economy was closed off. I remember how eagerly I, along with my cousins, would wait for uncles and aunts visiting from abroad—inevitably, their suitcases would arrive stuffed with Toblerone chocolate bars and packets of chips. The Indian community has spread its roots across the world, from the eighteenth-century indentured laborers who were shipped to Southeast Asia and Europe to the immigrants to the Commonwealth through the 1950s and the engineers emigrating to the United States in the 1970s. So far and wide has the community spread that, as the writer Parag Khanna noted, "The sun never sets on the Indian diaspora." And these Indians have been a ready conduit for the country's soft power, in terms of our film, literature, art and music.

Our attitudes toward our NRI community have changed as our econ-

*It would be amiss not to add that some Indian firms still remain highly connected with the government, thanks to their sheer size and clout in major industries—such as energy and mining. However, the number of such firms so far makes them the exception rather than the rule.

omy has globalized. Dr. Vijay Kelkar remembers how Indira Gandhi arranged a conference of senior Indian economists in 1980 to discuss the problem of "brain drain" from India—the government considered skilled Indians leaving for jobs abroad a major problem. Today, however, the government regards the Indian community abroad as a key asset; it has become a source of access into new markets, capital and knowledge, as Indian companies compete internationally, branch outward and establish new markets.

Globalization: Our peculiar challenges

India's real challenge when it comes to globalization is an intellectual one. Independent India has had three dominant strains of economic thought—Gandhi's swadeshi movement, Nehru's Fabian socialism and the Hindutva brand of nationalism. But we have had no prominent, popular champion of economic openness and reform in our politics. Our single prominent reformist party, the Swatantra Party, lost its way after C. Rajagopalachari's death. "The one big opportunity for a popular leader who supported global markets," Dr. Kelkar recently said to me, "was Rajiv Gandhi, but he died too soon." As a result the idea of trade openness in India has been pushed more by intellectuals like Manmohan Singh and Montek Singh Ahluwalia than by popular politicians, and this has kept support for it narrow and limited.

Our automatic hostility to globalization blinds us to the differences between "good" and "bad" global integration. The international financial meltdown that took place in September 2008 was a sign that all integration is not "all good, all the time." Financial globalization, for instance, can be dangerous when it is weakly regulated—this drives speculation up and encourages "electronic herds" who stampede into markets all at once, and also panic and pull out together, making stock markets and currencies across countries extremely volatile.

Despite these caveats, India's two decades of growth and the expansion of the country's entrepreneurs across international services and manufacturing have helped transform attitudes toward market openness across Indian industry. One upside in India is that globalization here does not present the complex political challenge that it does in the West. Kaushik Basu notes, "As an emerging market, globalization for India is definitely more a story of opportunity." Openness for us seems like a no-brainer, especially considering that a still-developing economy needs multipliers like trade to give our entrepreneurs the markets they need to expand and our price-sensitive consumers the widest possible choice of goods.

And considering that India is set to cash in on its massive demographic dividend, it would be bad policy indeed to turn trade opportunities away. Trade has become especially important for our *sustained* development and for sufficient long-term employment and income growth. With the vast number of people expected to come of age and join the workforce, India will not be able to provide jobs through its domestic market alone. The lack of jobs for such a large surplus workforce could shake India at its very foundation, and create large-scale political and social instability.

The opportunity world markets offer us is a chance for us to return to our roots and to become, once again, the fearless, outward-looking country of our past. But we cannot afford to sit around twiddling our thumbs. We must not forget that this is a time of "kaleidoscopic comparative advantage" for countries—as both jobs and capital become highly mobile, India can quickly lose the multitude of economic advantages it now holds relative to the global economy.

Right now, the confluence of our demographics, entrepreneurial prowess, financial flows and technology is forming a golden bridge to world markets. But to cross the bridge, we must deal with our internal stresses against liberalization and further reforms.

India within

A microcosm of India's challenges with globalization lies in the experience of a Tamil Nadu fishing village near Tiruchendur and its brush with globalization. In 2001 the villagers here found that a new fiber-reinforced plastic boat based on foreign know-how was available in the market. It was more durable and could go into deeper water than the timber ones they had, but only the rich fishermen could buy it. Income inequality rose as fishermen with the fiber boats saw fish hauls that were one and a half times those of the others. This continued for a long time, till the poorer villagers were able to save enough to buy the new boats. Once they did, inequality dropped to levels lower than ever before. The key here was access. The poorer fishermen lacked easy sources of loans and this kept them from buying these boats. If such options had been available, incomes would have grown much faster and more equitably. The benefits of globalization would have been more immediately apparent.

That this access did not exist has many reasons. Since economic change in India had come out of crisis, with no intellectual tradition to support it, people saw it as the only way out—a decision India's leaders saw as the unhappy choice we made in order to draw us back from the edge of a cliff.

Consequently, the push toward reforms in India has been dominated by economic forces rather than political ones. Globalization in particular has allowed Indian reforms to deepen their initial hold. Since India has begun to weave itself into world markets, it has seen a push from the outside in our economic policy, as India's financial markets have rapidly interlinked with global ones and as Indian companies, first in IT and then across sectors, have integrated with international supply chains.

But the progress remains complicated by the lack of political buy-in. Where economic reform has clashed with politically powerful interest groups, it has stalled, limiting above all the most dramatic, access-creating reforms—such as labor law changes that would transform access to employment and jobs, and to capital that encourages innovation and entrepreneurship.

Even such seemingly small limitations on access can thus have disproportionate effects on incomes. Globalization under such conditions tends only to intensify inequality and undermines the effectiveness of trade in driving growth.

Lack of broad access has also allowed a strident lack of concern among governments for the rights of the poor and of weaker groups. It has been visible in the political thuggery when the government hired police to beat up nonviolent protestors of the Enron agreement in Maharashtra, and more recently in the insensitive treatment of villagers and farm owners living on land bought for SEZ projects.

Partly, it is globalization itself that will enable the more difficult changes in political processes. Former prime minister P. V. Narasimha Rao had said, "The full freedom to dream the way you like came only in 1991, not 1947." In India reforms have enabled a rapid shift in attitudes—a growing middle class, for example, is demanding better public systems and services. The rise of the market economy has also been instrumental in driving a demand for better education, access to IT and better infrastructure across economic classes to take advantage of economic growth. Abhijit Banerjee remarked to me how villagers have begun to oversee public road works in their areas. "Old men will sit by the side of the road, watching the contractors," he says, "and if they mess up on the tarring and levelling, they make them fix it."

In the long term, world markets also have the power to improve governance standards. The integration across industry sectors with global supply chains has brought in international scrutiny and standards for local businesses, such as in food safety laws. It is also driving governments to respond to supply chain inefficiencies, which are bringing in reforms in agriculture, port and highway infrastructure, and a push toward less draconian controls in manufacturing. Across these sectors, openness is weeding out both government apathy and inefficiency.

The rise of a powerful and internationally connected Indian media of private news channels has also turned the spotlight on weak governance, and the string of "sting" news operations and colorful scandals have both angered governments and forced them to answer some uncomfortable questions. In addition, the spread of IT, which has gained a foothold in India through the software industry, is transforming access and transparency in government systems. And as businesses broaden their involvement into sectors such as education and health, it is providing an alternative to state systems. For instance, a villager without access to a good government school is able to access either a rural private school or education provided by a long-distance tutor through one of Sriram Raghavan's IT kiosks.

Group-based entitlements—in education, employment and infrastructure—are also becoming less difficult to sustain as the private sector expands and the country links itself with global supply chains in infrastructure and labor. Dr. Madhav Chavan, cofounder and director of the NGO Pratham, tells me, "Workers in Bombay are refusing to join unions on minimum wage, since they can negotiate directly with a company and get jobs at higher incomes." This is creating broader support for markets and economic reforms and is also slowly bringing down the strength of interest groups such as teachers unions in schools and of unionized employees in the public sector.

BUT THERE ARE LIMITS to what economic momentum alone can do in reforming ineffective systems. As Nayan Chanda says, "In today's economy, trade is a fast train that stops only at certain stations—the one with the infrastructure and the factor advantages to support it." In India we have already seen this in rising imbalances across Indian states—Gujarat, Maharashtra, Karnataka and Tamil Nadu are seeing rapid gains from globalization, while Bihar and Uttar Pradesh are not. Here we have a conundrum: global trade might enable better governance, but the states that should benefit most from such reform are so weak that they do not see global markets stopping at their particular "stations."

Additionally, globalization in India today benefits the educated far more than it does illiterate labor. Abhijit notes, "The returns from education have become a steep curve, with the illiterate seeing income levels similar to what they were in the 1980s, while for the highly educated, incomes have gone through the roof." To sustain gains as well as to ensure that the returns are broad based, Indian states must rapidly build and expand their infrastructure and improve the quality of their workforce through better investments in education and health. In this context, Roopa says, "If India manages to achieve the education standards of the other BRIC countries such as China and Brazil, it would see much more than the five percent average we predicted—the growth would be closer to seven percent a year."

These, however, are where the most-difficult-to-enact reforms reside and where our old, entrenched interests have grown deep, stubborn roots. And uprooting these requires nothing less than massive popular will.

I believe, however, that there is a momentum now building toward this kind of change. Even as the debate on globalization continues to contribute to the gridlock of our politics, Indians have cast their vote in its favor. Students are going abroad in droves to get the education they cannot get at home. The construction worker is going to the Middle East to make his fortune. The software engineer is busy solving intricate problems for the world's largest corporations. The young girl in a call center is walking an aggravated customer through a credit card transaction. The gardener of a floriculture company in Bangalore is getting thousands of crimson roses ready for export in time to accompany chocolate boxes and dinner invitations on Valentine's Day. The Indian entrepreneur is trawling the globe in search of new markets and acquisitions. The children of postreform India have no time to listen to tales about conspiracies of the "foreign hand"—they are too busy tapping into the vast opportunities that are emerging for them.

A friend of mine who runs a BPO tells me that he sees Indian youngsters today untouched by the tentativeness that marked my generation's interactions with the West. "They are assertive," he says, "and they are always confident of doing things their way, certain that the solutions they've learnt here will work." Our successes so far on the global stage have allowed us to move from being seen as a "wounded" civilization to one where people have enormous confidence in our global advantages.

As a result our political leaders are today demanding a role at the head table—be it a seat in the Security Council of the United Nations, playing a key role in WTO negotiations, or getting a greater voting share in the IMF and World Bank. This new assertiveness is not coming from a demand for reparations for past injustices, but rather from a sense that India is expanding its economic role and its influence around the world, and the global order should reflect this.

A while ago, I directly experienced the shift in the world's perception toward India. The night of January 28, 2006, was the occasion of the grand soirée at the Annual Meeting of the World Economic Forum at Davos. This was the finale of the "India Everywhere" campaign, a Confederation of Indian Industry (CII) and India Brand Equity Fund (IBEF) initiative to put Brand India on the world map. I had conceived the idea and orchestrated its rollout, with the enthusiastic support of India's biggest entrepreneurs. As the crowd danced to a vibrant Bollywood beat, it was clear a new India was being showcased, which was young, confident, diverse and entrepreneurial. In the midst of the soirée an American diplomat came up and yelled into my ear above the din of the music, "Congratulations . . . India has arrived!"

But even as the world is acknowledging India's new promise, the opportunity of the global economy has highlighted our internal differences—between the educated and the illiterate, the public and private sectors, between the well- and the poorly governed, and between those who have access and those who do not. In this sense, even as we Indians define ourselves in the context of our home and the world, we face incredible contradictions. Never has the external circumstance for India been so fortunate. And never has the need for resolving the internal conflicts been so urgent. The challenge for India is really within—in the decisions that will emerge out of our political struggles, our debates and our tempestuous democracy.

THE DEEPENING OF OUR DEMOCRACY

The unexpected country

Leo Tolstoy once wrote about India, "What does it mean that thirty thousand people, not athletes, but rather weak and ordinary . . . have enslaved millions of freedom loving people? . . . Do not the figures make it clear that not the English, but the Indians have enslaved themselves?"

The Indian subcontinent was indeed a region that the British captured and dominated with surprising ease. The historian Tarinicharan Chattopadhyay remarked in 1858 of the humiliation that British rule implied—that a region of such size had fallen under the sway of a tiny island.[1] But in reality, the unity of the Indian subcontinent was a tenuous one: it comprised mostly small, battling kingdoms that, absorbed as they were with their rivalries and resentments, fell piece by piece to the British.[2] Even when there was resistance against British rule, it remained small and localized, especially through the nineteenth century—such as the rebellions in Chota Nagpur among the tribals, or in the early 1850s in Bihar and parts of western India. The largest of these resistances, the 1857 mutiny, emerged within a relatively cohesive community—the Indian army.

So we could not easily dismiss the British claim of having "invented India"—the British shaped the country's boundaries from a deeply divided region. There was no dearth of economists and writers who suggested at the time of India's independence that this "artificial" nation, so intensely fractured along so many fault lines, would not be able to hold itself together for long.[3]

After all, the very concept of the nation-state, that post-Renaissance ideal, had its roots in liberalism and the rise of an educated middle class. But India, like the many "new democracies" that emerged in the 1940s and 1950s, was a largely poor and illiterate country that had little history of a widespread, liberal movement. We were a country that underneath the surface was what it had always been—a region riven by factionalism, whose caste and religious divisions seemed to be written in stone.

But the sum of India, as it were, remained greater than its parts. As it crossed its sixtieth year of independence in August 2007, India was praised around the world as a rare and heartening example of an Asian country where democracy has thrived, and as a nation that has managed both political unity and high rates of growth.

But our commitment to democracy has been neither natural nor easy—it has been hard-won. Since independence, India's leaders were careful to frame our economic and political policies primarily around our commitments to unity and democracy. Secular principles were paramount across our laws, and early governments unrelentingly opposed ideas that specifically threatened India's young, democratic institutions. Nehru, for instance, despite his strong belief in a socialist economy, rejected "full-blooded socialism" because it undermined democracy—"The price paid," he wrote, "is heavy."[4] As the political scientist Atul Kohli tells me, "Considering our history, India's leaders could have chosen a system that was half-hearted in terms of democratic and civil rights. Many of us didn't recognize how exceptional the untrammeled democracy we got instead was. It was a gift."

Building toward a democracy

India's path to democracy—from an outright feudal, chaotic region to Britain's jewel among its colonies and finally to its independence in 1947—was not an evolution that encouraged liberal and secular ideas to take root. In the two hundred years that India transitioned from a patchwork of kingdoms to a democracy, the essence of its society changed very little. Under the British government, the region remained both divided and feudal.[5]

The British viewed India more as an economic possession than as a political entity—India was one part of the broader Empire, and the administration even celebrated "Empire Day" in the colony, which fell on May 24, Queen Victoria's birthday.[6] Their attention to India's social divisions was unapologetic, partly because they never really envisioned India as a single community, but as a hotchpotch of disparate groups and regions they had stitched together into a colony. The Empire's governors and census officers emphasized the country's hierarchies, particularly caste, in its imperial surveys, and district gazetteers used caste identities to classify Indian populations.[7]

Elections in India under the Empire only hardened the caste, religious and class divides that already existed. Some form of elections had taken root as early as 1882, through Lord Ripon's resolution that allowed privileged Indians such as zamindars, princes and the wealthy merchant classes to elect candidates into municipal councils.[8] Caste lines came into sharp relief in voter eligibility—during the 1920s' elections in Bombay, for instance, "a Brahmin was a hundred times more likely to possess the vote than a Mahar," the caste that Dr. B. R. Ambedkar belonged to.[9] A report by Montagu and Chelmsford on these early Indian elections worried that this voting model was teaching Indians to "think as partisans and not citizens."

So much then for the "civilizing effects" the British claimed to have brought to India. It turned out that instead of the occupiers transforming Indian attitudes, it was the British officers who absorbed the caste and regional distinctions within Indian society, and they tended to stereotype Indians accordingly—into the "bigoted julaha," the "brave Sikh," and so on.[10]

IT WAS THE INDIAN LEADERS who brought real passion toward the idea of remaking India into a democracy. The leaders who emerged through the early twentieth century emphasized national unity above everything else, an approach that they hoped transcended the distinctions of the region's communities. For Indians, this focus on unity was a necessary choice if they were to mount a coherent dialogue with (or, if it came to it, a unified resistance against) British rule.

For these Indian leaders, the provincial elections of 1937 were an important mobilizer and unifying force for the Indian electorate. Lord Erskine, governor of Madras, commented in the 1930s that the Congress leaders were "panting for office."* But it was the impassioned, involved campaigning these Congress leaders did for the elections that enabled a nascent, nationwide political awakening.[11] Nehru in particular, although he did not contest the elections, focused on getting as many people to vote as possible—he traveled eighty thousand kilometers and spoke to 10 million people, addressing in some places gatherings of more than a hundred thousand.[12] He later described how the headquarters of the provincial governments attracted hundreds of curious viewers: "Hordes of people, from the city and the village, entered these sacred precincts and roamed almost at will . . . they went into the Assembly Chamber . . . even peeped into the Ministers' rooms."[13] Perhaps this was an effort to evoke the sense of a radical beginning, a parallel to the entry of the peasant revolutionaries into the palace of Versailles in 1789 and into Russia's Winter Palace in 1917.

The focus among Indian leaders on building a national electorate meant that they strongly protested against the British characterization of caste and religion as core parts of the Indian identity and especially objected to any kind of religion- or caste-based privileges. For instance, when Ambedkar reached an agreement with the British government in 1932 to create separate electorates for scheduled castes under the Ramsey McDonald Communal Award, Gandhi vehemently opposed it. He eventually forced the Dalit† leader (by going on a fast, which Ambedkar called "moral blackmail") to sign the Poona Pact, which maintained general seats with reservations for scheduled castes.

But it was difficult for India's independence leaders to knit together a truly unified front against the British. Large parts of the middle class—so critical to an effective freedom movement—remained ambivalent in its support for independence. India's business class, for instance, was concentrated among the Bania caste who had expanded into large-scale industry, trade and banking under the British. The propertied classes had also flourished under British rule through the zamindari-style revenue systems, and the arrangement the British had with the princely states had preserved the wealth of much of India's royalty.[14] The zamindars formed the British Indian Association as early as 1851, and the British secretary of state E. S. Montagu wrote of its head in his *Indian Diary*, "He has a fierce love of the British

*This snark was unfair—Nehru, for instance, refused to stand for these elections, stating that they were not fully democratic.

†Dalit was a self-adopted title of the "scheduled castes" and means "a broken people."

connection . . . a firm belief in it." Among these groups, loyalties were divided, and fence-sitters numerous.

BUT INDIAN LEADERS eventually managed to garner some support from these communities for the independence movement; the slogan of swadeshi, for instance, was at its heart a protectionist policy and found immense favor with Indian business. But the need to build bridges between various groups meant a lot of pussyfooting around the country's very worrying social challenges.

The strategies that Congress leaders championed sometimes unintentionally strengthened the very structures—caste and religious divisions and exploitative rural systems—that would later conflict with independent India's democratic vision. Gandhi, for instance, mobilized farmers into the national freedom movement, but his emphasis on nonviolence emasculated them in their ability to fight predatory groups such as moneylenders and zamindars.[15] Similarly, Congress leaders often resorted to religious analogies and symbols while drumming up support for the independence struggle;[16] they would compare the independence movement versus the British as support for "Ram or Ravan," and the red color of Holi with the blood of national sacrifice.[17] In one Congress poster, the rape of Draupadi* was reimagined with India as Draupadi, her attacker as the British and Lord Krishna as Gandhi.[18] The intensive use of such Hindu symbolism resulted in Muslims complaining of feeling shut out.

But for Indian leaders it was imperialism that was the enemy, not feudalism. Nehru even wrote in an article for *Foreign Affairs* magazine in 1937, "No one [in India], whatever his political views or religious persuasion, thinks in terms other than those of national unity." But as independence neared, these divides grew more apparent, and religious party leaders became especially vocal and provocative. For instance, there was the Muslim League's demand that they represent every Muslim political candidate in India, which alienated the League and the Congress even further. At the same time, Hindu leaders such as M. S. Gowalkar were demanding that India's minority religions ought to "remain wholly subordinated to the Hindu nation," and even Congress

*Draupadi was the wife of the five Pandava brothers in the Mahabharata, who was gambled away by the eldest brother in a dice game—this leads to the Rape of Draupadi scene.

leaders such as Abul Kalam Azad suggested that "there will be nothing left with us if we separate politics from religion."[19]

There was clearly a tug-of-war emerging in defining the Indian state—whether India would be ruled by its divisions or by a still-foreign secular ideal. The educated leaders made their case for India in the language of secularism and equality, which was very different from the "language of blood and sacrifice . . . of ancient, God-given status and attributes" that the rest of the country spoke.[20] Indian leaders worked so hard to deny these social realities that they considered the country's major ethnic fractures—its religious, regional and especially caste divisions—far less critical than its class divide. This allowed socialist policies, focused as they were on class and poverty, to gain traction.

But in defining our class divides entirely separately from these other cleavages, Indian leaders ignored the particular nature of our poverty. The political scientist Ashutosh Varshney has noted that India's class divides were a "ranked ethnic system" that combined both caste and class, similar to the apartheid systems in South Africa in that bloodlines would be a fair predictor of where you stood in the society in terms of income, respect and authority. As Varshney tells me, "The poor in India were not just poor—they were overwhelmingly low caste."

This relationship between class and caste held strong across Indian communities. As the writer and journalist Harish Damodaran observed when I put this question to him, "The business classes in India were dominated by the 'Vaishya castes,' and the business networks they built were around family and informal caste connections. These were tremendously difficult for an outsider to penetrate."

Harish himself is an interesting example of our past and present attitudes on caste. Harish, who recently published a book titled *India's New Capitalists*, has intensively studied the dominance of certain castes across Indian industry. He is the grandson of E.M.S. Namboodiripad—the leader of the CPI(M) in Kerala, who like many in his generation had dismissed the relevance of caste in India.

Apron strings: The monolithic state

It is remarkable how much India's political and economic policy was shaped not just by the dreams of our leaders, but also by their fears. In trying to kill

India's divisions by denying that they existed, our leaders, postindependence, created secular policies that erred on the side of control, sometimes to the point of being undemocratic. It showed quite decisively that being secular and being democratic were not always the same thing. "The secular ideas that the government embraced were not necessarily popular ones," Atul Kohli says, "and the government had to take on a top-down structure to implement them."

The central government also refused to recognize uprisings that went against its core beliefs, and popular demands for preferences based on caste and religion got a sharp rap on the knuckles. In the 1950s, for instance, the government initially ignored the clamor for language-based boundaries in the Bombay and Hyderabad provinces, and gave in only when pushed into a corner as violence and protests escalated. Popularly elected governments at the state level were dismissed by the center if they were not secular or liberal enough. As early as 1953, the Delhi government imposed President's Rule in Punjab, dismissing a government it saw as sympathetic to secessionism, and did it again in 1959 when the communists came to power in Kerala.[21] And in Kashmir the government made antidemocratic decisions in the name of unity and secular identity, which have come back to haunt it: beginning with the arrest of the state's chief minister, Sheik Abdullah, in 1952, and his replacement with sycophants. This was a leadership that was obviously uncomfortable with stirrings at the grassroots.

In fact, for a long time, Congress leaders in Delhi saw their party as the lone bulwark against India's feudal urges—Congress was the sole "agent of destiny"[22] that could fulfill India's vision of a democratic nation.* To ensure this, the government in Delhi created a culture of center-driven, top-down governance that may indeed have protected the ideas of secularism and liberalism from popular erosion. But this also allowed bad ideas to stand longer than they should have—such as the quasi-socialist policies that by the late 1960s had already proved to be weak and ineffective.

Ambedkar had observed that democracy in India was a mere "topsoil" that lacked any deep roots, and the one advantage, perhaps, of this was that the Indian government did not face many challenges in the early years of democratic rule—the majority of Indians were politically illiterate and un-

*Even much later, the Congress party continued to hold onto this idea and viewed opposition movements as a betrayal of national interest—as when, in the 1980s, Rajiv Gandhi made frequent insinuations about the loyalties of political parties opposing Congress policies.

aware of their rights.[23] This gave the Congress, Atul notes, plenty of elbow room and decisive majorities to enact secular, democratic policies in a country not necessarily committed to these notions.

But the prescriptive state that came into being also allowed a large number of weaknesses to creep into India's democracy. It allowed the government, for example, to ignore the realities of Indian society far longer than it should have. The first Indian government went to the extent of eliminating the caste factor from the 1951 census, and the writer Christophe Jaffrelot notes that when it was compelled to categorize the backward castes besides the scheduled castes and tribes, it termed them the backward "classes," pointedly avoiding the word "caste." In 1953, when the Backward Classes Commission estimated that the lower castes dominated the numbers among India's poorest communities, the government, alarmed at these implications, rejected its findings.[24]

Through these years, the Indian government swept these ethnic issues under the carpet, in favor of unity and nationalism. But they remained intact and resilient nevertheless. Ambedkar—who was the most perceptive of India's leaders of how vicious our fractures really were, having personally suffered from them—had predicted that democracy would not be the bed of roses that the Indian government envisioned. Instead, he said, "In political life we will have equality and in social and economic life we will have inequality." And, as it turned out, he was depressingly on target.

In part, India's fractures were not overcome because the government, too, fell victim to them. Even as the Congress at the center rejected the relevance of caste and community privileges, its formidable organization rapidly adjusted itself and its election strategies to local realities. So we would find that in canvasing for and recruiting candidates the party was aggressive about courting groups such as the upper agricultural castes, who could assure block votes from the tenant and peasant communities.[25] And by aligning with these caste elites to win elections, the Congress created governments that allowed dominant castes to "colonize state systems with their kin,"[26] keep governance all in the family and distribute public resources on the basis of bloodlines.

As Kanchan Chandra notes, this resulted in schools and wells built only where the dominant castes of the village lived, the segregation of election booths for "upper" and "lower" castes and the marginalization of Muslim communities in Hindu dominant areas. When the other backward castes (OBCs) and Dalits demanded land rights and access to state resources, they often faced violence—sometimes aided by the local government. In many ways, this was a heartbreaking letdown after the early promise and possibility of the democratic vision.

The ground heaving upward

The top-down style of Congress governments and the party's unchallenged hold at the center through the 1950s and 1960s would eventually be its own prison. Despite the government's ineffective policies, the Congress party got reelected to power in each election, and this meant that economic growth—which would have had the most powerful, scouring effect on India's feudal structures—did not take place. And without broad-based growth, India's various communities only grew angrier at the ineffectual state and clamored harder for special privileges, state benefits and patronage.

The Congress's struggle to maintain a secular stance in a feudal country also chipped away its popularity. The writer Baldev Raj Nayar traces how the party tied itself up in knots in Punjab in its efforts to alternately pander to the state's Sikhs and then the Hindus. The Congress in Punjab had initially opposed the formation of a Punjabi Suba (a state for Punjabis), but in 1957 it changed its mind and the pro-Suba Akali Dal aligned with the Congress party to form the government. But in 1962 the Congress again opposed the Punjabi Suba demand.[27] The compulsive flip-flopping of a secular, ineffective party angered pretty much everyone and allowed other niche parties willing to mine these ethnic fractures to gain popularity. In Maharashtra, in 1965, Bal Thackeray's magazine *Marmik* began to publish statistics of the Marathi population in Bombay and, for easy comparison, the lists of top officers in the city's businesses and bureaucracy, most of whom were south Indian. The paper bemoaned the "spectacle of Marathi *manus* . . . relegated to the job of coolie or peon while the clerical and management job went to others."[28] The party that Thackeray went on to found has since then been unequivocal in its position of keeping the state's jobs and education seats for ethnic Maharashtrians.

Even parties ideologically devoted to the notion of class war were aware of how India's other divisions dominated the country's consciousness. The Communist Party of India (CPI), for instance, made the claim that its symbol, the ear of corn and the sickle, was "the image of Goddess Lakshmi."[29] And when the CPI(M) came to power in Kerala in 1957, it was buoyed mainly by the support of the Ezhava caste, rather than any broad-based, working-class appeal.

The year 1957 also saw the Indian sociologist M. N. Srinivas make a speech at the Indian Science Congress, which predicted that democracy in India would not fulfill the great hope of a "casteless society." Srinivas, who in this speech contradicted much of the popular wisdom of the time, noted that caste in India was far from dead. He observed that the Indian Constitution notwithstanding, castes in states like Gujarat had printed their own "constitutions," and the country was witnessing a growing "manipulation of the processes . . . of democratic politics by caste lobbies." He coined the phrase "vote bank" to describe how this was playing out in villages—people were coalescing together around politicians of their own castes in return for public goods and services.[30]

By the mid-1960s, caste was becoming firmly established in Indian democracy. There was an emerging consciousness during these years among India's lower castes and a growing prominence for regional politicians. The green revolution had come to India and turned many midlevel peasant castes into prosperous communities, who aspired for a political voice that matched their new economic strength.[31] These changes were accompanied by a rising tide of frustration with Congress governments, who after two decades had little to show in either economic or social progress.

The spreading dissatisfaction also turned democracy from a light touch into something akin to a forest fire. The 1967 elections indicated that Congress support was beginning to crumble at the state level, when the DMK won for the first time in a Congress state on an anti-Brahmin platform, while in the north the Jan Sangh was making inroads into urban areas and key states.

The clamor soon reached the center's ears and unsettled them in their chairs. Indira Gandhi responded by fashioning herself as an antibusiness populist, trying to appeal to the electorate as one mass—the poor—even while she did little policy-wise to fix their problems. The dismal economy, meanwhile, only hardened local movements. Radicalism took off, triggering violence, standoffs with police, blood on the streets. The differing concerns of the All Assam Students' Union (AASU), the Naxalite insurgents and the

Dalit Panthers indicated discontent that was widespread across regions and castes.[32*] The platforms of these movements revealed an anger that would not be denied, anger at being relegated to the sidelines economically and politically; their language was of "total revolution," "liberation" and of "becoming rulers."

Indira Gandhi resorted to coalescing power at the center, demoting the authority of state Congress leaders and governments and violently suppressing these emerging movements. The Emergency that the government finally declared in 1975 was in many ways the last gasp of a center trying to force India's regional, religious, class and caste divides back into the bottle—Indira herself justified the Emergency as a means to "preserve and safeguard our democracy."

In retrospect, the 1970s was a red-letter decade for India, a time when democracy was virulently attacked from all sides, was upended dramatically by the prime minister, and yet proved itself resilient. These years saw Indian democracy truly come into its own—the post-Emergency elections in 1977 marked the beginning of the end of a long era of Congress-led, one-party rule. From then on, Atul notes, the decline of India's once-dominant Congress party, while drawn out, would also be decisive.

Since then, it is politics aligned around India's divides that has emerged triumphant. The government that followed Indira's was a defiant medley of peasant-based parties—the socialists, the Swatantra Party and the Jan Sangh. And this government brought the issue of caste-based policies and rights to the center of the debate for the first time with the appointment of the 1978 Mandal Commission.

Our new polycentric state

"The endurance of its democracy," Atul tells me, "is what makes India stand apart. It's a given, and completely unquestioned in the country."

For a long time, Indian leaders saw the rejection of our divisions as essential to the survival of our democracy. But the truth has turned out to be the opposite—Indian democracy has had to absorb its divides to survive. The

*The major cause of the AASU was against immigrants from Nepal and Bangladesh taking up jobs in Assam. The Dalit Panthers was mainly a Maharashtrian group fighting for greater social and welfare rights for the Dalit community.

coalition-style governments that have dominated since the late 1980s, and the regional and caste parties that have emerged at the state level have directly contradicted fears that these parties would threaten secular rule. These movements in fact have shown a respect for democracy—as the social scientist Sudipta Kaviraj notes, they have only "wished to enter, not to shake the structures to dust." Suppressing such movements and Indira's attempts at "government by willfulness" were the real threats to Indian democracy. Such repression only encouraged more violent groups, as in Punjab, where militancy flared up around the demands for an independent state. This escalated rapidly in 1984 when Indira's government initiated Operation Bluestar to flush out militants from their hideout within the Golden Temple in Amritsar. The operation came to an appalling end, with more civilian worshippers than militants killed, and less than six months later Indira's Sikh bodyguards assassinated her.

While Indian democracy has progressed a great deal since the 1980s, the tendency of our governments toward repression still exists, and it has contributed to a drawn-out struggle against terrorism in India. Governments in India have made it a habit to respond to breakouts in violence with a heavy and indiscriminate hand—both Indian and international media have covered the many abuses of the Indian army in Kashmir and in Assam in their fight against militants. Laws such as the Terrorist and Disruptive Activities (Prevention) Act (TADA) that the Rajiv Gandhi government passed in 1985 to handle violence in Punjab and the Prevention of Terrorism Act (POTA) that the NDA government introduced after the 9/11 attacks in the United States also massively scaled back civil rights for terrorist suspects. These laws, now repealed, allowed forced confessions in court, phone tapping and censoring mail, and gave prosecutors significant powers when it came to detaining and questioning people. Such draconian responses, and the abuse that civilians in terrorist-hit regions have suffered, only helped create sympathy (and recruits) for militant movements.

What is worrying is that the recent spasms of terrorist attacks across India have revived calls to bring back POTA and similar laws. But what we truly need to end such attacks is still missing—reforms in the systems of our police and judiciary, and in our intelligence agencies, which are now damaged and deeply politicized. Laws such as POTA are a weak substitute for this and inevitably capture civilians along with terrorists into their net thanks to the vast powers they give police and prosecutors to detain and interrogate—and they have a much higher chance of backfiring with more violence than catching the real terrorists.

THE YEARS SINCE the 1980s, however, did see progress elsewhere. We began to see the two conditions for a true and effective democracy—voter mobilization and political rivalry—emerge, especially with the rise of regionally powerful parties. This transition from top-down to a bottom-up politics has rapidly reshaped the face of Indian democracy. For instance, the 1989 Janata Dal–led coalition government had an explosive effect on caste politics when it gave a new lease on life to caste-based reservations and implemented the 1978 Mandal Commission recommendations. Such caste-based demands for economic rights have since then become an effective way to bring the backward classes together into a reliable voter base.

The parties that have come into prominence across India ever since have been based on outright caste, regional and religious appeals—for instance, the Shiv Sena with its "sons of soil" rhetoric and also a strongly religious tilt, the Telugu Desam Party (TDP) with the support of the Kamma caste and the Rashtriya Janata Dal (RJD), a party split away from the Janata Dal, supported by the Yadav caste and the Muslims.[33] The sloganeering of these parties has been highly confrontational—the RJD campaigned with pitches like "Rome belongs to the Pope and Madhepura to the Gopes" (Gopes being another name for the *Yadavs*). The TDP in Andhra Pradesh also capitalized strongly on regional sentiments during the 1980s and 1990s—the state's film-star chief minister N. T. Rama Rao fashioned himself as a wounded lion by complaining of snubs by the Congress at the center and declaring that New Delhi's leaders had insulted "the honor of the Telugu people."[34]

This in-groupism has also shown its ugly side in discrimination and backlash against specific castes and communities. In Ahmedabad, for instance, after the Mandal Commission riots, around 300 "only-Dalit" residential societies came up as other cooperatives refused to rent or sell to Dalits. Such caste- and religion-defined ghettos are pervasive in towns and cities across north India, even in Delhi and Bombay. While riding on Bombay's suburban rails, it does not take more than a fleeting glimpse to know—from the crowds and the lingo (especially within the older parts of the city, toward Dadar and Haji Ali)—which areas are dominated by Hindus and which by Muslims. The landscape of these ghettos is a sobering reminder of the ugly possibilities of our divides.

And who can forget Qutubuddin Ansari, the Muslim man who was caught on a journalist's camera during the Gujarat riots, pleading for his life in front of a Hindu mob? The photograph captured the zeitgeist of the 1990s and early 2000s, a time that saw the rise of religious politics as a significant challenge to the secular state. During these years, the Ayodhya issue and the "we shall build the Mandir" slogan of the BJP turned the party into the most prominent national challenger to the Congress for the first time since independence. Religious parties have managed to tap a deep vein of partisan religious sentiment through such rhetoric and ordinary Indians have paid the price for it—with the Bombay riots in 1992 and 1993, followed by the bomb blasts months later, and the Gujarat riots in 2002.

Parties such as the BJP have employed a form of religion-based politics familiar to conservatives in many parts of the world—a blend of religion and reform-friendly policies that enables them to whip up mass support and retain a populist appeal, while also promoting development. But Indian democracy itself has played a critical role here in tamping down extremist grassroots sentiments. The mainstream press and politicians have been unsympathetic in describing the people involved in religious riots as "miscreants," and even those who support such movements have to do so covertly. India's secular identity thus fortunately forces even communal politics to play by certain rules. The writer and professor Mahesh Rangarajan pointed out to me that when the BJP came to power at the center in 1999 with the support of regional parties it could not make radical moves on the Babri Masjid issue that it had promised earlier, and insisted instead on the need for a court decision.

Nevertheless, the rise of rath yatras,* the Ayodhya issue and the Gujarat riots are signs that religion-based politics in India has significant momentum. "Religious themes work quite successfully in the politics of the west and the north," political scientist Ashutosh Varshney says. "It's something we must still work through."

Our new freedoms and discontents

If we look back for signs of when our more spontaneous, bottom-up politics took off, we see a remarkable surge from 1985. It was from that year, as the

*The rath yatra or chariot festival became a powerful tool for L. K. Advani, president of the BJP, as he went on his own cross-country chariot tour to mobilize support around the Ayodhya issue.

first phase of reforms gave more autonomy to states in economic decision making and power, that our politics began to see real churn.[35] States fell one by one away from Congress rule and regional parties were on the ascent. Maharashtra was the last state to leave the old era and the Congress behind, when the Shiv Sena emerged as the second largest party in 1990 and formed a government in 1995.[36]

In fact, looking at India's trends of political fragmentation and reforms, cause and effect are pretty difficult to separate. A big problem for central governments through the 1960s and 1970s was the growing resentment of the states, which lacked authority over revenues and taxes. Of course, without economic power, there was also little responsibility—states were fighting with what money they did get from the center, giving it away as freebies. Political competition between the center and the state only worsened this dynamic; rival parties at the state level that emerged in Tamil Nadu, West Bengal and Uttar Pradesh could blame the center for underdevelopment, killing local support for the Congress party. The central government was recognizing the political price it paid for being solely responsible for the country's growth.

There may have been another, more direct link between fragmentation and reform. The need to control an internally fractious country, along with concerns around Pakistan, compelled the Indian government to double its defense budget during the 1980s. The 1989–90 budget froze defense spending at $8.5 billion, though the actual figure has been calculated to be as high as $11 billion. The imports of defense capital equipment and aircraft contributed to the balance of payments crisis in 1991—a high price to pay for control.* And in this sense, India's political fragmentation influenced the shift to reforms both indirectly, to limit the damage of low growth to the center's political credibility, and more directly, by aiding the rise of the fiscal crisis.

We have seen different things unite India at different times and these forces brought the country different orders of stability. Our early, monolithic state managed to create both unity and a slow-moving economy where little changed, and little was expected to. But in the last quarter century, the things that have come to unite India—a rising aspiration, connected with our rapid

*It is not surprising that the biggest scandal of this decade was the Bofors scandal—when the government was accused of receiving bribes to award army supply contracts to the Swiss company Bofors AB.

growth—while potentially more sustainable, are also shaping a more turbulent nation.

India's particular challenge, as Varshney tells me, may be one of sequence. "Capitalism came to Europe before democracy," he says, "but in India it's the reverse. So the private sector faces political pressures that Europe and the U.S. didn't experience."

As a result economics is clashing somewhat messily with politics in India, and it has come up against regional, religious and caste loyalties. But even as India's political turbulence is impacting the rise of our markets, the growth we have already seen is realigning India's political equations. Across countries, the disappearance of feudal feelings has tended to emerge as trade and business bring people from diverse groups into contact and bind them into large-scale, interconnected social and economic networks. In this sense, secularism and capitalism are woven of the same thread.

The need for social capital and mutual trust in India's market economy—to form working networks, supply chains and nonfamily business relationships—is reshaping India's divisions across religious, caste and regional lines. The penetration of the supply chains of big retailers into the countryside is taking farmers away from the old, informal and often caste-dominated networks of middlemen and commission agents and connecting them to more organized and "caste-neutral" relationships.

And as capital and talent became widely available in India's free markets, the family firm has also become less ideal—after all, if you were stuck in a family business with your clueless cousin, you lacked the conveniences of a contract-based relationship and the freedom to appoint the talent you needed. And indeed, postreform many family firms began to untangle—the Ambani brothers have divvied the company up between themselves and parted ways; the Mirchandani family, which owns the firm MIRC Electronics, and the Mafatlal family group of companies, found themselves in the midst of bitter feuds; the Birla conglomerate and the DCM group, both of which had built up massive enterprises in the decades before 1980, also broke up. The ties of blood in business—among both family and caste—are rapidly thinning.

Improved education and social indicators are also affecting perceptions on the importance of caste and religion in politics. Even some minimal effects of growth have had significant social impacts. For example, during the 1980s the new affordability of synthetic shirts and trousers made them popular across castes and classes, eliminating the earlier dress differences—"the coarser khadis, sometimes shirtless outfits"—that had marked backward castes.[37] This has only grown more intense since the 2000s. Across the cities of Delhi and Bombay, you find tailors whose shops carry denim material in every shade and texture. At a fraction of the price of Levi's, they stitch you a replica, difficult to tell apart down to the rivets on the label.

This trend was already visible in the south, where improved access to the economy and higher levels of growth—combined with better education and health achievements—has impacted political trends. "You tend to see a greater level of caste consolidation in the southern states," Kanchan says. "Castes are willing to partner with each other behind particular political parties, giving a lot more coherence to the region's politics and its economic policies." As a bonus, Varshney points out to me, this consolidation of castes has given the south more power at the center. "In the 1950s and 1960s Tamil Nadu was something of an outsider in Indian politics, at the periphery of the center's concerns," he says. "But today, Tamil Nadu parties are a powerful force in every coalition at the center."

Such shifts are now gradually making inroads in the north—the rise of development-focused governments in Bihar and Orissa, and more recently with the rise of Mayawati in Uttar Pradesh, who came to power on the back of an alliance between upper castes and Dalits. Additionally, as Kanchan notes, "The Seventy-third and Seventy-fourth Amendments* are bringing in grassroots power and influence, which can enlarge the role of local development concerns in politics." This can potentially not just shift electoral concerns toward development issues but is also contributing to a growing clout for women in politics. "The thirty-three percent representation for women in local *panchayat* positions," Dr. Vijay Kelkar tells me, "is making women far more visible as leaders." There are now 1 million women elected *panchayat* representatives.†

India's growth through the 1980s and 1990s has also added a new wrinkle to the class issue of Indian politics by triggering the rapid growth of a

---

*These amendments, passed in 1992 while Narasimha Rao was prime minister, drew a roadmap toward more power for urban and rural local governments. Before these amendments, the authority of local governments had gone unmentioned in the Constitution.

†Their success is, however, mixed in many of India's backward regions. In *panchayats* across states such as Rajasthan, Uttar Pradesh and Bihar, the "pradhan pati" has emerged, where it is the woman's husband who actually heads the *panchayat*, while his wife holds the position only on paper. Nevertheless, studies of women leaders at the local level have shown increased empowerment, with women leaders often reelected to their positions and linking up with self-help groups and women welfare NGOs to assist in village development activities.

middle class that now numbers close to 300 million. The impact of this group of Indians is most visible in the urban areas, as the sociologist Yogendra Yadav notes. "Class politics is taking concrete shape in our cities," he tells me. "Even religion- and ethnicity-based parties now must deliver something extra when they campaign in the cities—to win votes, they have to recognize the rich–poor discrepancy, and respond with better policy."

The educated middle class has begun to play a powerful role in the push for a better politics and to assert its civil rights. Many of them have turned to the legal system to hold corrupt institutions and people, however powerful, accountable. An instance of this is Neelam Katara, who went to the courts to get justice for her son. Nitish Katara, a graduate from the Indian Institute of Management Technology in Ghaziabad, was allegedly murdered in 2002 by D. P. Yadav's son and nephew, Vikas and Vishal Yadav, for having fallen in love with Vikas's sister, Bharti.

D. P. Yadav wields enormous power in western Uttar Pradesh—a powerful politician with nine murder cases against him, he served multiple times as minister of state in the Uttar Pradesh government and is widely regarded as someone who could not be touched. But Vikas and Vishal Yadav, after six years, were finally convicted, even though witnesses—including the inspector who arrested them and heard their confession—retracted their testimony. A big factor that led to the conviction was not just Nitish's mother's insistence to see the case through year after year, but also the widespread coverage of the case in the English and international media, and the public outrage in its wake. Though this case remains an exception in our legal system, where many perceive political power as a get-out-of-jail-free card, it is a testament to the power of the educated middle class and its possibilities.

The rise of the middle class is also impacting Indian politics by enabling the emergence of a vibrant third sector of civil society organizations and NGOs. Sanjay Bapat, founder of IndianNGOs.com, tells me that the growth of the sector has been especially significant since the 1980s. "Many of the early NGOs were caste based or religious organizations," he says. The exception to this were the Gandhian NGOs, which probably came closest to the "civil society" idea in emphasizing welfare across caste and community lines.

The NGO sector of the last two decades, however, is very different both in scale and in focus. Many NGOs are not affiliated with caste and religious denominations or particular ideologies. The emphasis of their programs is also more obviously class based and focused on issues ranging from child and maternal welfare to health, education and food. These organizations are beginning to influence policy decisions, especially over the last decade. They have achieved this both through direct advocacy and through "showing by doing"—for instance, Akshaya Patra's efforts in improving midday meal schemes impacted Karnataka's midday meal policies, and Vijay Mahajan and Al Fernandez's work in microfinance has shaped the center's approach to self-help groups and microlending.

There is also a new awareness among the NGO sector of the diverse roles it can play. Many NGOs are focusing on not just empowerment of the poor but also on strengthening awareness of civil rights. One of the people involved in such an effort is Trilochan Shastri, civil activist and professor at the Indian Institute of Management Bangalore who has been instrumental in creating new standards of information disclosure for election candidates. "We managed to get the laws changed only by igniting public support for it," Trilochan tells me. The impact these activists and organizations have had on legislation such as the Right to Information Act, child labor, the midday meal for schools and court rulings on environmental issues points to a young, powerful force that is shaping India's social and political debate.

The growth and activity of these NGOs is a sign of the changing nature of India's democracy. This bottom-up civil consciousness, nonpolitical and nonpartisan as it is, is a sign of a new kind of democracy in India. These organizations are emphasizing an approach toward political democracy that is rooted in the idea of "civil society" rather than in the divisions that now dominate India's politics. And while it is still early days here, this trend carries a great deal of promise, especially when we consider that the growth of such NGOs has been enabled by a middle class with an active interest in political reforms. This ever-widening group of middle-class Indians is using NGOs to come face-to-face with India's poorer and working classes, and to plant the ideas of secular rights and liberties across these communities.

For people like Trilochan, the media has also become an important aid of reform, enabling them to create awareness around fundamental rights and voter power. "Television has been indispensable for our cause," Trilochan tells me. The media is helping create the bottom-up demand necessary to drive change by popularizing, for instance, the ideas of education, better infrastructure and income mobility. "Even in villages, television is changing attitudes quite rapidly," the economist Sir Nicholas Stern remarked to me. "It is making people conscious of what life is like outside the walls of their village."

Not only is the Indian media affecting our social attitudes, it is reflecting these changes back at us. At one time, nationalism was just another key part of political maneuvering—especially with Indira, for whom appealing to nationalist sentiment was an easily available excuse for imposing President's Rule on opposition governments, and to tamp down on dissent. But as Jaideep Sahni, the boyish script writer of films such as *Company, Bunty aur Babli* and most recently *Chak de India*, points out, the success of his films has been based on a changed sense of nationalism—the kind that is from the grassroots. "Among film audiences now, what I sense is both a new curiosity and an understanding of people across state borders," he tells me. "There's always been a pride surrounding our particular regional identities. But now there is an emerging pride in being Indian."

"Barbarians at the gates"

For too long, the unchallenged authority of a set of quasi-socialist ideas took India on a path of low, disappointing growth. Nevertheless, while India's top-down political system allowed bad policies to last far longer than they should have, in the early years of reform it also gave enterprising bureaucrats such as N. Vittal, Sam Pitroda and later Manmohan Singh the opportunity to drive the policy agenda. These years were thus somewhat insulated from our politics.

Since then, however, India's democracy has changed and deepened. Untrammeled acceptance of ineffective policies and bad ideas is no longer possible. And, on the flip side, coalition politics has worked its magic, and India's potential bureaucrat-visionaries now have too many feet in the aisle ready to trip them over. The shift to bottom-up political power has meant that India's reform agenda has become far more tentative, as policies can be derailed or slowed down by political parties with even small national clout. What was once marginal has now become central—the only possible strategy now is alliance, agreement, coalition and accommodation. India's reforms are now firmly in the hands of its voters, in the shape of individuals, voting blocs and interest groups.

Critical reforms in areas such as labor, infrastructure, education and health remain tangled up in the politics of coalitions and blocked by powerful interest groups to the detriment of broader development. And unfortunately enough, it is the most controversial reforms that will also create the most access and broad-based benefits—such as labor reforms that will bring in labor flexibility and expand employment opportunities, or the removal of monopolies in the agricultural sector that keep crop prices stagnant and limit choices of sellers for farmers. The deadlock here worsens our existing inequalities, limits the benefits of growth and sustains inefficient subsidy systems. In the long term, it also hurts widespread support for reforms, since large numbers of people see no benefits from them.

I encounter many bureaucrats, academics and entrepreneurs who are dismayed by this state of affairs. The new political status quo and the rise of politicians who speak in the language of the demagogue has been seen, especially among the old-guard bureaucrats I had the opportunity to speak with, as a case of "barbarians at the gates."

But this period of stonewalling, backtracking and accommodation is essential—we must have this debate. It is the only way we can frame policies that are truly sustainable and also difficult for just one person or one government to revoke. And this approach, despite its sometimes infuriating slowness, also enables a system where all parties are responsible for policy, and bad policies come back to haunt them.

The need for this was pointed out in a different context by the Sapru Committee in 1937 while discussing universal suffrage. The committee noted that it was, despite its dangers, necessary for its "educative effect," even if the average voter's "judgment may be faulty, his reasoning inaccurate, and his support of a candidate not infrequently determined by considerations removed from a high sense of democracy."[38]

From khadi to silks

The form of political democracy we have today is still young—many of India's political parties mobilized and gained strength only since the 1970s, and it was only in 1977 that the first non-Congress government came to power. And as a BJP worker pointed out to me, it was only in 1998, a bare decade ago, that the first non-Congress government lasted its full term at the center.

And these new parties, despite their weaknesses and populism, represent a real break from the past. The holy cows of the freedom movement—the focus on swadeshi and socialism, for instance—were liberating, powerful ideologies in the fight against British rule. But postindependence, despite the fact that these policies outlived their usefulness, the Congress party held on to them, as they still connected and defined a potent history. Even the parties that emerged in the 1960s and 1970s embraced these symbols, which was not surprising since these were parties often led by former Congress leaders, such as Charan Singh who founded the Bharatiya Lok Dal and Biju Patnaik who formed the Utkal Congress.[39]

But the regional parties of today make a point of distancing themselves from the Congress ethos, and the most significant instance of this is perhaps the Dalit leader Mayawati and the Bahujan Samaj Party (BSP). Mayawati, with her legendary fondness for pink silks,* is indifferent to the idea of clothing herself in khadi or making other symbolic gestures toward the swadeshi/socialist ideology.

While Mayawati may not seem the ideal example of change for the better, she represents a breaking away with the past—which in time will hopefully allow us to debate our policies on their merits, instead of embracing them for what they symbolize. And as our debates today have the educational effect that the Sapru Committee championed on our politicians and voters, it will in all likelihood emerge that some of the crises in moving reforms forward is teething trouble. The politics of populism that we see now is necessarily a short-term strategy, and voters will grow impatient if these policies fail to deliver sustainable economic gains. The change is already visible in infrastructure, where people angry about bad roads and constant power outages have consistently voted out governments. In response, political parties have now slowly begun to favor more effective infrastructure solutions that rely on public–private partnerships and tariff-based models over state monopolies and power freebies.

This is also impacting how critical caste and regional loyalties are in determining elections. "Parties are shifting from pure interest group and partisan politics to a strategy that combines development concerns," Atul says. This, once seen only in the south, is also becoming visible in the north. For instance, as Yogendra pointed out recently, "The CPI(M) and SP have flirted

*After she was elected chief minister of Uttar Pradesh in 2007, officials also had major parts of the state's capital city, Lucknow, painted pink, her favorite color.

with liberalization, and the BSP talks about 'sarvajan samaj' [society for all people]." The latter shift is quite a transformation from the 1990s, when BSP's leaders—Mayawati and Kanshi Ram—shouted slogans like *"Tilak, taraju aur talwar, unko maro juthe char"* (Brahmins, traders and the warrior caste should be kicked).

This somewhat agonized movement in our policies does make it look like we are moving, slowly, to a politics that is based on ideas. But India's challenge right now is the environment the average voter lives in, which has influenced our political allegiances and dramatically shapes the way we vote. Illiteracy in particular has had a huge impact on voting preferences, since it limits access for voters to information on policy positions and ideas, and people consequently vote based on what they know—family and community loyalties.

This incessant focus on caste and religious identities has effects that ripple much beyond our economic policies: it sidelines national identity in favor of these others. Once reservation policies and vote-bank politics encourage Indians to fence themselves in within their own communities, people begin to see themselves as belonging to their caste or religion first, and country second, a dangerous theme in a nation so diverse. This also makes Indians susceptible to the extreme ideologies of terrorism in the name of their religious allegiances and communities. I believe there is a direct link here: in recent years, as we have seen more middle-class and educated Indians express more radical views on religion, we have also seen software engineers and doctors emerge among the ranks of domestic terrorists.

Rising populism and the framing of our democracy on caste, regional and religious lines have no quick fixes. After all, issues such as more effective primary education, better infrastructure and a focus on improving and integrating India's markets require long-term investments and taking on powerful interest groups. But they are the only policies that will be both sustainable and irreversible in the impact they will have on the quality and nature of our democratic debates.

But now more than ever, we have cause for optimism. To win, politicians trade on getting people excited and fired up in the moment, and they are finding that doing this now increasingly requires speaking the language of policy. In the short time since reforms, the expectations of our voters have changed dramatically. People are now making precisely those demands—in education, infrastructure and income mobility—which will force the government toward better policies. In fact M. N. Srinivas, who had been so perceptive on the role of caste in 1957, wrote an essay in 2003 predicting the uprooting of caste as a result of the rise of markets. In his "Obituary on Caste," Srinivas pointed out that the death of caste-based division of labor—thanks to the new emphasis on income mobility, as well as democratic and economic rights—is leading to a breakdown of a once pervasive social system.[40] In the last decade, this breakdown may have speeded up. The politician Jay Panda offers me an example of this trend. "A rapid change is occurring, especially as backward caste women enter the workforce. This is one among many forces that are enabling caste boundaries to dissolve, and it's creating a faster than ever before rise in inter-caste marriages."

As a country, we are still struggling toward our democratic ideals. But these past two decades have been a time of immense hope. The move to bottom-up democracy has brought with it a far more topsy-turvy politics than we have been used to. But the clamor has come with more access than ever before and carries with it an immense potential for change, new answers and better policy.

We now represent a truly unusual country, one that thoroughly embraced what was once an entirely alien idea and held on to it through upheavals good and bad—through growth and crisis, despite missteps. In this sense, democracy in India has shifted from being "essentially foreign" to being, simply, essential.

A RESTLESS COUNTRY

TWO DECADES AFTER REFORM, India is no longer an adolescent state, insecure and uncertain of its survival. Popular angst with bad policy and impatient voters have helped trigger fundamental changes in our economy and enabled new ideas that are now at the core of our growth. The widespread resistance to coercive population control, for instance, has driven our present demographic opportunity. The demands of people across the country created a groundswell of support for the English language, aided the rise of technology and Indian entrepreneurship, and made global markets increasingly critical for growth.

Our successes here, however, are creating new urgencies—for solutions to manage our cities better, to tackle the weak infrastructure that hampers the economy, for education that will allow people to access the opportunities of a fast-growing country.

Here as well our answers lie in the pressures that citizens can bring for change. In India we have already witnessed the dramatic impact that ordinary citizens can have. Bindeshwar Pathak's invention of the dry toilet—the Sulabh shauchalya, built to function with little water and a self-cleaning pit—has done more than any bans on discrimination in helping put an end to the sordid work of manual scavenging that the Dalit Bhangi caste had been forced into for centuries. In Ahmedabad, Rajendra Joshi's organization Saath has helped transform slum areas into functioning neighborhoods and helps slum residents set up schools, install sewer lines and lobby municipal corporations for electricity, water and better roads. Across India, change is coming through in these million ways, large and small—entrepreneurs setting up English coaching centers, connecting Indian farmers to global agricultural chains, setting up IT kiosks and innovating new services for India's poor, and activists demanding public services as well as protection of civil rights for the underprivileged.

It is these pressures that will decide our future success in implementing new ideas. We are still struggling with many issues—for instance, even as Indians across the country are demanding better schools, our progress in building them has been dismal. As more people gravitate to our cities, urban India teeters near collapse and is often unable to provide even basic services to its citizens. And while Indians across the country struggle with bad infrastructure and have made it the litmus test in evaluating their governments, progress here is still choppy and limited. Our ability to implement these ideas effectively will continue to depend on the pulls from below: the power of citizens to bring about change both individually and as a collective force, and push ideas through—through the noise, our distractions and our divides.

Part Two

ALL ABOARD

Ideas in Progress

IDEAS IN PROGRESS

THERE WAS A certain Indian gesture instantly familiar to anyone who had stayed in the country long enough—the shrug. Indians did it when the light went out—a power cut, which may have been scheduled, or not. It happened when villagers found that the water connections promised during election time failed to appear. We did it in the face of more news about failing schools, and across our cities it was our response to delayed trains, broken sewer lines, the mounds of garbage on the road.

Increasingly, though, we are finding ourselves much less blasé in the face of these problems. In fact, as the key ideas of the first part of the book have helped shape the dynamism of today's India, our progress has thrown up our remaining weaknesses into sharp relief. These include our challenges around primary education, urbanization, infrastructure and a unified common market—issues where there remains much to be done. While there is now broad consensus on the importance of these issues, our persistent weaknesses in implementing them are limiting the promise of India's future.

These ideas gained popularity with the rapid acceleration in India's economic growth and the rise of people's aspirations. For many years, for instance, the progress on primary education was desultory and defined more by pious intentions and policies on paper than actual action. Today, however, most parents across urban and rural India are acutely aware that it is vital for their children to have an education. Similarly, we now recognize that the dilapidated nature of our cities is coming in the way of our progress and raising our economic productivity. Both in the cities and in the villages, the lack of infrastructure, whether it is rural roads or modern airports, is impeding Indians from accessing education, health, markets and employment. And finally, every Indian, whether he is looking for a job or a college, or is a customer, now wants to tap opportunities across the entire country.

My own sense of how these ideas have come into the mainstream has evolved since the time I was heading the Bangalore Agenda Task Force (BATF), and working on the reforms we needed for the city's urban renewal. My early approach was a technocratic one, where I mainly focused on "getting things done." It took me a few years and some frustrated initiatives to realize that our cities were being held back by political and financial weaknesses, not just weaknesses in operational issues. I made some progress, but in 1999, rejuvenating our cities was still seen as an elite task and the popular take was that India's "true reformers" worked in the rural areas. A decade later, however, urban reform has become the policy bandwagon everybody is clambering on, and every progressive minister across the country wants a piece of the urban development pie.

As these various ideas become priorities for our voters, we are seeing large investments earmarked for them. Primary education is getting an unprecedented amount of money under new initiatives. The Jawaharlal Nehru National Urban Renewal Mission (JNNURM) is the first major thrust to revitalize Indian cities with significant money and a reform agenda, and the eleventh five-year plan (2007–12) has earmarked $500 billion for India's infrastructure. And the buoyancy of our direct-tax revenues has enabled the government to pave the way toward a unified, single market.

But the allocation of funds is just one aspect of what it takes to implement an idea whose time has come. As the funds for our various initiatives have appeared, it has quickly become obvious that the delivery mechanisms for converting our goals into concrete results are badly damaged, and we need a complete overhaul in processes and capabilities if we are to execute these ideas effectively.

If we miss out on the fundamental reform of our execution processes, progress here will depend on having the right person in the right place, and in a democracy, that is not practical—we will stall time and again when the political weather shifts. I experienced this firsthand when in 2002 the power ministry had an enterprising, enthusiastic minister, Suresh Prabhu, heading the office. He asked me at the time to chair a committee on using IT in the power sector, but by the time we got the report out his party had recalled him. Our report sank without a trace—until Jairam Ramesh shifted to the power ministry as minister of state in April 2008 and suggested that we dust it off and update it for him.

So yes, we have gone back and forth in ways that have set back the agenda on these ideas. We are still straining toward a coherent strategy here, even as our economy moves smoothly elsewhere. The ease, for instance, with which Infosys can seamlessly set up software centers all over the country has been at odds with the single-market challenges my farmer cousin in Sirsi faces, as he is forced to sell his produce at a specified price in a specified local market.

Implementing these ideas effectively will require a more prominent role for India's private sector, as well as enlightened regulatory policy that taps into private capital while enabling public services that are not just efficient, effective and of high quality, but are also equitable. And right now, we have quite some way to go before all these bits fall into place.

S IS FOR SCHOOLS

The Challenges in India's Classrooms

BY THE TIME I meet the economist Dr. Jeffrey Sachs in Delhi, he has been in India for a few weeks, and is somewhat sunburned, his cheeks a bright apple-red. I find him inimitably cheerful and enthusiastic about his trip—he has been touring villages across Uttar Pradesh, studying the progress of the government's new school education initiative. But when I ask him about his impression from visiting the village schools, his answer is cautious. "There is a lot of change," he says, "but I wonder if there is enough of it. India has a lot of ground to cover on education, and very little time."

I am familiar with this tone of wary optimism—I have caught it often in the remarks of NGO workers and the bureaucrats working with India's schools. Despite some signs of progress, our dilemmas in school education are very real; they are the small print that accompanies India's rise as a knowledge economy. We have some pretty shocking statistics when it comes to education: India produces the second largest number of engineers in the world every year, as well as the largest number of school dropouts. Even as India is building a name for itself in intellectual capital, a third of its population remains illiterate. Across cities, some of the best-equipped schools—with swimming pools and air-conditioned tennis courts—and the worst, lacking even a blackboard, exist across the street from one another. It is our schools that now delineate our class lines most prominently—even as middle-class parents compete to get their kids into the privately run Delhi Public School in RK Puram, parents in the RK Puram slums can do little more than place their children in the single-room slum school, or in the crumbling, dismal government school round the corner and hope for the best.

If this is our Achilles heel, it is significant enough to make the whole of us fragile. Few things are as wide-ranging in their impact on the economy as education. The collapse of our schools is a deep crack in India's foundation, and it impacts everything from our health achievements and fertility rates to our economic mobility and political choices. The evidence of our education failures is brought home to us every day—in the children selling magazines on city intersections, students dropping out from failing schools and accompanying their fathers to work, and companies facing shortages in educated workers in a billion-peopled country.

The crisis of our education system is not a new problem. Schooling in India has been a struggle, both before and since independence. But what has now changed is the growing awareness about education and a demand for it that cuts across income groups. "The poor used to talk about education in a very vague sense ten years ago," one literacy worker told me. "They saw it as something that was 'good' to do. Being educated was like being pious—it added to your character. But now there is a real sense of what people lose in incomes and opportunities from not attending school." And this shift is driving some remarkable changes in our education policy.

The British-educated Indian

John Milton's *Paradise Lost* was only one among numerous British literary works that referred to the "Orient" as a culturally infernal place—the East and India for the British was a region of "barbaric despotism."[1] By the nineteenth century, running down Indian culture was a popular intellectual exercise; British writers like John Stuart Mill described India as depraved, immoral, wild and populated by lost souls.

Our moral and cultural problems could only be addressed, in British eyes, by transmitting their culture to the country—through education and English schools. India was depicted as a "sad, sleeping beauty" that needed new life: the kiss of British education. Charles Grant, making his pitch for British-style schools, called the Hindus malevolent and evil, adding that "the true cure for darkness is light . . . the Hindoos err, because they are ignorant and their errors have never been laid before them."[2]

The writings of these English administrators and historians greatly influenced Thomas Macaulay, the chairman of the General Committee of Public Instruction in India in the 1830s. With typical modesty, Macaulay asserted that Indians had "no books on any subject which deserve to be compared to our own." Thanks in part to the tirade that was his Minute on Education, the British resolution to bring English education to India was passed in 1835. But while this gave a new stress on British education, there was little initiative toward a *universal* system. Three universities were established by 1857, and approximately fifty English schools took root. Beyond that, growth was slow.

One reason for this apathy was that the very idea of universal education was far-fetched among the British. England did not have universal schooling—it was a privilege for the sons of squires, for the nobles and the rich. It was the last country in Europe to adopt compulsory education and passed the law only in 1881. In India the British also did not have the money for it—the tiny parliamentary grant allocated for education to the Indian colony was just enough to set up the first universities and schools.

The British had dived in and built their schools in India with the hope of creating a class of British-educated Indians who would enact and translate their agenda for the rest of the Indian population. But the educated Indians that came out of these universities saw themselves not as brokers for the British but as brokers for the Indians—one Indian leader remarked in 1898 that they were "the brains and conscience of the country . . . spokesmen of the illiterate masses." This class of educated leaders immediately saw the potential of British education in social emancipation. Indian education had often been exclusionary and limited to the "twice born" across Indian gurukuls, and leaders such as Raja Ram Mohan Roy applauded the possibilities English education offered, in eliminating the social evils of sati, caste discrimination and dowry. The backward caste leader Jyotirao Phule similarly wrote of the potential of British schools to "construct a new society" and end "Brahmin domination" by offering a window to liberal ideas.

These Indian leaders took note of the sparse network of the British schools and began to pitch for schooling that was more accessible and widespread. In 1911 the Congress party leader Gopal Krishna Gokhale presented his universal education bill before Delhi's Imperial Legislative Council. He made an impassioned plea to the Council members. In a delicate reference to the salt tax, he said, "It's a smaller evil that my countrymen should eat less salt, if that money could be spent on education." And Lala Lajpat Rai, well aware of the British obsession with security, noted that inspiring Indians with patriotic thoughts "through education" would be more effective than deploying armed guards and erecting barricades. But the council did not bite.[3]

With no real solutions forthcoming from the government, Indian leaders began to try out alternative education systems.* In 1920 the Nagpur Congress session passed a resolution toward building "national" schools and colleges. These schools would offer education in a "nai talim" form suggested by Gandhi, where schools focused on teaching real-life skills, "through the medium of village handicrafts like spinning and carding."[4] Calling the British system "satanic," Gandhi toured the country to persuade students to drop out of British schools and join this national system. The effort was, however, a rather spectacular failure, since these schools were not recognized by the government and the economic rewards of British-style education were substantial.

Gandhi was relentless in his support for "basic education" that would translate into practical use. The Wardha committee of basic education in 1938 again recommended village handicrafts for boys, while offering, rather unfairly, domestic science for girls. Fortunately—since such education would have been very limited indeed—these ideas did not prevail and invited criticism from the National Planning Committee, as well as from other Congress leaders.[5] The writer Mulk Raj Anand wrote that such schools would only create "morons that vegetate within the limits of their self-sufficient village communities."[6]

Forgotten ambitions

It was a tiny part of the nation that could read the headlines and the unfurled banners declaring India's independence in 1947. By that year, the disparities in education were huge abysses—they stretched between the rich and the poor, women and men, and the backward and the privileged castes. Literacy

*There were political compulsions here as well—many leaders in Congress (and especially Gandhi) opposed the "indoctrination" that was going on in English schools, and the teaching of Latin and Greek; they wanted an alternative more oriented toward Indian education and culture.

in the country was a low 12 percent, and enrollment in schools averaged 40 percent.

The limited access to schools meant that education in India became more or less an inherited trait. One study of IFS officers showed that nearly half of the recruits during 1947–56 and 1956–63 had had their fathers working in the civil service.[7] Most of the educated employees in both the public and the private sectors were graduates from a small, privileged circle of approximately fifty prominent government and public schools, and a select group of church- and convent-managed schools.

Indian leaders were acutely conscious of what these disparities meant. The first Education Commission in its 1954 report—which helped frame the national education policy—remarked that "violent revolution" and chaos during India's economic development could be prevented by only one thing: education. But as the former member of the Planning Commission L.C. Jain notes, "The government had other concerns." In the years leading up to independence, Jain was a student political leader, working undercover against the British Indian government. At the time of Partition, he helped manage the camps of refugees from Pakistan and house thousands of displaced people. This kind of experience was shared by many of the leaders in India's early governments, and it shaped their priorities—their focus was mainly on trying to unify a turbulent young nation, one already wounded by the creation of Pakistan and whose cities and towns were being periodically swallowed up in violence and riots. The stability required for successful education schemes was missing, and Partition had especially frayed the nerves of the country's first education minister, Maulana Azad. Azad as a result, Ramachandra Guha tells me, "sat sulking in his tent," busy with relatively lightweight pet initiatives such as the Sangeet Natak Akademi and the Indian Council for Cultural Relations.

As Abhijit Banerjee points out to me, if we consider the early ambitious visions Indian leaders had, it was unusual for the government to not concentrate on education. "Many visionary leaders, from as far back as Napoleon, have found the idea of building a nation through education a very attractive notion," he says. But India's legislators did not really get that chance, thanks to the regional divides across the country that made a single, coherent education system impossible.* Delhi's focus on education and literacy got especially

*In fact, the Kothari Commission suggested a single system in the 1960s—a "Common School System" across the country, a hot rod of a recommendation that no minister dared to touch.

muddied when the states were allowed to teach in regional languages in their schools. And with education as a state subject, the center's role in setting school standards and regulation became very limited.

Besides, budgets were terribly tight. "The money allocated to education was just pitiful," Jain says. "Defense expenditure took a large bite out of the budget, over a hundred crore, while education had three or four crore." He adds, "The lack of money was a real tragedy. We had dynamic education secretaries who were just thirsting for resources." The pint-size amount allocated to schools worried ministers such as C. Subramaniam, and soon enough, with both money and a sense of urgency missing, education languished, kicked to the curb as India pursued other priorities of development.

Worse, education in India lacked a clear vision. Gandhi's ideas on schools—that schooling for the masses needed to be practical, of the "life skills" sort—had affected the views of many leaders. In this vein, Nehru suggested "one-teacher schools" across India that would give "basic, not literary education . . . the education codes should not apply there."

There was a real divide here between what the leaders said and the words of the Constitution. The dominant idea among India's early legislators was that the "masses" did not require the full scale of school education, even though the Constitution had made a commitment in Article 45 that the state would provide within ten years "free and compulsory education for all children until they complete the age of fourteen." In fact, in the assembly debates over the Constitution in 1948, the MP Lakshmi Kanta Maitra had demanded deleting the statement in Article 36 that said, "Every citizen is *entitled* to free primary education," since education, he argued, was not a fundamental right. Another member denounced the same constitutional article as "pious hopes and pious wishes . . . meant to create trouble for the provincial Ministries."[8]

This was in stark contrast with what India's neighbors were up to. In China, Mao pitched education as central to creating "new men" motivated and fully literate in the party ideology. In East Asia, the Confucian ethic emphasized the need for education, and literacy was a necessary virtue for the deeply religious. In the island country of Sri Lanka, the Buddhists were a strong force in encouraging literacy and education.

The religious and ideological momentum for education in these countries was similar to what had happened in most of Europe, where Martin Luther's growing influence had coincided with the rise of the printing press.

This enabled the mass production of texts, and the rise of the Bible as a hugely popular book printed in languages other than the inaccessible Latin. The trend was helped by the sentiment that, to be truly faithful, people had to read the scriptures. Such religious forces were an immense boost toward mass literacy, especially among the rural classes who would not otherwise have seen the point of being able to read and write.

In India, however, religious traditions almost demanded the opposite. Among Hindus, religious stories, songs and literature were sung and recited, and you could be, if you wished, an illiterate person of faith. Besides, the rural "upper" castes considered the idea of "lower" castes learning to read texts—especially religious texts—sacrilegious. This was especially pronounced in the north and east of the country, where the odious idea of literacy as a privilege for certain castes persisted well into the 1970s, and dropouts among backward caste students were especially high in schools. In West Bengal in the 1970s, for instance, four out of every five students enrolling in schools belonged to the upper castes, and in secondary schools the figure was 98 percent.

The dynamics of caste within villages only made things more dismal. Illiterate rural labor was a class of people that the landlords could easily dominate, especially since these workers depended on their landlords to handle government officers and manage their paperwork. The landowners, obviously keen to maintain the status quo, protested with a straight face that effective schooling created unreasonable expectations among the backward castes for better jobs and empowerment.[9] The government remained indifferent to these inequities, despite ambitious statements on education—in part because the political support they derived in rural India during the 1950s and 1960s was primarily from these large landowners and *jotdars*. It was a collaboration toward apathy.

For the poor, educating their children also meant enormous trade-offs. The reality of poor students in government schools, especially in the villages, was of "pupils in rags, unwashed, their hair red from sun and malnutrition, and made stiff and blond with dust."[10] For a family coping with meager shelter, hard to come by meals and regular movements from place to place due to temporary jobs, schooling was an issue fraught with too much sacrifice. Sendhil Mullainathan, the Harvard economist who has taken a close look at poverty in his work at the university, tells me, "Few of us can comprehend the day-to-day tragedy that the poorest people face. You have a limited daily wage, and your choice lies between everyday, urgent needs versus spending money on school books and uniforms to send your child to school. That's not an easy call."

Another factor that education officials regularly brought up while defending low enrollment rates in schools was the reluctance of parents to give up money that working children earned. In poorer families, it was expected that children would be earning members; the writer Suma Chitnis remarked how students in a Bombay municipal school were absent en masse "each time the neighboring factory had a peak of production." Many unorganized industries in India—bangle and glassware, matchsticks, fireworks, garment factories—hired child workers, some as young as three, in droves.

The social scientist Myron Weiner pointed out that this compulsion of poor parents to send children to work was used as a rationale by governments to not enforce compulsory education in India. Trying to teach these children, according to many education officers, was like hammering on cold iron—with parents unwilling, there was not much they could achieve. Time and again, these arguments ignored the interest and rights of the child in favor of the parent—perhaps this was a depressing reflection of the fact that the child, after all, could not vote.

School policy also presented Indian governments with a rather difficult and nuanced challenge. "Education" of real and tangible value requires a mix of factors, ranging from qualified, inspired teachers to up-to-date curriculum and effective testing. But the Indian government's education approach has been clumsy and unwieldy. Through the 1960s and 1970s, the focus of governments in school education was on building infrastructure, with little emphasis on teachers' training, educational achievements and performance measurement. As a result the total number of illiterates continued to grow, even as states haplessly built school after ineffective school—schools that were hollow promises, with little teaching taking place within the buildings. Our education policies, as the writer Amit Varma put it, "have funded schools, not schooling."[11]

The disappearing middle

Ateeq Ahmed, an IAS officer who has worked for years on Karnataka's education initiatives, is a tall, quiet man who dresses meticulously, with his hair carefully brushed back, and given to considering his answers for a long moment before he responds. Ateeq is a picture of contradictions—he is incredibly mild-mannered, yet speaks his mind on the weaknesses he has witnessed in our school policies. One of the biggest challenges he says that we face in Indian education is that everyone but the poorest and most illiterate parents have abandoned our government schools. "The parents that still place children in such schools," he says, "don't really know what a good education is."

Unfortunately, institutional reform in a country is usually the outcome of pressure from the middle and educated classes. The opinions of the working poor get underrepresented in public debates due to their illiteracy, and their lack of access to information also limits them when it comes to comparing good and bad systems and demanding reform.

The middle class often has both numbers and public voice in their favor, and their participation in India's state education systems was critical in maintaining education and teaching standards. But the language policy introduced in India's government schools had middle-class and educated parents fleeing the premises. In the first flush of regional pride postindependence, most Indian states had picked their own languages as the medium of instruction in state schools, especially at the primary and secondary levels. Much of the middle class, who wanted their children to be educated in English, pulled their kids out of these schools and put them in private schools.

These private schools were a hybrid mix—Italian-origin Montessori chains, the numerous church-affiliated, often single-sex convents, schools run by private trusts and by Hindu missions, such as the Ramakrishna and Chinmaya chains. Even government employees were guilty of distancing themselves from state and municipal schools—"Central" schools were set up for children of central government civil servants, and Sainik schools for children of military personnel.[12]

This has turned India's government schools into education of the last resort, the final, desperate measure for the children of the poor and the illiterate, who are left to the terrible mercy of state bureaucracies and teachers' unions. As a result the standards in these schools across indicators—the quality and relevance of textbooks, the monitoring of student achievement—have rapidly stagnated. Today, 90 percent of the public expenditure in Indian schools is on the salaries of the teachers and administration. And yet we have the highest rates of teacher truancy in the world—across our state schools, teachers simply do not turn up, and one in four government teachers is absent on any given day. Not surprisingly, students drop out in droves; as one education worker told me, "What's the point of sitting in an empty room?"*

Different strokes

As Indians, we shy away—and rightly so—from generalizations. It is impossible to frame a single picture of India: the reality of India depends on where you stand. This has been particularly true of our track record in education; since it was a state subject, India's states tackled the challenges around education in their own ways and came up with very different results.

The states that did succeed in making progress in school education were the ones that addressed the challenges of educating poor students head-on. The charge was led by the south, which had a history of mass education. The southern kingdoms of Mysore, Travancore, Cochin and Baroda had long emphasized schools for the poor, and their maharajas had made grants toward mass education and funded schools through the treasury. In both Travancore and Cochin, an emphasis on basic education across castes helped establish *pallikudams* and *kudipallikudams*, the equivalent of kindergarten and primary schools, in the nineteenth and twentieth centuries.

This meant that postindependence governments in the south tended to emphasize schooling for the poor far more than those in north India. The Tamil Nadu chief minister K. Kamaraj implemented the midday meal scheme, which the Madras Presidency had pioneered in 1923, across the state's schools. The scheme took on the responsibility of providing one cooked meal to schoolchildren, as well as uniforms and textbooks. This was expanded by the chief minister M. G. Ramachandran, popularly known as MGR, and by 1984 the scheme covered all Tamil Nadu students ages two to fourteen. The scheme was also rechristened with what is probably the longest abbreviation for a government scheme in India, the PTMGRNMP (Puratchi Thalaivar MGR Nutritious Meal Program).

The spending for the program initially triggered enormous opposition from state secretaries and legislators within the Tamil Nadu government, but

*It is an especially staggering indictment that more than 80 percent of government-school teachers send their own children to a private school.

MGR persisted, saying that the scheme came out of his own childhood experience, "of extreme starvation, at an age when I knew only to cry when I was hungry."[13] The effort triggered a spike in school enrollment across the state—enrollment shot up by 15 percent, a surge that cut across income groups and castes.

In Kerala, school education was influenced by a motley collection of progressive movements—led by the churches, the Ezhavas, the Nairs and the communist parties—and the state placed an early emphasis on making schooling universal. The state introduced an amendment in its very first Legislative Assembly to make education free and compulsory, and rapidly involved grassroots organizations and parents in the drive toward universal schooling.

Education in other Indian states, however, had a very different trajectory. Today, only six states of India account for two thirds of its children out of school—Andhra Pradesh, Bihar, Madhya Pradesh, Rajasthan, Uttar Pradesh and West Bengal.

The problems that have plagued these states stem in large part from their histories. Regions such as the BIMARU states had severe social problems, and they tended to infect state education schemes with them. These states, thanks to their histories of zamindari-style agricultural holdings, had created a predatory system of tyrannical landlords and serflike, indebted peasants. This left a legacy of bitterness and anger among these communities, enabling what Abhijit calls a kind of "revenge politics" that persists to this day. The focus here in these zamindari areas is on vendetta—and the politics in these states, Abhijit says, is "obsessed with retaliation for what someone's grandfather did." As a result, he says, "The voters here have so far been much less concerned with achievements in education, health and infrastructure investment."

The caste tensions in these states seeped into the schools, especially in the villages, where the schools are divided between the backward and "upper" castes. André Béteille notes that this segregation only got worse as state investments were divvied up along caste lines: "Ministers catered to their particular caste groups, so you saw government schools being built in specific community areas which 'outside castes' could not access." As a result half the OBC and ST villages in Madhya Pradesh and Uttar Pradesh do not have a single school.

These states, steeped in dysfunction, put school education on the back-burner, spent the least of their budgets per capita on the sector and ignored the incentives for poor students that had worked well in the more successful states. The results, as expected, were dismal. In Bihar the average number of schooling years among children who enrolled is 3.5; in West Bengal, Madhya Pradesh, Andhra Pradesh, Uttar Pradesh and Rajasthan, the average number of schooling years is fewer than five. The challenge for these governments was summed up by the Madhya Pradesh governor Dr. K. M. Chandy in 1985 when he said, "In terms of education, we will have to reach the twentieth century before we think about the twenty-first."

Both central control and local control of schools come with some advantages; and of all our decisions in school policy, the decision to place control of our schools in the hands of the "middle" government and the state bureaucracy may have been the worst. It limited any standardization possible from the center and also cut out the accountability to parents and local communities that more local power would have ensured.

State governments have since found that their most successful education schemes—such as the Education Guarantee Scheme (EGS) in Madhya Pradesh—were the ones that decentralized school management to local governments and *panchayats*.[14] However, the social scientist James Manor tells me that efforts to make such changes permanent were often scuttled in the tug-of-war for political power between state and local governments. In Madhya Pradesh, for instance, the Digvijay Singh government retreated from policies that gave increased power and authority to the *panchayats* when state legislators and school unions protested. This also happened more recently in Karnataka, when the state government attempted to clip the wings of local bodies by placing a "committee of MLAs" to manage their funds.

In fact, one of *the* biggest barriers—what Abhijit terms unequivocally "the biggest barrier"—to decentralizing power over schools to local bodies has been the teachers' unions. Teachers' unions in India have held remarkable political power at the state level and have grown rapidly over the years as an organized influence. Their political power is the somewhat unfortunate and unexpected result of the good intentions of early Indian legislators, who saw teachers as a valuable pool of educated citizens in a mostly illiterate country. The legislators decided to give this group a boost in political representation and provided a constitutional guarantee for teacher representation across India's Legislative Councils (the upper chamber of the state parliament).* Increasingly, the district-level chiefs of major political parties, especially in the north, came from the teaching community, teachers who were "not only 'master sahib' in the classroom, but also 'netaji' [politician] in the state."[15]

This idea of teachers as sober, reformist entities in government has since then been disproved quite thoroughly, as in the case of such corrupt legislators as Om Prakash Sharma, teacher and member of the Legislative Council of Uttar Pradesh. And even as teachers grew ineffectual in schools, it was difficult for local bodies to take them on—any letters of appeal they wrote to the state government would after all probably land at a teacher-legislator's desk.

New demands and changing choices

"I am a recovering communist," Madhav Chavan tells me. "I have had my share of protests, strikes and Marxist study groups." This ex-Marxist professor, whom I am meeting on a typically sultry Bombay afternoon, has been closely connected with the recent efforts toward education reform.

We meet at Gajalee, one of my favorite old haunts, a Bombay restaurant in Vile Parle that serves excellent fish. The place looks exactly as I remember it, down to the inexpensive menus and the 1970s décor—mirrors lining the walls, pink tablecloths, fussy napkins and brocade chairs. Here, over steaming prawn curry, Madhav charts out India's school crisis, and the government's changing attitudes toward it. By the mid-1970s, he notes, the central government had noticed the ineptness with which many states were handling education investments. Education shifted from the state list to the "concurrent" list† in 1976, as part of the omnibus amendments Indira Gandhi introduced into the Constitution during the Emergency. It was only because of the leeway that her Emergency powers offered that Indira was able to see the amendment through—Parliament committees as early as 1963 had recommended some central jurisdiction on education, but failed in the face of

*This guarantee once applied to all states, but no longer. Uttar Pradesh is among the only four states in India that still has a Legislative Council with such a guarantee.

†The concurrent list consists of the areas where India's state and central governments share responsibility for policy, budgeting and execution.

massive resistance from the states. But political chaos soon returned to Delhi, and it took another decade for the government to turn its attention back to India's school crisis.

It was the Rajiv Gandhi government that finally turned the glare onto the state's cobwebbed education departments in 1984. Rajiv announced a new National Policy on Education* and hoped to transform India's government schools through schemes such as Operation Blackboard, as well as teachers' training and improving and standardizing textbooks. The government even quietly acknowledged the terrible state of its schools by opening a separate network of rural schools for "meritorious students"—the Navodaya schools. But, as Madhav remarks, "The schemes quickly went down the tubes when the government lost the next elections and the bureaucrats changed."

Nevertheless, these efforts bred a later, more successful initiative. In 1986 Madhav had been invited by Rajiv's education secretary, Anil Bordia, to work with the National Literacy Mission. He left the initiative once Rajiv's government fell but found the idea of transforming India's education sector a far too compelling one to let go. In 1991 he cofounded Pratham (First), which took off with support from the United Nations Children's Fund (UNICEF). Pratham started as an effort to send every child in Bombay to school. In the beginning, it had a few *balwadis* or preschool centers across the city, but it has grown since then to a network of more than three thousand *balwadis* today, and its surge has coincided with a new interest among the poor for education.

"What happened to education was India's economic growth," Madhav tells me. "In the seventies and eighties, with jobs hard to come by, the jobs the poor wanted were in government—it guaranteed lifetime security and easy hours. Many of the state jobs that were accessible to them did not require education—the work was of sweepers, cooks, janitors." But as the economy took off, growth was everywhere, and there was a surge in the demand for educated people.

"For the first time people saw a direct connection between education and the chance for better employment," Madhav says. This change in attitudes compelled the poor to look closely at the schools their children were

*Rajiv's National Policy on Education was based on the recommendations of the 1966 report of the Kothari Commission, which had led to the formation of the National Policy on Education in 1968. The 1968 policy was, however, abandoned halfway and the report allowed to gather dust.

attending—to see a system collapsing around their ears. The general apathy that had allowed government schools to languish for so long began to dissipate. As a result, even as enrollment soared through the 1980s and 1990s in government schools, so did dropout rates.

Abhijit concurs, "Even in places such as rural UP and Rajasthan, there is now a growing demand for better schools." A number of state initiatives have taken off in response to this new demand for better schools. Key state efforts—such as the Lok Jumbish in Rajasthan—pushed literacy rates up, and 2001 was the first time India's illiterates came down in absolute numbers, from 328 million to 296 million. Education policy became, for the first time, politically fashionable. A tipping point here was probably Prime Minister Vajpayee's Independence Day speech in 2000, when he envisioned full literacy by 2010. Vajpayee, in his long career as a canny statesman, was always politically astute, and the hunger for education was something he noticed and rapidly incorporated into his rhetoric. Declaring that "Independence is incomplete without social justice," he pledged that his government would ensure that "no child . . . will be deprived of primary education."

With this announcement, the government set off a chain of events. In 2001 the Ninety-third Amendment gave education the status of a fundamental right for children between six and fourteen. That same year, a landmark Supreme Court ruling in the People's Union for Civil Liberties vs. Union of India & Ors case mandated the implementation of the midday meal scheme nationwide. This has turned the Tamil Nadu initiative into the largest school lunch program in the world, where more than 120 million children are being served food across Indian schools. Government schools across states also began reaching out to NGOs to manage their midday school meals. One such effort is being led by one of Infosys's own, Mohandas Pai, who has helped take Akshaya Patra (Inexhaustible)—an NGO project that provides hot, cooked and, as Mohan points out, "unlimited meals" to students—to more than two thousand schools across India.

Of course, these are small steps. As Madhav says, "The midday meal can only help in bringing children into school. We haven't done much in terms of keeping them there." So while we now see school enrollment rates soaring past 90 percent, two thirds of the children who enroll drop out by the sixth year; 90 percent drop out before they reach high school. What that leaves us in human capital is small change.

The Vajpayee government met this problem with a well-funded and highly publicized government effort, the Sarva Shiksha Abhiyan (SSA) or Mission for Universal Education, a package of "mini-interventions" for state schools. The scheme includes plans for local participation in school administrations, with village education committees and parent–teacher associations taking up a large role. The UPA government has since retained the scheme and turned it into a full-scale charge on the education sector—making it a rare, truly bipartisan effort. The government has also ramped up funds for the scheme through a 2 percent "primary education" tax cess, which was implemented in 2004, and a 1 percent cess for secondary education implemented in 2007.

Cesses are a bad government habit, but we are seeing new urgencies in these old twitches—never before has education received so much attention and funding from across India's political parties. Altogether the SSA was propped up with funds of more than Rs 131 billion for 2007–8, and the total target for school education in the year was more than Rs 250 billion.

But the real challenge for education in India is now not in political attention and funding, but in carving the path toward truly effective, well-functioning schools. And here, success is far out of sight.

Moving out into private schools

"Our government schools," Ateeq says, "have not responded effectively enough to demands for education. So people have looked elsewhere."

By the end of the 1990s, the poor had begun to do what the middle class had done three decades ago—search for alternatives to government schools—and cheap private schools surged across the country to cater to the new demand. Across states such as Punjab, Haryana, Kerala and Maharashtra, enrollment in state schools has fallen steeply, as students shift to private schools. More than seven thousand government schools in Karnataka are now empty, according to Ateeq, and in Maharashtra the government is handing over failed municipal schools to NGOs to run. "Even in the rural areas," Ateeq says, "as many as one third of students are now in private schools."

One of the people who studied this shift to private schools in India is James Tooley. James started out his career as a researcher at the University of Newcastle in England and authored a landmark paper on the trend in Indian schools, "Private Schools for the Poor." The media he got—thanks in part to a World Bank/FT award* for his study—brought him to the attention of an investor, Richard Chancellor, who provided him with the funds to set up schools in Hyderabad. He is now competing for students with the same entrepreneurs he had studied.

Tooley tells me that when he first came to Hyderabad to observe the city's education sector, "I was astonished—there is a very large and vibrant industry of schooling here, and there are private schools on virtually every street corner." These were often nothing more than what Tooley calls "mom-and-pop schools," one-room enterprises with ambitious names: "Oxford School," a tiny signboard next to a paan shop would declare. But Tooley found that these schools performed better than government schools on student tests. "In both math and reading tests, students in private schools scored on average 15 percent higher than government school students," he says. Little surprise then that even the poorest families were choosing private over state education—in Hyderabad, two thirds of students are enrolled in private schools.

"There wasn't even much difference in performance between the recognized and unrecognized private schools," Tooley tells me. It must be a typically Indian quirk that the lack of official recognition does not seem to impact quality much. After all, these schools remain illegal mainly due to the long, tedious tap dance with bureaucracy that is necessary to gain a license. Recognition of schools can consequently take years and involves, in Delhi, for example, fourteen licenses from several different authorities.

Tooley tells me, "What hope I have for India's education lies with the entrepreneurs. The teachers in these schools turn up on time and make an effort to teach their students. Whether these classes are held in backyards or slums, education is happening."

It is true, as Tooley says, that "what counts is what works." But I wonder how comprehensively this bottom-up shift to private schools can address our education challenge. The particular disadvantages that the poor suffer in education opportunities—in the illiteracy of their parents and their unique challenges in paying for private tuition, additional textbooks, a steady schooling experience—all add up to enormous hurdles in obtaining an all-round and effective education. It is a challenge that the market cannot address by itself. Some public role is necessary to provide for the twin goals of access

*I was on the jury panel for the award.

and equity in school education. And schemes such as the SSA, which are driving significant funds down the pike to government schools, at least signal a willingness to repair the system.

New dreams and schemes

To discover where exactly we now stand in education, seven years after Vajpayee and two decades after Rajiv, I turn to Rukmini Banerjee, who has worked for Pratham in the education sector for the last decade and is one of the people responsible for the immense dynamism around education reforms. As a friend, I have found her a live wire, always restless, and prone to big belly laughs that catch you off guard. She also serves up great anecdotes from her travels across India's villages and small schools—of wizened farmers and poor construction workers passionate about their daughters' education, and of slum children who have learned to read English and do arithmetic with impressive skill.

One of the first things Pratham did was try to measure real student achievement in India, a task the government had never attempted at the national, state or district level. Pratham's Annual State of Education Report (ASER) found appalling results around reading and maths—half of the Indian children tested lacked any skills in both—and this compelled the organization to focus on basic reading skills. I ask Rukmini if she sees any change in how the government is approaching the problem. They are, after all, pouring money into schools; are the big bucks bringing in results? "There is a focus in the government now beyond just enrollment," Rukmini replies. "Fourteen states across the country have MOUs with Pratham to work on learning reforms. Governments are worrying about retention and quality of education for the first time. That's a big shift, a foot in the door in favor of change."

But what about that old bugaboo—emphasizing the schemes that work, and doing away with the ones that do not? We face a real danger in repeating past mistakes: Indian governments and their big, stumbling bureaucracies have little institutional memory of failed education schemes, which keep receiving funds, while the most successful schemes at the state level have not been taken up as center-led initiatives.

Some state education officers suggested to me that the SSA has promise in the way it has focused on empowering local governments, *panchayats* and village communities to carry out education reform. But Abhijit is cautious. "The SSA scheme is facing the challenge of translating big visions into the little details that matter. State governments are unconcerned about the intricacies of the scheme—no one is running the village education committees properly, or enforcing the new standards."

He adds, "When we did a survey of SSA implementation in UP, we found that 25 percent of parents in the village education committee didn't know they were in the committee, and 80 percent of committee parents were unaware of what the SSA was." No one in the state education departments, Abhijit points out, wants to get down on their haunches and figure out the details. "One state education secretary wasn't even sure, when I asked, how the SSA committees would be constituted."

Neither the original goal of the SSA—of having all children in school by 2003—nor the revised target of bringing all children to school by 2005 has been achieved. In 2005 a quarter of children at the upper primary level had already dropped out. And of course, the usual vices of corruption and ineffective management have affected the initiative.

As it now stands, SSA has only enabled the pumping of more money down a very leaky pipe. While the midday meal schemes drove school enrollment up, the success of SSA in achieving the next step, retention of students, has so far been dismal.

The possibilities of literacy

What is heartbreaking about the thousands of children across India who go to hopeless schools is not just what we lose in terms of their potential, but also its broader political and social damage. It is difficult to overemphasize how education can trigger cultural and social change—this is already evident from India's past, when the educated class became the pivot on which our independence movement turned. Literacy has always had a revolutionary impact, and throughout history, universal education led to rapid, widespread social reform—rural schools created literate peasants and enabled the *zemstvo* or teacher-led revolution in imperial Russia; a newly literate class led campaigns for universal voting and women's rights in Britain; and educated blacks faced up to Jim Crow in the U.S. Civil Rights movement.

Where education has occurred in India, André Béteille points out, it has acted as a "solvent" of barriers between caste communities, especially in the villages. In his book *Caste, Class and Power,* Dr. Béteille describes a Tanjore village where the primary school was situated inside the *agraharam*, the Brahmin quarters that the Dalit elders would dare not enter for fear of "polluting" the place. But their children entered and left as they pleased, free of the terrifying and debilitating reluctance that their parents experienced.

Education goes a long way in helping people move away from knee-jerk feudal sentiments and embrace India's more secular ideals. This is particularly critical in our case, since our Indian identity is neither easy nor effortless, or based on a single language or religion. Rather, it depends in the long run on a progressive and literate mass of citizens who understand the language of a country based so strongly on the unfeudal ideas of secularism and equality before law.

Limiting education also limits the ability of poorer people to increase their access to resources even in successive generations—and it shuts the poor out of economic opportunities. It fences them within unfair social systems and limits their ability to question them.

But while the government has now ramped up spending on our government primary and secondary schools to never before figures, we are still struggling to spend these funds effectively. Making progress here requires us to address politically uncomfortable questions. For example, as Ateeq notes, it is impossible to tackle our school crisis without taking on the problems of accountability among teachers and administrators. Governments in India have attempted this through decentralization, which brings teacher and administrator accountability under local governments rather than those of the state. This has met with mixed success due to resistance at every level of the government, the lack of awareness among local and elected ward members of their powers and the sheer political clout of the teachers' unions.

A key reform to address this issue of accountability, which could also potentially converge the roles of state and private education, is school vouchers. This idea was suggested by Milton Friedman in 1955, and different kinds of voucher programs have seen successes in some U.S. states as well as in Chile, Sweden and Ireland. The basic idea of an education voucher is that the government funds students instead of schools—a transfer of power, since the money follows the student rather than the institution, and allows student choices to determine where the government's education funds go.

The voucher system not only removes ideological tilts toward either private or state schools but also brings in competition that can improve both these school systems, making one less exclusive and the other less bottom of the barrel. It also gives rich and poor students comparable opportunities to exit bad schools and provides a compulsion for reform in the government school sector. As Madhav notes, "If the government schools are empty, it doesn't matter how often a teachers' union calls a strike."

Such reform effectively removes ideology from funding and implementation and makes it easier, say, to hand over management of existing and failing government schools to the private sector, if this will attract students. This can bring the private sector and NGOs into already existing school infrastructure and government school buildings, instead of the current approach where we are constructing an alternative, private school system from scratch.

There are still challenges to such solutions; for example, direct benefits like school vouchers are effective only if there are competing education providers, and this is a high bar to clear in the rural areas. Governments may have to specifically target such regions through incentives such as gap financing options for school entrepreneurs.

A truly competitive market in education that involves both private and state schools offers a unique advantage—a rapid dissemination of best practices and effective teaching methods. Schools would invest in improvements not just to attain but also to exceed standards, so as to attract the best students. In India's private school systems, there are a number of institutions that are already providing an unusual, widening range of educational choices—such as Sriram's kiosks, which offer long-distance video classes and tuition for school students in far-flung villages. Another example is a branded chain of $2 schools that have been launched across India, called "Spark School-in-a-Box." The Spark schools would be owned and operated by entrepreneurs, who would be provided with a "plug-and-play package" that comes with everything required—from curriculum to fee structures to infrastructure design—to start and run a low-end school. It is a model meant to assure both quality and low-cost education to poor families. Similar approaches are also being tried out by Tooley in Hyderabad and William Bissell in Rajasthan.

Blowing in the wind

My wife, Rohini, visits a lot of government schools as part of her NGO reach-out. One of the questions she most likes to ask the kids is what they would like to be when they grow up. The answers are varied—"engineer," "teacher," "policeman" and, increasingly, "computer" [sic]. But even in the rural schools, one aspiration that they never express is "farmer"—their parents hope that the lives of their children will be different from the subsistence livelihoods that they as farmers have endured, and they and their children see these schools as their way out.

Private school entrepreneurs as well as organizations such as Pratham and Akshaya Patra are responding in their own ways to this massive change of heart. And governments, no matter what their ideology or which political line they toe, are likely to have their feet held to the fire by voters if they do not respond to the surging aspirations for good education that cuts across class and caste. Politicians are tapping into the changed sentiment across the country—as when in West Bengal Buddhadeb Bhattacharjee speaks of the need to combine the "push factor" of economic growth with "the pull factor of education."

We have had the goal of universal education in our crosshairs for a pretty long time—the target year for attaining it was first 1959; that commitment was later deferred until 1970, then until 1980, 1990, 2000, and now 2010, a date that according to the Comptroller Auditor General (CAG) we will not keep. Our schools have been in the crossfire of bitter arguments India has had over languages, religion and the ideology of control, and the fights continue.

Right now, however, we have a significant opportunity to reform India's primary education—thanks to a perfect storm of education demand that is cutting across economic class, political response and government funding. Jairam Ramesh remarked to me that with such a large amount on the government ledger dedicated to education, "the government cannot afford bad outcomes."

Since 2001 education has also received the constitutional ballast it needs, and voters can now demand real, concrete outcomes as a right. Since then, education initiatives have been delegating control of schools to *panchayats* and local bodies, and empowering local communities to interfere, criticize and praise. NGOs as well as philanthropic and civil society organizations across India have made education their first port of call and financing from these groups is a strong force toward education reform.

Across India—among the poorer families, in the rural country, and in the brick and tin shacks of city slums—the demand for education is rising in a single voice. This idea is now firmly rooted in the country. It is now really a matter of executing on our hopes. The ability to implement our education goals will decide what the large majority of Indian children are capable of in the future—increased economic mobility versus lost opportunity, access versus closed doors, the ingenuity and talent of millions of people lost or gained. Children across India today are attending schools with the full weight of their parents' hopes on their shoulders. The poorest families are setting aside as much as one fourth of their incomes toward school fees. The outcomes of these efforts will become clear only a few years on—as the poor discover if such education has brought them real economic gains, and whether it has turned out to be a stepping stone or a stumbling block.

While the demand for better education is at new highs, our failing schools and our dismal dropout rates have long ceased to shock us. Our schools now present us with the kind of crisis where the point of no return can slip silently and irreversibly past us. There will be no outcry or three-inch headlines on the front pages of our newspapers when this happens. But our success or failure here will, more conclusively than any other reform, determine India's economic future. We cannot forget after all that the toughest questions around education are now rearing up even as India's demographic dividend ramps up. Our response will make all the difference between the world's largest lumpen community of illiterates in an uncertain nation, and a country with a large pool of talented human capital that can fire up the economy to new levels of growth. Our opportunity to choose between the two is here, now, and transient.

OUR CHANGING FACES

India in the City

I SPEND A GOOD amount of my time in planes, and the view of our largest cities from a height of three thousand meters is an exhilarating experience. From the sky and at night, the shimmering, dense constellation of lights that is Bombay or Bangalore appears as a landscape of immense economic promise. On the ground, however, our cities are a very different story.

What I often find striking as I move across urban India is how diverse the country's geography is outside our urban centers, and yet how eerily similar our largest cities look—in their infrastructure, their crumbling edges and their appalling, disheartening urban problems. For Indians the images that dominate our idea of the city are those of disaster, and of neglect. We recall the torrential rains that caused many residents of India's financial capital, Bombay, to wade through waist-deep water; or we describe Bangalore's half-finished flyovers, Delhi's riots for water and of course the inescapable chaos of traffic snarls, broken-down pavements and disintegrating public systems that define our urban, everyday life.

We can trace back much of the crisis in urban India to our ideas of the city immediately after independence. These perceptions ensured that in the early constitutional battles for control, India's cities lost decisively. Since then, our cities have largely been exiled from the Indian imagination—our idea of

India is of a country rooted in its dusty heartland, village settlements and farms. But India's growth has gradually brought our cities into the spotlight, and what it shows up is a scarred landscape in dire need of reform.

A tale of two cities

I visit the Centre for Policy Research (CPR) in New Delhi early one morning, traversing wide, empty roads that the rain has just washed clean. The office is located close to Diplomatic Enclave, and sits in the green, well-planned part of New Delhi—it is just one face of our capital's many identities.

I am here to meet Dr. K. C. Sivaramakrishnan, chairman of CPR and author of a number of books on India's urban growth. I am especially curious, I tell him, about the marginalization of the city in Indian politics—it seems counterintuitive, since many of our prominent Indian leaders from Vallabhbhai Patel, Nehru, Subhas Chandra Bose and Mohammed Ali Jinnah, and earlier, Lajpat Rai and Surendranath Banerjea, came from India's city corporations. "But it was the nature of the colonial cities," Dr. Sivaramakrishnan tells me, "to alienate the Indians, and this included the Indian leaders."

While the Indian villages were dominated by zamindars presiding over local affairs, the stamp of imperial rule was apparent all over the city, where its officers lived and the British administration held complete control. Indian leaders in the city corporations chafed under British imperiousness—Lajpat Rai, who had worked in the Hissar Municipality, described the head of the city commission, a European officer, as an "extremely mischievous and tyrannical man."[1] During his time at the Ahmedabad Municipality, Vallabhbhai Patel was astonished to discover a fiefdom, "a people's organization acting under the orders of the collector and commissioner."[2]

The very aim of the colonial administration in Indian cities was to inspire awe, to make the power of the Empire concrete and visible. As the British architect Herbert Baker wrote to his friend and architect Edwin Lutyens, advising him on the plans for Delhi, "It must not be Indian, nor English, or Roman, but it must be imperial." The result was looming, Edwardian-style government buildings and tree-lined avenues and roads. "Edwin Lutyens' inscription on Delhi's colonial buildings said it all," Dr. Sivaramakrishnan says, "that, 'Liberty will not descend to a People; a People must raise themselves to liberty. It is a privilege that must be earned before it can be enjoyed.' "

The cities were also where the divides between India and its imperial heart were clearly mapped—Civil Lines of cities were reserved for British officers and affluent businessmen. One Indian observer remarked on the British parts, and their "spaciousness, wealth of color, peace, restfulness and beauty . . . none of this belonged to us."[3] Many of the buildings in these areas were in fact faithful imitations of what the British had left behind—English-style homes were built with large verandas and windows, which had to then be shuttered and draped with thick curtains to keep the heat and insects out.[4] The government buildings were similarly meant to remind the officers of those back home.[5*]

Britain's urban planning had little role in the cities beyond distancing the rulers from their festering colony. Indian cities were segregated to the point of having separate railway stations, such as in Bangalore, where a vast patch of grass set apart the "native" City and the "European" Cantonment stations.[6] Nehru made an attempt to phase out these urban divides during his tumultuous stint as chairman of the Allahabad Municipality between 1921 and 1923. Ajay Mehra describes Nehru during this period as an idealistic young chairman trying to push through a land tax regulation that would bring in more revenues from the richer city, "where most of the Big Noises and Little Noises lived," thus funding improvements for the rest. The district magistrate, however, overruled him, and the law never passed.

The neglect of the older, "native" city led to its widespread decline. Here, encroachments on public lands were common and in the absence of sewage lines people "constructed privies opening into public streets."[7] The wide roads of the Civil Lines wound their way into narrow lanes and dead ends in this part of the city. These urban parts, filthy, ignored and expanding without control or plan, would, as it turned out, be the unfortunate blueprint for the modern Indian city.

Besides the capital cities and industrial and trading centers, the British also built several towns across India to suit their needs. India's tropical summers, for instance, compelled the British to make a run for the hills—Shimla was Delhi's alternate summer capital, and for the British "a settled place for the heart in this perplexing conquered land."[8] Other seasonal capitals were

*These state buildings were, however, more like showcases, and built with far cheaper material than the original buildings. Lord Curzon noted that the Government House in Calcutta, supposed to be a replica of Derbyshire's Kendleston House, was a ripoff: "The pillars of one are alabaster, the pillars of the other lath and plaster."

Darjeeling for Bengal, Nainital for the United Provinces, Mahabaleshwar for Bombay and Ooty for Madras. There were as many as sixty-five such hill stations to which the British beat a regular retreat from the burning sands of the plains, where they could luxuriate in English-style cottages and weather. Gandhi, in his characteristic style, criticized this habit as "Rule from the 500 hundredth story."[9]

By settling in and loosening their ties in a city setting, the British led Indians to associate India's urban identity with the colonial one. Gandhi went as far as to say, "I regard the growth of cities as an evil thing . . . certainly unfortunate for India." India's leaders were eager to shake off the dust of these colonial cities; for them they were inextricably linked with a past they longed to forget.

So it was that immediately after independence, the government marginalized the Indian city. "The cities became constitutional orphans," Dr. Sivaramakrishnan says. "Independent India's new government essentially recognized two tiers—the center and the state." Taxes were also split among these two, with the center collecting income and excise taxes, while the state collected sales tax, stamp duty on properties and excise on alcohol. The city governments were cut off. In fact while the Constitution made provisions for rural, local institutions, the entire document mentioned urban local governments exactly twice, and neither time to their advantage—the urban bodies went under the state list and were stripped of their independence.[10]

This may not have seemed such a bad idea at the time. With independence, India's most prominent city politicians had attended the clarion call of forming new governments at the state and center, and the municipal halls were emptied of their most capable hands. But political calculations in a democratic, independent India stacked the deck even further against the metropolis. Ashutosh Varshney has pointed out that democracy, when introduced into a country before an industrial revolution takes hold, dramatically tilts power to rural areas. This tilt was decisive in India postindependence. With 80 percent of Indians living in villages, the move to a rural, "sons of the soil" rhetoric among politicians was fast. Across India, the narrative grew of the rural country being the far more "authentic" part, and price controls on agricultural goods (attempts to control inflation and food prices) led to cities being depicted as "a vampire that drinks the blood of the countryside."[11]

But the real stake in the heart for city politics was still to come. The idea of the city as "the result of conflict" is particularly true in India. In the emotionally fraught battle that occurred in the 1950s over dividing states along linguistic boundaries, India's cities got caught in the crossfire. No state could really lay claim on the provincial cities, which were community and linguistic melting pots. This was especially true of Bombay—the city that was India's prize jewel, the richest in the country. Who would possess it was the resounding question when the Bombay state was carved up into Maharashtra and Gujarat. It was the Gujaratis who dominated trade and commerce in the city even though it lay deep within Maharashtrian territory. The States Reorganisation Commission suggested that Bombay remain the capital of a bilingual state. But the politicians supporting the "Bombay for Maharashtra" cause objected, saying that "everywhere the principle of language has been recognized, except in this one case."[12] In an effort to rescue the city from the linguistic battles, Nehru suggested that Bombay should become a separate, bilingual area directly administered by the central government, an idea supported by some Bombay politicians such as S. K. Patil.

It was support they would soon regret. To put it mildly, the Maharashtrians did not welcome the idea. Mobs surged across the city's streets, shouting, "Bombay is ours" and "Death to Nehru!" They smashed statues of Mahatma Gandhi—his identity as a Gujarati, in this period of mayhem, superseding that of national leader—and attacked Gujaratis across the state. The rioters tossed rocks and electric bulbs filled with acid—the latter a protest weapon of choice since the 1940s Calcutta riots—blockaded roads and railway lines and looted shops. And when a European photographer stopped to take a picture of Nehru's vandalized posters, the crowds cheered: "Take it, take it, and show the world what we think of Nehru."[13]

The government was forced to back down, and any suggestion that the city would be carved out from the state was abandoned. The battle over Bombay permanently changed and challenged the city's dominance and marked the beginning of its retreat within a politics held spellbound by India's villages.

Nehru dreams

During my trip to Delhi, I visit the home of Dr. O. P. Mathur, the soft-spoken, diminutive academic who is one of India's foremost experts in urban development and growth. His house is a wonderland of art—it is hard to tear my eyes away from the gorgeous, surrealist prints of Miro and Kandinsky lining his walls.

Dr. Mathur, however, does not let me linger. In our chat on urban India, he concurs that our cities were dealt a pretty unlucky hand. But Indians were far more optimistic about the possibilities of urban life during the Nehru years, he tells me. From the moment of India's independence, Nehru was bent on transforming the country from its ugly duckling status of a poor former colony to a swan, a soaring, industrial economy, filled with the visible and spectacular signs of development. Nehru envisioned powerful industrial cities that would be a marvel of execution and state planning.

But the Empire had left its fingerprints all over India's older cities—Delhi, Calcutta, Bombay, Madras had all been baptized into urban life by the British and cluttered with their architecture. Nehru called New Delhi "un-Indian" and was in search of a new Indian city that would be free of the burdens of colonial rule and legacy, a "new town symbolic of the freedom of India."[14]

Nehru got an opportunity to test his dream of a new Indian city with Chandigarh, the new capital for Punjab. Le Corbusier, the temperamental French architect, designed a city after Nehru's own heart—carefully planned between residential and commercial areas with each sector named, quite unromantically, with a number.

Chandigarh was meant to be just the first of many planned cities—the target in fact was three hundred by the end of the century—that would dot India's plains. Nehru had been terribly impressed by how Russia had built the steel city of Magnitogorsk under Stalin, and the Indian steel city of Bhilai was in a way Nehru's remembered reconstruction. A large number of new Indian capitals also sprang up—besides Le Corbusier's Chandigarh, we had Otto Koenigsberger's Bhubaneswar, and Gandhinagar and Dispur. And in tandem with Bhilai, the industrial centers of Durgapur, Barauni and Sindri were also being built.[15]

But India's dismal reality—of a poor, struggling, rural economy—would soon render this vision threadbare. By the early 1960s, driven to the trenches and addressing basic food and security concerns, we saw our plan of building a modern, urban India fade.

But one wonders how much of the dream would have been realized, even without the crises. For the Indian state was busy committing a laundry list of missteps in the name of urban planning. The cities in independent

India were still essentially symbols, as they were for the British—Chandigarh was the sparkling spire on the hill for Indian socialism, "a city of government rather than of industry, meant for politicians, bureaucrats, administrators." The industrial cities too were weighted with symbolism.[16]

The Indian government had missed the essential relevance of the city in the context of the market—failing to see them as vibrant, living systems that sustained economies by becoming centers of large-scale, efficient production, and that, as people coalesced in large numbers, also became spaces for innovation. Indians had never seen our cities that way; as Dr. Sivaramakrishnan notes, besides India's ports, the biggest cities for both the Mughals and the British were primarily displays of power, driven more by the logic of empire than of commerce. The disconnect was well captured in the 1951 census report, which stated that India's towns and cities were "accidents of history and geography."[17]

Swati Ramanathan—who with her husband, Ramesh, forms the passionate, reformist team that heads Janaagraha, an NGO emerging as a think-tank on urban policy—tells me, "Our first Town and Country Planning Act was based on Britain's Town and Country Planning Act of 1909. But while they have revised their act and urban planning laws over eight times, we have held on to ours as if they have been carved in stone."

But while the concerns of urban India may have held little interest for Indian legislators, the city lights were beacons of hope and promise for the masses of India's rural poor, the dispossessed and the unemployed. As agriculture stagnated, people left the countryside in droves. It was migration as escape—for many people, it meant leaving behind lives that entailed "three months of work per year and then hunger, terrible hunger . . . it was like a heavy hand on my heart."[18]

The surging crowds were soon choking the cities and towns, wearing their resources thin. Bombay city, once called "Bombay the Beautiful," an urban vision against the Arabian Sea, atrophied so rapidly postindependence that such a label is now unimaginable. The complicated layers of state administration made it especially difficult to manage such rapid urban growth. This administrative weakness had been in full view during India's Partition, that intense, bloody amputation of the Indian subcontinent which saw the displacement of hundreds of thousands from the northwest into India. While this mass migration led to the creation of new urban spaces that resettled these people—such as Faridabad, Kalyani and Nilokheri—the bureaucracy impeded the growth of these cities, throttling any strategy for planned growth with its "everything in triplicate" sentiment and its snail-like pace.

L. C. Jain, former member of the planning commission who participated in the building of Faridabad, tells me, "We had angry refugees, trigger-happy Pathans, and chaos at the government level. Much of what we managed was with local initiative." Urban growth was a fast-moving tide that hit the walls of a sleepy administration again and again. In independent India, city master plans usually take years to be prepared and published. By the time they are out of course, they have all the relevance of an old photograph and look nothing like the existing city itself. Karnataka's state government, for instance, released its 2005 plan for Bangalore city two years late, during which time the city expanded with chaos as its ruling theme. Urban planning in India has become little more than a performance piece, with both the state actors and the audience—the urban citizens—aware that once the lights go off, life will go on as before.

"The city slickers have left town"

By the late 1960s the city was well and truly relegated to the background as the drumbeat of rural politics reached fever pitch, and Indira Gandhi's "abolish poverty" movement gained momentum. By then the green revolution had created new rural wealth, leading to the rise of a powerful class of rural statesmen and regional parties with a strong kisan, or farmer, base. Among these were the Akali Dal, which was powerful among the rural Jat Sikhs, and the Janata Dal, with its leaders coming from middle-level peasantry and the rural, backward castes in Bihar and Uttar Pradesh.

Dr. Mathur tells me that the infatuation with rural India reached the point where, in order to corner resources and funding from the central government, "we had state governments labeling their urban areas as rural ones." He speculates that our urban growth as a result might easily be underestimated by 5 to 10 percent, with surging towns disguised as dusty hinterlands and hidden away from the center's eyes.

So irrelevant did urban growth seem that a ministry of urban development was established only in 1985, and in the next two decades, it did little to inspire faith—it focused on tending Delhi and its gardens, allocating houses for ministers and managing the machinations of the Delhi Development Authority (DDA).* "The urban concern in India," Dr. Mathur says, "has remained a Delhi concern."

Abandoned by the center, the cities were also skewered by the states. State governments in independent India wasted little time in exercising their new power over city governments and squeezed them dry. Always wary of competition from the grassroots, states made sure to keep party sycophants at the municipal level and limited the power of city bodies by pruning the size of their wallets. Major taxation resources of the municipalities were limited to property taxes and octroi, while the state collected the rest. This meant that the riches of the cities translated into little in its coffers, and urban officials had to wait for stale crumbs from the state treasuries.

Gandhi saw cities as a sponge on the village's resources—its edifices, he once alleged, were "built on the blood of the villages." Our approach to cities seemed to be attempting the reverse—a sacrifice that may have been worthwhile if there had been tangible rural development. But the government's focus on the villages was mainly to sustain them with dole-outs and ineffective subsidy schemes. The battered rural districts remained backward and painfully poor. As Vijay Kelkar tells me, the economic health of these rural areas only grew worse as global trade dynamics worked against them. "The third world entered the global market in one swoop in the 1950s and 1960s, flooding it with agricultural products." As a result there was already a global surplus in what rural India produced, and this impoverished them further.

Invisible men

"The problem of our city governments," Dr. Mathur tells me, "is obvious in the fact that we can't name any of our mayors or city councillors." If money were running on correct answers here, most of India's urban residents (including me) would lose every time.

This is mainly because accountability in our city governments has moved up, not down. The municipal commissioner in the cities was an IAS officer appointed by the state government. The commissioner was an unfortunate individual indeed, caught between two tiers of government, subject to de-

*Till the 1980s, the ministry of works, housing and supply managed urban development.

mands made by elected corporators and also answerable to state ministers looking over his shoulder. The position of the city mayor was even weaker, with fewer powers at the local level than the ceremonial governor of the state.

It is no surprise, then, that no one has heard the names of the mayors of Bombay, Delhi and Bangalore.* This is quite unlike many other countries—Mayor Bloomberg of New York and ex-Mayor Livingstone of London, for instance, have been nationally known, powerful figures. Mayor Giuliani of New York became an especially popular figure after leading the city's response in the wake of the 9/11 attack—a level of responsibility impossible to imagine for an Indian mayor. In China, as well, cities are run by strong mayors who often move up to the highest positions—such as Jiang Zemin and Zhu Rong Ji, both Shanghai mayors who went on to become president and premier of China.

In Indian cities, however, political power has been amputated at every level. City-level decisions in India are subjected to a multitude of state-level checks and balances, for everything from creating new posts to passing the budget and selling property. The very existence of the municipalities has often depended on state goodwill, turning them into little more than the vestigial organs of the state body. Dr. Sivaramakrishnan tells me that the majority of India's municipal corporations "were superseded by the state at one time or the other. The Calcutta Municipal Corporation was superseded as early as 1948."

Instead, a range of bureaucratic state agencies mushroomed across Indian cities, elbowing out the municipalities. These agencies typically took over the investment and tax collection functions for the cities, with local bodies relegated to "operation and maintenance"—housekeepers for urban infrastructure. As a consequence, municipal expenditure has remained a tiny share of state GDP, ranging from 1.84 percent in Maharashtra to the chump change of 0.1 percent in Bihar.

Local governments with little authority, and state governments that were powerful but unaccountable to city residents: the Athenian ideal of democracy, where policy decisions are local and face-to-face, has been clearly buried deep down in the cities. The lack of a powerful elected body has meant

*In fact one of the few times a mayor of Delhi did make headlines was when his wife kissed him in public, inviting the disapproval of many politicians. "Only men," these ministers said, "may kiss the mayor." They added, "Unless the mayor is a woman, in which case only women may kiss her."

that city resources became prizes to be quartered among powerful interest groups in the state. And city development has become both opaque and ad hoc—as when governments in Delhi, Bombay and Bangalore up and conduct demolition drives on encroachments every few years but fail to enforce building regulations the rest of the time.

Our "unintended cities"

By the 1970s a pork-barrel politico could not have had it better in the city. A series of well-meaning but horribly counterproductive laws passed during this decade, which gave an immense leg up to interest groups in the city. The rent-control legislation and the Urban Land Ceiling Act had effects that, in the best of socialist tradition, were just the opposite of what they had intended. The rent act, by stating minimal leasing periods and strict eviction limits, basically gave renters carte blanche to squat and quickly took unoccupied housing off the market, and the land ceiling act shifted large amounts of land into the illegal market.

In Delhi the Delhi Development Act of 1957 forced out private players in real estate, making government agencies like the DDA the sole developers in the city. In Bombay a tiny group of developers and trusts eventually came to control all available private land by the 1990s, creating a deeply oligopolistic market where land was released in small quantities when prices were high.

At the same time, the "floor area ratio" restrictions limited urban density and sent cities sprawling across the landscape. As a result, through the 1960s and 1970s, land in cities and especially in Bombay, the business heart of the country, was dearer than gold (and that's saying a lot, since gold was dear as well) and was controlled by a nexus of politicians, bureaucrats and city developers.

When I moved into Bombay city for my first job in 1979—fresh out of IIT, rough around the edges—the decline of the city was already well under way, and the urban chaos was clearly visible in the rise of the shanties and slums on the city's margins. Such temporary housing was the only answer in a city where regulation had created a chronic shortage of real estate. On my salary, the only thing I could afford in 1979 was a bed. This two-by-six-foot space was in a tiny room located on Mumbai's Grant Road, which I shared with two other people who were, like me, just out of college and in their first job. I perched there for two years until I got engaged, and then I panicked. Renting an apartment was unimaginable, and it was an uncle—in the Indian tradition, he "knew someone who knew someone" with an empty apartment—who found me a place to stay.

I was lucky—such networks of well-connected relatives were not available to the vast majority of people who came to the city to earn a living. The rise of slums, then, is no surprise; people have merely carved out spaces for themselves where there is none. Two thirds of Bombay's population lives in such housing.* Inventively built with plastic tarp and tin and cardboard sheeting, and occasionally with more durable material like concrete and brick, these slums are an architectural marvel. They are dense and tiny homes, built wall to wall and one on top of the other, defying gravity and as delicate as a house of cards, and sometimes, like a final flourish, have dish antennae sticking out of their roofs. They are a testimony to urban survival; many cram eight people and more inside a tiny room. These slum neighborhoods manage with decrepit infrastructure and tap electricity from the main lines, and it is not uncommon for a thousand houses to share one working toilet. Life here is tenuous, as vacant spaces here go for Rs 100,000 and more, and tenants stay at the slum lords' pleasure.[19]

These slums are the saddest symptoms of our urban failures. Our 170 million slum dwellers alone surpass the populations of all but five countries in the world. With so many of the city's residents housed in these shanties, the influence of the slum lords and the mafia touches every part of the city, including its government. The writer Suketu Mehta notes that 40 percent of Bombay's policemen live in its slums, which essentially makes them the slum lords' tenants and the mafiosi's neighbors.

The chaos in our land markets has fed on itself—in the absence of any coherent land regulation, outfits such as the D-Company, the city's largest mafia organization, have exploited shortages to squat on and lease out public land. Such unplanned encroachment has not been limited to individuals and private players—the government has waded into the chaos as well, often claiming land resources for development without assessing the impact on the

*The richer classes in Bombay's slums earn as much as Rs 14,000 a month, which means a substantial part of Bombay's middle class lives here.

city's environment and its resources. My city, Bangalore, for instance, was long known as the city of lakes—which was actually a vast network of more than two hundred manmade tanks. Over the years, the government has slowly encroached upon and developed these waterbodies. The Shivaji Nagar bus stand was built over such a tank, and the massive residential complex built for the National Games in 1997, the National Games Village, was constructed over a large tank that linked into the ecologically critical Bellandur Tank, one of the largest wetlands in Bangalore. These developments have hurt the water table and threaten the city's long-term, sustainable access to water resources.

The consequence of too many rules has obviously been that everyone has agreed to ignore them. Across cities, our roads and pavements are dug up and left open for days on end, inconveniencing pedestrians and traffic. Every so often, children fall into these open ditches and get badly hurt—and recovering them out of these storm drains, holes and open wells becomes a human interest story covered by newspapers and TV. In the early days of the Bangalore Agenda Task Force (BATF) we thought we could solve this problem in Bangalore by having a "road cutting protocol" that would help us coordinate the work of these agencies. We were sadly mistaken. We found that there are many service providers who needed to dig up the roads for different reasons, because there are no ducts to lay pipes or cables. So the road could be cut open for water supply or sanitation, for installing telephone lines, electric cables or gas pipes. While all these agencies took permission from the municipal authorities, there was often no time limit on the approvals they granted. And what usually happened was that the municipality would contract out the work order for digging the trench to one provider and of covering the trench to another. We often saw a road dug up for a water pipe, then repaired and dug up again immediately after by another service provider.

Many public services in cities have actually worsened in recent years, and informal, nonstate solutions dominate the housing, security, water supply, health and education sectors. While India's urban rich and middle class are seceding from the public sector by investing in gated communities and private guards for security, pumps and borewells for water, private generators for electricity and private schools and hospitals, the large groups of the urban poor are seceding in other ways. City slums, for instance, have developed intricate local governance that provides utility services for a fee.

Slum lords provide a variety of services from sewage facilities to water and electricity—the latter usually by siphoning from public distribution systems; they also act as fixers with connections to the government and help procure state resources such as ration cards and land records.

Such secession, however, worsens our inequalities. The government houses in Lutyens' Delhi consume thousands of liters of water a day, while slum residents struggle to collect or buy a few liters. And slum lords are not too reliable when it comes to security and land rights, since they are not above razing homes and reselling the land if it is profitable. The alternatives for the poor as a result are both inefficient and lack any real protections.

The urban facelift

Jeffrey Sachs recently commented on the state of Indian cities, which has made it impossible to take a jog, or even walk from place to place in an Indian city. "The broken pavements, the chaos of the roads," he told me, "endanger the casual pedestrian."

There was a rare glimmer of a well-planned Indian urban space in the building of Navi Mumbai across Bombay's harbor by Charles Correa in the 1970s. Correa, who later headed the National Commission on Urbanization under the Rajiv Gandhi government, believed in the ability of urban spaces to shape culture and living, and in Navi Mumbai he created a remarkably planned minicity for two million people, which juggled community spaces, schools and hospitals. As the years passed, however, the project got mired in bureaucratic wrangling, and the planned shift of the government secretariat and Mumbai's wholesale markets into the new city fell through. The vision has since been muddied further by the typical challenges of failing urban maintenance, the rise of unplanned areas and growing encroachment. Right now, the problems of Navi Mumbai are clearly in the early stages of a very familiar affliction.

To figure out if our urban policies have changed in recent years, I meet Ramesh Ramanathan, the other half of Janagraaha's leadership, over coffee one sunny afternoon in Bangalore. I reach late for our meeting thanks to traffic, but there could not be a more understanding audience for my apologies. Ramesh is in his forties, and his boyish smile under a head of silver hair is both incongruous and charming. I ask him about the possibilities of a new urban vision and he says, "We are making progress in the typical Indian way—two steps forward, one step back."

India's urban transformation, as Ramesh points out, had begun with the policies of Rajiv Gandhi's government. Rajiv represented a dynamic shift for Indian policy on a number of fronts, and one of them was his attempt to give cities in independent India a measure of power. With his Nagarpalika bill, Rajiv pushed for the empowerment of local bodies both in the cities and in the villages. But his bill failed by three votes, and it took until 1992, after his death, for it to finally pass under the Narasimha Rao government as the Seventy-third and Seventy-fourth Amendments.

Dr. Sivaramakrishnan tells me that the real focus in these two amendments was on empowering the village bodies and the *panchayats*. "The city," he says, "was an afterthought." But even to the hardened skeptic, these reforms came with promise. With these amendments, the Constitution of India formally recognized the city as the third tier of government and abolished the powers of the states to suspend or dissolve city governments.*

The amendments proposed some revolutionary changes in the powers and functions of the urban local bodies. For the first time, the laws freed city governments from the state's apron strings and gave them new powers ranging from urban planning, regulation of land use and construction of buildings to infrastructure management and provision and tax collection. The amendments also provided for the setting up of a State Finance Commission (SFC) in each state to advise on money transfers from the state to local bodies.

But the big weakness of the reformist Seventy-fourth Amendment was that the states had to pass the necessary laws empowering local bodies. So while these reforms have been exceptional, implementing them has been exceptionally difficult. Escalating political tensions between the center and the states—worsened by the rise of regional parties—mean that state parties view city empowerment as an effort to weaken their own power. The states have protested that city reforms would result in an "hourglass," where the state would be the tiny waist, "with an immense center at the top and the city government at the equally wide bottom."

Such suspicions were not entirely baseless. Sunil Khilnani noted, for instance, that Rajiv Gandhi's enthusiasm for Nagarpalika was linked to his

*It is a different story that this rule has often been violated by state governments.

effort to bring about more grassroots challenges to regional movements that were chipping away at the once mighty Congress party.

Not surprisingly, there has been an intensifying tug of war over giving new powers to city governments. "Concrete shifts in urban policy are yet to happen," Ramesh says. "We are still struggling for episodic wins." While some states such as Kerala and Karnataka have taken steps to pass responsibilities to local bodies, in most states these powers remain tangled up with the multitude of state-managed agencies. State governments have also implemented the SFC recommendations half-heartedly and sometimes not at all. Govinda Rao, director of the National Institute of Public Finance and Policy (NIPFP), tells me, "The state governments have not really accepted the role of the SFCs, so the governments ignore the commissions' requests for the resources and information they need to function properly." Regardless of reforms, we have held onto the basic power dynamic between the state and city governments—that of a hammer and an anvil. As one *panchayat* worker in Rajasthan recently pointed out, "The state government allows us to tax any vehicle in our jurisdiction—which is not motor driven. That leaves us with camel carts."

Another major challenge is simply weak management. "Cities have got a bum rap when it comes to skills in urban management," Ramesh says. "We lack a history in running complex, well-coordinated urban systems." For instance, the major source of tax revenue for city bodies—the property tax—is a mess of complicated valuations, legal disputes and rents ceilings. The BATF that I led focused in part on property tax reform and helped revamp the Bangalore corporation's accounting systems. The eGovernments Foundation I support is also using IT systems to streamline property tax and accounting systems in city governments across the country.

Improving management to garner more revenues becomes especially critical now as an old tax, the octroi, is being abolished in nearly all states. Local bodies are now searching for new alternatives in their financing, such as municipal bonds. These have become especially important in the light of the Jawaharlal Nehru National Urban Renewal Mission (JNNURM), which requires investments from municipal bodies of well more than Rs 300 billion in the next seven years, up to half of which can be market borrowings. This is compelling municipal corporations across cities to obtain credit ratings from agencies such as Credit Rating Information Services of India Ltd (CRISIL), ICRA and Credit Analysis and Research Ltd (CARE).*

A change in attitudes

"Our cities have gained new political relevance with our economic growth," Ramesh says. In part, the changing attitude has to do with the rise of Bangalore—the surge of IT/BPO industries here and elsewhere has put immense pressures on urban India's infrastructure and resources. This has been an industry with unusual and demanding urban requirements: as a fast-growing sector that relied more on human capital than any other resource, it had to be concentrated in cities. The industry's 40 percent annual growth through the 1990s—a blink-and-the-size-would-double rate—also created a new class of relatively rich, "high-impact" urban residents with their two-wheelers, cars and apartments and their demands for shopping malls and restaurants. This was a very large class of consumer-citizens, more than a million today, who needed effective urban infrastructure—infrastructure that was on 24/7.

The sudden, unprecedented pressure from these IT/BPO firms galvanized the demand for better urban infrastructure. It was also an early sign, a weathervane of how economic reforms would transform the way the states viewed their cities, as they began to compete for private investment. Money, both Indian and foreign, was searching out cities with good infrastructure, and this compelled Indian politicians to look twice at their decrepit capitals and towns. This pressure is likely to only ramp up further in the light of the SEZ projects that are coming up across the country, once cities have to compete with these regions for investment.

As India has emerged as a power to reckon with on the world stage, its cities have also come into sharper focus globally, and are often negatively compared with the booming Chinese metropolises of Shanghai, Beijing and even its young city of Dalian. When I traveled to Beijing recently, I found it difficult not to be awed, or feel like a provincial visitor to a futuristic city.

---

*Bangalore can lay claim to pioneering bond issues by cities in India—India's first such bond issue was by the Bangalore Mahanagarapalika in 1997 of Rs 1 billion, with a coupon rate of 13 percent.

The Beijing master plan is in marked contrast to the Indian versions—every building and park is exactly where it says it should be.

But Ramesh points out to me that if we contrast India's and China's cities, India's urban story has some unexpected advantages. "If we look at our cities in terms of a 'night sky shot,' the lights of India's cities and towns are far more spread out across the country." This creates possibilities for a far more balanced path to urbanization. We have the chance to adopt a sensibly planned, sustainable urbanization strategy that is oriented toward five thousand cities across the country, which would keep both migration and environment stresses at manageable levels.

The political winds in India are also now finally beginning to change direction in favor of urban India. One of the major shifts has been brought about by the Delimitation Commission, which recently revised Parliament and state assembly seats to reflect updated population numbers. The share of electoral seats for urban India had been previously based on a census three decades old, and the new Delimitation Commission, with its basis in the 2001 census, took into account thirty years of urban growth.

As a result the number of Parliament seats for Indian cities has gone up significantly, especially in highly urbanized states like Tamil Nadu, Karnataka and Maharashtra. Bangalore, for instance, currently has twenty-eight out of 224 seats in the Karnataka assembly, up from sixteen, and rural Bangalore has ten, up from eight. With the share of the smaller cities added in, urban concerns now have greater weight in our state legislatures, and the results are already showing—while campaigning for the 2008 Karnataka elections, the former chief minister H. D. Kumaraswamy included highlights of the government's achievements in city infrastructure and governance. The party that won the elections, the BJP, was also the one with the most coherent, well-thought-out urban manifesto, and the party had emphasized the theme of urban development throughout its campaigning. These changing political and democratic compulsions mean, at the very least, that rural spin no longer holds the same political magic. In Andhra Pradesh, Y.S.R. Reddy, the "rural looking, farmer friendly" minister has referred to the need for "rural and urban, rather than rural or urban," and pledges a greater focus on city development.[20] Ministers across states as varied as Gujarat, Kerala and Tamil Nadu are interleaving urban concerns into their stump speeches.

Much of this is coming together in a shift toward a more clear-eyed policy approach for urban renewal—the JNNURM. The BATF gave many of us who had worked within it what I would call a "worm's-eye view" to how cities functioned. When the task force ended, I and its other members went on a road show around Delhi's government offices to push for a broader, national focus on urban change. We had interested politicians from the left and right, all of whom thought that the urban issue was an urgent one. And we went through the whole trip without being labeled as out-of-touch elitists! The national mission on urban change eventually took shape with the JNNURM, and our experience with the BATF helped us a great deal while helping shape reforms toward improving disclosure laws for urban bodies, strengthening citizen participation, introducing more effective financial accounting and aligning city organizations better. The urban renewal mission has a provision of Rs 500 billion, and adding in the contribution of states and municipalities, the amount goes up to Rs 1250 billion over a seven-year period. The JNNURM has also adopted an effective carrot approach, mandating various reform preconditions for states, including changing rent control and land ceiling acts, overhauling urban property-tax systems and rationalizing stamp duties, in order to access its development funds.

Our urban consciousness

"You can sense it in the air," Swati tells me, "there is a new concern, both in the government and the private sector around city growth. The local bodies are flush with JNNURM money, and there is a new interest in our urban issues." What may also help in creating new awareness around the state of our cities are private projects—in the form of gated communities. These projects and our emerging SEZs are showcasing themselves as small-scale models of how cities ought to be run.

Right now though, as state governments remain one of the big bottlenecks to urban reform, we are tackling our urban problems through center-funded schemes, and a combination of NGO and civil activism. Across cities, large networks of NGOs and private organizations are providing services from garbage collection to schooling to health services. But while the emerging ecosystem of NGOs and voluntary organizations are filling in some gaps, it is difficult to imagine a coordinated, large-scale and well-funded effort akin to a working city government, and this also fragments the capacities of the urban class to drive change.

My experience in leading the BATF and the eGovernments Foundation bears this out. Organizations like these are able to bring about specific reforms and can sometimes enable dramatic improvements in city infrastructure. But permanent change is difficult without a coherent public voice in urban government. There is really no substitute for powerful, elected city governments with the financial and political wherewithal and accountability in providing infrastructure, managing security and addressing the complaints of urban citizens.

In fact the ability of cities to have a clear, powerful political voice has implications far beyond urban India. It has been fashionable in our cultural commentary to refer to India's cities as places of vice, corruption and the loss of innocence. But cities are and have historically been a powerful catalyst for political reform—it was in Calcutta that political dissent against imperial rule emerged and where an educated middle class first began to struggle against the British. Through their political and social ferment and their crowds, cities have tended to be the primary centers of new ideas and intellectual thought, across science, arts and economics—the Renaissance began in Florence, Venice and Naples, the Industrial Revolution took root in London and the information technology revolution started in Palo Alto.

Leaders such as Dr. B. R. Ambedkar recognized this and found the Indian city liberating after the "sink of localism, the den of iniquity" that was the village. As André Béteille tells me, a big reason caste discrimination in India persisted decade after decade had to do with the kind of resources you owned (or did not) in villages. "The upper castes in villages owned most of the land, and it passed to their sons and stayed in the family," he notes. "Land was economic power, and the upper castes fenced in much of that power through family ownership."

But in urban areas, wealth is flexible and market led, and not limited to land—people can get wealthy in a number of ways, including by running a business, or through occupations from construction work to professional careers. Upward mobility for the backward castes is therefore most tangible in our cities, and it has had a significant impact in caste relations. It also becomes difficult to enforce the silly notions of caste purity and pollution in the forced proximity of city buses and trains. Some of the inane and repressive caste rules prevalent in parts of rural India—for example, that upper caste members only address the lower caste while standing on a higher platform—become especially impossible in a city environment. And it is difficult to enforce caste preferences while hiring in the relatively flexible, high-demand urban labor market. The Dalit activist Chandrabhan Prasad says, "What I tell rural Dalits is to leave the village, get out, go. In the city, life is freer."

The Indian city thus brings with it the promise of liberation, simply because its population is so mongrel and crowded in. It is difficult for a city politician to woo the hodgepodge of urban voters based on caste and community, fragmented and mixed up as they are. There is consequently the hope that our cities can help transform the face of group-based politics in India.

But to enable this, we must empower our cities further. Else the continued marginalization of the city will have the opposite effect—urban anger among communities deprived of resources and an effective democratic voice can give rise to the kind of festering politics that we are now seeing in cities like Bombay. Here, as the poor are deprived of an urban identity that brings them any kind of benefit, they are turning to the markers of religion, community or caste, if these can bring them resources. In fact the rise of extremist parties in Bombay is linked with their efforts in providing medical and educational services to the city's poor. Broken-down urban environments give rise to violence that prowls the narrow streets and by-lanes in overcrowded slums. India's urban slums have, for instance, been a breeding ground for parties such as the Bajrang Dal. Overcrowding and the fight for resources also make city populations especially insular and hostile toward new migrants, as existing resources become even scarcer and more precious. This has contributed to the anger against immigrants in Maharashtra, and policies such as the move toward carrying ID cards in Delhi.

Urban legends

It has taken some time, but I think we can confidently say that India is no longer imagined as an essentially rural country. The city is edging into our political, cultural and economic thought, as it becomes home to more Indians than ever before, and as urban problems are becoming both personal and national issues.

But even as urbanization takes on mainstream appeal, it faces many challenges in execution. The investment required to rectify decades of neglect in the city will run into billions of rupees, which will have to come from both public and private funding. The federal structure will have to be reexamined to give cities more autonomy and taxing powers. Archaic laws will have to be scrapped. Land markets will have to be reformed. Urban planning will require a whole new approach that accounts for sustainability, climate adaptation and public health. Regulations will be required to ensure that the poor get their share of public services. Finally, there is the challenge of scale, as thousands of municipalities will all have to gear up simultaneously and need people, technology and providers of goods and services for the transformation to happen.

It will take courageous reforms to heal our urban landscape. But with the growing realization of how much economic growth depends on cities, and how much we stand to lose from broken city structures, some progress is being made. The shifts in political power for the cities, thanks to the new Delimitation Commission, have heightened our urban awareness. Economic growth has also exposed the popular idea of the "two Indias" for the old wives' tale that it is. In fact as entrepreneurs venture in, this distinction is beginning to get quite fuzzy—economists such as Roopa Purushothaman have shown the strong connections that exist between the rural and urban economy. "A two and a half dollar increase in spending on consumption in urban India," she tells me, "increases rural household incomes by just under one dollar."

Ground truths

The release of the urban voice could be India's biggest strength in meeting the challenge of city reform. Our cities have become a fertile space for the rise of a literate and middle class, who are demanding change both through structures such as NGOs and more confrontational petitions in India's courts. The resulting small triumphs in civil voice—the clampdown on illegal establishments and pollution in Delhi, the use of the Right to Information Act by Shailesh Gandhi in Bombay and the NGO Parivartan (Change) in Delhi—are hints of a new impatience and are harbingers of bigger changes.

We now see funds pouring into the cities through the JNNURM, and our political debates are tinged with the recognition of an emerging, urban India. Manmohan Singh pointed out that the day is not far off when half of India will be in its cities, and that "we need to prepare for that day." The Planning Commission may have referred to urbanization as an "unhealthy process" in the 1970s and 1980s, but in its recent remarks, it referred to city growth as "a natural outcome of the growth of the economy."

The number of states using JNNURM funds in 2007 reveals how the idea of urbanization has caught on across our political parties—they include Gujarat's BJP government, the DMK in Tamil Nadu, the NCP-CP alliance in Maharashtra, the Congress government in Andhra Pradesh, and the CPI(M) in West Bengal. City development is increasingly seen as a "popular" concern, and urban investments are loudly publicized by the ministers—in West Bengal Buddhadeb Bhattacharjee exhorts his ministers to focus on "Bengal shining" by bringing in "integrated development" for the state's cities, and in Tamil Nadu Karunanidhi describes his vision of growth as establishing satellite towns and well-planned cities across the state. Behind these words, there lies a real, tangible shift in the city's place within the Indian landscape. The day is turning, and the sun is rising on the city—the place where, as many of us are beginning to recognize, our biggest successes will take shape.

THE LONG ROADS HOME

THE ECONOMIST AND WRITER Shankar Acharya and I are having lunch at the India International Center in Delhi, among somewhat musty but reassuring surroundings, chipped plates and barely attentive waiters. Shankar hands over his most recent book, a collection of the columns he writes for the *Business Standard*. I read him often, and remark that India's infrastructure crisis has been a favorite topic of his. "Yes," he says, smiling, "I am a killjoy. But I think that India's growth rates have made us perhaps overly cheerful in the face of some obvious weaknesses. And somebody has to say it."

He is right, of course. There is no escaping our infrastructure problems, even here in India's capital city—the Delhi newspapers during my visit have been full of headlines on the city's power outages. A single day that week, as one outraged journalist wrote, had seen "10 periods of 'load-shedding.'"

In fact this particular bit of bureaucratspeak we use, "load-shedding," reveals how a growing economy has found it difficult to look its crisis in the face.* Our bad roads and power cuts are a reminder of our prereform years—it is here that we can most clearly see the evidence of India's old structures,

*As a technical term, "load-shedding" means power cuts to tackle spikes in excess demand. But what India faces is consistent and severe power shortage.

the tattered vestiges of socialism in an emerging free-market economy. As a result India now presents us with a bewildering landscape—of vibrant, private enterprise choking up as it meets crumbling public infrastructure. Our tall, glass-fronted office buildings are powered by private generators, entire neighborhoods rely on private wells for water and shopping complexes, technology parks and well-run housing communities sometimes have little more than dirt roads leading up to their gates.

But it is only in the last decade that infrastructure has become a big concern for our middle class, entrepreneurs and farmers. We are far behind the United States, Europe and China on connecting the country—in the West, people refer to the Internet as the fourth big stage of infrastructure expansion, after the nineteenth-century growth of rail systems, the networking of red copper telephone lines in the early twentieth century, the road expansion in the early and mid-twentieth century, and the dramatic rise of air travel in the 1950s. In India, however, all these infrastructure expansions are only now taking place, and in parallel to one another. We have had a rail network that the British passed down, but we barely expanded it till the 1990s. Our road network was a patchy effort, with more than 80 percent of our roads narrow, unpaved tracks; our teledensity was stagnant at 0.6; and much of the rural country was in darkness, unconnected by power lines.

Only since the late 1990s has there been a spurt of growth, with new investments in infrastructure that cut across rail, road, air, telecom and the Internet. Yashwant Sinha, the finance minister under the NDA government, has remarked that all centuries coexist in India. This is certainly true of our infrastructure landscape, where everything is changing chaotically, and all at once.

All roads lead to the Empire

Imperial India's approach to infrastructure shows up the differences between empires and democracies. For British India, infrastructure meant building roads and rail that focused on colonial requirements, rather than as responses to popular demand.

It was trade with Britain, and the ships leaving India's ports stocked with indigo, tea, wheat and cotton that shaped infrastructure expansion in the early imperial years, and the East India Company's focus was to get these goods moving faster through the country. For instance, the British built the Bombay to Thana rail line in 1853 after the Lancashire mill-owning community lobbied to move the transport of raw cotton from the backs of donkeys to trains. India's ports and port cities rose to promote trade with Britain, and city roads, water supply lines and sewage systems were built mainly where the Empire's officers lived and carried out business.

But after the 1857 revolt, security became British India's core obsession, and it triggered a massive expansion of rail infrastructure.* Rail connectivity grew from zero trains in 1850 to a network spanning close to 10,500 kilometers by 1875. The rail stations around these newly laid tracks were grim, guarded buildings—virtual fortresses with security towers overlooking the stations.[1] The only thing missing were the moats. For British officers, these newly fortified cities and railway stations were protective Edens, against which "the chaos of India beats, outrageous as a sea."[2] But such security imposed quite a strain on the exchequer—the railways were built at a cost of £18,000 per mile, compelling Charles Trevelyan, the then governor of Madras, to complain that India's rail systems were "eating the British out of house and home."

Infrastructure growth in India during this period thus came to emphasize power and control. Even the intricate rail network symbolized power and was compared to the triumphs of other empires, "surpassing the aqueducts of Rome, the pyramids of Egypt, the Great Wall of China, and the . . . mausoleums of the Great Mughals."[3]

Occasionally in later years, infrastructure growth—in terms of irrigation projects and rail connectivity—did happen in response to persisting famines and droughts. But the idea that infrastructure is essential to governing—one that comes naturally to democracies—took some time to arrive in India. One of the rare instances the British attempted such a "popular project" in infrastructure was in the Punjab province when it built extensive canals that

*This view of roads and railways as an investment toward safety—to move people and goods in and out quickly, and avoid being cornered by enemies—has plenty of precedent. The Romans built Britain's major road systems when they had occupied the restive island, and many of these still exist. Another parallel was the Eisenhower-era expansion of roads in the United States during the Cold War, to ensure the rapid rollout of the army in case of an attack at home.

brought 4.5 million hectares under crops from 1885 to 1947.* Elsewhere, infrastructure as popular policy took hold only when the Congress party used local projects as patronage, to win the provincial legislatures. For that matter, connecting rural areas through roads and rail actively went against the colonial interest, since it would have allowed farmers to bypass the state and sell their crops to markets directly. What infrastructure the British put in place here were chains of powerful middlemen—a bureaucratic system of revenue officers, and below them their rural intermediaries, the local zamindars and landlords. These caged the villages and ensured a monopoly of buyers linked to the government.

Much of rural India as a result stayed unconnected throughout the colonial years, and the countryside remained static and unchanging, a world unto itself, isolated from the rest of India. The British government's efforts to counter the growing nationalism of the early twentieth century did trigger some isolated instances of rural infrastructure investment, such as the work of the Willingdon administration, which allocated Rs 10 million for rural infrastructure and exhorted its officers to "know your villages."

Postindependence: Out of focus

"We are making great things," Le Corbusier, the architectural adviser to the Government of Punjab, said of India's infrastructure efforts in 1953. "It flows as the music flows in Bach."

Our great plans for infrastructure immediately before and after independence were seen all over the massive blueprints of the 1927 Jayakar Commission—it stressed the development of a rural road network, and the blueprint led to the Indian Roads Congress in 1930, which released its first road plan in 1943. The ambitious agenda for roads was meant to be carried out over a period of twenty years.

These early, enthusiastic plans, however, soon gathered dust. Instead, between 1950 and 1970, while passenger and goods traffic increased more than thirty-fold, road length went up only five times. The rail network in-

*This project significantly affected the provincial elections—Punjab was the only province where a political party that was sympathetic to the British, the Unionist Party, won when competitive elections were introduced in 1937.

creased at less than half a percent every year in the 1950s, falling to a barely detectable growth of 0.2 percent in the 1960s and 1970s. Well into the 1980s, much of the rail network remained what India had inherited from the British—which excessively focused on Indian ports, barely skimming rural areas. The first major railway project since the British left India, the 750-kilometer Konkan Railway on India's western coast, came up only in the 1990s.

The government was filled with good intentions when it came to infrastructure—the first five-year plan had envisioned a spate of new dams, irrigation projects and steel plants across India. It was, according to Haravu Raj Iyengar, governor of the Reserve Bank of India, a plan for change and rebuilding, "as important as the French, Russian or Chinese Revolutions."

But India's infrastructure vision was top-down, and the government got carried away with trying to prove to the world what India was capable of. The urgency to turn a desperately poor country into a gleaming industrial power had prompted the state to emphasize higher education over primary schools, power plants, steel factories and massive dams over rural roads, and building new cities over reforming the older urban "pestholes."

The result was infrastructure comparable to diamonds in a paper crown. India had islands of triumphant, modern factories that towered over you unexpectedly in the midst of vast rural landscapes. The town of Kalyani, which was planned as one of India's industrial townships, went into slow decline in the absence of highways and roads to network it effectively to cities and ports.[4] "The government had its blind spots—it saw product markets as the main drivers of growth," Jairam Ramesh tells me. "It didn't really consider the gains we could make from connectivity and networks."

The government's growing impoverishment also dampened these plans. Government policy came adrift in the wake of India's financial crises through the 1960s, and the government struggled to meet the bare-boned demands of "food, clothes, housing."

But it is also impossible to ignore how the Congress party's overwhelming, almost suffocating dominance in these years—Myron Weiner once remarked that the fondness among voters for the Congress amounted to "veneration"—affected its infrastructure investments. Spending on bridges, roads and railways is usually a big way for parties to build popular support—they are political investments and great voter-bait. But in the first two decades the Congress party could instead coast on its organizational prowess and its links to the independence movement. This in turn allowed the government to prioritize the projects that appealed to it ideologically, which were mainly more industrial investments and new city development. Infrastructure for villages and rural India in general also suffered from the antimodernity views of some of India's leaders. For instance, Gandhi had viewed British rail systems as responsible for "India's greed." He wrote, "I am not aiming at destroying railways . . . though I would certainly welcome their natural destruction." Gandhi's logic provided a foil to politicians slow at providing their constituents with essential services—water, electricity and roads.

"We've had a nirvana of anarchy in infrastructure," is how Shankar Acharya puts it. "It's where we need the government the most, but where our government has been present the least."

Indira Gandhi in particular killed any pretense of an infrastructure policy in her years as prime minister. In its place, she took up a strategy of intensive, ramped-up subsidies—in food, fuel, electricity, loan waivers—which elbowed out investments in more universal public goods such as hospitals, roads and railways.[5] This has also set off an enduring political tradition in India. Subsidies are always tempting—they guarantee instant payoffs for governments, and this has been especially true since the 1980s, when Indian politics became more turbulent. As the economist Sumir Lal pointed out, India since then has remained in "perpetual election mode, as every year one or more major states face the voters." And infrastructure projects, where political dividends take time to mature, are unsuited for such chaos.

Instead, short-horizon Indian governments have favored short-horizon initiatives, expanding subsidy policies and freebies that have an immediate, big bang in PR, even if the real effect is a whimper. For most governments, investments in infrastructure were anyway a lose-lose option: the often zero tariffs in power and incredibly low user charges for road transport and railways meant that when it came to such projects the more the state built the more it lost. And with governments so unstable, it was likely that the next government would take credit for what you did.

Indira's years as prime minister also left us with another legacy. Her paranoia—both real and imaginary—over threats to her power compelled her to stack the public sector, including infrastructure institutions, with her acolytes.[6] The politicization of infrastructure providers killed the morale of lower administration across the sector; the bureaucracy here was increasingly filled with cynical officers who had one eyebrow cocked and one hand extended out. The writer and bureaucrat S. K. Das quotes the words of Kautilya's *Arthashastra* while describing the ethic of these officers handling public works: "Just as it is not possible not to taste honey . . . when placed on the surface of the tongue, so it is not possible for one dealing with the money of the king not to taste the money in however small a quantity."

Infrastructure policy was thus caught in the maw of bureaucrats and contractors who circled the wagons when it came to executing projects. Das notes that bureaucrats regularly handed over road contracts to contractors unable to execute them, and in terms of "leakage" the funds allocated were sand through fingers. And the dilapidated, delayed projects—roads that were obstacle courses, half-built bridges that soared up like stunted children, water pipelines that were laid down and dug up again—were awarded and re-awarded to different contractors in a game of musical chairs. The looting of raw materials, disappearing funds and bureaucratic apathy meant that flats that the Delhi Development Authority (DDA), the government body meant to manage the city's development, built would crumble a few years after construction. Large-scale rural infrastructure schemes such as the "million wells project" saw across districts the same well being dug in the same spot over and over as the funds flowed in. The Rajiv Gandhi drinking water scheme, after twenty years and billions of rupees spent, had the same percentage of villages as before—twenty—unconnected to drinking water supplies.

The infrastructure shortages that were emerging across the country also made it a prize to be doled out to favored constituencies. Infrastructure bodies as far down as water and road committees for villages and city wards were caught up in these bounty politics. In the rural areas, villagers fought desperately for frugal resources—a water pump or an electricity line—to be installed within the areas their own communities dominated.[7] James Manor has noted that this also led to the rise of "fixers," especially in rural areas, a vast network of middlemen with political ambitions of their own who lobbied on behalf of the villagers with state legislators for favors, such as water and electricity lines and small-scale irrigation projects.

The lay of the land

"When you talk about building highways, canals and rail in a country like India," Vinayak Chatterjee says, "you come up against a big constraint—land." Vinayak heads the consultancy Feedback Ventures Ltd and has years of experience working with the government and private sector on infrastructure issues.

Land has been an especially charged concern in our politics. The 1950s and 1960s land reforms had failed across most of the country with the exception of Kerala and West Bengal. The landowning zamindars were politically powerful, and in most states the loopholes in the legislation had made the reforms largely impotent. At the same time, rent control policies imposed massive restrictions on urban land, taking it off the market. The 1950s controls around land markets only grew worse when Indira introduced land ceilings and limits on the height of buildings in the mid-1970s. These laws, as Vinayak notes, single-handedly exacerbated overcrowding and lack of urban space in India several times over. By the mid-1980s, India had the highest percentage of population in the world unable to afford housing, and a growing number of landless poor were improvising their own houses out of bits of cardboard, tin and plastic on illegal land.

Land shortages and the rapid rise of illegal settlements also dragged proposed infrastructure projects into quarrels over property. The fallout of this was that in 1983 the DDA was receiving land for development that the government had notified for acquisition in 1956. The illegal, mass settlements on public lands gave immense leverage to politicians with a taste and talent for populism. Arjun Singh, the Madhya Pradesh chief minister in the early 1980s, manipulated the politics of illegal housing by handing out "pattas" or land rights to illegal settlements, giving his political image a pro-poor patina. Other governments, such as A. R. Antulay's in Maharashtra in 1991, dived off the opposite end, executing "Operation Eviction," which transported thousands of slum dwellers in trucks and dumped them in places far off from their homes. Such cycles of pandering and eviction from one election to the other have been visible across our cities and towns.

Slow steps

Dr. N. Seshagiri describes the politics of infrastructure in India that emerged by the 1980s as a case of "ten quarreling men holding each other's bits of hair, and no one is willing to either pull or let go." The gridlock brought new public construction to a virtual standstill. By the 1980s the shortfall in infrastructure across India was intense, public-sector enterprises in railways and power were veering close to bankruptcy and the Congress party remarked that these shortages were having "a crippling effect on production in numerous industries."

Some change did begin to occur with the sixth five-year plan in 1980, which was essentially a "power, coal and transport plan."[8] During this period an idea—supported by the success of the green revolution—began to take hold in the government: if the state focused on building the foundations and the infrastructure of the economy, the private sector would take care of growth. The national highways across India were built under this plan, and the government made new investments in the power sector. By the mid-1980s, the Rajiv Gandhi government was straining against the leash to address the infrastructure crisis. But, Dr. Seshagiri tells me, some gaps seemed unbridgeable. "We soon saw the distance that existed between what was needed and what was possible for us." Long-existing holes in roads, railways, power had to be plugged, but wider and bolder reforms that the government needed to enable this were out of bounds for a government limited by capital—in both money and political support. The government ended up doing little in traditional infrastructure sectors such as roads and railways, but took steps to improve connectivity and access in areas such as telecom. With the advent of Sam Pitroda's telephone exchanges, PCO/STD community phone booths became ubiquitous across much of urban India. The computerization of railways was another effort the government made to reform infrastructure indirectly, without upsetting the reigning power equations and the hold of the bureaucracy.

Captain Gopinath, the founder of Air Deccan, India's first low-cost airline, has had a colorful life—after his stint in the army, he lived in a tent for a year on a patch of barren land he was trying to farm on, then tried his hand at growing silkworms, and eventually won awards for his eco-friendly agricultural practices. But he met his match when he went to Delhi to get an aviation license, and walked into a maze of red tape. "Our push toward better infrastructure," he says, "could have been much faster and more intensive. We lost too many hours sitting in Delhi offices waiting for permits, submitting project proposals and getting rejected."

The 1991 reforms have been seen as a silver line for India, one that has separated the old country from the new. But there was no clean break in ideology when it came to India's infrastructure sector. Infrastructure actually touched a new low in the postreform period. The focus during these years was on rapidly expanding the role of private enterprise, including in infrastructure—it was a thirst long denied, and it had to be slaked. In the eighth five-year plan (1992–97), the government drastically cut back its own investments, leaving the glass half empty in the hope that private funds would pour in.[9]

But the money failed to arrive. Even as government spending in roads and ports fell in the late 1990s, businesses remained wary of entering the sector, and private investment in infrastructure hovered at less than 1 percent. At the end of the eighth plan period, the addition to power generation capacity was a little more than half of the target, and India's roads and ports remained in deep disrepair. The fallout of this was evident—even as industry exploded, cities and towns have lagged badly in keeping up with the growing demand for roads and power. Rural India has remained sparsely connected even as new entrepreneurs began to target the rural market. Through the 1990s and 2000s, the delays in highway and flyover constructions alone exceeded the total planned duration of the project. A major flyover project in Bangalore—connecting Koramangala, HAL and Indiranagar, which finally opened in 2007—sat half-completed for more than two years, its iron skeleton exposed and rusting, surrounded by piles of debris, and a half-built road that rose up on pillars and ended mid-air.

Corruption in public works and awarding contracts has played its part here, but another big reason for our dismal showing is that Indian governments have failed to take into account the problems with private investment in public goods. Infrastructure investment has been a roller coaster of policy in most countries, as when Britain nationalized its utilities in the 1940s, but later reversed it and introduced private but regulated systems in the 1970s and 1980s. France has also experimented with private provisions for urban systems, even while it nationalized electricity, telephone and water. In Latin America, private investments since the 1980s have sometimes succeeded, and sometimes failed spectacularly.[10]

Markets do not work as well in infrastructure, and this springs from the nature of public goods—which are "expensive, durable, and immobile."[11] This makes private infrastructure players vulnerable—after all a company cannot recall a road if it proves to be a loss. And because of this, governments may be tempted to break promises with companies by reneging on the terms of public–private partnership or forcing them to lower tariffs.[12]

On the other hand, it is also incredibly easy for private infrastructure companies to become monopolies—since the idea of competing rail or road systems is pretty impractical. This makes both independent regulators and clear, transparent guidelines around public–private partnerships critical pieces in infrastructure reform, both of which were missing in our postreform economy. Their absence led to the unmitigated mess in the private infrastructure projects that were signed in the early 1990s, such as the independent power projects of Enron in Maharashtra and Cogentrix in Karnataka, all of which got mired in problems of transparency, costs and, as one infrastructure expert delicately put it, "ministerial preferences."

Untying the knots

"Sunil Mittal of Bharti Airtel says that people use their mobile phones the most when they are in a traffic jam," one entrepreneur tells me. "So the fact that telecom is far ahead of the rest of India's infrastructure has brought him a lot of revenue!"

The telecom sector, which has emerged as Indian infrastructure's poster boy, has seen quite a transformation in the last decade. The change did not come all at once—the Indian government loosened the strings on telecom policy with some reluctance. "The first policy changes were around mobile telephony in 1993, but they were quite half-hearted," says Rajeev Chandrashekhar, former chairman of BPL Mobile and currently a Member of Parliament. The regulations allowed a limited number of mobile phone operators to do business, but the licenses carved out particular regions for each of them, constraining both scalability and competition. Rajeev notes that despite these restrictions, both Indian and foreign entrepreneurs immediately recognized the sector's promise, and the bidding was fierce. "Everybody and his uncle wanted a telecom license to operate in India." The following years, however, were a hard slog. "We hardly saw any growth for a long time," Rajeev says. "To make things worse, the rupee devalued by over 10 percent in 1995, at a time we were importing all our equipment. Interest rates went through the roof, to 19 percent. We had to charge for even incoming calls, so pretty much no one wanted our mobile services."

The government, focused more on retaining control, had yet to recognize the potential of the sector. People still saw mobile phones as an elite product, something the masses could not afford. The idea that there might be something bigger in the market dawned only in 1995, when a major Indian telecom entrepreneur sold off his license for Rs 5 billion. The size of the sale created a "just a minute" moment for the Indian government. "They realized that they were sitting on a gold mine, a sector which could bring the state a lot of revenue," Rajeev says. The state expanded the market to twenty licenses across the country. The idea of having national operators, however, still did not catch on, and the costs of doing business stayed discouraging. "The inertia was frustrating," Rajeev says. "Our growth came to a dead halt."

It was the 1999 reforms that gave a shot in the arm for telecom—the new policy that the NDA government pushed through broke down the fences, allowing carriers to embark on national coverage and compete across regional circles. It triggered a fever of building—of new transmission towers and the laying of fiber cables across the country. The telecom expenditure per person in rural areas alone was Rs 44 in 1999, up from Rs 14 in 1993. The explosion of private players has led to what has become the most rapid and sustained expansion in teledensity in the world, and we have a network that now covers close to half of India's population.

One critical step in telecom reform was the government's appointment of an independent regulator, the Telecom Regulatory Authority of India (TRAI) in 1997. It clarified the rules of play, made allocation of spectrum more transparent and resolved a key conflict of interest by removing the government from the role of both player and police—of being the operator as well as regulator in the sector. Telecom still faces some policy kinks in the transparency in allocating spectrum to market players and squabbles over regulatory independence. Nonetheless, reforms here are years ahead of other infrastructure sectors. As the Planning Commission adviser Gajendra Haldea notes, the very existence of an independent regulator is a major step that other infrastructure sectors have yet to take. The National Highway Authority of India (NHAI) in roads, the Indian Railways and the Airports Authority of India all operate and regulate the sector, and this tilt in favor of the public competitor has discouraged companies from diving in.

Turning points and missing pieces

But it is only since the late 1990s that the popular demand for better infrastructure became more strident. The rapid growth of markets across the country triggered this, as people across income classes and states attempting to participate in India's surging economy found themselves facing massive bottlenecks in roads, railways and power. "As markets grew, people were clamoring to access them effectively, and angry at the long queues, traffic breakdowns and power failures everywhere," Ramesh Ramanathan tells me. "In the villages, people would call up buyers at the mandi and get an excellent price for their produce, but the lack of a road meant that fruits and vegetables would spoil, and delays hurt their ability to bargain. These issues have created a big spike in demand for roads, telephones and better connectivity from the villages and the rural areas."

In the cities, the rise of the middle class (who for the first time in India were educated as well as increasingly wealthy, engaged consumers) helped sharpen the focus on India's hopelessly dilapidated urban infrastructure. "The consuming class noticed that they could buy a house, but they didn't have sewage or water connections, or garbage disposal systems," Ramesh says. If they bought a car, they had to drive it on terrible roads, and if they chose to walk, they found they could easily fall into an open storm drain or a random hole in the sidewalk that had been gouged open to lay pipes and then forgotten. The people in the city were living in an environment where the front end of private goods had largely fallen into place, while the support infrastructure at the back end—transport, water, power—was in a shambles, full of ominous creaks and missing pieces.

This same demand for infrastructure from two audiences, rural and urban, that rarely echoed each other, gathered steam through the 1990s. It made politicians sit up and take notice. The political support for infrastructure got a boost under the NDA government, whose prime minister, Vajpayee, had a penchant for announcing infrastructure projects with poetic flourishes at Independence Day events. "Vajpayee made infrastructure politically fashionable, something that it had never been before," Vinayak says.

The expansion in infrastructure had another big impetus. There were growing security concerns in India at the time, owing to the sanctions the United Nations had imposed on India following its nuclear tests. The government wanted to minimize the bottlenecks that throttled growth, since the world, they feared, would be much less willing to help out in case of a fiscal or economic crisis. Additionally, transport and power inefficiencies were also a risk in the light of a security threat from Pakistan, a country with which the NDA government had a tense relationship. In this sense, Eisenhower and Vajpayee were statesmen separated by decades and geography, but strategically on the same page.

"Vajpayee saw how infrastructure could be a unifying force," Sudheendra Kulkarni says, "and that is how he pitched it in his speeches." When I meet Sudheendra, I experience that jolt of meeting people you knew in college many years later—of having to face the truth of their aging and yours. His face is still familiar and mostly unchanged, but he is plumper and the thatch of hair I remember is missing. He is an IIT contemporary of mine, who has traveled across the political spectrum in his career—he shaped his early political views with the works of Karl Marx and Lenin but now works with the BJP. He tells me that Vajpayee was fascinated with what infrastructure development could symbolize for the government. The prime minister announced his Golden Quadrilateral project in 1998 and portrayed it as a way to "join the four corners of India" by widening and laying thirteen thousand kilometers of highways in a planned span of fifteen years. The addition to road length since the initiation of the project has been almost equal to what India achieved in the first forty-four years of independence.

"It became Vajpayee's signature style to pump up each major speech with a new infrastructure project," Vinayak says. The government's focus on infrastructure continued with the National Telecom Policy, the Pradhan Mantri Gram Sadak Yojana (the prime minister's village road scheme) to connect villages with rural roads, the "garland of ports" or a "Sagar Mala" to improve port infrastructure, and a scheme for interlinking India's rivers to resolve regional droughts.* A 1997 law also transferred the management of all surface irrigation systems to local farmers, who found themselves included in water users' associations for the first time ever. The Electricity Act—which had

*The Sagar Mala and the river interlinking scheme plans eventually did not get implemented. The sheer buzz that the announcement of these infrastructure projects generated, however, had the Congress party attempting to claim some credit for having thought of the river scheme first, in 1972.

long languished in the Parliamentary Committee, the place where unfavored bills went to die—was finally passed in 2003. This was a landmark for power infrastructure, bringing competition in distribution, issuing standards of performance, including financial penalties payable to customers.

Another key innovation of the NDA government was the highway cess consumers paid on all fuel to fund the national highways. This created a separate revenue stream for the NHAI to build roads. The UPA government used a similar strategy when it levied a cess on air travel to support airport development. The change in political sentiments toward infrastructure has also been obvious across states—a number of state governments, for instance, approved power sector reform, from the AIADMK-led government in Tamil Nadu to Amarinder Singh's government in Punjab. Election promises have moved from the *roti, kapda, makan* (food, clothes, shelter) rhetoric of the 1970s to slogans around infrastructure. Across state elections in Rajasthan and Chhattisgarh, parties have won on infrastructure promises, particularly on what legislators have called the "BSP" promise—*bijli, sadak, pani* (electricity, roads, water).

The demand from voters for better roads and ports has only intensified with the pressures of India's markets—from export-oriented industries, which are growing at annual rates of 20 percent—and with the rise of manufacturing firms that have found their cost competitiveness compromised by delays and costly electricity, water and transport systems.

The emphasis on infrastructure has therefore continued despite the change in power at the center to the rainbow coalition that is the UPA government. Prime Minister Manmohan Singh placed infrastructure among the *saat sutras* or seven aspects essential for growth and, à la Vajpayee, announces major infrastructure projects on Independence Day, such as the Bharat Nirman (renew India) scheme to irrigate 10 million hectares of land and provide electricity to 25 million houses.

An especially telling trend has been the new willingness of different parties to continue the infrastructure schemes of previous governments—as in the Golden Quadrilateral project, which the UPA government embraced as its own. Both the NDA and UPA governments have also attempted to address the delicate issue of land for infrastructure with bills to amend the one-hundred-year-old land acquisition act to ease up land purchases.

Interesting changes have also occurred in the aviation sector under the UPA government, through reforms brought in by the man once known as

Vidarbha city's Beedi King, the civil aviation minister Praful Patel. Praful, always impeccably dressed, his designer sunglasses placed casually on his desk, is brimming with ideas, and spins quite a vision for air travel when I meet him at his office. "Infrastructure growth has happened more by default than by design in our country," he tells me. "We build a flyover only when our roads are completely jammed, and people are agitating for it." In fact, in his first days as the aviation minister, Praful attempted to trigger a similar outpouring of demand for better air infrastructure. "Our private airlines had to get permissions from the government each time they wanted to buy a plane," he says. "I gave each airline in-principle approval to buy up to five hundred aircraft." The surge in airplanes created immense pressures on ground infrastructure and airport capacity—in 2007 India's airports handled ninety million passengers, up from fifteen million in 2004. The rapid growth turned India's airports into a major bottleneck and made them notorious for their crowded lounges and serpentine queues. There were even several cases of cranky, exhausted passengers getting into scuffles with front-line staff over delays. This helped push forward airport reforms. "When airport reform became demand-led," Praful says, "the strikes against these policies were met with little sympathy." The reforms included the revamping of Delhi and Bombay airports, after which they will be able to handle more than twice the passengers they could before—40 million in the Bombay airport and 37 million in Delhi. "We are also modernizing fifty nonmetro airports," Praful tells me, "and we have gone from fifty airports to eighty across the country. My vision is for five hundred airports." The recent rise in ticket prices, however, has probably tempered Praful's hopes. This industry is now seeing a slide in revenues and traffic. High fuel costs and heavy taxes have discouraged fliers—it is a repeat of the pre-1999 telecom approach in how the government has limited the rise of a still fledgling industry.

An important trigger for the sector's early growth was Air Deccan, the budget airline Captain Gopinath launched, which transformed flying in India (at least for a time, before airline and fuel taxes soared) into a reasonable and affordable choice for a growing number of Indians. "Our idea was that planes were not just for the politicians and businessmen," Gopinath tells me. "A great moment for me was when C. K. Prahalad called me from the Delhi airport and told me that he had just seen a group of tribal women carrying mattresses climbing on my flight." The entry of Air Deccan also rapidly expanded the routes that planes could ply—Gopinath, on examining survey maps from the 1930s, found more than 500 abandoned airfields across the country, and some of these have since been developed into airports, such as in the town of Tuticorin. "We are also planning new airports in Navi Mumbai, Pune, Goa and Nagpur," Praful tells me.

In railways as well, the UPA government oversaw a transformation helmed by Laloo Prasad Yadav, the RJD minister who played up his rustic, son-of-the-soil image into a powerful, effective electoral strategy in his state for nearly two decades. The fact that Laloo—a minister who defined the essence of his reform measures as, "The Railways is like a cow, you need to milk it well"—has focused on improving rail infrastructure is a potent sign of its broad appeal today. Sudhir Kumar, secretary to the railways minister, notes that the sector, which was written off as "a debt trap in the terminal stages" in 2001, had nearly doubled its operating margin by 2007 and had profits of Rs 250 billion in 2007–8, even as it has started running more trains and expanded the scope of public–private partnerships. That the Indian Railways—India's oldest infrastructure and the one most deeply rooted in its old systems, way of working and labyrinthine regulations—is adapting to market realities is probably our most telling sign of change.

Gathering steam

I have often heard of China being referred to as a "nation on steroids" thanks to its rapid and dramatic infrastructure growth. While in India it seems a big deal that in just two years we have doubled the share of infrastructure investment in the Indian budget to 4 percent, China spends roughly three times as much, as a percentage of GDP.

Our impromptu, rough-and-tumble economy is groping its way toward better infrastructure in a demand-driven, "grow first, build later" model, in direct contrast to China's slickly top-down, supply-driven approach. However, we are finally beginning to see some glimmers of coherence, as sectors such as telecom, and increasingly road, rail and aviation, see new growth. "Even with the glitches," Vineet Agarwal, CEO of Transport Corporation of India, says, "the new Golden Quadrilateral highways have made a big difference. Where we used to take three days in travel time, we now take one." Vineet, whose father started the Transport Corporation of India in the 1950s out of nothing more than a one-room office and an optimistic company name, has seen his business grow more profitably since 2000 than ever before, thanks to the slow smoothing out of bottlenecks. We can now even claim outright success stories here—such as the Delhi Metro, the best-run mass-transit system in South Asia, executed ahead of schedule and on budget. The metro is serving as a new bar of execution for other mass-transit systems across Indian states, and state ministers with mass-transit systems in the works make it a point to visit it and pose for photo-ops while riding the rails.

That infrastructure has become one of those concerns that is both rural *and* urban has not just made it impossible for politicians to ignore it but is also making the connections between the city and the village far more apparent. It is becoming less fashionable, and it does not work as well politically, to dismiss urban India in favor of the village, and to frame the country's identity as a mainly rural one. It is increasingly obvious that what we need instead are well-connected states that diminish the distance between the two—the vitality of both the city and the village hinges on our infrastructure. Productivity in rural India will only improve with stronger supply chains and multiple ways to connect people, both within rural India and with urban areas. So far, India, and particularly the countryside, has not yet experienced the immense productivity gains that will emerge from the "network effect" of being well connected to markets through telecom, roads and rail. To date, our policy makers have underestimated the impact of building these connections. But as India's fishermen who use mobile phones and farmers who use Internet kiosks have shown, giving people multiple means of connectivity can trigger a level of economic growth that we have so far underplayed.

From how talk around roads, rail and power is changing, it is obvious that the new focus on infrastructure is here to stay. The UPA government stated its plan to raise infrastructure spends to 8 percent of GDP, and the finance minister P. Chidambaram termed this as "simply essential" to meeting India's growth targets. The eleventh plan in particular, in the words of Manmohan Singh, has aimed to be "historic" in its focus on infrastructure. And increasingly, the hope for infrastructure in India resides in partnerships with the private sector, which will provide one fourth of the planned $500 billion in infrastructure investment over the next few years. We are seeing what Montek Singh Ahluwalia calls "private funds for public infrastructure rather than public funds for private infrastructure."

The government's efforts to better define contracting and outsourcing norms have also triggered new public–private partnerships based on the build-operate-transfer (BOT) and build-own-operate-transfer (BOOT) models in roads, railways and airports. These are bringing new efficiency and completion standards for projects. Crucially, the government has also agreed to let market realities decide in issues such as toll rates for roads. The state's budget has also provided for viability gap funding for some projects and waived import duties on building equipment.

Other incentives to change are piling up. Competition among states to attract the private sector has compelled them to look twice at the state of their roads and power. Karnataka, for instance, began ramping up investment in infrastructure when Andhra Pradesh emerged as a rival for new business investment. Narayana Murthy sees such competition as having made a big difference—in 2000 he had found working with the Karnataka government in his role as chairman of the Bangalore International Airport Limited project a deeply fraught affair. "Even though government ownership in the project was 26 percent, they acted like majority partners," he says, "and they were highly suspicious of the private sector." Now, however, he notes, "working with the state on such projects has become much easier."

One major weakness of the states has also, somewhat perversely, become an advantage for infrastructure reform—their precarious fiscal situation. Through the 1990s, many of the largest states were waist deep in red ink and met their expenditures by cycling debts or evading payments altogether. Their finances became so shaky that most, as the economist Steven Wilkinson notes, failed to fund the pensions promised to their retirees (to the point that many filed court cases against the state) and had resorted to borrowing from provident funds.[13]

This meant that these states could not even maintain existing infrastructure. What money they did have to spare they directed toward subsidies—an addiction that grew steadily worse through the 1990s. Financially on the brink, the state governments have been forced to look toward the private sector for infrastructure investment. (This, ironically, has also allowed these governments to keep high-rolling their subsidies.) Private sector participation can have especially large benefits in the sectors where governments are experiencing their worst losses—such as power, where public enterprises are veering toward bankruptcy due to freebies and power tariffs much below their costs.

"The horse before the cart"

"We make our plans and announce our schemes," Montek says, "but the potential of our plans and their real successes have been very different."

Our investments in infrastructure today get plenty of political enthusiasm. The buy-in is present across the political spectrum, as seen in West Bengal's CPI(M) government pushing for the upgrade of the Calcutta airport and announcing a new airport at Durgapur. Even while India's left parties officially opposed airport privatization, Nirupam Sen, West Bengal's commerce and industries minister, said private participation in the state's airports was welcome, adding, "We will not sacrifice modernization at any cost." In Kerala, another left government agreed to a Rs 12 billion loan from the Asian Development Bank to improve the state's urban infrastructure and objected to the center blocking the Chinese from investing in a port project.

But right now, we still face a wide "rhetoric–implementation gap." India is playing catch-up from far afield, and infrastructure is finally getting the funds it needs—but the problems spring up when it is time to build.

The much-celebrated Golden Quadrilateral project, for instance—in many ways the talisman of the new proinfrastructure mind-set—has struggled to get off the ground with the UPA government. Even the basic plan of highways connecting the main cities (called NHDP–I) remains unfinished, and eight years past the deadline, 130 kilometers of roads remain unbuilt. That is a pretty embarrassing result and quite a letdown after the shining promises that both central and state governments made about the project. One challenge, as Vinayak points out, is that we still do not have the basic systems to evaluate our progress. "We don't even know precisely how much we invest in infrastructure," he says. "Even our best numbers are good guesses. How can we tell how high the fever is if we don't have a thermometer?"

The lack of a coherent approach has allowed some infrastructure sectors to surge ahead, often thanks to a well-funded, central scheme supported by a minister passionate about these reforms, such as Laloo Yadav in railways, Praful Patel in aviation and Atal Vajpayee in telecom. Sectors such as roads, power, water and urban transit systems have on the other hand languished for want of champions and are plagued by corruption, bad incentives and weak institutions, which torpedo well-funded schemes. And each infrastructure sector has worn blinkers with regard to the growth of others. As a result, even as port infrastructure expands, a system that coordinates road and rail connectivity between port terminals and cities is absent. So we have islands of reform springing up around our bottlenecks—as Vineet notes, "The new highways allow our trucks to move faster, but at the end of the trip, we still get stuck in a line at the state border for two days."

States are also opting out of the toughest reforms. For instance, the Electricity Act, thanks to the flexibility it gives states on reform implementation, has been at best a ragged tourniquet on our power losses and inefficiencies. States have enacted reforms on billing collection and control, but backed away from metering, supply regulation and tariffs. "Power has been a dismal failure so far," Vinayak tells me, "and it's probably our most worrying bottleneck."

These distances between what the center suggests and the state gets done has created quixotic results. As Vineet says, "We have six-lane highways without a single bypass, forcing interstate trucks to crunch through cities and towns on narrow, crumbling roads." We have just six thousand kilometers of highways, a whisper of asphalt compared to our neighbor's forty thousand kilometers, and speeds even on Indian highways average thirty kilometers an hour. Our mass-transit systems are overcrowded and falling apart. In Bangalore, as a consequence, Infosys spends $5 million a year on transporting our eighteen thousand employees to and from Electronics City. And the salaries of the traffic coordinators along the Hosur road, the highway that connects the campus to the city, are paid by the Electronics City Association.

The lack of independent regulators also continues to give government agencies far too much elbow room. While two thirds of proposed investments in our ports now come from the private sector, these investments are held up by delays on bids. So far, of the stated investment goal of $60 billion over five years, the government has cleared only half. And new private, independent producers of power have to count on deep-in-the-red state electricity boards to pay the bills.

The gaps between our public statements on infrastructure and the real results in both rural and urban India was visible when Karnataka's former chief minister visited a village in May 2007. There, he was presented with the sight of not the original village, but a Potemkin one—with plastic sheets hiding the old buildings, a newly built Western toilet, freshly tarred roads and the family of a farmer who had committed suicide sent away for the day.

Groping toward answers

"Our debate around infrastructure," the economist Ajay Shah tells me, "boils finally down to whether the Indian citizen gets economic 'rights' or 'opportunities.'"

At its heart, this challenge addresses a fundamental choice for our emerging paths to growth. Infrastructure and the lack of it lie at the heart of the inequalities emerging within India's markets—a person living in a village without a road leading out faces a very different kind of access to the Indian economy compared with someone living in the middle of Bombay city's fertile chaos. And his income possibilities fall accordingly.

The complaint of one West Bengal chief minister in the 1980s that "repair workshops were covering up the heart of the city" unwittingly underlined an important fact of Calcutta's potholed roads: that even a bad road creates an opportunity! A road, a railway track, an electricity line and reliable water supply all have a wave of effects much beyond their immediate use. For farmers and entrepreneurs alike, effective infrastructure lowers the cost and entry barriers to participating in markets. Praful says, "Farmers in Kashmir tell me that if they could send their flower harvests into Indian markets by air, it would massively cut their losses from decay, and expand their reach across India." Telecom and road networks also mean the chance for farmers and fishermen to negotiate prices in markets directly and discover market trends as opposed to depending on support price mechanisms and middlemen networks. Better irrigation networks mean not having to rely on a fickle-minded monsoon or free electricity for pumps—and this has a big effect. Sixty-nine percent of people in nonirrigated areas are poor, while in irrigated areas this figure falls to 2 percent. Similarly, a million rupees on roads lifts an estimated 123 people out of poverty. In other words, a million rupees spent on roads can reduce poverty seven times more effectively than the same spends on antipoverty programs.

Unfortunately, when people find themselves without the ability to access the economy, self-educate or self-start through effective infrastructure, nanny states are what become popular. The challenge now of getting infrastructure right comes from this tug-of-war between roads and railways, and our long-entrenched legacy of handouts.

Our existing infrastructure failures make this worse, by keeping old-style subsidies both inevitable and politically attractive, as in Andhra Pradesh in 2004, when in the midst of droughts the Congress chief minister Y. S. Rajasekhara Reddy reversed his predecessor's tentative tariff reforms in the power sector and reintroduced free power to farmers. This was repeated later the same year in Tamil Nadu and Punjab. This model of dole-outs has been highly porous and ineffective—for instance, in Uttar Pradesh's drought-prone areas, people have sold their ration cards for food, and free power means little when farmers face blackouts of more than twenty hours a day. Corruption does not help. One economist described to me how in a village "I found desperately hungry people without 'Below Poverty Line' ration cards, while a man who owned a motorbike had one."

But until our infrastructure is good enough for people to prize it over subsidies, governments will not feel the pressure to get rid of subsidy programs. I believe that this tipping point—when the benefits of accessing markets more effectively outweighs the pluses of sticking with old, broken systems—is approaching fast. The rise of effective infrastructure through the system of public–private partnerships across sectors is a hopeful sign, as is the growing investments by Indian firms into retail networks and supply chains, expanding telecom and Internet networks, and rural financing. As such networks take root in the rural hinterland, we are likely to see big changes in not just what people want, but also in what they are willing to give up.

Today we are seeing people's priorities across economic classes changing. Just a decade ago, the focus was on getting private goods—televisions, scooters, better housing. Now, the focus is on public goods such as infrastructure. What was once a narrow concern among people who owned cars or ran businesses has now become a powerful rallying idea for the "masses."

This is reflected in the change in electoral promises politicians make—and one that has persisted across states and parties. In Andhra Pradesh, Rajasekhara Reddy, who succeeded the reformist Chandrababu Naidu as chief minister in 2006 on a very different, rural platform, continues the government's emphasis on road building, irrigation and communications, and defines Andhra Pradesh's "key USP" for investors as its investments in infrastructure. The Karnataka chief minister pitches state-of-the-art roads and power for smaller towns and districts. In Madhya Pradesh, Shivraj Singh exhorts his bureaucrats to form a "Team Madhya Pradesh" to promote investment in infrastructure, "across our roads, power and telecom." The burgeoning kitty at both the center and the state levels also means more funds for such investment, and the maturing of the public–private partnership model is driving investments into the sector.

As the idea of infrastructure has become both important and urgent, we face as usual plenty of challenges in getting it done. The sectors most intractable to reform will be power, water and fuel, where a culture of subsidized services and an over-bureaucratized public sector has deep roots and a long legacy. And despite emerging models for infrastructure, such as public–private partnership projects, Indian governments are still struggling with how to manage the problems of exclusion that come with public goods being provided by private firms—of denying access to roads, power and water if you cannot pay for it. Road tolls, for instance, restrict the vehicles that can use highways built through such projects, and may require governments to construct smaller, parallel roads that are open access.

Besides tackling these issues, we will have to channel huge amounts of capital into infrastructure, which will require in turn other reforms in our bond and pension markets. Each area of infrastructure, from power to telecom to water, will also need effective regulation. Scarce resources like land and spectrum will have to be equitably and fairly allocated, and with due process.

For now, despite our dreams and schemes, our infrastructure efforts remain chaotic, a struggle every step of the way. An example of this lies in the entrepreneur Ashok Kheny's effort to build a 150-kilometer expressway between Bangalore and Mysore—a project that became mired in land disputes, court cases and bureaucratic fights. More than a decade later, if you travel down the road, you encounter long stretches of a well-built highway that suddenly, after several dozen kilometers, comes to a dead halt, with flat, barren land stretching ahead.

It is a visual shorthand for our country's infrastructure challenge. The people who live around the completed sections of the road call it "beautiful."[14] They wait for the road to be finished, to see where it will take them.

ERASING LINES

Our Emerging Single Market

HARISH HANDE, whenever I run into him, comes across as a man in a hurry, a bit rumpled and restless. The founder and managing director of SELCO, Harish is one of India's many new entrepreneurs and also among the most innovative. His company provides low-cost solar lighting systems to small entrepreneurs and rural business groups. While describing his innovations for cheap lighting, Harish tells me of a group of blanket makers whose productivity went up dramatically thanks to solar lights that let them work on their sewing machines well into the night. As a result he says, "These workers ended up with many more blankets than they could sell. So we found a hospital that needed a regular supply of blankets, and introduced the workers to them."

When I chat with India's new breed of can-do entrepreneurs, I find this a common theme—to be successful, companies must often devise unorthodox solutions to reach and connect people within India's highly fragmented markets. It is an essential part of doing business here.

India has been routinely described as a land deeply fragmented, with divisions within divisions, and I think this description especially suits our markets, which are splintered all over the place—fragmented at the state level thanks to policy differences, and locally because of regulation, weak infrastructure and information networks that still cover only half the country. In fact, while India has managed to sustain a political unity that has defied all expectations, economic unity has been far more difficult for us to achieve. And it is only in this past quarter century that this has begun to change.

No easy choices

India—always difficult to govern and hugely diverse—defied the attempts of its many kings and empires to unify and control the region. Invaders who came in with their swords blazing and conquered parts of India found it to be a slippery possession. Even the powerful Mughal Empire only partly succeeded in running the large territories under its rule, and tended to cede authority to local powers. These local leaders would slowly grow ambitious and start plotting to overthrow the kings. The key threats to the kingdoms in the subcontinent were consequently mostly from within, and it was these petty kingdoms weakened by a thousand internal cuts that would finally fall to the British.

The British in turn resorted to a centralized, authoritarian government with a shallow reach, which formed alliances, as the Mughals had done, with a variety of "local despotisms." Despite this history of centralized rule, there was a strong sense of local roots among Indian leaders, even within the highly nationalist Congress party. For instance, during a visit to the United Kingdom in 1895, the major Congress leaders identified themselves primarily as heads of their respective regional associations.[1] The Indian movements of the period had a strong tradition of decentralized management, and the most prominent politicians emerged first as local and city leaders who thrived on regional support and kept these interests close to heart. Once the imperial government passed the Montagu-Chelmsford Reforms in 1919 allowing representative government in India, these leaders took steps to ensure that voters were represented regionally, and the Congress adopted twenty-one provincial committees based on linguistic divisions.[2]

But as independence became more a reality than a hope, Indian leaders started to favor a strong center. Nehru wrote in 1936, "It is likely that free India may be a Federation, [but] . . . there must be a great deal of unitary control."[3] This vision completely contradicted the constitutional framework the British had pitched for independent India, which had even suggested that states be allowed "to maintain their own armies." A big reason for this change of heart in India was the growing worry over the nation's security—a young state with its independence so freshly minted was jittery of its external and internal threats.[4]

Nehru and his ministers could not ignore how fragile the country they had to govern seemed. The varying interests of the Indian states were pulling them in different directions, with the ones furthest from the center threatening secession. The idea for a centralized state consequently gained the support of key leaders in a March 1948 conference, which had convened in the backdrop of Gandhi's assassination, the events of Partition and "an India out of control." Congress leaders and especially Nehru emphasized that "we are not concerned with any possibility of attack from outside. Our fear is of violence amongst ourselves—of internal conflict."

India's legislators believed that a centrally empowered government would limit this "tendency toward disintegration."[5] A big influence that shaped India's centralized framework was another powerful center—the British India government. "The 1935 Government of India Act had a big impact on our constitution," Dr. Govinda Rao tells me. But this was an act tailored for the colonial government and meant to give the British massive control over the Indian-run provinces. "Constitutional articles such as Article two," Dr. Rao says, "even allowed the center to abolish a state or create a new one—it only had to inform the state that it had done so." The 1935 act thus became a refuge for India's leaders, a restraint on an independent—and perhaps headstrong—young country. Nehru hoped that a strong center would help India weather the challenges of freedom, "however high the winds, or stormy the tempest."

But political issues in India soon muddied this picture. The government's hopes for a powerful center were tamped down somewhat by the passionate regional sentiments that rose across newly independent India. The 1948 Dar Commission had already warned that "Indian nationalism is deeply wedded to its regional languages; Indian patriotism is aggressively attached to its provincial frontiers."[6] Delhi had to give in to the regional passions that lay behind the fiercest, most vehement protests postindependence—the fast unto death in 1952 of the Telugu leader Potti Sriramulu in his demand for a separate state for the Telugu-speaking population, the violent Bombay riots and the clamor in the south, especially Tamil Nadu, against Hindi. This decision to carve out new states based on linguistic boundaries eventually allowed regional parties to emerge as powerful political forces, wielding significant clout in Delhi.

Of the two things the government wanted—political and economic coherence—India effectively managed the former, in part by drinking deep from the nationalist sentiment that prevailed after independence. The aim of economic coherence, however, slipped from its grasp.

A poor, unconnected economy

Both India's early democracy and its growth surprised observers—in the remarkable success of the first and in the disappointment of the second. Even as India came to be rated as one of the few enduring and "continuous" democracies in the world, our governments' inability to create growth became near legendary in its failure. Both resulted from our policy of control.

Dr. Parthasarathi Shome is now the "former" adviser to the finance minister, having left the role in early 2008, but when I met him he was still with the ministry, steeped in its politics and its policies. Despite the changes outside, the North Block and South Block in Delhi, where the major ministries are housed, still keep to their particular culture. It is not just the furnishings, which, while luxurious, are worn around the edges, from the faded carpeting to the paint peeling off its cream walls. When you enter these buildings you are struck by the decades-old Delhi ethos of "support staff"—after you get past the polite security, you are surrounded by a hubbub of assistants carrying handwritten notes from one office to the other (email has yet to make much headway here), liveried men carting trays of teacups and bureaucrats making their way through the corridors with their arms full of files.*

I sip sweet tea in Dr. Shome's office, while he dissects the mind-set that has made it so difficult in recent years to integrate India in an economic sense. "Indian governments believed they could direct economic growth in a top-down model," he says. The focus among India's early governments was on a unified approach to economic policy, and the five-year plans were built around this. The centralization of policy was aided by the Industrial Devel-

*A glance at these files is enough to tell you how set in its ways these offices still are—these are the kind of folders that have loops on either side and threads to pull them closed. While they are old-fashioned and a little inconvenient, I still find them deeply charming.

opment and Regulation Act in 1951, as well as the industrial policy resolution in 1956—which Dr. Shome calls "decisive" in the shift in control to the center.

Directed policy, it was hoped, would enable a coherent economy to emerge out of the ruins of a highly feudal colony, but it ended up doing just the opposite. At independence, India was a low-technology, agricultural market that lacked the unifying effect of industrialization. What we needed to link the different parts of India's economic terrain was industrialization in parallel with infrastructure investment.

But investment in infrastructure was lagging badly, in part due to the lack of funds. The government also made a variety of concessions to local powers and players, which impoverished it and fragmented markets even further—for instance, as the Congress found widespread support among the agrarian elite and the midsize and local landowners, the government refrained from taxing these groups at a time when agriculture contributed to 50 percent of India's economy.[7] The feudal systems also kept these markets fragmented—landowners maintained their power over local communities and small farmers, which hindered rural areas from getting information from and access to outside markets. Demands to impose new limitations on market links became a lobbying cause—pesticide distributors, for example, could successfully plead to the government to prevent farmers from directly contracting purchases with manufacturers. Similarly, Uttar Pradesh's cane reservation regulations restricted sugar cane growers to not just selling only to local mills, but also often tied the farmers to just one mill, allowing local monopolies to flourish and killing off market networks. Much of rural India as a result remained villages that were isolated and apart. And the government, while neither buyer nor seller of the crop, has insisted on setting sugar cane prices, which makes little economic sense.

Specific laws further throttled the growth of wider markets. Dr. Rao notes that laws such as the Essential Commodities Act, which had entered the books to manage war scarcities and famine, survived as they were written long after independence. "The act restricted the movement of agricultural produce across state and even district borders, and limited the amount of extra food a trader could keep in his store backrooms," he says. Agricultural markets imploded to local networks.

There were other problems that thwarted the rise of interstate markets.

The absence of physical infrastructure and cold chains made the movement of goods difficult and that of perishable goods near impossible. While the rail network was the one transport system that could pass through states unhindered, its snail-crawl expansion led to an emphasis on road freight.[8] This gave immense power to state border patrols that held the interstate movement of goods virtually hostage while regulating the traffic of trucks. Some states levied a "path kar" or road tax on the entry of all commercial vehicles, which further complicated interstate movement. Additionally, as the states regulated transportation licenses, each truck carrying goods had its papers checked at the state border. Vineet Agarwal tells me, "The focus on 'checking' trucks itself is a big drain on our costs and the time we spend on roads."

Labyrinths of taxes

"A big reason why states tightened their borders so much in later years," Dr. Rao says, "was because they were struggling for revenue."

The restrictive state border policies had come about in the same way all unnecessary laws did—as "traps for money." At the time of independence, Indian states had ceded a great deal of their tax-levying authority to the center. This made them overly dependent on center–state transfers for revenues—such transfers covered as much as one third of their expenditure. But as the center grew cash strapped in the 1960s, these money transfers began to dry up, and the states were forced to levy their own taxes on their borders and internal markets to stay solvent. Income from interstate taxes eventually amounted to more than 60 percent of the state's revenues. And unable to tax consumption and production directly (as this power belonged to the center), the states also levied various indirect taxes on goods.[9] Every few years, that percentage crept a little higher. By the 1980s, the average indirect tax incidence on goods in India was one of the highest in the world, varying anywhere from 30 percent to 40 percent of their total value.

These taxes that the states imposed on interstate trade directly contradicted the spirit of the Constitution and the early hopes of the Indian government.[10] "The Constitution was quite clear in its preference for a single market," Dr. Shome says. For instance, Article 301 stated, "Trade, commerce and intercourse throughout the territory of India shall be free."* But a related constitutional article that had been written in the war years had empowered Parliament to impose restrictions on this freedom in the "public interest"—a loophole that gave tax-happy legislators plenty of legroom.[11]

The final result was a complicated, hydra-headed tax regime, which would unleash a cascading array of taxes as material moved from state to state into a finished product. The myriad state taxes on goods made interstate transport and production incredibly difficult.

The limitations on interstate trade were an especially big thorn in the flesh for India's central states. The economist Paul Collier has pointed out the critical importance of accessible markets for regions that are landlocked; in Africa, for instance, landlocked countries became trapped in poverty since they were surrounded by equally impoverished countries with high trade barriers, and they had virtually no one to sell to. In contrast, landlocked countries like Switzerland had accessible markets in Italy and Germany, which allowed the country's domestic economy to flourish. This is also borne out by India's landlocked BIMARU states, all of which struggled due to their lack of access to ports, as well as high interstate barriers which limited their access to neighboring markets.

The market forces of supply and demand are usually great unifiers of local and regional markets, as businesses build supply chains and support infrastructure. But the Indian industry faced a market cluttered with limits on production and investment, licensing rules and tax rates that were "progressive with a vengeance"[12]—taxes hovered at around 60 percent for companies in 1970. This discouraged any spending businesses would have made in expanding their networks across the country. "Going through our tax policies was simply mind numbing, they were so hopelessly complicated," Dr. Shome tells me. "There were pages and pages of exemptions, additions, extra levies. For any business, getting it all straight would have been a nightmare."

These strategies of control, which had served the government so well in the political sphere, only crumbled India's economy into local, inefficient

*The Constitution was in fact pretty clear about the need for a common market, adding in Article 286 that "no law of a state shall impose, or authorize the imposition of the tax on the sale or purchase of goods where such sale or purchase takes place (a) outside the state, or (b) in the course of import of goods into, or export of goods out of, the territory of India." But this was also elbowed to the wayside through the Sixth Amendment.

markets. The market also proved slippery and difficult to pin down, and a large, informal economy across labor, land and capital that evaded regulations took root. Rent control and land regulation acts pushed large parts of land into the black market. The flourishing black market for goods, under one estimate, was as much as one third of the legal economy. And tightened labor laws meant that the workforce across industries was mainly made up of unorganized and contract workers.

The vast network of regional restrictions often puzzled—and thwarted—foreign buyers in India. One senior manager of a large, European furniture firm (which is now entering India) told me in passing that this was not his first attempt in doing business here. "I came here in the 1980s looking to source furniture from India. I had found the designs and work the craftsmen did here quite exquisite." But he wanted to buy the wood in Punjab and the brass fittings in Uttar Pradesh and assemble them in Maharashtra. "I found that the logistics for doing it was impossible," he said. "There was simply no reasonable way where I wouldn't be stuck with clearances for weeks each time I wanted to move something. I had to drop the plan."

Our regional imbalances

The Planning Commission in Delhi had come in with a sweeping vision in 1950—to ensure that India's economic growth was "regionally balanced and socially equitable." But in reality, the budget allocations for states from the center have long depended on the states' ability to bargain effectively with the Delhi government and the skill of their local industry to negotiate with the bureaucracy for licenses.[13*] With the rise of coalition governments, such negotiations between governments at the center and states only grew more pronounced—for instance, Andhra Pradesh's state party, the Telugu Desam Party (TDP), had twenty-eight seats within the NDA coalition government, making it the BJP's single largest ally. This gave the TDP enormous bargaining power for benefits and investment for its home state in return for its continued support. Andhra Pradesh as a result had the highest allocations for rural development among states, and also got the biggest share of subsidized schemes—such as the food-

*After 1969, however, distribution of revenues was done on the basis of a consensus formula called the Gadgil formula, decided by the National Development Council (NDC).

for-work program—within the NDA government. Personal interests of ministers have also counted for a lot when it came to receiving funds—the Amethi constituency in Uttar Pradesh, for instance, has prospered due to its Nehru–Gandhi connection and Haryana could snap up the Maruti project thanks to "the personal intervention of Sanjay Gandhi."[14]

Such sops and benefits for specific states created immense opportunities for arbitrage in markets across the country. One bureaucrat described how a 50 percent subsidy on pesticides in Uttar Pradesh meant that a truck carrying a cargo of pesticides from neighboring states would travel back and forth several times with the same load across the border, collecting the subsidy each time. Vineet points out that the free hand for officers at checkpoints means that these regulations remain pretty ineffective, becoming little more than tools for taking a cut and extorting bribes. "Officers at border checkpoints and some truckers share code words to trigger the exchange of cash," he tells me. "This gives contraband a free pass, while legal traffic gets slowed down and stopped due to constant checks."

Other policies created massive problems of regional inequity at a single stroke. The priorities of India's five-year plans—such as their focus on energy and steel production—diverted large investments to states such as Maharashtra and Gujarat. One particularly ill-considered policy was the Freight Equalisation Act, which kept freight costs the same no matter where the goods were transported from. This act was a body blow to India's mineral rich eastern states, and relocated resource markets closer to the port cities. Bad policy is nearly always the result of powerful lobbying, and Dr. Vijay Kelkar notes, "The Freight Equalisation Policy was at the insistence of the industries located in Gujarat and Maharashtra, who found themselves shut out from cheap resources, once import substitution came in." As a result states on our east coast such as West Bengal, which had dominated industrial growth in colonial India, saw their fortunes slide both as a resource center and as an industrial center through the 1960s and 1970s.

A house of cards

The fortunes of the single-market idea in India have been closely tied to the relationships between the governments at the center and the states. Till the mid-1960s, both India's center and state elections were usually nothing more than the routine reelection of the Congress. In fact in the first three general elections to the Lok Sabha, Congress won three in four seats, and it dominated in all the state governments except for the brief gap during 1957–59 in Kerala. But weaknesses began to emerge—spreading, hairline cracks in popular support—in 1967, and the state ministers sensed an opportunity for more power when the Congress lost eight state elections that year. They began to challenge the authority of Indira Gandhi, the new prime minister, and the Tamil Nadu chief minister K. Kamaraj remarked, "No person would be able to fill the void left by Jawaharlal . . . the party would have to function on the basis of collective leadership, collective responsibility and collective approach."[15]

But center–state power equations were not going to change easily. Indira was no pushover, and she saw these suggestions as villainous attempts to undermine her position. She made her objections to this clear—through a rapid centralization of power within the Congress organization that left her state ministers barely hanging on to their chairs.

Indira's focus on control also caused her to pass a series of laws throughout the 1970s that redefined the nature of markets in India. She tightened labor, land and investment regulation, and prioritized smaller companies through laws that essentially favored the bazaar over large-scale industries. But while these policies further undermined a common market for goods, Indira's efforts to access people directly and bypass the state machinery led to policies such as the nationalization of banking and insurance. This quite unexpectedly shaped a streamlined market around services. Thus—in her attempt to build more direct and mass-based political power—Indira created national markets in these sectors. In this sense, services in India operated in a national market, manufacturing in a state-level market and agriculture in local (*mandi*) markets. It is no wonder that the relative growth rates are so different. In fact localized markets in agriculture have strongly discouraged productivity growth—since, as the tailors' dilemma of extra blankets made clear, in a limited localized market, increased productivity only resulted in surplus goods and falling prices.

Additionally, the free movement of people was never restricted in India. The investment-heavy states such as Maharashtra and Gujarat have, for instance, attracted immigrants from across the country, from construction labor to doctors in city hospitals. These easy crossovers of people across state borders have been reflected in India's film industry. Bollywood and regional movies in India have seen many actors and actresses become icons in states outside their own, and who had to initially cram their dialogues, unfamiliar as they were with the state language. Some of the most admired actresses in Hindi films through the 1970s and 1980s, including Rekha, Hema Malini and Sridevi, were Tamilian, while Kushboo Khan, a Muslim girl from Bombay, became such a star in Tamil movies that fans built a temple for her in the town of Thirichirapalli and a popular dish in the state goes by the name "Kushboo idli."

This easy movement for labor has created a national market for both organized and contract labor. This sets India apart from countries such as China, where the Hukou system requires people to have a work permit to move to the cities.*

Breaking borders

India is not alone in our politics shaping the nature of our markets. Across large economies, regions tend to become territorial of their markets, as politicians respond to local interest groups and frame gatekeeper policies that limit access. The rise of a common market is consequently often a gradual one. In Europe, the growth of the common market was an attempt for peace in a region that—with the exception of relatively peaceful years from 1815 to 1914—had seen almost constant war. A move toward the European Common Market in 1957, an agreement first brokered between Belgium, France, Italy, Luxemburg, the Netherlands and West Germany, was part of the effort to end the regional skirmishes that had resulted in a continent full of shifting boundaries and small kingdoms for centuries.

In India our early political equations had, while hindering the movement of goods, unwittingly enabled a national market for services by gradually establishing central institutions that regulated the services sector. Thus, India's Reserve Bank has regulated banking since preindependence days and the Forward Markets Commission has regulated commodities trading since 1953. Other services sectors also had central oversight, including the airlines sector

*Migration has, however, reduced the pressure on low-performing states to grow, as enterprising people simply left—villages across Bihar, Uttar Pradesh and Orissa are full of families without their men, who have left the state to work in Bombay, Delhi and Bangalore and send back money.

under the Airports Authority of India and the media under the information and broadcasting ministry.

More recently, postreform institutions such as the Insurance Regulatory Authority of India (IRAI), the Securities and Exchange Board of India (SEBI) and the Telecom Regulatory Authority of India (TRAI) have emerged as central regulators of India's insurance, stock exchange and telecommunication sectors. The uniformity these institutions have brought to these services is a huge competitive advantage and they are among the fastest-growing sectors in India today.

India has been fairly unique in this seamless services market. Each state in the United States still has its own insurance regulator, which has to give approval for any new insurance products, and this results in varying standards and portability problems across regions. In China, each province has to issue permissions for performing financial services, which has created a complicated system of entry approvals for every region. In Europe a regional streamlining of financial services happened only recently, with the MiFID, Markets in Financial Instruments Directive, and there still exist significant barriers to a single market in other services, including audit and transparency standards, company registration and laws, and rail and air transport.

The rise of the single market in the European Union, however, is an instance of its enormous potential. Not only has it eliminated the tit-for-tat capital and labor policies that debilitated Europe through the 1920s and 1930s, it has also brought in significant efficiencies, with the rise in productivity and trade growth adding half a point on average to the region's GDP every year for the last decade. And despite the "Polish Plumber" fear that came with low income, cheap labor countries such as Poland and Hungary joining the European Union, the free movement of people and goods helped create an estimated 2.5 million new jobs across the continent's otherwise staid labor market.

The worm turns

When it came to the balance of center–state power in India, what had seemed like only mildly threatening shifts in the political landscape in the 1970s became an avalanche by the 1990s. As Sunil Khilnani points out, India's reforms, by releasing the center's grip on economic regulation and giving increased decision-making authority to the states, upended the equations of center–state power, and the relationship between the government in Delhi and the states began to tilt in favor of the states.

The post-1990s rise of markets also created new buzzwords: efficiency and productivity, which gave momentum toward reducing interstate barriers. "Before the reforms, single market debates among Indian analysts and economists alike were pretty rare," Shankar Acharya tells me. Dr. Kelkar concurs: "Until the mid-1990s, we hadn't used the 'single market' phrase in any government document or speech. But by the end of the decade, the idea was everywhere." A definite shift here was seen with the BJP-led NDA government at the center and its highly nationalistic approach to the Indian economy.* For this government, the idea of a common market seemed a natural one.

"Connecting India—both in the physical and economic sense—was a big policy concern for Vajpayee," Sudheendra Kulkarni tells me, and the NDA government began to aim its policies toward removing the many barriers to the growth of a uniform market. Their efforts toward making more markets accessible included the new openness in telecom policy, the Golden Quadrilateral Project and the reforms in ports. And perhaps the most remarkable achievements for Vajpayee's government were its directives to abolish the much-loathed octroi and dismantle administered prices and the middlemen haven that was the Agriculture Produce Marketing Committee (APMC). The government also directed states to get rid of the Urban Land Ceiling Act (ULCA) and appointed the Kelkar committee to work toward a unified tax system.

"One ring to rule them all"

In Allahabad† the confluence of the rivers Ganga, Yamuna and Saraswati is called "Triveni," a site holy for many Hindus. Here, several leaders of Uttar

*In part, this was out of political necessity. The NDA coalition lacked the natural appeal of the Congress party's history, which the Congress had long capitalized on—of leading the independence movement, and with the Nehru–Gandhi family among its senior leadership. The NDA leaders had to resort to broader themes of unity, connectedness and national pride, both in rhetoric and in policy.

†Taking a small detour into Indian mythology—Allahabad, the "City of God," has one of the most charming mixed origins when it comes to its religion. While the Mughal emperor Akbar gave it its present name, Hindus also give this city special religious status, as the place from where Brahma (the First of the Trinity) made his first sacrifice after creating the world.

Pradesh's trading bodies gathered on New Year's Day 2008 to carry out what they called a "buddhi shuddhi" (mind cleansing) fire ceremony. The ceremony, they hoped, would "unite their minds" and help them present a single front while protesting against the implementation of the value-added tax (VAT). It was not going to work. Their state was the last holdout against VAT but implemented the system four days later over protests and strikes.

These traders ought to have had a conversation with Bhoothalingam. He was part of the first Indian government committee that mooted the VAT—in 1968. This obviously did not go far. In the 1980s the Indian government again began testing the waters for tax reforms. This policy if it came to fruit—of bringing the country under one national tax, first through the VAT* and then a goods and services tax (GST)—would allow the idea of the single market in India to truly come of age.

But as Bhoothalingam and others discovered, champions of such tax reforms faced pretty rough political odds from the word go. Indian states have been immensely wary of such tax reforms—it meant losing their tight control over their borders, and reform efforts here were immediately torpedoed.

India's tax reformers learned to take the small wins when and where they could. The first successful step to a national tax in India was the state-level VAT, a convoluted and contested reform that started in 1997 and was negotiated every inch of the way. It involved two central governments, all the state governments with their many, divided loyalties, several enterprising bureaucrats and a couple of holdout states who resisted the reform well into 2007. All in all, it is a tale of a few good men negotiating and maneuvering the reform for the better part of a decade, through the labyrinth of the government and its bureaucracy.

"The NDA government did something really smart," Dr. Shome tells me. "It put the responsibility of the tax reforms directly into the hands of the states." The central finance minister Yashwant Sinha took a step that was a masterstroke in reducing dissent. He appointed the West Bengal finance

*The big advantage of VAT is not just its simplicity—the payoffs in tax revenues are big, because it is very difficult to evade it. The advantage of VAT is that, as Dr. Shome points out, "It only taxes the additional value of your input and labor at each step of production. You can claim tax credits on the rest. But a seller downstream the supply chain can only claim tax credits if the person he bought from does the same." The domino-effect of the tax thus compels people across the chain to disclose their revenue.

minister Asim Dasgupta to head the empowered committee of finance ministers for the VAT, thus making the minister of one of the states more ambivalent to VAT the man in charge of steering the reforms through.

Yashwant Sinha effectively sums up the transformed attitude of the central government in this decade. "Trying to steamroll these policies over the protests of the states would have been a very bad idea," he tells me. "Our approach was instead to build consensus and not rush policies through." He adds, "An MP from our own party representing the traders promised us that blood would flow on the streets if these policies went through. But discussions with each group to address their concerns helped us ensure that these leaders didn't take their arguments—at least too vehemently—into the streets."

Nevertheless, the government did have some advantages here that its predecessors did not. For instance, the only reason it was possible to get the states to the table to negotiate was that they were less dependent on state taxes to stay financially afloat. Many of the economists and policy experts I spoke to admit that state governments earlier had little elbow room for reform. Thanks to the continually strained finances in Delhi, there was not much money coming from the center, and the states depended on indirect taxes for as much as 80 percent of their revenues.

But through the 1990s, direct-tax revenues surged, and 2006 marked the first time direct taxes took more than half of the total tax pie, in a windfall for the government treasuries. The new wealth of the 1990s gave the central governments the leeway to drive structural changes in policy, issuing more transparent guidelines for grants and loans to states and making states more secure about letting go of indirect taxes. The rise of markets were also changing how state governments looked at taxes—the competition between states for private investment through the 1990s had forced them into a race to the bottom in corporate tax sops. It was not a surprise, then, that they were giving the idea of a national tax system a second look.

The big fear for the states about moving toward VAT was that it would reduce their independence, and the center would appropriate their revenue and tax collecting powers. The UPA government took up VAT reforms where the NDA government left off, but the challenge in convincing the states remained. Dr. Shome tells me, "Chidambaram met the resistance from some states against VAT by offering to compensate them for any losses." The finance minister was able to offer the states a comfortable cushion, more than making up for state losses. "Chidambaram pointed out that the fastest growth in tax revenues the states had experienced in the last five years was 12.5 percent," Dr. Shome says, "and he told them that if any state got less than 17.5 percent in tax growth, he would make up the difference."

Dr. Shome adds, "At the meeting with the empowered committee, I was sending him memos saying, stick to a 12.5 percent compensation. But he looked up at the state ministers and offered 17.5 percent!" Chidambaram then passed a paper to Dr. Shome that said, "Partho, sometimes in life, you have to take risks." But without the financial comfort that India's burgeoning economy gave the finance minister, it would have been a risk that he would have been unable to take.

The third path toward a streamlined tax has been through the service tax reforms. The service tax is now collected, as Dr. Shome points out, only at the center level, thanks to a constitutional amendment in 1994. "When the bill for the tax was first introduced, the states didn't recognize the revenue implications, since services hadn't fully taken off," Dr. Shome tells me. "Only when the money started flowing in directly to the center did they realize how much they were missing out, and they've pushed strongly for this reform." This tax is now set to be aligned at the state level.

And thus we have reached closer and closer to the GST. The final step toward the GST system would mean enfolding the CENVAT (the government's tax on manufacturing), the service tax and the VAT into a dual GST at the center and state. "Passing the GST will need a constitutional amendment," Dr. Shome says, "but I am optimistic about our 2010 deadline."

Faster and faster

The shift to a single system in taxes would be enormous in its impact for the Indian single market. It would take us from the status quo of evasions, tax distortions and dodging the taxman to a self-regulated, uniform system. Something fair and all-encompassing like the GST would also eliminate the lobbying across Indian industries for exemptions and local monopolies, which has very effectively constrained the growth of efficient market networks across the country.

With the milk and honey of tax revenues closely linked to the health of their markets, states have also become more concerned with the efficiency and growth that the single market brings. This has compelled them to invest more in infrastructure and in the health of their cities.

And as regulations eased up, market players have brought in remarkable synergies into the rise of a single market. Freeing up the private sector has allowed entrepreneurial energy to work its way through infrastructure barriers and connect markets, thus building innovative, interlinked networks from scratch. For instance, the NSE is fast linking India's disparate and remote capital markets, while the NCDEX is networking agricultural bazaars across the country. This is creating unprecedented market access—as Ravi Kumar, chairman of NCDEX notes, "The commodity exchange means that a farmer has a choice of selling his produce to any of the seven hundred and fifty *mandis* across India." At the same time, models such as the Honey Bee network, which is focused on documenting innovations and new ideas from across rural India, aims, as the founder Anil Gupta tells me, "to tap and interconnect India's knowledge bases." He says, "The vision is to create a national idea network that anyone can access, and which can enable best practices and regional innovations to quickly spread."

Indian firms are building business models that can connect producers to far-flung consumers more effectively than ever before. ICICI Bank, Madhabi Buch tells me, is linking old infrastructure such as post offices with IT, to build networks that eventually reach "even the smallest village." And national chains are emerging in everything from organized retail to agricultural produce, health services and education. India's newer, small companies have been especially ambitious in their all-India approach—Sanjeev Bikchandani, the founder of the jobs site Naukri.com, tells me that the company sees itself as a market unifier, a firm that "ties India's regional labor markets together into one seamless pool." The rise of such national market models is fast establishing single-market standards across sectors, such as the Delhi Public School, which has established a 115-school network with a shared school curriculum across cities and towns as varied as Bangalore, Jammu, Siliguri and Calicut. And K. S. Kohli, CEO of Frankfinn, an airhostess training school, tells me that as his firm—which now has more than a hundred training centers—branches out to smaller towns, girls have begun to pour in from nearby villages. "We are able to tap into a lot of latent talent, thanks to how intricate our network is becoming," he tells me. This single-market vision has also spread to the NGO sector—Madhav Chavan's vision for Pratham is to teach 60 million children across India to read, and Akshaya

Patra wants to cover a million children across India's schools in its meal scheme by 2010.

India's surging national market has also made indirect taxes such as customs and excise duties secondary to direct taxes in government revenues. This has given India the breathing room to slash these levies across sectors and connect its internal markets more seamlessly with the global economy. The rise of such access to the global market has encouraged Indian companies to invest capital into building the supply chains and networks to source and produce across the country. The company Calypso Foods, a growing agricultural exporter, has linked more than 5,000 farmers in the south and 1,000 farmers in the east to its supply chain network. Its founder, Debashish Mitra, tells me, "We are building cold chains to transfer the fruits and vegetables to the markets and ports for exports, and we use mobile phones to communicate with our 'farmer-partners' on fertilizer use, planting patterns and harvesting times."

The new focus on single-market synergies is also driving reform toward national policies and infrastructure around critical sectors such as energy. For example, the freeing up of the distribution market around energy is making a national gas grid possible. Krishna Kumar, chairman of Turbotech, is especially enthused about the infrastructure investments around gas—he tells me that firms such as GAIL, Reliance Industries and the Gujarat State Petroleum Corporation (GSPC) are "building a gas pipeline that will grow from six thousand kilometers to over twenty-four thousand kilometers across India by the end of 2008." India has also benefited from a national oil market governed by a central regulatory policy, with a seamless retail and distribution network across the country. And the Electricity Act of 2003 has envisioned a uniform tariff policy across electricity markets, as well as a single regulatory framework.

Moving cracks

"The Congress party," one of its party workers says to me, "is in holding operation. Our glory days are past." India's early years were marked by political unity but economic fragmentation. Since the 1990s, however, we have moved toward the integration of India's local and regional markets. But in parallel, India is seeing a rapid splintering in political power—even as regions are becoming less distinct economically, they have become more prominent politically. This is the decade of the state party in power.

This shift in fragmentation has immense implications for Indian policy. For a long time, India was a country that Indians experienced in the abstract, and its geographical and economic span was unfamiliar to the large majority in the country. But since reforms, the ubiquity of the print media and television both in the cities and in the villages has made different aspects of India, and its variety of socio-economic classes and communities, far more familiar.

The growing opportunities and economic benefits of a single market have also become powerful incentives for a stronger national consciousness. We have already seen the evidence of this in the rise of the European Union and in the long queue of countries from Croatia to Turkey eager to join it. These countries are willing to endure the long-drawn qualification process for European Union membership for the benefits of job and trade opportunities, and new investment that the region's seamless market will provide.

In India similar, emerging single-market benefits have been critical in tamping down secessionist movements in the country's far corners. Through the 1950s and 1960s, states such as Tamil Nadu, Nagaland, Mizoram and Jammu and Kashmir were economically marginalized and attracted little investment from the center, and their sense of alienation had given immense power to local, messianic movements for independence. Getting negligible benefits from being part of the larger Indian economy, these states felt that they traded in their independence for little in return.

The Tamil Nadu minister C. N. Annadurai had put the case for secessionism well when he spoke in the Rajya Sabha in 1963 on why Indian states such as his own wanted to secede—Tamilians, he noted, were unhappy that they had to depend on Delhi for policies to address their economic backwardness and poverty. "Psychologically," he said, "we would not have so much of solace as we would have if we were to separate." He added, "Today, our riches are plundered and our prosperity sapped." In an effort to weaken such secessionist demands the center amended the Constitution in 1963 to ban "secessionist propaganda and activity."[16] But the rise of the single market—with the growth of national employment opportunities, the fall of interstate market barriers and the rise of internal trade—has been far more effective in curbing these movements. It has given states powerful economic reasons to remain within Indian borders.

"Three Café Coffee Day outlets have opened up in Srinagar," Jairam Ramesh tells me, "and I think attracting such Indian investment and capital is more important than anything else when it comes to discouraging support in these areas for militants." Similarly, many immigrants from the northeast have found jobs in the services sector across urban India, thanks to their fluency in English—many northeast Indian men and women run beauty salons and work in large numbers in Bangalore's BPO sector, in shops across Bombay and in Delhi's hotels and restaurants.

Dr. Nicholas Stern labels this change as India's "internal globalization." He says, "At the most basic level, connecting India's villages to the Indian market is as big a challenge as connecting to the global market—India is a huge country, massive in its opportunities."

Paths to growth

Mahesh Rangarajan underlines the major challenge to the single market today as a political one when he tells me, "We are going through a period of some political chaos. And the impact it will have on single-market reforms is pretty difficult to predict."

The reality is that our national consciousness and economic cohesion are emerging even as our politics shifts toward more local and state leaders. Even as the economic importance of our state borders has begun to fade in the emergence of a single market, the fast-integrating Indian economy faces other, less visible boundaries—of caste and regional groups and their political demands for privileges. The national economic consciousness is coming up hard against these interest groups.

Coalitions, for example, have skewed the political game significantly in the favor of smaller parties, which now possess disproportionate bargaining power at the center, allowing, as Omkar Goswami notes, "the tail to wag the dog, and an emerging politics of compromise across our policies." This also enables them to squeeze more resources from the central government for particular regional interest groups—a tendency that has been clear during our coalition governments, where regional partners extracted sops such as high support prices in wheat and rice for their farmers and specific state development packages.

Such bargaining within coalitions has compelled other governments to install breakers against such powers—as in Germany, where parties are allowed to vote out governments only if they have an alternative, credible coalition they can attach themselves to. But in India this is, for now, wishful thinking. We have to work with the government we have, and it is becoming increasingly clear that the remaining key reforms to an efficient and effective single market lie in the hands of the states, and in the back and forth of negotiation and slow steps toward reform.

At the state level single-market reforms are finally now finding political favor. For instance, states now admit to the need for better connectivity and infrastructure across urban and rural areas. The move toward a more rational tax system also has broad buy-in, especially following the success of VAT, which, on average, doubled the growth in tax revenues for states to 24 percent. Flush with cash, states are eliminating many market-distorting taxes such as octroi. Nevertheless, some specific taxes—such as the state excise tax on alcohol—have been reform-resistant, since these provide substantial revenue; in Tamil Nadu, for instance, revenues from alcohol taxes amounted to more than Rs 85 billion in 2007–8.

Governments are also accepting the gradual move toward organized retail markets and supply chains that link both local and out-of-state producers. In West Bengal, the chief minister is promoting his state as "a logistical hub." In states such as Uttar Pradesh, politicians trumpet industrial and private investments in infrastructure, which is leading, as one minister exulted, to the "unleashing of unlimited potential" of the state.

But state governments are also closer to their local interest groups—the farmers and industry sectors that receive sops and subsidies, and the constituencies eligible for grants. The rise of effective, accessible market networks, as a result, has been tangled in numerous political considerations and has turned some critical reforms toward a single market into nothing more than lip service at the state level. For example, APMC members and *mandi* owners in Uttar Pradesh and West Bengal have stalled the reforms aimed at removing the monopoly of the state marketing committees and enabling contract and direct farming. Even the VAT reforms caused traders to object, as this would amount to their being included in the tax net—forcing, as Dr. Shome notes, "the state finance ministers to promise a benign tax regime toward traders, with no tax raids till they adjusted to the new tax system." Consequently, as Ashutosh Varshney points out, it has been easier to liberalize trade and simplify investment—concerns of the central government—

than it has been to revise labor laws and drive infrastructure reform, which are state subjects. "The reforms around state issues such as education, infrastructure and agriculture are where we now lag the most," Yashwant Sinha concurs.

Central governments have attempted to drive reforms in these "single-market enablers" while working within the boundaries of its now more limited political power. For example, the proportion of tax transfers to the states has steadily increased, while that of grants has declined. Dr. C. Rangarajan, chairman of the twelfth finance commission, notes, "The center has made attempts to link debt relief from the center with fiscal reforms, with states that adopt Fiscal Responsibility Acts receiving substantial debt relief." Such an approach compels states to choose development and reform-oriented expenditure in areas such as infrastructure and market efficiency, instead of throwing freebies at vote banks. The central government has also resorted to specific-purpose transfers that require states to pass certain reforms. This has included centrally driven schemes such as the JNNURM program, where states are required to execute specific reforms in urban governance and financial management before they can access funds.

Cess-funded schemes from the center such as the Golden Quadrilateral Project are also attempting to connect markets better. But the reluctance of states to pass key reforms has also compelled the center to sometimes pass policies that actually undermine the single market—such as the SEZ policy,* which establishes isolated economic zones governed by relaxed labor laws, less regulation and more streamlined supply networks and costs. Other moves, such as the area-based exemption package that Delhi granted to India's "hill states," including the northeast, Uttarkhand and Jammu and Kashmir, exempt businesses in these areas from income tax for five years and from excise duties for ten. These steps are highly retrogressive—such isolated exemptions bypass the gains we would see from an interlinked, efficient national market. It also short-circuits the difficult but necessary debate the states need to have on the merits of reforms in labor, infrastructure and regulation, which is necessary for long-term political buy-in into the single market. And the strategy of exemptions that the central government has resorted to is a death spiral in itself—these policies penalize developed states with better infrastructure and labor quality, and artificially prop up backward regions. The state government

*Full disclosure: Infosys has investments in Indian SEZs.

of Punjab, for instance, has already sued the central government for job and investment losses from capital flight to neighboring tax-exempt Himachal Pradesh.

The execution of the idea of India as a single market has several dimensions. The GST will take the extremely ambitious reform of indirect taxes to a close. With services like banking, telecom, stock exchanges and insurance already a national market, the GST will close the loop on goods. Yet there are still missing pieces to the vision of the single market. Agriculture, for instance, needs reforms that allow the farmer to sell his produce anywhere in any market. This will be aided by the spread of electronic commodity and spot markets. The alignment of stamp duties in property and securities will enable national markets around them. Creating a common market for alcohol will become imperative as ethanol gains acceptance as a biofuel. Land titling systems will create a countrywide market for land. The national electric grid should enable us to buy and sell power anywhere in the country. Octroi will have to be abolished. All "enclave" approaches like area-based excise exemptions, the tax breaks of the SEZs and other such policy detours have to stop. The entire highway network should have one interoperable system for paying tolls. Products and produce should be able to move smoothly between different modes of transport. And national standards and information utilities for drivers' licenses and vehicle registration will ensure electronic exchange of information at state boundaries, reducing time and hassles.

Border crossings

Right now, our consciousness in terms of a single economic and cultural identity is still evolving. But there are signs that both at the regional and at the national level our ideas on our identity might be converging. Jaideep Sahni tells me, "People now travel across India for work and education even from the smaller towns and villages, and they constantly come across people from other states and regions who help break down the stereotypes they hold. Additionally, with Hindi and English as increasingly shared languages, people usually find they are a lot more alike than different."

Even as our politics have fragmented, our economics has become a unifying force, bringing people from all corners of the country together in the cities, connecting them through networks and linking them to the larger, national market. And Indians in every corner are eager to tap into the opportunities such a market presents. But meeting the demand for connectivity and economic cohesion here depends on how fast and well we will be able to execute our goals in primary education, urbanization, infrastructure and single markets.

While people are impatient for improvements on the ground, these reforms have taken years to go from proposal to implementation. "Maharashtra took many years to implement the Urban Land Ceiling Act reforms," Yashwant Sinha points out. "Reforms around the APMC have been extremely slow, and even the policies we successfully passed, such as VAT, took a very long time to be implemented." Ateeq Ahmed notes, "Education schemes such as Sarva Shiksha Abhiyan are still not addressing the roots of our school crisis. We are sidestepping the most difficult reforms for creating teacher incentives and reducing dropouts." Similarly in infrastructure, the knots are not fully unwound, and as a result, as Chidambaram points out, "We are allotting significant funds for roads, but we see enormous delays and expense in constructing every kilometer of them."

Our slowness in implementing these ideas remains our greatest challenge. And our shuffling and backtracking around the reforms here is especially painful to watch considering the speed with which we implemented other policies. We brought in free markets at a single stroke in 1991, incentivized our IT and knowledge industries, and opened up to global trade. Now the economic successes enabled by those policies are coming up short against our slow progress in this second set of ideas, and we cannot stall any longer. Else, the reality of India will remain a strangely bipolar one. We are a country that is now fast growing yet constricted, with entrepreneurs who eye the global market yet find the infrastructure and regulatory barriers to expanding their business into, say, Uttar Pradesh difficult to overcome. Our surging reputation as a knowledge power is threatened by our weak and crumbling primary schools. Our cities struggle for better governance even as they expand outward and millions of people pour in. And in the world's seventh largest country, we seem to be running out of space to grow.

MOVING DEADLINES

PLAY A WAITING GAME with an Indian, and you will always lose. Indians—inured to serpentine queues, traffic jams, foundation stones laid for bridges never built—have long adapted to an economy that moves slowly and that has, in key reforms, struggled over the last mile. India's policy makers and politicians have been great at forming agendas and presenting blueprints, and our five-year plans have been nothing if not exhaustive. Our big weakness has been in execution.

When it came to the goal of attaining universal education, the country has moved its target year time and again, all the way from 1959 to 2010. We will miss it this time as well. In our infrastructure projects, we have regularly faced time overruns that were longer than the initial planned completion time. Several years ago, the government had put up a large green board next to a bridge that was under construction in Bangalore with a date marking the beginning of the project and the planned completion date. Initially, the second figure said 2002. As 2002 came and went, a sticker appeared over it that said 2004. Another sticker finally appeared over the earlier faded one, this time also specifying the month: June 2006. The bridge eventually opened a year later.

We have become used to these moving deadlines across some fundamental reforms. This challenge of implementation we have faced across the economy—in our infrastructure, the growth of our cities, our schools and single-market reforms—has invited many unfavorable comparisons with China. Ministers like Kapil Sibal have been frank about admitting this difference, saying, "We can't [unlike China] build a Pudong overnight." Rather than executing with vision, India, unlike China, executes with crisis—as states are forced into action by market pressures building up. This response-led strategy has not been a good model for growth. It has made chaos the rule in our crumbling cities, our highways that meander into dead ends and mud roads, and in schools with failure rates of 100 percent.

Considering how popular these issues of infrastructure, connectivity, better cities and schools are now among Indian voters, implementing them should have been a no-brainer. But the state here is in a struggle with itself; the government's ability to execute its plans and targets has been overwhelmed by interest groups and a slow bureaucracy, of which Lord Curzon had complained, "Round and round like the . . . revolutions of the earth goes file after file in the bureaucratic daily dance, stately, solemn, sure and slow." Change has been painful, and hard-won.

In essence, while the Indian economy has changed over the past twenty-five years, the state has not. Our public institutions function under the same rules and incentives as they did in 1980 and under standards that date back to colonial India. What is required is a fight to remove long-rooted interest groups and bring about fundamental changes to our governance. This is where our most passionate disagreements now lie.

Part Three

FIGHTING WORDS

Ideas in Battle

IDEAS IN BATTLE

THIS IS WHERE it gets messy.

So far, the debates on our various issues have been fairly straightforward to write about. But we have two kinds of ideas in India now—those we can discuss calmly and somewhat coherently and those where our debates rapidly derail into white-hot, emotional arguments, deeply rooted in ideology and beliefs so long held they have become a matter of faith.

The ideas that the country has become more optimistic about over the last sixty years—demographics, entrepreneurship, the English language, the role of IT, globalization and democracy—have been the foundation for an expanding economy. They have also led to a kind of catharsis—it now finally looks like India has escaped from its sense of persecution and the limitations of its history. This change in our mind-set has in turn led to a growing demand for new ideas on primary education, urbanization, infrastructure and a unified single market. While the new popularity of these latter issues has created pressures for change, we face big challenges in implementing them.

However, the most frustrating part of my experience with Indian policy has been in the ideas where we still have such fundamental disagreements that we simply fail to see the logic of the other side. In areas such as higher education, the role of our markets and labor laws, Indian politicians and voters alike have held some very specific and stubborn beliefs. And this has created a deadlock on arguably the most critical issues—by affecting our ability to balance fairness and competition, meritocracy and egalitarianism, and the included versus the excluded in our economy.

Across the world, there is a familiar line that divides people in terms of our economic opinion, which places us on either the left or the right. But India is far different from most countries when it comes to such partisanship. Our arguments at the left and the right are not really ideological, in part because of how young our economy is. Outside our unions, for instance, there is no large bloc of voters that has formed to demand social security, or are arguing in favor of comprehensive health care, education, energy solutions or infrastructure. India's fragmented caste system has instead redefined partisanship mainly around caste lines. The pet issues of the Indian left and right focus on affirmative action and caste reservation; these have forced the debates on broader reforms in, say, labor education deep into the sidelines.

These appeals to caste and the politics of identity have also hardened people's opinions, with their you're-either-with-us-or-against-us approach. Both within the government and in our advisory committees and task forces, there is now little more than sharp partisanship.

Indian policy makers are also struggling with a popular animus to the idea of more reforms—resistance that has come from the many Indians who have felt shut out of the economic gravy train because they lacked access to the right education, jobs and infrastructure. And in response, reformers in our governments have been increasingly reluctant to come out of the closet and publicly endorse good ideas. Even as India's central government sold off equity stakes in public sector companies to private players, the word "privatization" has been taboo. The NDA government preferred to call the process "disinvestment" and the UPA government has suggested renaming it (in the hope of disemboweling the opposition against it) "listing." This is reminiscent of when computers were brought into banks undercover and labeled ledger posting machines.

The different forms of pushback we are facing across these ideas underline an important truth about developing markets—that the transition from a developing country status to a fully developed one is not automatic, whatever long-term forecasts may assume. The road to a developed country is instead fraught with pitfalls and significant risks that we may backtrack toward populist policies to create "inclusive growth."

This has been true in Brazil and Argentina, which saw years of dramatic growth before flatlining and sliding back into a state-centric approach. During my visits to Latin America, I cannot miss the similarities many of these countries have with India—in our struggles with education, infrastructure, income inequalities and even in the *favelas,* the urban slums that circle its biggest cities. Recently, some countries, including Brazil, have been staging a comeback. While Brazil has a socialist government under President Luiz Lula da Silva, a trade union leader, it has adopted liberal economic policies. When I asked one of the former ministers in his cabinet how Lula managed this balance, he told me it was because "[Lula] treats it like a violin. He holds his voters in his left hand and plays the government in his right hand!" This balancing in itself shows that politics in Brazil is beginning to move beyond destructive partisanship—a place where India has yet to reach.

The best guarantor for sustainable reform is inclusion of people who are now shut out from our markets into the process of development. But we face a catch-22 challenge here, since the present lack of inclusiveness and rising income inequalities have created a bad environment for precisely those ideas that would be their palliative.

This deadlock has led to policy shortcuts and populist measures, especially when elections loom near. Our free markets exist alongside a complicated structure of subsidies, loan waivers, handouts, tax exemptions and government-sponsored jobs and reservations. And people who have watched the economic boom from the sidelines and are skeptical of fundamental change in their favor see these concessions as their best options.

The challenge we now face is in passing these reforms so that growth and development continue unhindered. In this, we confront the paradox of a nation that is blessed with the most talented and diverse entrepreneurs, but which still does not trust the market to deliver on broad-based development. We are struggling with constrictive labor laws even as the economy is rapidly creating more jobs and markets worldwide are eager to recruit India's young people. We are battling growing shortages in higher education as we face a crunch in skilled workers. And our battles for better ideas here require us to vanquish a monster with many heads—of old ideology, deep-rooted caste groups and the many temptations of short-term populism.

It is here that we face a fork in the road.

THE SOUND AND THE FURY

Our Biggest Fights

The quarrels within

"One thing that leaps out at me about India, especially when I compare it to its East Asian neighbors and China," Dr. James Manor tells me, "is that India has seen reforms arrive cautiously, slowly and with limitations."

India is the world's new economic darling—newspapers around the world have editorialized about the country's transformation, and its sixtieth Independence Day celebrations got widespread and unprecedented coverage. Forecasts have predicted that India's twin forces of a free market and a secular state will ensure uninterrupted growth and a steady move toward liberal economic ideas. But I have noticed that people outside the country often sound far surer about where we are headed than Indians themselves. In this, India is a bit like a Monet painting—from a distance, the picture seems clear. It presents an image of an increasingly liberal, outward-looking country that is eager for the opportunities that are now within its grasp. But close up, our reality is less straightforward. Many Indians stay cautious about our economic future and fiercely disagree on fundamental policies.

Our most profound disagreements stem from our history. India has been, more than anything else, a country based on an idea. A disparate group of communities was knit together under the vision of unity and growth that our early governments offered. It was no accident that the "Tryst with Destiny" speech Nehru made in the country's first hour of independence spoke of the "dreams" and "ambition" that would bring Indians together.

But the collapse of the semisocialist vision since the 1980s left Indians bereft. Without the unifying forces of a paternalistic government and its massive five-year plans, India's economic approach has looked a lot less coherent and visionary. And it is a big reason why we have not let go of past ideals easily.

This struggle between our past ideas and our present challenges animates our most divisive arguments—the debate on the role of the government versus markets, in the policies that will work most effectively for education, and the need to create more jobs and better infrastructure. As a result we have not progressed much in these ideas beyond the extravagant yet unspecific promises that our politicians offer time and again, for "better education," "more jobs" and "better roads."

Our hesitation around these urgent issues has meant that India has remained far below its potential in growth, productivity gains and in creating employment, and a large sector of the economy—agriculture—continues to stagnate, skimming the bottom in incomes and dragging down our overall GDP growth.

These yet unanswered questions will determine the path of income growth for individual Indians—whether it remains a narrow, rocky path, difficult to ascend, or a broad, accessible route to economic mobility and wealth. So far, there has been no resolution in sight. And even as we fight over these ideas, Indians, especially the poor, have grown impatient with the slowness of change, which has significantly limited their income opportunities, the future of their children and their access to products and services. While so many see us as the economy that has taken flight, in terms of our most critical reforms, we seem to be flying in circles.

Doublespeak: Our left and right

"It's been difficult for many Indian politicians to let go of our history," Raghuram Rajan tells me. "Many of them remain nostalgic for the idea of the state that dominated our prereform years—as the provider, the *mai-baap*." Raghuram has spent several years outside India in his role as the chief economist of the IMF and his long stints of teaching in U.S. universities. He tells me that every time he returned to India, he was impressed by the changes since the

1980s but was also surprised at the things that have stayed the same—especially the reluctance in our politics to publicly let go of our socialist ideals.

But then, India's quasi-socialist policies were closely intertwined with both the freedom movement and the early hopes of a newly independent country. This lumping together of Indian socialism with our triumphant political years has left us with plenty of emotional baggage and created a weird hall of mirrors in our debates. Our arguments run high on passion, and we linger with the socialist rhetoric that connects us with the hope and idealism of the Nehru years. Our politicians still argue for "swadeshi" principles and publicly decry reforms as "prorich." The Constitution still defines India as a sovereign, democratic, secular and socialist republic. Every political party has to, at least on paper, identify itself as socialist if it wants to contest elections—a rule that was recently challenged in the Supreme Court, which proved to be too queasy to strike it down.

While pointing out the advantage of our slow pace of reforms, Dr. Manor says, "India avoided the massive social dislocation that happened in countries like China, where thousands of people were displaced from land, livelihoods and jobs as the country plunged headlong into capitalism." But the compulsions that slowed down India's reforms have also warped our debates and allowed proponents of both provably good and bad policy to argue as if on a level playing field. Quite disconcertingly, we have seen politicians hang onto ideas that have dismal records in reducing poverty and in creating employment—such as free electricity and job-guarantee schemes—and these are still pitched as more "propoor" than reformist approaches. The sharp partisanship around these issues also drags down the debate to name-calling. For instance, during my time with the National Knowledge Commission, we took a stand on the debates over increasing reservations for backward castes in India's central education institutions. We came out publicly against it, voting 6-2.* Leftist politicians—especially the communists—and academicians descended on us, calling us "elitists," a favorite pejorative. In the same vein, India's reformers have been painted as "capitalist stooges" and "puppets of the IMF."

This inability to argue out our issues without being tagged with such cartoonish labels has allowed a cobweb of bad ideas to persist in our approaches to the economy. In fact, besides the punchy rhetoric, it has been difficult to

*Two members—Dr. André Béteille and Dr. Pratap Bhanu Mehta—eventually resigned when the government decided to go ahead with the new caste quotas.

smoke out the alternative economic positions of ministers opposing reforms. When it comes to their economic beliefs, for instance, the antireform left parties have shifted their stance a great deal over the years in their dominant state, West Bengal. The writer Rajat Ray has noted that when the first left-led government came to power in West Bengal in 1967, one of Jyoti Basu's early moves as transport minister was to nationalize the Calcutta Tramways.* His last decision in 1996, however, was his controversial effort to privatize a state institution, the Great Eastern Hotel.[1] And in 2008, the West Bengal chief minister, Buddhadeb Bhattacharjee—who speaks of Basu as his "political mentor"—has been unapologetic about the need for private investment in the state.

Despite such a marked shift, West Bengal's ruling party has often retreated behind ideological, communist-line rhetoric, especially in its former, scrappy role as supporting partner to the UPA coalition government in Delhi. One issue that roused its opposition was the India–U.S. nuclear deal that Manmohan Singh signed with George Bush in 2008. The resistance was despite the fact that the deal would bring significant energy benefits to India, and without it India's nuclear plants are set to run out of fuel. The left opposed it on the rationale that such a deal with the United States would bring American influence over India's foreign policy, a closeness that would be akin to "dining with Satan." In West Bengal, on the other hand, the left government invites "any investment, be it Tata, Birla or American investment . . . as long as they generate jobs and benefit the state."

Even as India's major left party has moved to the center at least in state policies, the space at the far-left is being filled by more radical strains of communism. One in particular runs a deep shade of red, colored with blood and violence. Since 1967 a grassroots Naxalite armed movement that proclaimed itself disillusioned by India's ruling government as well as by the "ideological sclerosis" of the old left has gained ground in central India. These militants have adopted a Marxist-Leninist ideology, assassinated landowners across India's central states and organized large areas of the region under "village soviets." Over the last few decades, the movement has strengthened across parts of central and southern India, and a "red corridor" runs through here, covering as many as 170 districts across fifteen states.[2]

Somewhat closer to the margins of India's left movement are the "new

*Jyoti Basu was among the most prominent members of India's CPI(M) party since the late 1960s and has been India's longest-serving chief minister—he held that post in successive West Bengal governments from 1977 to 2000.

left" leaders such as Medha Patkar and Aruna Roy, whose beliefs overlap somewhat with the global Green Left movement. These leaders have condemned the rise of "global imperialism" in India—they regard multinational corporations as corrosive—and instead stress the need for community institutions and rule from the grassroots. The new left in India are, however, not linked to a large, popular base, and they have limited themselves to civil activism.

INDIANS HAVE HAD a fondness for colorful characters, both in our movies and our politics. In Indian films, there has always been a special fondness for actors gutsy enough to go totally outré with their outfits and their roles. Rajnikant cleaved bullets with his knife, Govinda made his name with bawdy jokes he delivered while wearing canary yellow suits, red trousers or checked blazers, and Anil Kapoor made the neck bandana and open shirt iconic for an entire unfortunate generation in the 1980s. In politics as well, we have had a thing for leaders who took pains to put on a show—MGR, with his soap-opera personal life and the signature shades that never left his face (even his statue in the Parliament complex has the sunglasses), L. K. Advani, traveling across the country in his "chariot," or Laloo Yadav, as chief minister of Bihar, honing his image of country bumpkin to perfection. Regardless of how effective they were in governing, these men are consummate politicians and campaigners. It is not superficial to say that in politics image defines us a great deal, and India's most prominent champions of reform have been intellectual politicians who would not look out of place in a university: Manmohan Singh, P. Chidambaram, Yashwant Sinha. This might be what Indians have in mind when we complain that our reformers "don't sell their economic arguments to the voters, and remain aloof." "What worries me most," Ajay Shah tells me, "is that many of them don't seem to have the heart to discuss their policies with the people."

After years of reform that cut our poverty rates by more than half, enabled annual growth of more than 6 percent and shaped a path for millions of people to enter the middle class, our reformers remain strangely reluctant to engage in a forceful, public debate on the economy. In fact, it is disconcerting to see the tentativeness of our reformers—whose programs engineered India's economic turnaround—as they spar with their opponents. In public, Manmohan Singh has offered careful, qualified praise for reforms and at one point even expressed concern over the "vulgar display of wealth" in postreform

India. In the UPA government, both Dr. Singh and Chidambaram have pitched programs and budget proposals whose reform agenda has been modest at best and heavily tilted toward sweeteners in subsidies and grants.

One problem is that populism may just sound better while stumping to a crowd. It is a message Indian voters have long become used to, and it is easy for a politician to distill a populist pitch for election. Indira Gandhi did this in style in 1971 when she coasted to a massive electoral win on her pledge to "abolish poverty," and in 2004 in Andhra Pradesh Rajasekhara Reddy rode his promise for "free power for farmers" all the way to victory.

An additional complication for reform-minded politicians is that policies toward more open markets cut out interest groups—it levels the playing field and connections and patronage lose their advantages. The defenders of closed, interest-group economies consequently fight tooth and nail to keep it that way, and governments find it difficult to resist their pull, and their voting clout. The hold of middlemen in India's agriculture sector, for instance, has blocked the rise of open networks in farming, and recent efforts to free the market and allow consumers to make direct purchases from farmers met with outraged protests and *bandhs*. Special interests—rich farmers, labor unions, the fertilizer and sugar industries and the bureaucracy surrounding our public distribution systems—have similarly ensured that subsidy reform is near impossible to push through, and no Indian minister as yet has been, depending on how you look at it, either courageous or foolhardy enough to annoy these lobbies through such policies. So significant is the power of these groups in India that Rajiv Gandhi, in a speech in 1985, publicly decried their "sanctimonious . . . cliques" and "their net of avarice."[3]

Even Manmohan Singh, whom *The Economist* once called "the genuine article" while referring to his role as a reformer, has as prime minister been cautious in promoting reforms. Reform in India has therefore been typically led by crisis or been carried out far away from the limelight by bureaucrats who, with the support of their ministers, quietly launched new initiatives. The bureaucrats who led such initiatives in key sectors—C. B. Bhave with NSDL, Rajiv Chawla with Bhoomi, Dr. Seshagiri and N. Vittal with IT reforms and Sam Pitroda with the early telecom expansion—tell me that the resistance they faced was usually enormous and united across the ideological spectrum. To get things done, these bureaucrats had to be adept, as Ajay Shah notes, "in political maneuvering—building consensus, dangling carrots."

So the 1990s may have been the decade for major reforms, but it was not one driven by the electoral programs of political parties. In fact the word "reform" has remained conspicuously absent from the election manifestos of India's parties—it is as if the phrase "reform" itself will doom campaigns. Instead, the pledges of politicians across the spectrum have stubbornly stuck with the *mai-baap* tradition of expanding subsidies and making clearance-sale promises of free water, electricity, free televisions and even free computers. This has been especially the case since the NDA government put its reform achievements at the forefront of its political message and got voted out in 2004.[4] The last few years also saw dramatic reversals in fortune for India's most prominent politician-reformers, which forced them back to populism—the former chief minister of Andhra Pradesh Chandrababu Naidu, who was once against free handouts, promised voters "free power" in his 2008 campaign.

Our Indian peculiarities—particularly that of caste—have further complicated our reformer–populist and left–right divides. The impact of caste is especially telling in the fact that India has never seen a powerful, mass-based left movement. "That's pretty unusual for a country with our per capita income and our level of poverty," Ashutosh Varshney tells me. The socialism-tinged approach of the 1950s and 1960s had been a top-down one, and India's communist party has been limited to two corners of the country, West Bengal and Kerala.* As Ashutosh says, "Caste has always trumped class" in India.

Even the rightward movement of economic policies in the 1990s that the BJP led was driven by a confluence of extraordinary events—antipathy toward new reservations for backward castes and the anger generated by Ayodhya—which mobilized large groups of "upper caste" Hindus to vote for the party that had draped itself in saffron. This obsessive focus in Indian elections on caste identity has amputated idea-based movements both on the left and on the right, and badly muddled our reform agenda.

A country without a revolution

India's self-consciousness around caste once compelled the French anthropologist Louis Dumont to rather incorrectly classify India and the West into

*The unique role that class and the communist left played in West Bengal was mainly due to the large-scale mobilization of Bengali sharecroppers during the Tebhaga struggles of the early 1940s, with peasants demanding a two-thirds share of their produce. This unusual mass movement left a rare legacy of class-based politics, which has remained unique to the state.

two human species—India, according to him, was *Homo hierarchicus* and the West was *Homo equalis*, or Indians concerned with hierarchy versus the West concerned with equality.[5]

Dumont had ignored the fact that India's hierarchies did have parallels with the West, in the "estates of the realm" that had flourished under Europe's kings until the eighteenth century. Across Europe, it took angry peasant revolutionaries—whose demand for representation fired up when mass literacy met the pamphlets of radical political writers such as Rousseau and Voltaire—who took axes and sticks to castles and enabled an often bloody, violent shift to secular rule.

Dumont had thus missed our real difference: India never had a revolution. India is in fact a significant exception in that it was a huge and poor country that transitioned into democracy without any dramatic internal upheaval and with our feudal structures intact. The British had even strengthened the caste structure in the villages over time and allowed the landed castes legitimacy in their titles of "Rai Bahadur" and "Rai Sahib."[6] India's own reform movements against caste took a backseat in the struggle for independence, as Indian leaders preferred to emphasize a unified resistance against the British. Congress leaders like Rajendra Prasad roundly criticized the more intense class efforts, such as the radical *kisan* movements against landlords. Nehru, too, preferred a peaceable revolution, and wrote that "if class conflict . . . could be avoided or minimised, it was an obvious gain."[7]

India's ancient, hierarchical pecking orders thus remained intact well past independence, and our systems of exclusion were well preserved. Real mass mobilization of the people has instead taken place in India slowly and painfully, decades after the country "officially" became a democracy. And through their early years such movements were often thwarted and repressed—the 1950s and 1960s were the dark ages for Indian secular rule as across states political parties shunted backward castes to the margins and limited their political power. In Bihar the state Congress took great pains in 1963 to prevent a minister of the Kurmi caste from becoming the chief minister.[8]* In Uttar Pradesh, the Congress MLA Sampurnanand stated that "opening the doors to the backward castes . . . will blow up the whole social

*The Kurmis were a backward peasant caste in Bihar, which in the 1990s became a powerful base of support for the Samata ("Social Equality") Party founded by a Kurmi politician, Nitish Kumar. Nitish Kumar won the assembly elections in Bihar in 2005, and became the chief minister.

structure."[9] And when land reforms took place in parts of Uttar Pradesh and Bihar, violence surged against Dalits and backward castes who were allotted land—a trend that continued well into the 1980s and 1990s in north India.

The rapid rise of such caste alliances deeply angered leaders such as Ambedkar, who felt that the government was making a mockery of political rights. He said, "People always keep on saying to me, 'Oh you are the maker of the Constitution.' My answer is I was a hack."

Burdened with this kind of history, political rivalry in India has become interest groups on steroids. The dominance of key castes meant that the government provided even basic public services and economic access selectively, as patronage for specific groups, at the exclusion of other, mostly backward castes. And when backward caste groups finally emerged as prominent political forces, they arrived battle-scarred, resentful and deeply angry.

These battles for control have turned government power into a tool for caste pride, and loyalty to clan and kin.[10] The writer Francine Frankel notes that family and caste loyalty has become a righteous foil that allows parties to justify all kinds of political shenanigans—from capturing voting booths to using hoodlums to intimidate candidates. As a result the other backward castes (OBCs) and Dalit parties that mobilized since the 1960s and 1970s have also focused mainly on getting political power and cornering economic benefits such as government jobs that were long denied them. Charan Singh's rise in Uttar Pradesh, for example, was greatly helped by his demand that 60 percent of government jobs be reserved for sons of cultivators.[11] In Bihar, Karpoori Thakur's 1967 election campaign was based on the slogan "Socialists have given their pledge; the downtrodden get 60 percent."[12]

Indian politics has thus been singularly concerned with what economic rights caste identities can win for you. Caste-based reservations in jobs and education dominate India's debates on how to make our markets more equitable. Dalit and OBC leaders have pointed out that decades of political discrimination have given the "upper" castes superior access to education and capital, and enabled them to dominate the rich classes and take advantage of the country's growing wealth.[13] But the Dalits in rural India have long been landless and were paid for their labor in food, which virtually chained them to the farms they worked in. The incomes of these Dalits have remained at subsistence level, and well more than 80 percent of the community is desperately poor.*

These realities make "fairness" a far more potent and ambiguous word in Indian politics than it first seems. And as a consequence, the battle lines around left–right arguments in India are defined mostly in terms of what is owed to each group according to their caste. The discussion on labor reforms focuses not on bringing jobs to the larger population but reserving them for particular caste groups. In higher education, the issue becomes not of improving quality, but of opening the gates to the OBCs and Dalits. And as Dalits and OBCs have become a powerful voting bloc, this approach to economic rights has received support from across the party spectrum, including reform-minded parties. Today, even the BJP has made support for reservations part of its party manifesto, despite having first come to power in the 1990s on an antireservation platform.[14]

Shut out and angry

"We do not have a single major Dalit entrepreneur in the country," Chandrabhan Prasad tells me, and his remark highlights the big flaw in our attempts to reserve parts of the economy for castes: they are not broad based enough in creating jobs and wealth for backward groups. "Caste quotas in India," Dr. André Béteille tells me, "have encouraged the upward mobility of backward castes through government hiring in administrative jobs, but discouraged it through markets." India's economic resources—property ownership, access to good schools and access to capital—remain unaffected by reservations and reflect age-old caste imbalances, especially in the north and in Uttar Pradesh, Bihar, Orissa, Madhya Pradesh and Rajasthan.† For instance, as Harish Damodaran says, "The Bania [business] caste dominates the

*The perception among the Dalits and OBCs that the upper castes have unfair advantages in markets only gained ground with the rise of the BJP since the 1990s. This party has historically had the support of the "Brahmin–Bania" vote (India's upper and merchant castes), and the BJP-led government's promarket policies confirmed the impression among backward caste leaders that market reforms benefited these groups and no one else.

†In fact, Dr. Béteille calls the reservations debate the "battle of the elites"—the people who benefit most from such policies are the "backward caste middle class," which explains why the issue of excluding the "creamy layer" or richer OBCs from reservation has often sparked massive objections.

moneylenders in north India's villages. This makes it difficult for backward castes and Dalits to take loans to start a business."

Well-known leftist economists and political historians such as Zoya Hasan have defended these reservation policies, calling them "essential to reverse centuries of accumulated discrimination." The same political power that landed and business castes once used to corner patronage, resources and government largesse, they point out, is now being employed by India's backward communities to access the economy. This turnabout, they argue, is about time and only fair.

I can see the need for corrections for groups that were both abused and sidelined. But I think that this is a dangerous road we are on—there are big downsides to the government taking up the rules of a feudal system, only to turn it around so that advantages go the other way. Divvying up economic rights on the basis of caste—and using government-mandated quotas to do it—effectively kills "the civic genius" of a people; it transforms us from a society into partisans of caste and minority. And it truly destroys the secular nature of our institutions by keeping an ancient discriminatory system alive while turning it on its head. Once it sets in, reservation politics is also incredibly difficult to uproot as it becomes the gift that keeps on giving, a case of never-ending hairsplitting. Across states—Tamil Nadu, Uttar Pradesh, Karnataka, Bihar—OBC reservations have devolved into demands for specific shares for "backward," "more backward" and "most backward" castes. In Madhya Pradesh the chief minister Digvijay Singh has pushed for reservations for the economically backward among the privileged castes. All this jockeying for reservations is taking place against the backdrop of a "backward castes" list that has ballooned from 2,400 castes in 1947 to more than 4,000 today. And a corrupt system is no help; one journalist recently managed to procure backward-caste certificates from the government for former prime minister Vajpayee, the general secretary of the CPI(M), Prakash Karat, and the UPA's human resource development minister, Arjun Singh—all of whom are "upper" castes.

Dr. Vijay Kelkar points out that there are better ways to correct years of backwardness, through solutions that ensure affirmative action while looking out for relative skill. "Adding an additional number to the exam scores of OBC and SC/ST students in entrance tests would give them benefits that balance fairness and merit," Dr. Kelkar says. He compares this movement from outright reservations to such "score additions," to our postreform shift from import quotas to tariffs. "Quotas are, in the end, a very crude mechanism for inclusion," he says. Yogendra Yadav has similarly recommended a point-based system where college and job applicants receive additional points for caste backwardness and low incomes, a system that closely parallels affirmative-action schemes in the United States.*

But it is much more difficult to establish such rules than to allow what is now happening—retaining feudal loyalties, only this time in favor of the Dalits and lower castes. And the recent rise in power of OBC parties that are tightly focused on caste pride and loyalty brings to mind George Orwell's warning that a corrupt system will, if unchanged, stay corrupt even if power shifts hands from its tyrants to its past victims—and soon enough, as he wrote, "it's impossible to tell which is which."

This recent upending in caste advantage in India has had some interesting results. In the 1920s and 1930s, the more backward Indian castes attempted to use the annual British census to reclassify themselves as "higher" castes, and would "sanskritize" their practices—turn vegetarian and adopt the holy thread—to gain such status. Today, however, India's caste communities are demanding that they be classified downward, with the Gujjars in Rajasthan and the Pahari people in Kashmir clamoring for the status of a scheduled tribe, and Muslim and Sikh communities requesting OBC classification.

How we navigate the politics of reservation will determine the direction the country takes, since it forms the heart of our left–right divide. Ruchir Sharma, MD of Morgan Stanley for Emerging Markets, points out to me that developing countries, despite their early years of growth, often fail to achieve the GDP per capita levels of developed countries. A major stumbling block for them is usually, he says, their inability to resist the pressures for politically popular but economically disastrous social policies in the wake of rapid growth. Brazil is one such cautionary tale—after an ephemeral burst of growth between 1960 and 1980, its economy sank under the weight of unsustainable redistribution policies, including high taxes on industry and large-scale social programs. The country's economy did not recover for two decades. In India we face a similar test in the choice we make between reservations and reforms.

*While the parliament does not support such cutoffs, the Supreme Court has made moves in this direction. While concurring with the judgment that cleared the OBC quota law, Supreme Court justice Dalvir Bhandari suggested that the cutoff marks for OBC candidates should not be less than ten marks below that of general candidates, "to maintain standards of excellence."

Leaving behind a half-done reform process

"Our weakest communities should ideally be the strongest supporters of reform," Chandrabhan tells me. Truly accessible, open markets after all bring with them powerful caste and class solvents—through education and job creation that is not tied to community identity, and through access to capital and infrastructure that does not depend on family or caste connections.

In just two decades, as Chandrabhan notes, the effects of even limited economic freedoms have been superior to an interventionist state. "Through the 1990s, the growth of the market economy has allowed many Dalits to escape suffocating rural environments," he says. "Dalits who were once bonded laborers can now go to the city and get a job, in construction or in retail. They can educate their children there, make money, buy property. No one can stop them."

But in India the market has not yet been a complete panacea for our problems. The overwhelming demand for reservations for college seats and jobs after all is a response to scarcity, and a sign of the massive weaknesses in our schools and in job creation. The reforms that are left over in these areas are the most urgent ones, which would provide an escape hatch to people who have long been languishing on the margins of the country's economic life.

James Manor tells me that there are certain reforms that will be especially difficult to pass, because they are simply unpopular among the political class. "In every country in the world—and India is no exception—you will see that in sectors such as education, labor markets and local government, interest groups are deeply rooted and have lots of political capital, which makes leaders wary of angering them," he says. In India certain reforms have consequently either failed to fully take off or not been on the radar at all. These include pending reforms in local governance, which would create fairer and more transparent systems to deal with problems of development, security concerns and investments in districts. Similarly, single-market reforms would cut down the dependence of poor farmers on tyrannical middlemen, and better education policies would make quality schools far more accessible.

"The sense I get of how the government is proceeding with these reforms," Dr. Parthasarathi Shome tells me, "is that of a walrus moving from side to side." Market reforms carried out halfway and then abandoned are far more damaging than none at all, since such limited reforms benefit people already positioned to take advantage. My friend and the former president of Mexico Ernesto Zedillo, coming as he does from another developing country, is familiar with the enthusiasm that a fast-growing, emerging economy can generate. He remains a cautious optimist about India, with the caution dominant. He confesses his key worry to me: "You can manage growth in the first decade, and even the second, without reforming completely. But in the longer run, I think half-done reforms give you a terrible result in terms of inequality, growth and political unrest."

In India the reforms that have been carried out so far, while dramatic, have clearly been a first wave—"probusiness" reforms rather than promarket ones. These policies have barely scratched the surface of the deep, pervasive inequality in our society—especially in our cities, where child hawkers sell us *Cosmopolitan* and *Maxim* magazines at traffic signals, ragpickers sort through massive piles of trash and large groups of migrant workers sleep on pavements and in shantytowns while building the highways and the massive offices where our educated middle class work. These men and women live as close as is physically possible to the new dreams of middle-class wealth in India, but in their chances of achieving it, they might as well be living thousands of miles away.

The next phase of reforms, the "promarket" ones, would be critical in actually opening up capital and market resources to people like them, and reducing the pull of interest groups. Better policies in labor and education are crucial here, considering India's incredibly young demographics and its growing army of workers looking for jobs. We need to overhaul our welfare benefits, turning away from subsidized goods like rice and kerosene, and move toward payments and vouchers that we can deliver directly to the poor without the middleman. We also need to clear the decks for more FDI to drive growth in sectors such as insurance and retail. Markets can only lift people out of poverty if these reforms are allowed to create the means for them to escape their circumstances.

But the problem now may be a lack of pressure. "India has become adept at finding our way around our remaining obstacles in policies," Omkar Goswami tells me. This strategy of taking detours around a country still not fully comfortable as an open economy has seeped into our everyday life. In cities we take routes through back roads—sometimes through neighborhoods where the houses hug so close to the median that the "road" may be a mere meter and a half across—to avoid potholes and traffic. We use generators to work through our power failures and pick private and foreign colleges in favor of our dismal, government-funded universities. Even the poor avoid public schools in favor of private ones. And Indian businesses go around labor regulations through both contract and unorganized labor.

But these detours around ineffective and unreformed systems are shaping a growth path for India that is very different from the one we intended. The threats for the Indian economy lie here, in these unswept corners of policy that we now avoid and step around, because they will determine the country India is set to become. We are now speeding toward a situation no one really wants. For instance, while we are, as Dr. C. Rangarajan notes, "approaching full employment," the majority of our labor force is reaching this goal along a path based on low-income, insecure work. As our cities crumble, people are cordoning themselves off in gated housing communities with private supplies of electricity, water and security. And our higher education systems are creating thousands of graduates every year who cannot string a coherent paragraph together—"educated illiterates" whose degrees literally are not worth the paper they were printed on.

"The urgency of now"

The part of the Indian economy that has probably been hit hardest from the lack of consensus on reforms is rural India. Agriculture as well as India's rural businesses lie on the fault line of our worst policies—weak incentives, infrastructure shortages, lack of access to information and education, capital constraints and labor imbalances have hit this sector the hardest. The dynamism that helped transform services and manufacturing in India has yet to take off in agriculture, which has languished under meaningless and largely corrupt subsidies. Constraints in getting reasonable loans have limited the rise of rural entrepreneurs and prevented farmers from expanding their farms and investing in new cropping strategies and technologies. Government price guarantees that encourage farmers across India to grow wheat and rice crops, regardless of soil and climate, have put a ceiling on their incomes, while the resulting overdependence on groundwater and fertilizer has degraded their land.

The future of this flailing sector rests on how we resolve our fundamental divide on future reform policies. Right now, we disagree vehemently on steps such as replacing subsidies with market-oriented incentives. For instance, in June 2008, even as the state-set price on fuel was costing India's state-owned oil firms—Indian Oil Corporation Ltd, Hindustan Petroleum Corporation Ltd and Bharat Petroleum Corporation Ltd—losses of Rs 6.4 billion a day, and with oil rationing a real possibility, members of the left opposed hikes in oil prices and opted out of the UPA government's coordination committee before the price was hiked. Such opposition hardens when agricultural incentives are at stake. When it comes to incentives for rural India, our budgets have prioritized free electricity and grain giveaways over better infrastructure, supply chains or sources for loans. A large part of rural India still lacks even a dirt road leading out of the village. And though linkages to commodity markets such as the NCDEX and the MCX are enabling farmers to derisk their farming strategies and access market information on future prices for crops, the government has taken steps to ban futures trading in several commodities.

A big challenge here is that the left and the right in India are looking at the same picture of a crumbling agriculture sector and are seeing entirely different things. Left economists such as Prabhat Patnaik blame inflation on the "rises in commodity prices." Reformers argue that rising food costs can be far better addressed by improving the efficiency of the supply chain between farmer and consumer, through, say, better roads and cold chains for produce, so that efficiency allows the producer to get higher prices and the consumer to buy at lower costs. These are not small gains—right now spoilage during transportation causes Indian farmers to lose one third of their produce.

But there is a lack of faith among the left in the ability of markets to decide price. The economist Abhijit Sen—who sits on the Planning Commission and is probably Montek Singh Ahluwalia's ideological opposite—stresses that the government has to offer minimum support prices to farmers as "the market continuously fails" to provide for them. Basically, what India's left politicians and economists support are price controls and subsidies, as well as bans on "speculative trading" in commodity indexes.

There is also a "policy schizophrenia" present in agriculture that has left reforms in limbo. Obviously, the best way to improve the lot of our farmers is to allow them to get better prices for their produce. But that creates higher costs for Indian consumers and also inflation. In a country where there are many poor people and where food eats up a large part of their income, such inflation can lead to deprivation and unrest, and usually results in incumbent governments losing elections handily. So what is good for the farmer is not good for the consumer and vice versa, and this means that our governments are constantly tinkering with their agripolicies to meet irreconcilable goals. For instance, the state procures wheat and rice and then distributes it to the poor, and in that process they have built the mammoth, porous and notorious public distribution system (PDS).

The state also sets the procurement price for key crops; and if market prices exceed that, the government prevents farmers from getting the best possible deal by passing ad hoc measures such as banning exports or prohibiting farmers from selling to private buyers.

But running interference in this way invariably backfires. When market prices rose above price controls—as they did in the 1950s and 1960s and again in 2007—it triggered large-scale shortages across the country, as traders hoarded inventory, told desperate customers that they were "out of stock" and sold grain in the black market at stratospheric rates. This has happened in India across subsidized and price-controlled products from kerosene to petrol to wheat. And the distribution system for subsidies is itself hopelessly broken. "The losses in the public distribution system across subsidized products," Chidambaram tells me, "are at thirty-eight percent."

When money does not disappear down the rabbit holes of the bureaucratic distribution system, it is badly targeted. It is difficult to see, for instance, how a landless laborer in rural India gains from a power or fertilizer subsidy—these handouts are inevitably a sop for the well-to-do farmers. It is the owners of India's medium and large farms who own a third of our tubewells and gain most from our power freebies. And besides, when such subsidies are guaranteed, like in water and power, they ensure that the utilities that deliver them become financially crippled.

What we need to do for rural India and agriculture is, first and foremost, carry out the "great unwind" of subsidies and move to a direct-benefit system. Right now, the subsidies on food, fertilizer, fuel and power are mounting by the day. "In 2007," Chidambaram tells me, "we spent more than ten trillion rupees on subsidies alone." That's Rs 10,000,000,000,000 funding some very bad ideas. And the bill will most likely be much higher in 2008 from rising fuel costs.

We ought to pause for a moment and consider what Rs 10 trillion could do for welfare in India if put to effective use, rather than being lost to "leakage" or given to the wrong people. A government willing to transform these payouts into direct benefits—cash payments, vouchers and lifeline subsidies—would see an impact that would be the Indian equivalent of the New Deal. It would create massive new wealth and opportunity for the middle and working class, and would give the party or coalition that implements it an endurance in politics that India has not seen since 1977.

Building such a direct and transparent benefit system is not difficult (besides getting the political buy-in we need, of course). One way to do it is to put money into citizen accounts for the poor, either as a negative income tax or as a copayment within a universal insurance system. This could use accounts linked to smart ID cards, which would cut out the clutter and chaos of the middlemen. A second approach that could accompany direct payments would be to give eligible citizens below a certain income level a noncash voucher that can only be used for specific purchases—food, education, health, fertilizer, fuel—with the vouchers valid among both private and public companies. These would not completely eliminate subsidies—a direct-benefits approach would also include a "lifeline" or a certain amount of guaranteed supply of electricity, gas and water, above which you would have to pay.*

These steps would hollow the subsidy system from the inside out. Once more effective and direct welfare mechanisms are in place, the kind that actually help people participate in the economy, the poor would be, I suspect, glad to see the back of a system that has long exploited them, and been more effective as election-day voter bait than as an antipoverty mechanism. As one farmer in Punjab once said, tellingly, of their extreme dependence on the state's price guarantees and the whims of local bureaucrats, "It is blood and toil for six months, and we cannot afford to annoy the officials."[15]

The shift to direct benefits would be a fundamental change and probably has its closest parallel in what happened with our tax revenues. Two decades ago, the individual citizen was barely represented in the government's revenues—direct taxes accounted for just 10 percent of tax collections. But in 2007, money from direct taxes crossed indirect tax collections for the first

*It has to be said, however, that cutting subsidies in electricity and water also requires making these public services more reliable and efficient in parallel, so that people are willing to pay for them. Farmers would be willing to pay for power if this assured them a regular and stable supply rather than the sixteen-hour power outages they now face.

time ever, and I believe that over the next decade the direct tax share will rise to 90 percent, a complete flip from 1980. This marks a radical change in how the government views its citizens: they have become crucial, individual contributors to the government finances. It ought to acknowledge this fact when it comes to spending money on its citizens as well: the move from indirect subsidies to direct benefits accepts that our voters are not undifferentiated "masses" with a single demand, such as for cheaper rice or kerosene. Rather, we are individual citizens who have unique needs, and the government has to cater to personal choice by giving people direct cash benefits to do what they choose with it. Such an approach also allows us to target welfare to make it more effective—providing direct payments, for example, to the women in poor families, who are more dependable when it comes to spending money on education, health and food.

Top-down or bottom-up?

In the decades before 1991, we grew used to comparisons of the country as "the mother" and its citizens as "her children." Such rhetoric and policies created a passive people who were empowered to do little and were hedged on all sides by an encroaching state. In the end, this did little to draw Indians out of their poverty.

But as Ruchir tells me, "India is unusual, different from any economy I see in how it votes out governments whether they reform or not, and whether they create growth or not." We are in an environment where politicians are still tripping over one another to promise freebies and government protections, and parties across the spectrum now jockey to support reservations in jobs and education. These strategies capitalize most on the fears of reformers, on their ability to fight and win in public opinion and with the voters. The treatment of reformers through the 1990s has made them nervous, and not without reason. "Now, politicians freely blame all our current problems on reforms," Yashwant Sinha tells me. "If prices go up or a drought happens, reforms are somehow the culprit!"

But it is possible that economic reform may not be as unpopular as our politicians think. More recently, populism's appeal has begun to show some cracks, as in Gujarat where Narendra Modi mocked Congress's electoral promise of free electricity in front of voters—to loud applause. Despite all his baggage and his unappealing Hindutva triumphalism, Modi may have been the first politician to demonstrate to his voters how markets could work better than any corrupt subsidy system in accessing electricity, water and roads. Before this, reformer politicians have not had a very good track record in implementing direct, market-aided schemes for the poor. Chandrababu Naidu, despite his reformer credentials, was seen as ignoring the problems of the farmers and the droughts across rural Andhra Pradesh—his opponent Rajasekhara Reddy campaigned and won the 2004 elections on the charge that under Naidu the state had become "Runa Andhra" (debt-burdened Andhra).

Similarly, the NDA government may have contributed to India turning into "an economic powerhouse," but it focused too little on the most critical reforms in water, welfare subsidies, district roads, education and labor—the policies that would have brought widespread, tangible results. "What I realized," Naidu tells me, "is that we have to consciously frame our reform agenda as an inclusive one. Right now, people consider our policies to be the opposite."

But there are signs that these attitudes toward reforms might be changing and that the populist politician has to wake up and smell the market. "It's not about reservations," Atul Kohli tells me. "The poor in India basically want to be treated at par in the opportunities they have for themselves and their children in education and employment, and they have been denied that for a long time."

Indian voters are well versed in the problems of government and know from experience how little has changed even with decades under the "benevolent" state.* They would readily embrace alternatives that show results. So far that has not happened, and since the 1980s voters have shown their unhappiness time and again by regularly voting the sitting party out and the opposition in. And the only time this trend broke was in 2007, when they voted the reformist chief minister in Gujarat back into office. As Madhav Chavan says, "When markets are effective, workers always choose them over guaranteed benefits." We see the proof of this everywhere we look—when

*Even the National Rural Employment Guarantee Act (NREGA), the much-touted employment guarantee scheme that the present government has pushed instead of labor reforms, is marked by all the weaknesses of the Indian state. One report recently noted that the target of a hundred families receiving jobs has been met in very few districts—and in some districts the scheme has not reached a single poor family.

even the poorest people opt for private schools and hospitals and choose employment in the private sector, over a government job.

A study on democracy by the State of Democracy in South Asia team has shown shifts in the Indian idea of prosperity since reforms, and that more Indians are happier about their economic situation compared with what they had before. Most Indians now also pay attention to the overall economic health of the country (rather than of just their household) and demand better solutions from their leaders. Even in the poorest states, this change, and the impact it has had on growth, is visible. "In the past three years, Orissa has seen GDP growth that is consistently above the Indian average, thanks mainly to new private investment," Jay Panda tells me. In Bihar and Chhattisgarh an economic turnaround—even if it is a nascent one—has also begun, with private investment picking up and unemployment in the states slowly falling.

It is not enough, however, for our reforms to work backstage. There is a truism that all that is needed for bad ideas to succeed is for enough good men to remain silent. We must publicly champion these policies and point out their successes—how, for example, the surging taxes from Indian industry are funding schemes like our primary education and health programs and how entrepreneurs in rural areas, such as Sriram Raghavan with his IT kiosks and Harish Hande of SELCO, are creating new job opportunities and access to valuable new products and services.

Chidambaram says, "Reforms that help us build a road to a village might bring the rural poor some benefits, but they are largely intangible. It's what we've completely held back on—reforms in welfare subsidies, education and jobs—that would make the biggest difference in the lives of voters." After all, policies that would enable a thousand successful and celebrated Dalit entrepreneurs would do far more to make economic growth seem more inclusive than reservation laws and trillions spent on subsidies.

This means that our reformer politicians cannot dodge and weave when it comes to support for these issues—the only way to sustain what reforms have won us so far is to implement these last and most contested policies head-on and support them openly. I think that the consequences of this would make it quickly clear that the reforms that attract such knee-jerk opposition are the very ones that bring the poor significant economic freedoms and power, the kind that would allow them to choose better schools, access welfare more effectively and have broader opportunities in both education and jobs. "There were nationwide strikes against my proposal to allow FDI in insurance," former finance minister Yashwant Sinha tells me, "but in the years since we allowed foreign investment, the insurance industry has created a million new jobs, and the market is filled with more insurance options for the Indian consumer than ever before. I now ask the people who led those protests—why did you do it? Don't you see how well the new policies worked?"

In favor, always, of more freedom

At the time of independence, India's leaders were clearly ahead of the people. The creation of a new, secular democracy with universal suffrage, anchored by the Indian Constitution, was a leap of faith the government took with an uncomprehending, yet trusting country. Sixty years on, however, it seems that the roles have reversed. The people have gained more confidence and are reaching for the stars. India's leaders, however, seem timorous—our politics has become more tactical than visionary and, as Montek points out, what we now see among our politicians is "a strong consensus for weak reforms."

Much of this opposition to reform has come from the loss of India's early economic vision, but our reformers now have the opportunity to frame an inspiring new one, tailored around a dream of economic mobility and opportunity. As Dr. Manor tells me, "The sophistication of 'illiterate' Indians is very impressive on policy, and they know what works and what doesn't."

The fear among our politicians of engaging the electorate beyond populist, please-all economic policies is probably because an earlier generation of leaders—Nehru's contemporaries—had dismissed the powers of India's divisions in religion, caste and regional loyalties. Their failures in surpassing these divides have made us both cautious and overwary, erring too much in the opposite direction, thinking solely in terms of interest groups and vote banks.

Our governments have also inherited to some extent our early leaders' distrust of the voter—who worried about the "massive ignorance"[16] of the Indian populace and treated them like errant children. Indian politicians have believed for too long that it is only the crudest pandering that will work with voters. The tragedy is that this has forced us to stall on those reforms that are finally the most inclusive of them all—in labor, education, social security—which could change the lives of Indians in the most fundamental, transformational ways. Once we do take the risk, the results may in all likelihood prompt us to wonder what we were so afraid of.

JOSTLING FOR JOBS

"THE HORATIO ALGER STORY," Raghuram Rajan tells me, "is not yet part of India's popular imagination. For me, that would be a sign that the sentiment around India has truly transformed." Raghuram is talking about the kind of stories that could be found in Alger's dime novels. They typically centered on one theme—of extremely poor young boys who struggle upward to build highly successful lives. This was the American dream distilled down to a simple tale of around a hundred pages, written by Alger during the heat of the country's industrialization, at a time when manufacturing had helped create a mass base of middle-class, blue-collar workers. This part of the economic story has been the missing piece in India's success, and it has made the country's mood, despite our growth, a bipolar one.

India's growth has taken off against the backdrop of a surging global knowledge market, where workers are becoming both more mobile and highly prized. The country has looked wonderfully placed to take advantage of this, and for global and Indian companies looking for large numbers of high-quality and affordable talent, India seems to have it all. I have had the opportunity to watch this up close—the bright, young engineers and analysts across our Infosys campuses have over the last two decades drawn the world's capital, attention and admiration.

Thanks to India's pool of skilled graduates, we have so far nailed the services story—a pretty rare win for a developing country. Usually, low-income, developing countries have lacked the skilled labor to build strong services-based industries, especially in the knowledge sector, and India has proved to be the astonishing exception. But when it comes to the industry that the rest of the developing world has excelled in, low-cost manufacturing, we have struggled.

This upside-down story in our job growth has been political kindling for our election campaigns. The question of job creation has always been a hypersensitive political issue in India, not surprising for a country that has been both overpopulated and poor, and where jobs have typically been hard to come by. Through the 1960s and 1970s, unemployment served as the main trigger for Indian militancy movements—the Naxalites attracted support and fighters with the rallying cry of "land and jobs," unemployed men were fodder for the recruiters of the Shiv Sena, and the All Assam Students' Union targeted its violence at migrants coming to the state to "steal our jobs." Throughout these years, masses of unemployed, desperate young men mounted frequent riots against governments both ineffectual and too broke to create investment or jobs. The numerous labor protests and the massive railway strike in 1974 also led Indira Gandhi to announce the Emergency. She had been watching these strikes with growing irritation, and the first thing she did with her newfound power was throw labor leaders into jail.[1] In those years, as India's economy tottered and unemployment grew, the government automatically responded by tightening labor laws and promising to expand government employment. By the 1980s, the list of central labor laws on the books in India ran to forty-six, and at the state level to more than two hundred.

Postreform, however, India looks very different—we are a vibrant economy hungry for human capital, and our labor costs are soaring faster than anywhere else in the world. The Indian worker has real bargaining power in this market. Politically though, we have not accepted this reality, and the years during which the government bunkered itself against the angry, rioting masses of unemployed have left an indelible imprint on our policies.

India's debate on jobs is now between those who are arguing for reforms—to ease up labor inspections and hiring and retrenching workers—in order to reflect our new economic realities, and those who are unwilling to let go of protections that they believe cushioned them from the worst of the economic downturns in the 1960s and 1970s. As a result our governments are forced to walk a fine line when it comes to employment policy. Our prime minister, for instance, has declared "Rozgar Badao" (increase employment) as the slogan for our coming decade, even though he faces an extremely hostile climate when it comes to any chances of passing labor reforms.*

Our early decades of economic insecurity and pessimism have defined our opinions on labor at a time we need to act quickly. Over the next decade, job growth in India—one million new jobs every year—is going to be far lower than what we need, considering the 14 million people who will enter the workforce every year. The effects of this massive shortfall are fundamentally reshaping India's path to growth and complicating our search for the ambitious, upwardly mobile everyman.

Shaping a movement

In trying to unravel our debates around jobs, we are forced to follow the shouting rather than the policy arguments. The labor unions dominate the debate on jobs in India, and while they represent a small fraction of our working population, they have defined the tone of our employment policies.

The classes of organized workers in India have long been a force to reckon with—they have been hugely vocal and inseparable from our politics, and governments have often found it difficult to put a lid on their activism. From the bifurcation of the Bombay state in the 1950s to the Emergency of the 1970s, the unions have often helped whip up popular fervor, bring out workers onto the streets and swing political decisions. In many ways though, the deeply politicized Indian labor movement is a creature that Indian leaders helped shape. Independence leaders intent on recruiting people for the struggle against British rule had recognized Indian labor as a potent force that they could tap to supply their movement with brawn, enthusiasm and numbers. These workers were, by the early twentieth century, a large cohort—the British had overseen the building of employment-intensive in-

*It is a little disconcerting that in his speech Manmohan Singh also compared this slogan to Indira Gandhi's famous, failed slogan of "Garibi Hatao," which was more successful in garnering votes than achieving results.

dustries in jute, cotton and railways, and by 1900 these businesses employed more than half a million people. The power of this mass of workers, if aroused, was obvious. The police commissioner of Bombay noted, as early as 1908, "If a combined movement against the government can ever be effected . . . the numbers engaged will be fifty or sixty thousand able-bodied millhands."[2]

There was also a deep vein of resentment here that Indian leaders could draw from, owing to the conditions in which these "millhands" and other workers toiled. Large-scale, speculator-style investment in Indian businesses—the British had "a thousand million pounds of capital"[3] invested in India—meant that labor welfare was a distant concern for India's factory and mill owners, compared with business growth. The managing agency system that the British used to run Indian businesses also resulted in a stepmother-like attitude toward the mills and factories, and their managers viewed the idea of labor rights as something in the realm of fantasy. Other problems only added to the general misery of the workers, such as the communication gap between the British managers and Indians, which meant that clerks and junior supervisors in the mills and factories had broad authority without accountability. These men, as workers complained, "got them in trouble with the management unless constantly placated by bribes."[4]

The discontent would soon give way to outright anger and powerful political movements—and it was about time. During these years, factories in both Europe and its colonies were vile, inhuman places to work in, where child labor and worker abuse were the norm, with people sometimes falling dead from overwork. It was a time when the excesses of the market were in full swing and entirely unregulated, and policies in favor of labor were essential. It was this form of capitalism—criticized by many as overly cruel and "vampirelike"—that gave so much power and heart to the communist and socialist movements of the early twentieth century. In India, as well, the idea of emancipation for labor was growing into an important cause.

Soon enough, the imperial government was warning its officers that "labor is growing more conscious of its wants and power, and is showing signs of . . . organization."[5] In 1920 India formed its first prominent labor union, and the number of strikes across the country soared. The Congress, attempting to make common cause here, declared in its party manifesto its goal to promote "mass solidarity" and incorporate both worker organizations and peasant movements into the independence struggle.

These labor strikes immediately after the First World War soon became closely intertwined with the broader nationalist movement. It was easy for the Indian leaders to take up the cause of the workers, and Gandhi's interjection on behalf of Ahmedabad's mill workers in 1917 (although Gandhi being Gandhi, he called the problems between the mill workers and management a "family dispute"[6]) and Nehru's hostility toward capitalists in general fueled support among Indian labor for the independence movement, and they rapidly formed a powerful core of resistance to the British. In fact it is not surprising that the 1926 Trade Union Act was enacted when it was—by the mid-1920s, India's independence movement was gathering steam and had gained powerful and charismatic leaders. The British government passed the labor law partly to prevent the grievances of the working class from infecting and strengthening the movement. But the protests only intensified as the years wore on, and in 1933 alone there were nearly forty strikes across Bombay's textile mills.

The priorities among India's labor classes, however, were soon evolving quite differently from the rest of India's independence movement, and to some extent this soured the honeymoon between the Congress and the workers. It was class politics after all that was paramount to the labor community—for workers, the fight was less against British-run businesses than against supervisors and managers, both Indian and British. Their resistance was thus soaked head to toe with the antiauthoritarianism that communist ideologies could make use of quite effectively. India's communist parties consequently made significant inroads into worker communities during this period. Congress leaders, however, were less focused on class conflicts. During the time Nehru was president of the All-India Trade Union Congress (AITUC), he remarked, "Of course, everyone knows that the Congress is not a labor organization . . . to expect it to act as [one] is a mistake."[7] And Gandhi suggested that while workers ought to be able to air their grievances, it had to be "according to the financial condition of their industry."

Soon enough, some parts of the worker movements began to break away from the independence struggle—a shift that became especially obvious once Congress governments came to power at the provincial level after the 1935 elections. The left-led working-class strikes across the cities of Sholapur, Kanpur, Bombay and Calcutta that occurred after these elections angered Congress leaders, and the Congress leader G. B. Pant wrote in a furious letter to his colleague Rajendra Prasad, "They are trying to discredit the Congress Ministry."[8] These strikes against the Indian provincial government meant that the tradition of working-class agitation against British governments would continue against the Congress-led one, something the Congress leaders saw as a betrayal.

As a result the provincial governments gradually distanced themselves from the politics of labor, and this affected how later Congress governments in India approached labor issues. Congress leaders were—except for their dealings with the government-run public-sector enterprises—unenthused by the intricacies of labor legislation, and these laws were shaped mainly in response to union and worker protests.

In the shadow of the state

"India has yet to shift away from its old mind-set of scarcity," Arvind Subramanian tells me. Our memories of our many crises have led us to focus disproportionately on security—by accumulating huge foreign reserves and emphasizing stockpiles in food grain.

Perhaps all our slow-moving caution on labor comes from this same concern and our inability to forget these past upheavals. The shortage decades of the 1960s and 1970s saw large-scale unemployment or underemployment across the country and a desperate jockeying for precious government jobs; the job of a worker in an economy seesawing through crisis after crisis was at best tenuous.

Like the rest of the country's economic problems in those years, the unemployment crisis stemmed largely from the government's embrace of the *mai-baap* and the "dharmshala model,"[9] where the state provided economic protections and guarantees for the "pious poor."

This responsibility weighed heavy on the Indian government, which, low on funds and its pockets full of lint, regularly fell behind in its promises of poverty reduction, employment and industry growth. India's labor laws were framed around this miserable past of growth slowdowns and production crisis, when workers termed their life in the factories and mills as one of "*kashtam*, pain and misery."[10]

It is only recently, in our latest wave of job growth, that these labor laws have truly begun to hurt. In the early decades after independence, India saw a surge mainly in organized labor, as it was mainly government largesse that drove job creation. The first wave of job investment after 1947 involved the expansion of the state and the Indian bureaucracy. In the coming decades, the state-funded gravy train created more than 4 million employees in the central government alone. It has been said that the British had turned bureaucracy expansion into an art form, but Indians were quick to pick up on it, and scale it up many times over.

The second wave of jobs that surged in parallel to the first occurred between 1951 and 1965. It happened in the "temples of modern India" that Nehru had envisioned, and the state's new power stations, irrigation projects and heavy engineering plants drove new employment across the country. These public enterprises, which formed the Indian economy's "sinews of strength," expanded from 5 in 1950 to 240 by the 1990s, and employed at their peak 2.3 million people. The third wave of jobs occurred when Indira Gandhi nationalized fourteen banks in 1969 and seven more in 1980, creating more than 1.2 million new state-funded jobs.

These waves of state-led employment growth melded quite well with the leftward trend of India's labor politics, and the number of Indian unions grew three times over in these years. But since independence, union interests also rapidly diverged from the realities of the factory floor and millwork. The unions that emerged prominently after 1947 were sponsored and nursed by political leaders, and the prominent labor union postindependence, the Indian National Trade Union Congress (INTUC), as Myron Weiner observed, pledged their loyalty first "to the Congress Party, then to the present (Congress) government, to the nation and last of all to the workers."[11]*

The dominance of the state in the Indian economy also affected the priorities of union leaders. Government-run enterprises were easy meat, since strikes in sectors such as railways and hospitals left the state worried and scrambling, eager to negotiate and reach agreements. Consequently, unions focused on the white-collar public sector, where workers were already well paid, and ended up looking for, as one writer put it, "luchi and mithai [savory and sweet] on top of bread and butter."[12] As the economy slowed between 1961 and 1975, the number of workdays that were lost grew by 500 percent mainly due to skilled workers striking—from employees in life insurance,

*The other unions were no exceptions to the rule, whether it was the AITUC, the oldest of the labor organizations, founded in 1920 and led at first by Congress leaders such as Lala Lajpat Rai, or the Bharatiya Mazdoor Sangh and the Center of Indian Trade Unions (CITU), which were linked with the BJP and the CPI(M), respectively.

nationalized banks, state and central secretariats, to airline pilots, doctors, teachers, engineers, steel plants and railways. The instability spared no one—as when Indira Gandhi's planned 707 flight to meet the United States president Lyndon Johnson was canceled because Air India's navigators were striking for higher wages.

The concerns of blue-collar workers and problems in manufacturing and industry were mostly ignored by the biggest unions. India's long-drawn textile-mill strike in Bombay in the 1980s was in fact a strike against the INTUC-affiliated Rashtriya Mill Mazdoor Sangh (RMMS) union—which the workers saw as tilted toward the management's interests—and the wage agreement it had reached with the mill owners.

The vacuum in leadership made India's labor politics unrelentingly violent. Businesses lacked an effective way to reach agreements with workers, making strikes the order of the day, and worker agitations incorporated everything from assault to murder. The characteristic of Indian labor protests became as they were in British India—the "lightning strike, which is unpredictable, short-lived and unsuccessful."[13] Work at public companies stalled again and again, and private companies avoided large-scale investment or hiring more workers. Such incoherence also gave opportunities for eccentrics to take advantage, such as leaders like Datta Samant, the "militant daredevil" whose career as a free-floating, swoop-in, swoop-out labor negotiator began in 1965 when he organized quarry workers to demand wage increases, and who played a dramatic and ultimately destructive role in the unsuccessful Bombay textile strikes.

No longer the "protector"

The track record of the Indian government in creating jobs has been patchy at best. By the late 1970s the disappointments of labor with the government had become part of a broader sense of betrayal that washed over the country. This was a time that marked the end of our great romance with the Indian state, after a decade and a half of food shortages, war, slow growth, inflation and, most significantly, of disillusionment, with the early promises of a visionary government gone stale.

The Emergency in particular hollowed out the popular idea of the state as a source of sustenance, and as protector and provider of jobs. Indira had banned labor strikes and filled up the jails with striking workers and their leaders. These Emergency-era policies to curb labor resistance have also left us with an unfortunate legacy—any effort toward labor reforms since then has evoked memories of that dictatorial period.

Indira, during her roller coaster years as prime minister, later tried to tamp down on the surging, helpless anger of labor by offering new sweetner restrictions on firing workers. In 1976 she introduced the provision that still hangs over the head of every Indian manufacturer who comes under the Factories Act: it requires companies with 300 or more employees to obtain permission from the state government before any worker could be retrenched. In 1982 she lowered this limit to cover businesses with 100 or more employees—legislation that, as Kaushik Basu notes, triggered a rapid retrenching of employees from firms that had more than 100 workers. But while India's politicians could discuss labor rights till the cows came home, one thing became increasingly clear through the 1970s: growth mattered more than labor protections. No matter how tough these regulations were, struggling companies would simply bypass them. Faced with a losing business, for instance, companies got around tough laws through lockouts or lapsing on their electricity bills, forcing their factories to close. It was a lose-lose deal, where both workers and companies felt shafted by a stagnating economy.

The need for growth

"When it comes to labor controls, the government is fighting a battle on the wrong side," Manish Sabharwal tells me. "Our policies are limiting employment in a country with a billion people and a demographic bulge!"

Politicians who oppose the unshackling of the labor market, and even favor new constraints, have often referred to India's workers as the "toiling masses," a homogeneous, beaten-down group who need the enveloping arms of the state. In this version of events, labor is a passive force that survives only thanks to the aggressive intervention of labor regulations. But this is no longer true. The idea of "mass," easily replaceable labor has foundered on the rock of India's rising knowledge economy. India's growth has also given labor new power and employment opportunities. At Infosys, we have our share of employees who come from financially constrained backgrounds—Prasad, the son of a rickshaw puller, and Fatima Bibi Sheik, a young girl whose husband, a street *pani puri* vendor, supported her education and put her through college. In India's present investment-friendly, high-growth market, such opportunities for financial mobility and an entry into the middle class have the potential to multiply and explode for our workers.

The change is felt even in the way workers are talked about today—the turn of phrase used for our workers is not "labor," but "human capital." Indian workers are no longer irrelevant in the global market—the competitiveness of firms now pivots critically on the competencies, skills and knowledge of their workers. The demand for such workers is spreading beyond the services sector—in manufacturing, as investment growth has soared, managers in factory floors and plants across the country are finding it difficult to find talent.

Another argument that the left has wielded is that the only worthwhile job is a permanent one. So Manish—who runs what is India's largest contract labor firm, which has ninety thousand people on its books and serves as a bridge between temporary and permanent labor, with 65 percent of workers becoming permanent within a year—has around a hundred lawsuits against him filed by the state.

But this narrative of the state being the watchdog over markets in creating and protecting jobs is quite a stretch. The government has been able to fund new jobs through schemes such as the National Rural Employment Guarantee Act (NREGA) thanks to recent revenue surpluses—surpluses that have come from the growth in tax collections paid by workers and entrepreneurs in the private sector, especially over the last decade.

In fact the government has been able to stick with an aggressive policy of cordoning off the labor market despite India's fast-growing young population only because a variety of other factors took the pressure off the state for job creation. One was the rise of the informal labor market, especially among blue-collar workers in the manufacturing, construction and heavy industries. India has also emerged as a country of entrepreneurs, big and small—a disproportionate number of Indians are self-employed.

Another release valve on the pressure for jobs was the rise of the global job market. Till the late 1980s much of the world grew faster than India, creating massive opportunities for labor arbitrage—Indian workers were willing to travel vast distances for the chance of earning much more than they could dream of at home. Migration from India into Britain has in fact helped double the number of ethnic-minority Britons in the last twenty years. Another wave of migration from India took place into the Gulf states in the 1970s and 1980s, as the oil boom created new money in these regions.

In the 1960s the United States opened up for skilled migration, and the country became a magnet for India's educated workers, and since the 1980s, for large numbers of India's IT specialists. More recently, migration has only diversified, with people going to Australia, New Zealand, Canada, Russia and across Europe.

Since 1991 the biggest driver in creating jobs has been the private sector in India. The rise of the market economy created a fourth wave of jobs utterly unlike the first three waves of employment, in that it was independent of the public sector. The tide of new private-sector jobs took off with the IT sector, which together with the BPO industry has created 1.6 million new jobs over the last two decades. The IT and BPO jobs have helped trigger a vibrant domestic economy and, particularly since 2003, a growing tide of jobs across industries. "The first surge of well-paid Indian consumers employed in technology and BPO helped create a chain reaction in new jobs," one financial analyst tells me. We can see this domino effect of new jobs across sectors such as insurance, banking, telecom and retail. The financial services sector alone is expected to employ more than 2 million people by the end of the year. Manish adds, "Sixty percent of new job openings in these sectors are coming in sales." These jobs carry profiles that require much lower educational achievements than what were required in either IT or BPO; sales jobs in financial services and retail, for instance, hire high school graduates.

Moving the goalposts?

"In a sense, the goal we've envisioned for the Indian workforce is already here," Dr. C. Rangarajan tells me. He expects "India's workforce to equal the labor force" by 2010, which means that for the first time in India's economic history everyone eligible for a job will have one. Indian governments have long searched for that evasive Holy Grail, and it has come by quietly.

Of course, we are nowhere close to the real ideal of full employment. Too many Indian workers are in the unorganized sector, which mostly offers seasonal, insecure work. And a large number of Indians have turned to entrepreneurship as a distress choice. For lack of other career options, people set up pavement displays, tea stalls, phone booths, kirana stores and small shops in a variety of markets. It is these groups that illustrate why we so urgently need to make our labor markets more flexible.

A big challenge in getting this done is the continuing focus of many economists on the Indian left over job security in our markets. Labor market flexibility, the economist Jayati Ghosh has argued, would only increase chances for workers to be fired, in both the public and the private sector. Studies by these economists have found that labor flexibility in India is not missing, as reformers argue. The economist L. K. Deshpande has pointed out that through the 1990s the manufacturing industry in India did not have trouble hiring or laying off workers, as they depended on the casual workforce.

But this, in truth, is the heart of the problem. Thanks to a stiff-backed labor regime, the risk of getting fired has been disproportionately less for the unions and organized workers, but at the expense of the unorganized sector. By leaning heavily on the vast pool of casual workers—who have little rights, no welfare and no guaranteed income beyond the ongoing project—our labor rigidities have protected some workers at the cost of many. Contract workers in particular must surf along the most volatile edges of the job market and having to constantly shift their places of work limits their upward mobility, stability, incomes and the ability to educate their children. As the economist Pranab Bardhan pointed out, the left in India, while taking aim at the "dictatorship of the proletariat, has given us instead the dictatorship of the salariat."

In India's revving economy, what the left has called "pro-people" policies have had the opposite effect, creating "a citadel of security and relative prosperity . . . with a regiment outside trying to scale its walls."[14] It has created huge numbers of unorganized workers who lack both income security and job protections, who work in a culture of exploitation. Today, India's organized labor is an estimated 30 percent lower than it could have been, thanks to the labor regulation we have in place. While every other nation is loosening its labor laws, the world's second most populous country is tying the hands of job creators and preventing enterprises from scaling up.

OUR LOPSIDED APPROACHES have ensured that our new economic freedoms are extremely uneven. Through the 1980s and 1990s, economic reforms released the shackles on India's entrepreneurs, allowing them new freedoms to both create and participate in economic wealth. But it has kept these shackles on its workers, limiting the jobs that could have multiplied incomes and created a newly wealthy working-class community. As a result, as Ajay Shah points out, "The agonies of our farmers have reflected our difficulties in creating non-farm jobs, and shifting people into manufacturing."

China on the other hand has been training and shifting 1 percent of its rural workforce into manufacturing over the last two decades. This has fueled the rise of companies making everything from toys to walkie-talkies and has turned China's coastal regions, particularly the Guangzhou delta, into the world's manufacturing powerhouses. India's agricultural workers have no such escape hatch, and this has ensured that our rural sector remains unprofitable, its productivity low, and full of distressed farmers and workers. The low productivity in sectors such as milk production means that it takes 75 million Indians to produce 100 million tons of milk, while in the United States 100,000 people produce 60 million tons of milk.

The pressures of growth

Our new awareness that growth is more essential than labor protections when it comes to creating jobs has changed how we approach strikes and lockouts. Since 2000 a number of court rulings point to a rising impatience with such union approaches. The high courts in the most union-friendly states in the country have ruled against such tactics: the Kerala High Court declared *bandhs* as illegal and unconstitutional in 1997, and the Calcutta High Court did the same in 2000.

The exasperating nature of our labor regulations has also compelled the Supreme Court to step in for key decisions. Besides upholding lower court orders making *bandhs* illegal, it has weighed in on cases filed by workers demanding their jobs back. The Uttam Nakate case, for instance, had a fired worker arguing for his right to nap on the factory floor. The Supreme Court did not see things from his perspective, and in other cases as well the court placed new standards of behavior. These are hardly overwhelming changes—the rulings have been along the lines of "don't sleep at work, and don't hit or swear at your supervisor." But they nevertheless signal a shift from the idea that job security is nonnegotiable.

With labor issues on the concurrent list, some states have also tried to dilute the more draconian regulations. Since it was difficult to take labor laws head-on, states have issued directives to limit labor inspection in firms. For example, in Uttar Pradesh, inspectors can enter factories only after the consent of a senior bureaucrat. Gujarat, Rajasthan and Andhra Pradesh have also reduced the scope of such inspections, and Gujarat's efforts in particular to simplify labor laws have led to a sustained rise in investments into the state.

The recent years have also weakened the hold of the unions, with the numbers of unionized workers stagnating even as the jobs have expanded considerably. The new industries of IT and BPO, for instance, have stayed tenaciously antiunion—one writer, researching on the trouble unions had in organizing BPO workers, remarked on the fact that even "BPO workers from West Bengal and Kerala," India's reddest states, "were dead set against unions."[15]

But even as the country's economy has transformed, the unions stick to old wisdom. The Indian unions and the left strongly oppose labor reform, and despite the share of unions in the Indian workforce now hovering around 2 percent, their political clout—and their ability to bring core public enterprises to a standstill when necessary—has given them considerable bargaining power with governments. India's labor laws remain fossilized and intact, a net of tripwires across the economy.

"If we were to follow the letter of the law in our labor regulations," one employer tells me about the more than one hundred different regulations he has to keep track of, "we wouldn't be able to hire anyone. Both the government and private companies exploit the loopholes." The NREGA itself violates thirty-seven laws, and much of Indian industry has been able to grow only because entrepreneurs have decided to ignore many of the more draconian regulations, while the state chooses to look the other way. This makes corruption the rule, and as one textile exporter told me, "We bribe the union leaders to stay away and pay the inspectors to not close us down."

During the 1980s, amid the height of hostilities between workers and textile-mill managers, a prominent textile entrepreneur drew attention to the lack of any logic to our aggressive regulations when he remarked, "Are these managers not Indians?" India's labor policies have, above everything else, had a militant attitude toward entrepreneurs, seeing them as little more than "antisocial profiteers or powerful exploiters." Recently, L. K. Chaudhary, CEO of the Italian company Graziano, was killed at his office in Greater Noida, and the labor minister Oscar Fernandes reacted by calling the death "fair enough" and blaming the company management—suggesting that the "simmering discontent" of the company's workers and fired employees had caused his death. It took a public outcry and criticism from leaders across Indian businesses (I made some remarks as well) for him to apologize.

The state has long approached India's labor laws with this classic point of view of the downtrodden worker versus the scheming entrepreneur, but in India, which is among the most entrepreneurial countries in the world, this is a terrible mistake. From our farmers to our street-cart vendors, our ubiquitous small shopkeepers and our urban and rural innovators, economic initiative and an appetite for risk is apparent across the country. And while large enterprises can pay to make state harassment go away, it is these people, the street entrepreneurs and small stores, who suffer the most from an overregulating state that intrudes on everything from labor issues to the myriad work permits and forms a small business needs to operate.

"Pro-people" policy is not about overregulating the economy; it is about freeing labor and entrepreneurs alike and limiting the very real harassment they endure in the hands of municipal officials and inspectors.

A showcase for how much these laws fall short is the people who live in the packed tin-and-concrete, brick-and-plastic shacks on the margins of Bombay city. The residents of the Dharavi slum are among the most disadvantaged communities in the world in terms of their access to education, capital or land. Many of them came to the city in search of work, and resorted to entrepreneurship when they failed to land a steady job. And most of their enterprises operate out of Dharavi, which has become the hub for an estimated fifteen thousand single-room factories with an annual output of $1.47 billion. This teeming community of entrepreneurs includes recyclers, potters, furniture makers, private schools, cable operators, as well as beauty parlors, pubs and businesses that provide water and electricity and help kill the slum's rats.[16] Dharavi is a symbol of both our successes and our failures in our approaches to labor. The people here are largely self-employed, and while many of them are successful, there are also many among these small entrepreneurs who have turned to businesses for want of steady work.

Unfortunately, there has been little impetus for change. India's unorganized workers have provided businesses with a way around the tangled forest of labor regulation, and industries with flexible work practices such as textiles and construction have taken up subcontracting and outsourcing in a big way to bypass tough laws. Companies have also figured out ways around retrenching workers through voluntary retirement schemes and the like. This has proved temporarily convenient to everyone—the left, the businesses, the unions and the government are content with the status quo. We have both deadlock and consensus. "The problem," Manish says, "is that these laws are a thorn in the flesh, not a dagger in the heart." As a result job creation in India now has no real champions in policy, and we have a situation where the most influential classes have made their peace with a labor system that exploits and denies access to its poorest workers.

The damage from this is long-term—the "thorn in the flesh" is a slow-acting poison to the economy. Labor regulations have drastically limited scale, and India has a much smaller proportion of workers in enterprises with ten or more employees than any comparable country. Capital intensity, a sign of machines replacing people in sectors such as manufacturing, is also unnaturally high for a country with so many available workers. In these sectors, companies see hiring permanent workers as a last option.

Our "Indian" solutions

"The problem with the debate around jobs in India," Omkar Goswami says, "is the distance between what our contending groups want. There's a canyon in between them." Manmohan Singh speaks publicly of the need for "broad consensus" on labor policy, a sign that at present there is none at all.

"It is a workers' market in India today," one employer tells me. "Companies are now desperate enough to say, 'Give me two hands, I don't care if a brain is attached.' " But despite this, we are in danger of turning our jobs story into one of exclusion rather than inclusion. We have the people, the potential and the opportunity, but apparently lack the permissions to take advantage of our expanding economy. We have embraced our identity as a services-led economy, rather than considering its very real implications. A population of India's size, and with its upcoming demographic surge, cannot rely on the services sector to create the mass of jobs it needs, and a large mass of unemployed and seasonal workers is a recipe for instability. As Sunil Khilnani said to me, "People in a growing economy are patient—for a while, even during long, early periods of unequal opportunity. But how long will they wait for jobs? Years? A decade?" Rapid and large-scale new employment is obviously a sine qua non both for stable growth and for the sustained rise of a domestic market. The model has been indispensable not just for China's growth but also for Japan and the United States during their boom years. The American entrepreneur Henry Ford had demonstrated how effective this approach could be when, in the early 1900s, he introduced mass-manufacturing and large-scale employment, which led to the rise of a new consuming class in the United States and drove soaring growth rates over the next few decades.

On the other hand, solutions such as the NREGA will in the long term not only suck away at the exchequer but also become a political hobbyhorse, and are at best weak alternatives to the kind of employment that triggers both economic growth and industrial productivity. So far, we have sidestepped the tough political moves we need for such growth. In 2001 the NDA government's finance minister, Yashwant Sinha, made a stab at it, proposing that requiring state permissions to hire or dismiss workers should apply only for establishments employing a thousand workers instead of a hundred. "The reform proposal was dead in the water because of trade union opposition," Yashwant tells me, "and many politicians were eager to paint it as anti-people." Governments since then have merely proposed tangential solutions, such as creating jobs through caste reservations—political parties such as the BSP are now seeking caste-based reservations as a ticket for entry into the much-prized private-sector jobs.

Such political responses to our challenges on jobs are filled with potential booby traps. Ajay says, "My worry is that programs such as the NREGA will have a toxic effect, thanks to our typical election-time fondness for adding sop over sop." The employment-guarantee scheme might as a result be expanded, remuneration increased and so on, until it becomes the symbolic, hugely gargantuan and monstrously inefficient solution to more jobs.

Across urban India, we see people flowing in, setting up their fragile homes on the city's fringes and setting out in search of work. People are arriving with a willingness to work at anything, and to learn in any way they can. "These people are hungry for opportunity," Jaideep Sahni tells me. "They will live in any circumstances, and move anywhere, for a chance at a job." And yet, instead of creating opportunity, our regulations have placed a glass ceiling on both the economic potential of these workers and India's overall rise. It has limited our mobility, growth and the individual hope of these workers—it prevents, in essence, the promise of the Horatio Alger story.

INSTITUTIONS OF SAND

Our Universities

"OUR UNIVERSITIES," Deepak Nayyar, former vice chancellor of Delhi University (DU), says to me, "are no longer ivory towers. They were meant to remain above politics but are instead at the very center of it."

It is true that our universities are now at the heart of a grim and fractious political scrabble that has pushed our most prominent deans and academicians into exchanging terse, public one-on-ones with our politicians. The path to this state of affairs has been a long way down. Early on, India's educational institutions were at the center of our most positive iconography—our universities were a source of great pride, which gave Indians, as Nehru declared, "a franker look and a straighter back." But forty years on, India entered the 1990s in the midst of massive protests against the Mandal Commission recommendations for caste reservations in colleges. Since then the debates in higher education have only become more virulent and now surround every aspect of university policy. Over the last decade and a half, the arguments here have been hijacked by questions on the ownership and control of our colleges, and seat reservations for backward castes among students and in faculty appointments. Watching these protests over the role and control of universities, one commentator and academic famously remarked, "It's not democracy, but democrazy."[1]

There are two big questions that lie at the center of this crisis around our universities: How much should universities reflect the agenda of the government? And to what extent should it focus on social justice and equal access—an institution that in its selection processes is at its heart, after all, an undemocratic one?

The high level of rancor and disagreement on these questions has allowed our universities to continue the slow collapse that began in the 1970s. The former vice chancellor of Delhi University Upendra Baxi described the unfolding tragedy when he wrote that our universities are in their "death throes."[2] Our higher education system has become inert and incapable of adapting to a rapidly evolving economy, and even its best central institutes—arguably Nehru's most enduring legacy to India—are in danger. Their weaknesses have become particularly critical with the rise of the knowledge economy, and as India's legions of youngsters enter institutions that seem less and less capable of giving them what they need.

A persistent legacy

The year that the first three universities came up in India, 1857, carries a particular note of hubris for the colonial empire. The British never suspected, when they established universities in Bombay, Calcutta and Madras the same year that they were going about stamping out the army rebellion so thoroughly, that they were setting themselves up for a far more intense, widespread protest against their rule. It is in these institutes that India's political awakening began and it is here that India's educated absorbed the ideas of freedom and democracy, inspiring them to eventually lead the struggle against colonial rule.

The focus in these first universities was on creating a small pool of aristocratic, English-educated Indian workers for the civil services and strengthening the foundation of British rule. But institutions often have a way of thwarting the aims of their founders. Sir Henry Maine, vice chancellor of the University of Calcutta, remarked in 1866, "The founders of the University of Calcutta thought to create an aristocratic institution; and in spite of themselves, they created a popular one."[3] And these universities *were* immensely popular. The demand for British-style college education grew by leaps and bounds, since it was a ticket to a job in a country where jobs were hard to come by. People crowded into the liberal arts courses to absorb English, Greek and Latin, all for a possible career as a government bureaucrat in British India's revenue and judicial departments, with its attendant promises of security and petty power.[4]

The British press largely dismissed this emerging new class of Indian bureaucrats—one journalist wrote in 1875, "The pliable, plastic, receptive Baboo of Bengal eagerly avails himself of this [university] system . . . partly from a servile wish to please the *Sahib logue*, and partly from a desire to obtain a Government appointment."[5] But these British degrees were also creating a new class of *bhadralok*, educated Indians, who lay outside the clutches of the traditional caste system and were evangelists for Western ideas of equality and liberty. By 1889 the British were aware of this growing force of educated Indians opposing British policies. Initially legislators such as Sir Antony MacDonnell tried to play down the problem, labeling India's Congress party as nothing more than "a preserve of lawyers and schoolteachers"—a small, educated minority with little influence in their attempts to foment unhappiness against colonial rule.

Of course, it turned out to be a little more than that.

On the flip side, these universities had an overwhelming tilt toward preparing students for government jobs, and most of the degrees the colleges awarded were in the arts. Faced with studying subjects that they could not relate to, such as European languages and British law, students focused mainly on "swotting"—cramming to absorb as much as possible, while understanding little. One Calcutta tutor noted that by the 1880s an entire industry had mushroomed to cater to the crammers, with the "extraordinary prevalence of 'keys' . . . meretricious aids to a degree, sold by every bookseller and advertised by every post."[6]

Another unhappy consequence of this narrow focus on graduate-bureaucrats was that science and technology were put on the back burner, hurting both innovation and new ideas in the long run. Some British administrators did recognize this problem, and governors such as Lord Curzon discussed the need to "rescue the . . . university from its corrosive narrowness."[7] But while policy papers on reforming universities came out by the sheaf, the British government did little to change the existing focus. There were a few efforts by Indians as well to counter the status quo and establish more competencies in science—the industrialist Jamsetji Tata, for instance, envisioned a unique institution for scientific research and study and set up the Indian Institute of Science (IISc), which by 1911 began its first courses in Bangalore. Mostly, however, these belated efforts tacked on science institutions and departments to the existing university systems, creating separate and segregated cultures of the sciences and the arts—which still persist.

Perhaps the most egregious problem was the singular focus on building universities—elementary and secondary schools were largely ignored. Instead of building from the bottom up, from elementary schools to the venerable universities, reaching upward brick by brick, the British had chosen to erect an edifice that amounted to university arches perched on stilts. The British India district magistrate A. O. Hume (who founded India's Congress party) summarized the effects of this when he wrote with some disappointment that "Indian education, like French liberty . . . has been more of a show than a reality. In our haste for results we have . . . tried the great Indian trick of developing in a single hour, the shoot, the plant, the flower and fruit and found alas! That we at least were no conjurors."[8]

But instead of reforming the system we were left with, we have chosen to hold it even closer to us, resisting change in any form. Our university policy has long failed to add up to a coherent approach, but our governments have been reluctant to redo the math.

Tinkering with policies

"We are a country propelled forward by crisis," one minister tells me. "We make tough policy changes only when faced with emergencies." As a consequence, in issues where it has taken a relatively long time for the danger signs to hit, bad ideas were left standing long past their sell-by dates.

This has been the unfortunate fate of our university policies, where an ineffective system has frozen into place, unchanged in imperial India for want of enthusiasm, and in independent India for want of political will. "The desire I see among people today to study beyond high school," S. Sadagopan, director of the Indian Institute of Information Technology Bangalore, tells me, "is quite massive and unprecedented. But it's a whole other story when we look at the quality of higher education available. Our capacities and capabilities are falling fast."

Our first governments had a unique opportunity to implement some changes—Nehru, for instance, was excited about the role universities could play in India's economic rise and was willing to invest in and promote new, better institutions. There was also broad agreement within the government that the center in particular would have to spend on and oversee the growth of universities, and the education minister, Maulana Azad, urged "central guidance, if not central control" for India's colleges.

Nehru framed his vision for India's institutes in soaring rhetoric, one in which India's colleges would be the catalyst that would transform the country from a backwater of superstition and old practices. In fact India's new higher education institutions such as the Indian Institutes of Technology (IITs), the Indian Institutes of Management (IIMs) and the All India Institute of Medical Sciences (AIIMS) were weighted with symbolism and the need for the young nation to prove itself. The site for the first IIT, IIT Kharagpur, was the Hijli jail where two Indian dissidents had been killed by the British. Nehru referred to the IIT itself as a fine "monument"—so wrapped up were these institutes in the symbolism of our past.

But despite such ceremony and intent, there was no clear-eyed focus on education policy. In 1944 the British had formulated an educational policy for independent India under the leadership of Sir John Sargent. Called the Post-War Plan of Educational Development in India, it envisioned higher education for one out of every fifteen students that completed secondary school, and vocational or technical education for the rest. While the Indian government rejected this approach, with good reason, as "needlessly conservative," fifteen years had to pass before it rustled up an alternative, national policy on education. Eventually, the Kothari Commission report—which was published in 1966 and ran into 615 pages—drew out an agenda for the government and recommended creating five or six major universities in India that would be global centers of excellence. These recommendations formed the basis of the 1968 National Policy on Education.

The government had several stumbles in its efforts to define a good policy and regulatory framework for its universities. While India focused on new institutions around technology and science, there was little progress on university reforms and the overhaul of the old systems of affiliation and regulation. Pressure from interest groups and drawn-out negotiations with university administrators muddled proposed legislation and regulatory standards for colleges. For instance, in the 1950s the minister Humayun Kabir introduced a major regulatory bill for universities, which among other things gave India's central government sole authority for university recognition. But

Kabir quickly found himself in the midst of a heated argument around the bill's provisions—vice chancellors overwhelmingly did not want much regulation or new standards. Kabir felt like "a culprit in the dock"[9] during these conferences, targeted by groups whose vehemence against the bill was clear and unsubtle.

As a result neither the government nor the University Grants Commission (UGC) gained effective authority over our institutes. The bill Kabir had pushed had contained two provisions: the first stating that no university could be established without the approval of the UGC and the ministry of education and the second giving the UGC the authority to derecognize any degree. But in the heat of the debates both these provisions were fought off. "The academicians in our universities," Pratap Bhanu Mehta tells me, "have fought against any regulation with real teeth. They've demanded protections and job safeguards of the worst sort—the kind without accountability." The eventual legislation was as a result weak and ineffective—universities could choose to forgo recognition from the center as well as the UGC—and the UGC was reduced to a regulatory body standing helplessly by as India's public university system crumbled.

"An immobile colossus"

"The decline of our institutes has happened quite literally before my eyes," Dr. Nayyar tells me with some feeling. "It's been painful to watch." I can empathize. Both Dr. Nayyar and I have cherished our years as students in Indian colleges—he was a graduate from St. Stephen's and the Delhi School of Economics (DSE) and I had studied at IIT and roamed around the vibrant DU campus, participating in its raucous intercollegiate debates and quizzes. We were lucky that during our time the rot had not yet set in. In fact Dr. Nayyar notes that when he arrived at Oxford for his doctorate from the DSE, the Indian institute was so reputed that the economist John Hicks asked him why he was at Oxford at all. Our standards since then have been in free fall—while the DSE remains respectable, one cannot possibly imagine comparing it with Oxford today.

Our growth in higher education hides more than it shows. There has been a rapid expansion of Indian institutes since 1947, from 20 universities and 636 colleges to 214 universities, 38 additional deemed universities and

9,703 colleges today. But it is an empty victory. "An immobile colossus . . . insensitive, unresponsive and absorbed so completely in trying to preserve its structural form that it does not have the time to consider its own larger purpose," was what S. C. Dube wrote, as he mercilessly summed up the state of India's universities in the government's 1985 State of Higher Education report. Others were even more cutting in their assessment—one vice chancellor recently suggested that more than half the expanding network of Indian colleges were "intellectual and social slums."[10]

The degeneration of our universities has paralleled the state's collapse. These institutes have long been abjectly dependent on government funding, and a decline in governance and state funding from the mid-1960s onward led to their slow fossilization—with money hard to come by, departments and labs in disrepair, faculty with little incentive to do research, a gathering of dust on everything, layer after layer.

The dependence of these institutes on the state's graciousness to remain solvent has especially had a corrupting effect. More than anything else, these institutions seem to have lost their revolutionary role, the mantle of independent thinking and change they wore so easily before independence. "Our universities," one college dean tells me, "have been handed over to political ideology." Dr. Nayyar says, "Our deans and administrators now hang on the spoken word of our politicians, and student unions and teachers beat to their drum. It's so entrenched that asserting independence in appointments and day-to-day decisions turns you into a radical, a rebel in the system."

Our bunkered institutions

During my visits to my alma mater in the late 1990s, what struck me most about the campus was its general sense of disrepair. By then, it was two decades since I had graduated and I was nostalgic for the place where I had spent some of the best years of my life. But on my return, I was shocked by what I saw. The IIT Bombay campus is nestled between the Powai and Virar lakes, and has always been green and beautiful, but the buildings themselves were depressingly dilapidated, and it looked nothing like what it was: one of India's top educational institutions. I resolved then to reengage with the institute and do anything possible to restore it. As an alumnus who had unexpectedly got lucky in the IT boom, I funded various initiatives, including the renovation of my old Hostel 8, the setting up of an IT school and a new IT incubation lab. IIT being a residential campus, the number of students that the institute could admit was constrained by the number of hostel rooms, and there had been no significant addition to the hostel capacity in decades. So the IIT management and I decided to cofund two new hostels that would add one thousand rooms, an increase of 30 percent. These hostels were built in record time—in less than two years—thanks to Dr. Ashok Misra, the dynamic director of IIT Bombay.

But to my utter surprise, the IIT management soon got a letter from the ministry of human resources development (HRD) under Murli Manohar Joshi inquiring why such a "lavish" hostel had been built, and whether the college had followed due process. And a few years later when the state of Gujarat offered IIT Bombay both land and money to build an extended campus, the HRD ministry under Arjun Singh inexplicably withheld permission for several months. Several other initiatives aimed at increasing the capacity of the IITs were also criticized and delayed.

Even as these institutes languish under the "HRD raj," Patna, the capital of Bihar, is seeing rare and booming growth in a related industry—coaching classes to train students for admission exams to the top universities. Among the most famous coaching institutes in the city is the Ramanujan School of Mathematics, run by the mathematician Anand Kumar. Every year thousands of students come to this school for coaching, and thirty of the best and the brightest are selected into the "Super 30" and put through a punishing eight-month coaching session to prepare them for the IIT entrance exam. As Anand Kumar says, these students "sleep, talk, walk and eat IIT" during this time. The boot camp appears to pay off—in 2007 a record twenty-eight of the Super 30 made it to the IITs.

This is a microcosm of the state of our universities. On the one hand we have our top institutes asphyxiated under regulations that are often as puzzling as they are suffocating. On the other we see a process of selection where more and more aspirants compete for a handful of seats at our best colleges, and for that shrinking chance of grabbing a place in the small patch of light and promise that these institutes offer.

HOW DID WE come from the early euphoria around education to this dismal state of affairs? It is true that the first few governments invested significant amounts in these institutes—even in the midst of India's financial crisis, Nehru managed to build the IITs with the help of German, British, Russian and U.S. funding. But the government's emphasis on "accessibility" meant that it was reluctant to charge the fees required to cover education costs. The aversion toward charging fees made state investments into our institutes a source of guaranteed deficits for the government, not exactly an attractive incentive for them to pour money into colleges.

To make matters worse, the routes through which these institutes could earn their own income—such as research—were cut off. The government was tunneling research work into institutions such as the Council of Scientific and Industrial Research, the Defense Research and Development Organization, Hindustan Aeronautics Ltd and the Bhabha Atomic Research Center, in sharp contrast to policies in countries such as the United States, where research funds from public agencies such as the National Science Foundation typically go to both research institutions and universities. The result was that research in academia—the university's soul—atrophied. Cutting-edge research not only attracts financing but also brings in both talented students and faculty, encourages innovation and new ideas, and keeps the academic atmosphere from choking in rarefied theory.

It was in the 1970s that the big decline began. As the government concerns shifted to famine, exchange pressures and simply keeping its head above water as the Indian economy ran into rough weather in these years, public investment into our institutes also began to dry up. These decades set the pattern for Indian policy as far as long-term issues such as education were concerned. Investments in higher education as a percentage of GDP fell from 7.4 percent in the first five-year plan to 2.7 percent in 1980. At the same time, student fees at institutes like the IITs remain unchanged from what the Sarcar Committee had recommended in 1950,[11] even as the inflation in the ensuing years made the real value of these fees one-fiftieth of the original amount.*

The thinning budgets of the universities could cover little more than salary expenses, sidelining new infrastructure, course reviews and research.

*P. V. Indiresan offers some detail: The Sarcar Committee in 1950 believed that even at subsidized fees the student should bear one third of the costs. It had estimated the cost of education in the Imperial College, London at Rs 1,480 and at the Massachusetts Institute of Technology, Boston at Rs 1,560, and therefore fixed the IIT fees at Rs 500 a year. That is where it remained decades later, in 1980. In the 1990s, the cost recovered from fees was 5 percent.

The state in the meantime explicitly frowned on competition among institutes, by prohibiting new institutes from setting up close to existing ones. Policies that cut out merit in everything from pay scales to university budgets resulted in underpaid faculty, a large shortfall of teachers and a lackluster administration. As André Béteille notes, this approach has turned our universities into mere "ABC factories," degree-giving institutions whose primary focus is not education but conducting examinations. Allowing affiliates to universities allows these colleges to get away with substandard teaching and infrastructure. "I call it the McDonald's model of education," Sadagopan says, "but without the quality control."

Our universities may be driving home the truth of that old adage of the road to hell being paved with good intentions: the socialist leanings of the Indian government were wholly unsuited to our universities, and it was a fundamental clash of ideals. In their best incarnation, universities emphasize the pursuit of new knowledge and nonpartisan thought, and for this they need independence, high, transparent standards and the best of human capital. But in India, the government has undermined funding, independence and the larger role of universities as knowledge creators. And the dominance of the state in the sector has come to mean interference rather than guidance, and politics rather than policy.

Our choices for change

"The eleventh plan," Montek Singh Ahluwalia tells me, "is more strongly aimed at education than ever before." Manmohan Singh has triumphantly promoted this fact—he has called the plan a "national education plan," in which for the first time India is shoveling money, lots of it, into both schools and colleges. Nineteen percent of the budget is allocated for education, quite a ramp-up from the 7.7 percent in the previous plan, and expenditure on higher education is, for the first time in decades, set to go over 1 percent of GDP.

This new enthusiasm is a long overdue acknowledgment of the immense value human capital holds in India's changing economy. Manmohan Singh often quotes Churchill when he talks about the need for better universities—particularly his remark that "the empires of the future are going to be the empires of the mind"—and he has an academic's fondness and understanding of education's place in the economy. But one thing is also clear: the state has made a choice between fixing the system and providing resources. The plan's approach has chosen to tackle the universities' money crisis, but the government is silent on the weaknesses that have warped our institutes, and for which money is little more than an ineffectual Band-Aid.

It is not that the Indian government has been unaware of the degradation of the university. The state set up reform committees as early as the 1960s, but the response was slow and reluctant. The 1962 Committee of Standards, for instance, took three years to file its report, by which time the government had changed and the recommendations were never implemented.

In 1985 the Rajiv Gandhi government suggested an overhaul of our universities in a 119-page document titled "Challenge of Education"—a report that minced no words in criticizing the dismal state of India's universities. Again, there was no action.[12] Even now, there continues to be no dearth of good ideas. Most recently, the National Knowledge Commission made recommendations on improving the independence and transparency of regulators as well as on addressing the challenge of creating enough quality universities to meet the vast demand.

But politically the reform suggestions were, and are, a fist-size pill to swallow. Governments have to handle institutes that have long been in the grip of pugnacious interest groups, from the politicians and controlling trusts to the faculty and the student leaders. As the planning adviser J. P. Naik noted, the existing power structure now "will do its damnedest to see that no radical reconstruction of education . . . takes place."[13]

Therefore, each time commissions have proposed reform, the spine of the state has been tested and proved wanting. So as one analyst recently remarked, reforms in the sector have amounted to "a Niagara Falls of reports on educational policy issues and a Sahara of action."

"The resistance among college administrations and the government to changing anything has been pervasive," says Dr. Sam Pitroda, head of the National Knowledge Commission. Our universities as a result have become islands untouched by the fast-changing economy that surrounds them. Their weaknesses have deeply undermined people's access to the skills and knowledge they need to take advantage of the jobs in a growing and rapidly changing market.

Despite the legions of our colleges, it is now a rare Indian university that makes it to the top four hundred in the world. As a result, when Indian graduates are held up to the glare of global competition and new standards, many are found wanting—one study deemed that 75 percent of our graduates were unemployable for the work they were ostensibly trained to do.

These failures are most conspicuous in our vocational education system. The estimated seven thousand vocational schools are nearly all in the public sector—the private sector has not entered here because it is not lucrative enough, unlike engineering and medicine. As a consequence, while industrial jobs have become more knowledge- and skill-intensive, vocational institutions have not responded. The relative supply of workers with vocational skills in India has actually come down since the 1990s, and many workers when asked about pursuing such education give a shrug of a response: "it's of no use."

The failures of the vocational sector have compounded the challenges of the rest of our education system, since many students who could have built a lucrative career here instead choose substandard graduation or engineering courses, getting degrees of little value and with little chance of employment. One labor market study estimates that 90 percent of employment opportunities in India require some vocational skills, but there is a huge mismatch in the labor available—90 percent of our college and school graduates have only "bookish" knowledge. It eventually becomes difficult for such graduates to take up what they come to see as low-prestige employment. "Many of them will outright refuse a blue-collar job," Manish Sabharwal tells me. "Even if they can't get white-collar jobs and the alternative offers them more money, they see it as beneath them."

But even as many of our colleges have become little more than cardboard cutouts, our politicians and academicians shy away from these difficult realities. We remain stuck with superficialities, arguing over the paint of the tower turrets while the castle crumbles: our public debate on our institutes is focused on two issues, privatization and reservations.

Indian ministers have been unrelenting in their opposition to a law allowing the entry of "profit" into our universities, and the National Institute of Educational Planning and Administration has favored a law that would ban "commercialization" in the sector. But even a short inspection of the nature of private investment in higher education, especially preindependence, belies the claim that private investment enables either "commercialization" or "commodification." The Tatas, for instance, were responsible for a number of venerable institutions focused on the fundamental sciences—besides the

Indian Institute of Science, they also set up and funded the Tata Institute of Fundamental Research and the Tata Institute of Social Sciences in 1936 and 1945, respectively. The family behind the DCM established the Lady Shri Ram (LSR) College and the Shri Ram College of Commerce (SRCC), which are now among Delhi University's top institutes. Similarly, the financier Dr. Rajah Sir Annamalai Chettiar* helped establish the Annamalai University in Tamil Nadu, first by setting up the main college and then funding the Madras government in the 1920s in their efforts to expand the university. The laws permitting minority private institutions also cleared the way for well-respected and privately funded universities such as the Aligarh Muslim University (AMU) and the Banaras Hindu University (BHU). Churches across India also established colleges that rate among India's top institutes, including St. Xavier's College in Mumbai, the Christian Medical College in Vellore, St. Stephen's College in Delhi and Xavier Labor Relations Institute (XLRI) in Jamshedpur. And institutes like the Hindu College—funded by Delhi's Chandni Chowk businessmen, who had made their fortunes in the Indian bazaar and the trading square—remain among the best early examples of the private sector role contributing to our universities. Since Indian philanthropists and entrepreneurs have set up what are now among India's most prestigious institutes, there is no reason why they would not do it again, if we make it easy for top-class institutions to come up.† Foreign universities will also flock to India if they feel there is a level playing field for such institutes in the country.

India should be welcoming such private participation to address its challenges both in quality and in quantity. As the National Knowledge Commission had pointed out, if we are to move up from an enrollment rate of 15 percent in higher education by 2015, we need at least 1,500 universities as against the 350 we now have. But the government's budget for the eight new IITs and seven new IIMs alone exceeds Rs 25 billion. The expenditure that we need is clearly not something the state alone can, or should, take on. A vibrant market here creates, in addition, a varied set of institutes that move past our standard-bearer degrees and provide students with opportunities to use their talents in emerging market niches, from animation to anthropology. Other once-reluctant governments have recognized this—the Chinese gov-

---

*He happens to be the grandfather of the UPA government's finance minister, P. Chidambaram.

†One of the initiatives that I am involved in and support is a plan to start a high-quality private university (The Institution for Human Settlements) to look at habitats, planning and urban governance.

ernment has already taken an about-turn from its Cultural Revolution–era hostility toward universities, and it is setting up more than a hundred "IIT-like" engineering institutes across the country to address the demands of its burgeoning economy. Since the 1990s China has also given its colleges greater autonomy in everything from admissions and finances to course content, and allowed foreign universities to erect campuses in the country.

But in India, the political tap dance that has guaranteed both an apathetic state and restrictions against private education has brought us to a very Indian state of affairs: de facto privatization, where plenty of private colleges have cropped up across the country and where several state legislatures have passed their own bills in their favor. Private investment in the sector has surged to five times that of public investment over the last decade. In fact bad policies dominate in our state universities, without the government being pressured for change, mainly because much of the middle class are voting with their feet and moving away from these institutions into private colleges. People are jockeying for seats either in India's elite central institutions such as the IITs—which have remained, not for want of effort on the part of certain legislators, somewhat above the political fray—or in the rising number of private institutes that have mushroomed across the country. The promise of white-collar jobs in the 1990s across Indian industry has especially driven the dramatic expansion of private engineering colleges and business schools in the last decade and a half.

In fact it is primarily the expansion of these private-sector colleges that supported the growth of the IT industry. The industry emerged mainly in the states that had allowed private engineering colleges before 1992—Andhra Pradesh, Karnataka, Maharashtra and Tamil Nadu—and more than 80 percent of the new capacity in engineering graduates over the last twenty-five years has been created by private institutes.[14]

Another factor that took the pressure off public higher education is that even as students opted for private colleges, the elite in India found foreign education accessible, especially with the country's postliberalization riches.* As a consequence, India today has the largest number of students abroad—nearly 200,000—who are subsidizing universities in host countries through their fees.

*I am one of those who seceded in this way—both my children are doing their college degrees in the United States.

However, the weak regulatory environment has encouraged private investment mainly from people looking to make a fast buck rather than provide effective education. Such creeping, unregulated privatization is dominated by religious groups and politicians exploiting loopholes in the law—hardly the recommended strategy for the market to participate in our universities. In fact somewhere around two thirds of these institutes are deemed below par, and less than a third qualify for recognition by the UGC. Professor Sadagopan recounts an anecdote of a "truck carrying books from college to college to fill empty shelves prior to a state inspection of college libraries"; there is a real danger of this soon becoming the norm rather than the exception. Reality is now worse than a Vijay Tendulkar* satire, as the opponents of laws favoring private education have created the very conditions they fear most—"exploitative," "for-profit" private education.

The sheer wrongheadedness of such an approach—where bad regulation has created a runaway private sector, even as the government hinders the day-to-day running of state colleges—was recently in full view in Chhattisgarh, where the pendulum on university regulation swung to one extreme and then the other. The 2002 Chhattisgarh Private Sector Universities Act (a badly written piece of legislation that was Swiss-cheese-like in its loopholes) created a wave of more than a hundred new private universities across the state, some of which were "operating out of corner stores and run-down apartments."[15] When the Supreme Court struck the act down, it also swung the other extreme and recommended that each new university in the state had to be created through a separate law, specifically authorizing it. As Pratap Bhanu Mehta notes, the ruling was like demanding that "every business have an individual law authorizing it to operate."

Some government role in higher education is inevitable and necessary. This is obvious even in the United States, which arguably has the world's most vibrant and successful network of private universities. American state universities and community colleges are subsidized by the federal and state governments. Effective regulation must focus less on the window dressing—private versus public ownership—and more on achieving a balance that gives

---

*Tendulkar's plays (which were mainly in the Marathi language), revealed a fascination with the ironies of conservative values and religion. His plays focused time and again on how traditional "moral values" and religion often caused violence, both in politics and within families. His work, as a result, often invited comparisons with Henrik Ibsen, another playwright who wrote in order to puncture illusions of virtue of traditional, "moral societies." Unsurprisingly, Tendulkar's work was often a target of censorship.

universities the independence to take critical decisions on hiring, pay scales, fees, student selection, course content and infrastructure. At the same time, an empowered, independent regulator must focus on monitoring the quality of institutional output such as patents, papers published and the employability of graduating students. And most important, such a regulator must be allowed to rate and derecognize institutions on the basis of these criteria. At the National Knowledge Commission, we had made some recommendations for such regulation that included eliminating the regulatory roles of the confusing array of statutory bodies such as the UGC and the All-India Council for Technical Education (AICTE), and establishing in their place a "super regulator" in the form of a single, independent regulatory authority for higher education. Such a body would bring about uniform standards and a transparent system of regulation, recognition and quality control. This would also make way for national-level assessment tests and scores that would carry weight in any university anywhere in India.

Such an emphasis on quantity and quality—with more private universities, foreign investment as well as smart regulation—would bring with it a fresh jolt of new ideas and investment, and a much needed shake-up to what is now a very complacent sector. These steps are also critical to end the politics of scarcity in our universities and the painful, hyper-Darwinian selection process that now exists, which has encouraged the "Kota mind-set" of cramming—and created a coaching industry worth Rs 10 billion annually.

The steps to increase the quantity of good colleges would go a long way in expanding access beyond the tiny sliver of our population—12 percent—that now attends college. Such a large-scale, short-term expansion has been done before: when the United States was faced with a million demobilized soldiers in the 1950s and 1960s after the world war, it rapidly improved access to colleges by offering cheap financing options for students and allowing the private sector to expand into universities across the country.

The democratic sense of our universities

In June 2008, St. Stephen's College, one of India's most reputed institutes, announced that it would reserve 50 percent of its seats for Christian students. The news channel NDTV invited Ramachandra Guha, a former Stephanian, to a panel to give his opinion on the decision, and I watched as his remarks opposing the quota were shouted down by an academic who said that "minorities deserve protections, and minority colleges are the right institutions to do it."* Ram pointed out that the Christians eligible for the 50 percent quota make up around 2 percent of the Indian population, and the quota decisively downgraded merit in admissions, setting the cutoff high school score for Christian students at 60 percent in a college that typically demanded well over 90 percent. More depressing, an institute famous for its diverse alumni, Christian or otherwise—Montek Singh Ahluwalia, Amitav Ghosh, Kaushik Basu—is now encouraging a policy that segregates religious groups within a secular society.

The movement toward such policies is now pervasive. Instead of debating the difficult but necessary reforms we need to improve access, expansion and quality in our universities, Indian politicians have stuck to the issue of reservations. In 2006 a constitutional amendment sanctified caste-based reservations in private universities, and a new law increased reservations in central institutions to include more caste groups. Nehru had trusted our universities with the ability to cleanse India of its "feudal pathologies," thanks to their influence through ideas that were both "secular and scientific." But with reservation the opposite is taking place—our universities are being shaped by the worst of India's factionalism and feudal ideas. Our biggest arguments are now over the share of different castes and communities in seats and hiring.

"Reservation has probably set us back several years in our ability to carry out the reforms we need to," Sam tells me. It has become a means of evading the questions of falling quality and low access by demanding community-based access to the few good institutions that remain. It has also preempted effective approaches where we could combine merit and financial aid effectively while expanding access to quality education. Needs-blind admissions—where a student's financial status is not looked at until after the admission is made, but no student would have to forgo education due to financial constraints—has not received the same attention as reservations, and neither have affirmative action policies that take into account both skills and background.

The reservations approach has embedded itself to the point that it now seems impossible to drive a stake into its heart. For many resigned observers,

*While St. Stephen's College is affiliated to the Delhi University and funded by the UGC, it was set up by the Church, and the Supreme Council which sets its policies is dominated by Anglican leaders.

the hugely popular support for reservation is in line with the general politicization of higher education. The 1986 National Policy on Education had virtually conceded defeat while remarking that all basic policy decisions in education had become "political in their essence." But by breaking down this wall between politics and our universities, we are killing the reformist capability of our colleges.

Though the various competing visions for our institutes seem bent on destroying each other, there is common ground among them—particularly in their need to ensure relevance, quantity and access. The reservation debate feeds on the major weakness in India's higher education: the lack of access to quality schools. Arjun Singh's recommendations for OBC reservations in central institutions was spark to dry tinder, igniting protests across the country, particularly because half of all the highly coveted seats in India's top colleges were now "reserved," making admissions even harder to come by for the "general category" students. Only when the Moily committee recommended an increase in the total number of seats, so that capacities in the general category remained unchanged, did much of the anger die down.

Our universities are now among the last remaining holdouts of the top-down state, where the government's word passes down the ranks, and is carried out by its bureaucrats. This sector may also be the hardest for the government to let go of, considering the central role universities are seen to play in shaping a country's ideas, and the power that reservation has in whipping up electorates into a frenzy. But the market economy is nevertheless pushing relentlessly against old systems, urging them toward reform, and penalizing policies that fail. The question remains, however, whether we can enable reform fast enough to leverage the opportunities we now have both domestically and globally.

Reform requires key, controversial steps: we need to move toward a model of light regulation, where we have an independent regulator distanced from government. The oversight of educational institutions must be transparent and allow new institutions to enter easily. An open system that welcomes private investment both from India and from abroad is essential to create institutions with ambitions to be world-class.

Investments without reforms will do nothing to counter the distortions that we see today. Entrepreneurs building institutes will continue to come up with combinations of nonprofit and for-profit organizations to evade regulation and taxes. The landscape will fragment into a highly regulated and a totally unregulated sector. The politics that are insidious to the sector will discourage those who want to set up top-quality colleges. The rich will send their children abroad to study. In the face of a lack of choice and capacity the battle over reservations and the bunker mentality of preparatory schools for admissions to top colleges will continue. And the students will remain caught in the middle of this harrowing mess.

The effect of reform here is likely to be electrifying. Universities are powerful centers for dissent and change. The Kothari Commission report had called them "the organs of civilization"—across countries, they have been the major source of new ideas, both economic and political. The most fundamental notions of secular identity and liberty had their roots in Europe's universities, and the most prominent technological advances and innovations of the last few decades have come from the tight cluster of colleges in the United States, Europe and increasingly East Asia. In India, during the years of colonial rule, our universities had fulfilled precisely this role. As André Béteille has written, these universities were "among the first open and secular institutions in a society that was governed largely by the rules of kinship, caste and religion."[16] They were the first places where thousands of Indians began to question and resist unfairness both in domestic tradition and in imperial policy.

Unshackling these institutions from the hold of the state and interest groups means that our universities, rather than being weathervanes for our political opinions and debates, can become important shapers of political opinion in themselves. This is especially true as we now move into uncharted territory in our environment, energy, health and pension challenges, and as we attempt to leverage technology more effectively for growth. Reforms in higher education cannot be bargained away—they form the bedrock for a vibrant economy, the place from where we can, given the chance, build powerful and sustainable new ideas for our future.

A FINE BALANCE

IN POLITICS, we often mistake stubbornness for strength and ideology for idealism—showing bullheadedness and portraying yourself as some sort of "immovable force," it is believed, is likely to bring rewards. And this stance has unfortunately become especially pervasive in our most critical ideas.

The failure of this approach became clear to me in the 1990s, while watching the arguments unfolding over the Sardar Sarovar dam on Gujarat's Narmada river. From 1989 the activist Medha Patkar—relentless, gutsy, unyielding—led the 200,000 peasants and tribals who were to be displaced by the dam in a protest movement, the Narmada Bachao Andolan (Save the Narmada Movement). It attracted media coverage and support from around the country but did little to persuade the government to back down. With half the dam already built, an outside group of Pune engineers studied the dam's logistics and came up with a compromise, in a better-designed model that would lower the dam's height and submerge much less of the surrounding environment. But both the NBA and the government rejected the option. The activists said the dam could not be built at all (even though the protesters were already agitating in the shadow of its large, concrete wall) while the state insisted on the original design. The final dam was exactly as the government envisaged, and the protesters' every demand was spurned.

Time and again, this extreme partisanship has dragged our battles straight into the ditch, with compromise rarely making any headway. This strikes me as very unfortunate, since I believe that the best path for our policies can never be at the far left or right. It has to be at the point where the state, the entrepreneurs and civil society negotiate over development decisions, where each can exercise some kind of control over the other. Right now, we are nowhere close to such negotiation, and this is a danger sign for the Indian economy.

Our changed approaches to the ideas dealt with in Part One laid the foundation of our rise so far, and took India past 8 percent growth. The ideas in Part Two are the ones that we need to execute effectively, and without which we will eventually fall back to a 6 percent growth rate or less.

But it is in our most contested ideas that our potential for double-digit and inclusive growth exists. Dr. Vijay Kelkar admits that these reforms need political courage. He tells me that during his stint with the NDA government as adviser to the finance minister and head of various task forces on tax policy, he attempted to persuade the ministers toward bold reforms by referring them to the mythological story of the churning of the sea.* As Dr. Kelkar pointed out, change and churn, as in the story, would have both good and bad consequences. Reforms, by triggering upheaval, would first bring out *halahala*, or poison, in criticism for the government, but would create massive political gains—*amrita*, or nectar, over a longer period. "The job of a visionary government is to accept these short-term challenges, since the political gains for them will be massive."

However, Indian governments have balked at implementing our most contested and visible policies, in labor and education and in bringing down entry barriers for entrepreneurs. In part, this is thanks to the lack of a vision on the role of the state in India's postreform economy.

The state in India typically encompassed two aspects: as provider of goods and services and as a regulator and decision-maker.

Our earlier, socialist-tinged take had given the government enormous power in both these roles, since the popular notion was that the government can provide solutions and results that are more equitable, inclusive and more effective than the market. But as we saw both in India and elsewhere, this

*In the story, a mountain was used as the rod to churn the "Ocean of Milk," while the king of serpents, Vasuka, served as the rope. A deadly poison or *Halahala*, came out early in the churning. *Amrita*, the nectar of immortality, came out last.

theory of government rarely mirrors reality. "There was so much money spent in the public sector and government driven development," Chandrababu Naidu tells me, "in the hope that this would address India's many problems." But a country's economic structures are finally run by people, and power held in a vacuum—either by the state or by markets—allows them to circumvent rules and tilt decisions in their favor.

We have often mistaken the reform agenda to be one where the markets replace the state as the key player in the economy, and the state relinquishes its earlier roles of player and regulator. But this would be egregious—the role of the state is indispensable. What our reforms must really envision for growth, and for inclusive growth in particular, is rather a golden mean where power is balanced between our various players and where no one can assume overweening control. A new vision for the state—whether as a provider of services or as regulator—is a search for this golden mean, a balance between government, markets and civil society.

A focus on such a balance means that even as the state is retreating from its dominant role in the economy with reforms, it cannot, must not, retreat too far. It cannot, for instance, abdicate its role in providing services in public goods such as health, education and infrastructure.

In regulation as well our vision for the government must focus on balance, taking care not to tilt power too much toward markets or allow market players to capture regulatory policy. The danger of allowing markets to innovate without regulation has already become apparent in the U.S. financial crisis of 2008. Deregulation here reduced oversight over large swathes of the U.S. financial sector, and when this coincided with the rise of opaque derivative products and markets flush with excess cash, the result was a financial meltdown. The cost of this has been an expensive "bailing out" of the sector with a rescue package that is likely to cross $1 trillion.

The government has to maintain independent regulatory bodies, promote open markets and limit oligopolistic businesses—especially in natural resources such as iron, coal, gas, oil and spectrum. It must encourage fairness between markets and civil society through independent, transparent stock markets and financial regulators, and a legal system that prevents mob rule and influence by businesses.

Such an approach, as Naidu points out, "gives more people a stake in reforms, and they become invested in implementing progressive ideas. Else people become mere spectators to wealth creation, who forever feel left out and sidelined." He adds, "We have yet to realize trickle-down economics in a substantial way, and without that we will not be able to keep implementing our reform agenda."

We have to embrace this idea of balance across our policies and realize that the more players in our markets and the more dispersed the power, the better it is, since it self-regulates against abuse.

From the farmers using India's commodity markets to the urban poor building their own homes in shantytowns, to the villagers, abandoned by weak state and local governments, instituting community cleanups under Apna Desh, people are in search of concrete solutions. This vision of balance and fairness can achieve progress that is sustainable and provides these cross-sections of Indians with real answers.

If we do this effectively, we will be able to frame an agenda of ideas that will focus clearly on inclusive growth. In fact this becomes especially critical when it comes to the "ideas of our future," which form the last part of this book. These ideas of the future—environment, energy, health, pensions and the use of technology—are the ones that developed markets struggle with today, and where the interplay between the state, markets and civil society become indispensable for alternative and more effective answers.

A vision for a golden mean will help us avoid building massive barricades between the group of people who believe in government and those who believe in markets. In essence, it can become a touchstone for both these groups to agree on better solutions.

And it gives us the means not just to resolve our differences, but to look far into our horizons and anticipate the challenges we are likely to face.

Part Four

CLOSER THAN THEY APPEAR

Ideas to Anticipate

IDEAS TO ANTICIPATE

IN THE 1960s the writer Leland Hazard, while on a visit to India, attended the Beating the Retreat ceremony and was fascinated by the ceremonials and the processions of tall, solemn Sikhs in their impressive turbans marching past the crowds. In the final moments of the evening, he stood waiting for the band to strike up "some esoteric Indian strains" that would end the day. The band started, and he found himself listening to "Abide with Me," a hymn by the nineteenth-century British poet Henry Francis Lyte, and one of King George V's favorite hymns.

In its symbolism, I found his story striking—in how India, despite our longing to leave our past behind, remained a country caught between the old and the new, with a large number of British ideas still holding on years after the end of the Empire.

As a young nation finding its footing in the tumultuous years of the 1950s, India pulled off some impressive achievements in a very short period of time. The majority of the Western democracies had become "full democracies" only in the 1940s, the culmination of a centuries-long journey toward civil rights that India completed within three years of independence. Such an accelerated change meant that instead of shaping our economic and social themes from scratch, we retained a lot more of British India's laws and ideas than we were comfortable with. For instance, too much of the Government of India Act of 1935, with its obsession with central power and control, seeped into the Indian Constitution. We retained the bureaucratic structures of British India, and imperial ideas influenced our approach to education, employment, health and the environment.

We did not make much effort to clean house or introduce new ideas in the years after independence. We could forgive ourselves this in India's early decades, as the country struggled for growth and remained in a near-constant state of crisis. But post-1991 and postreform, India is a very different country. As a nation that is now the world's fastest-growing democracy, a child of the global networked economy and possessed with a large share of human capital, India should be an emerging hub today for provocative and innovative new ideas.

After all it is usually the countries that lead the curve on growth that take the lead in shaping the ideas of the era. Most of our early ideas around markets, wealth creation and citizen welfare, for instance, came from thinkers such as Adam Smith and John Stuart Mill, who helped shape Britain's policies during its growth in the seventeenth and eighteenth centuries. The United States similarly shaped its most dynamic and enduring ideas on growth as industrialization peaked through the mid-twentieth century. These ideas drove up productivity and created massive new wealth for these economies by expanding their workforce and by creating a new, surging middle class on a scale never seen before. These new ideas turned these countries—the United Kingdom, parts of Western Europe, the United States and Japan—into the powers of the modern age.

But while India is now on a similar and even steeper growth curve, we have fallen behind when it comes to new, innovative solutions. Here, we are battling an age-old statism that has gone deep into the grain of our governance and our state. Our most enterprising bureaucrats and politicians encounter this resistance at every turn, coming up smack dab against a tradition of this-is-how-we've-always-done-it. When I visited Sudhir Kumar at the railway ministry, what struck me was that a big part of his job was battling this inertia within the bureaucracy and in railway regulation. He described his astonishment when on a visit to the Rail Museum he found documents and weight standards for rail tracks dating from 1922 that were exactly the same as the standards the Indian Railways use now. "Many of our capacities and standards," he told me, "have not been revised for decades, even as our building materials, technology and track capacities have changed."

This is a risky mind-set to have when India faces challenges that are both unique and daunting in our health, pensions systems, environment and energy. Right now, these are the issues that occupy our periphery, barely visible in the glare of our day-to-day concerns over our schools, subsidies, our infrastructure and job markets. We pay them lip service on anointed days—when the government releases an energy report, or when the Employee Provident Fund releases an update of its latest dismal numbers—and then go back to business as usual.

I have noticed, however, that these very issues we ignore so thoroughly are the ones that are now widely debated in the global conference and speaker circuit—they represent major crises in the developed world. For a long time I thought of these issues as "rich nations' concerns," believing that India had more urgent things to worry about in our poverty and growth rates. But as I heard experts going on about climate change, pandemics, obesity and the aging crisis in the West, I realized that not only are these problems relevant to India, but we have to address them proactively to eventually come to a workable solution.

As a late bloomer, India has had the advantage of listening in to developed countries as they discuss what worked for them and what did not. This is not a trifling advantage on issues where the wrong approach has created a whole host of challenges for the rich nations.

Much of the West, for example, is now struggling with the fallout of pensions and health policies framed in the 1930s and 1940s, and are facing emerging crises in their environmental and energy resources. Many of these problems ballooned in advanced countries because the consequences were not anticipated, it was not fully understood how people would respond to incentives, and technology was inadequate to design better solutions. By adjusting our own approach, India could actually take steps now that would eliminate or minimize such future crises.

In India, however, we have not yet started to frame new solutions around these issues. After all, for a young country, pensions are the last thing on anybody's mind. Our development challenges eclipse concerns over the environment and clean energy solutions. Even as we worry about infant and maternal mortality, we tend to dismiss obesity and diabetes as the concerns of the well-to-do, outcomes of private, bad habits rather than a public health matter. And we treat technology as the technologists' concern and not a fundamentally transformational force.

But why would we choose to go into these issues deliberately blind, stumbling in the very places the countries before us did, and repeating their mistakes one by one? We can already see, from where we stand, a route to development that is cleaner, healthier and more sustainable than the one other countries chose. We do not need to create a plethora of lifestyle diseases before we realize that wellness from a balanced diet, exercise and a moderate lifestyle is a good idea. We do not need to burn through our forests and drain our groundwater before we realize that abusing the environment has awful consequences. We do not need to grow addicted to oil before we realize the potential of renewable energy. We do not need to grow old before we realize that the state's pension liabilities have become unsustainable, and we can avoid clumsy forms of governance by using information technology.

Mahesh Rangarajan tells me that for India this lack of innovation seems to be the default mind-set. He adds a remark that is now instantly familiar. "We are a country," he says, "that has embraced lethargy except in crisis." So far, we have all but dismissed the advantage of foresight, and we are losing out on an opportunity to attempt solutions that could uncover new efficiencies and trigger big leaps in growth. The entrepreneur and venture capitalist Vinod Khosla has said of our emerging challenges in energy and environment that "a crisis is a terrible thing to waste." This has a certain resonance, considering that India is exceptionally well placed to provide answers to these new, hot-button problems—as a latecomer to development, we are not burdened with the legacies of old technology and entrenched behavior. We have, for instance, yet to pick up developed-country habits such as a fondness for gas-guzzler vehicles, for meat-oriented diets or for social security paid up by the government.

But we have not yet committed ourselves to these issues. In health and pensions, we are following set models; in energy and environment, we are taking our cues from the developed world. We have yet to recognize the full possibilities of IT. India now stands evenly balanced between our reluctance to change in the face of immense challenges and the possibilities we have if we do tackle these issues head-on. The consequences of these two choices are in extremes—in the long term we will either become a country that greatly disappoints when compared with our potential or one that beats all expectations.

ICT IN INDIA

From Bangalore One to Country One

A hole in the wall

A decade ago, on January 26, 1999, the scientist Dr. Sugata Mitra watched as his team cut out a hole in the wall of the Delhi NIIT campus. On the other side of it was the Kalkaji slum, a closely packed, messy confusion of small concrete and brick homes.

The slum's neighbors had regarded it as such an eyesore that the government had been busy building a five-foot-high fence to cordon it off. But Dr. Mitra saw the slum—whose clusters carried hopeful names like "Nehru" and "Navjeevan" (new life)—and spotted an opportunity. Through the hole they had carved out, his team provided access to a computer for the slum's kids, who quickly figured out how to use it. And soon enough, Dr. Mitra found that children using these computers were demanding "a faster processor and more RAM"[1] and teaching themselves English.

Experiments like the one initiated by Dr. Mitra, whose project the government has since taken up as part of its literacy efforts, are shaping a face for information technology in India that is very different from anything anyone expected when IT first made inroads here.

When IT first made a serious debut into Indian economic policy—with its coming out party in 1984—it might as well have been the most unpopular kid in class, greeted with brickbats and managing to survive only thanks to its passionate champions in the Rajiv Gandhi government. Rajiv had great faith in the possibilities of these technologies and as prime minister had announced the New Computer Policy just twenty days after he took office. But if anything, electronification started off disappointing the expectations of both its critics and its admirers. Some of the early initiatives were enormous successes—the telecom policy introduced by Sam Pitroda had an immediate impact, as public telephone booths mushroomed across the country, making phones truly accessible for the first time in India's cities and towns. The electronification of banking processes across India's public banks made the jobs of those at the front office, the tellers and clerks, far easier. And the computer policy put wind in the sails of small IT companies, including Infosys, which were targeting the international software market. Indian IT companies such as ours—despite early clients who seemed interested but anxious about our ability to deliver—took off.

But other efforts fared badly; Rajiv had emphasized, for instance, that IT was key to tackling India's challenges from poverty to education, but computers supplied to schools with no electricity were little more than curios, and most departments in Delhi strongly resisted the IT initiatives the new government introduced. Overall, the technology remained on a slow simmer. Its effect on the lives of ordinary Indians was mostly indirect—some industries such as banking and telecommunications were adopting these tools in a big way, but few Indians had come in touch with such technology themselves.

But sometimes, change can sneak up on you, completely underestimated in the impact it will have. Around the 2000s, the impact of electronification in India began to change. It started to rapidly evolve from a top-down system driven by government policy and industry into a force surging up from the grassroots. Indian entrepreneurs big and small were at this point focusing on the possibilities of building a unique business approach—based on the idea that you could vastly expand the pool of Indian consumers if you were willing to focus on extremely low-cost products. When IT met this strategy, its presence exploded. Even as Hindustan Unilever Limited (HUL), P&G, Nirma and Cadbury began selling everything from shampoos to soap, detergent and chocolate in tiny, "single serve" packets costing a rupee or less, banking firms such as ICICI began to offer "micro" loans, and hospitals such as Aravind Eye offered targeted, low-cost health services, technology entrepreneurs began offering low-cost Internet and computer usage to villagers across rural India.[2]

As the possibilities in such low-cost technology began to explode, firms across retail, banking and communications found that IT could well be their missing link in connecting with people who were often illiterate and located in distant villages, dirt-road miles away from the nearest market. And reform-minded bureaucrats found that such technology, untouched as it was by the legacies of the sarkar raj, could be a powerful leverage for better public services. IT could play a bigger and more powerful role in the economy than anyone had guessed or attempted before.

Beneath the surface

You might wonder about my *two* chapters on electronification—it may look like nothing more than part indulgence and part compulsion on my side, a nod to my long role in the software industry.

But I think that electronification is still incredibly underestimated in India in the changes it can bring. In the first part of the book, we talked about how our changing attitude toward technology, from being regarded as an alien and forbidding thing to something that has a huge impact on our daily lives, has been one of the ideas that helped reshape the Indian economy. But we have yet to scratch the surface of the possibilities that electronification offers us, partly because we have looked to the West for guidance in using such technology.

The evolution of IT worldwide has given us a whiff of its potential. Since the invention of the transistor, technology has evolved to astonish even its most optimistic champions. Computers and other forms of digital technology are becoming more powerful, smaller and cheaper every year—and more ubiquitous. We are now seeing the rise of immense computing power, almost unlimited storage capacity and numerous small yet powerful devices that can tap into this. This has enabled a high-speed "digitization" of all kinds of content, where voice, books, music and video can be transmuted into ones and zeros and carried on the network. At the same time, networks transmitting this information have become intricately intertwined and ubiquitous, especially with the rise of fiber-optic and broadband technology. Communication is becoming wireless, lighter than air, with cellular telephony and an alphabet soup of technologies such as Wi-Fi and WiMax. But while these electronification trends triggered dramatic change in the United States and Europe—and no book has described these shifts better than Thomas Friedman's *The World Is Flat*—we have seen them evolve in these countries mainly as another layer over traditional models, complementing fixed-line telephones, dead-tree content and established ways of doing business.

India is different. For all the benefits India has seen from expected trends in mobile phones, electronic voting and modern stock exchanges, there is a lot more that is likely to unfold around our technology revolution in the next decade. As virgin territory, India could be a testing ground for something far more radical. India is not yet a "settled in" economy—our supply chains and infrastructure are not nineteenth- or twentieth-century structures and systems, and our market systems are little more than a quarter century old.

Combine the still untapped potential of technology with India's possibilities, and I see a path to a very different kind of country a few decades from now. Even if I were to extrapolate only from what is happening in the present, we can expect a transformation. We can, first of all, reasonably assume that within a few years we should be able to have ubiquitous connectivity to cover every Indian home, hamlet and town. The trends toward this are already obvious: mobile phones are set to pass the 50 percent penetration mark and many mobile operators hope to cover 95 percent of the population in a few years. Falling prices for handsets has helped make them popular, as the price has come down from around Rs 15,000 for the cheapest handset in the early 1990s to less than Rs 700 today. And even as mobile telephony gets more sophisticated and networks move from 2G to 3G, high-bandwidth and wireless connectivity will allow us to transmit both voice and data with ease.

The second implication of the rise of increasingly low-cost technology is that it will be possible to put an electronic device into the hands of every citizen and in every village. It could be a low-cost computer, a smartphone, a smart card or a PDA, and it will be both practical and cheap enough for the person to buy or the state to provide.

The third implication is that we will have the computing power and storage capacity to store an unprecedented amount of information that could be universally accessible. While this may conjure up the picture of an Orwellian Big Brother for some, in truth the power from ICT and access to information flows both ways, as many governments have found out to their disadvantage. For instance, news on unpopular policies and state scandals spreads much faster, and so does dissent. The combination of ubiquitous communication, cheap devices and unlimited computing and storage means that everyone will have a way of communicating with one another, and of storing vast amounts of such information, accessing knowledge and entertainment and being connected to a "national grid."

So powerful are these tools becoming that I believe India's revolution, when we see it, will not be like the one carried out in Europe, with peasant revolutionaries storming the castle gates with farmhand tools, but through low-cost technology models that put the power of digital information and networks in the hands of everyone.

But so far what I have described will happen one way or the other. This part of the revolution is already inevitable, thanks to falling costs of technology, global competition and the emphasis Indian governments have placed on making these tools accessible. But there is a lot more we must get done in terms of our underlying structures in order to have a truly effective, wired nation in place.

To have any kind of national-level, working approach to technology, we must start with the government. But when it comes to computerization within the state, we cannot build new systems over a creaky base—we have to first reinvent our state processes to increase our efficiencies rather than merely computerizing what exists. We also need to ensure that people can actually access these systems effectively; else IT-enabled governance will be little more than a showcase project. And we have to take a long, strategic look at the information infrastructure we need and all the possible services we can deliver across this structure.

Getting rid of our phantoms: Single citizen I.D.

A big source of heartburn for those running banks, managing elections and regulating the stock market in India is that the country is filled with people who are virtually invisible. "The one thing that gives me sleepless nights," ICICI's Madhabi Buch tells me, "is the inability of us Indian bankers to put a name to a transaction."

Today Indians can have a multitude of numbers with which to identify ourselves, depending on when and where we interact with the state. When we get a passport we get a passport I.D., a ration card gets us another number, when we pay taxes we need a permanent account number (PAN), when we register our vote we get a voter I.D. card, and on to barcode infinitum. "Our databases are in these disconnected silos," the chief election commissioner N. Gopalaswami says. This makes zeroing in on a definite identity for each citizen particularly difficult, since each government department works a different turf and with different groups of people. The lack of a unique number has given space to plenty of phantoms—in voter lists and in below-poverty-line (BPL) schemes and holding bank accounts with multiple PANs. One academic tells me, "The number of BPL ration cards circulating in Karnataka is more than the state's entire population, let alone the number of BPL families."

India's ministries and departments are also quite isolated, with separate fund flows and intricate, overhyphenated authority levels. As a result these systems require paperwork-choked processes each time citizens approach the state. A common technology and process platform for government schemes and departments—especially now that they have such large budgets—would be a huge improvement in coordinating information between departments and getting rid of redundancy and triplicate forms. Identity systems linked up with an IT-enabled process that interlinks our various departments would, besides making citizen information and identity more verifiable, make the relationship between the state and the citizen infinitely less traumatizing in both time and energy wasted.

Such a "national grid" would require, as a first and critical step, a unique and universal I.D. for each citizen. Creating a national register of citizens, assigning them a unique I.D. and linking them across a set of national databases, like the PAN and passport, can have far-reaching effects in delivering public services better and targeting services more accurately. Unique identification for each citizen also ensures a basic right—the right to "an acknowledged existence"[3] in the country, without which much of a nation's poor can be nameless and ignored, and governments can draw a veil over large-scale poverty and destitution.

The use of IT and the rise of such unique number systems are closely correlated. In the United States, for instance, the Social Security Administration (SSA) was the first federal bureaucracy to require the use of computers, because of the overwhelming complexity of processing the social security numbers and data of its 200 million–plus citizens. The bureaucracy was a massive complex of wall-to-wall file cabinets managed by hundreds of clerks. It was the early IBM 705 computer that helped transform and streamline it. This mainframe approach quickly spread to European bureaucracies in the 1960s and 1970s. The transparency and flexibility of such computerization also enabled other reforms—such as laws that introduced individual citizen accounts for benefits and welfare payouts, a step that both opposition parties and citizens in Europe and the United States would have been deeply suspicious of under the earlier, less transparent and bureaucracy-run system. In China as well, IT has helped the government transform its social security systems from a local network to a national, increasingly interlinked process.

In India the government has made some attempts toward such a single citizen I.D. number. This had a lot of traction in the previous NDA government as well, albeit for reasons that were less financial—they saw it as a way of identifying illegal aliens and refugees. UPA's finance minister, P. Chidambaram, has on the other hand seen it as a way to address the identification challenges of Indian banks and the financial sector. A stop-gap arrangement that the government has put in place requires the PAN as "the sole identification number" during bank transactions. But of course, with just 60 million people with a PAN, this does not come close to a broad-based citizen I.D., and Dr. Arvind Virmani, former principal adviser at the Planning Commission in New Delhi, tells me that the government has been working on a "smart-integrated I.D. card" that would serve as a unique I.D. As things stand, a regulatory authority along the lines of the SSA in the United States, Chidambaram says, is likely to be approved.

Too often, though, we see issuing smart cards as the main challenge of implementing such a system. But building these intelligent little stripes is the easy part. It is in making the back-end infrastructure secure and scalable, providing a single record keeper for the whole country and integrating the agents who issue these numbers that it gets tough.

To do this, we need a sustained and multipronged effort that cuts across governments as well as companies. For example, issuing this number to each citizen, say, during a census would be extremely onerous, as it is a painful task prone to errors as census officials spend long days walking through neighborhoods and knocking on doors. It would be a lot more effective to issue these numbers when citizens come to the government. This would mean issuing citizen I.D.s when individuals come to a public office for an identification document—a passport, birth certificate, caste certificate, driver's license—when they come to collect a benefit such as a BPL card or when they have to make a financial transaction, such as pay taxes, open a bank account or buy into a mutual fund. The government can also easily recruit private companies such as telecommunication and financial services firms to become intermediary issuers to their large numbers of customers.

Each of these paths to identifying the citizen and bringing him into the database would cover different pools of people. The PAN covers all tax payers, voter I.D.s all registered citizens over eighteen, birth certificates all newborns and BPL cards the poor. Using the databases to issue I.D.s to different groups of people means that the initiative would ramp up to near-universal, accurate levels very quickly. And if necessary, such efforts can be complemented with a census.

A national smart I.D. done at this level could, I think, be transformational. Acknowledging the existence of every single citizen, for instance, automatically compels the state to improve the quality of services and immediately gives the citizen better access. No one else can then claim a benefit that is rightfully yours, and no one can deny their economic status, whether abjectly poor or extremely wealthy. More than anything else, this recognition creates among all parties concerned a deeper awareness of their rights, entitlements and duties. It becomes far more difficult for both the citizen and the government to dodge any of these.

A key piece of infrastructure that must sit on top of an interconnected grid is the electronic flow of funds. This will require that each uniquely identified citizen or organization has a financial account into which money can be transferred from the state. This could be an account in a bank, a post office or with a self-help group. And within this system, the I.D. smart card can function as a mobile, nontransferable electronic passbook.

My guess is that the impact on inclusive growth and India's savings rate from implementing this would be massive, considering that an estimated 80 percent of Indians today do not have a bank account and therefore lie outside any sort of banking system besides perhaps the one represented by the exploitative moneylender and his steel box of cash. "The weakest aspect of India's economic reach is in financial access," Dr. C. Rangarajan agrees, "and its impact on inclusive growth has been severe." For instance, people need savings to invest in education, spend on health care, or to feel secure enough to move to a city, leaving their home and land to take up jobs in a place where they have no real assets.

Linking smart cards to such accounts can open up the banking system to hundreds of millions more people. It also introduces the possibility of offering direct services, from pension and benefit payments to trading accounts to an unprecedented number of people.

Distribution channels

It does sound premature to talk about the transformational potential of IT when our Internet penetration nationally stands at 2 percent. Without real access, our fond dreams for technology in India are just that. But IT penetration can ramp up very quickly with the right models. For an electronification strategy to be effective in India, we need an approach that does not stress traditional mechanisms of IT penetration but is tailored to our disparate and dispersed geographies, and that can expand with speed, efficiency and, most critically, at low cost.

Right now the greatest danger we face is of creating a divide in IT access that parallels the other divides in accessing infrastructure, capital and information that exist between India's rich and poor, educated and illiterate, and urban and rural people. To avoid this, we must target a variety of distribution channels for spreading technology. Already, mobile phones have spread rapidly and linked up with other technology-based services such as the NCDEX for live commodity prices and the NSE for live market movements. There are other, not immediately obvious ways of communication that can be invaluable in building complementary technologies that get information to people. Community radios, for example, can disseminate information to large groups, regardless of literacy levels. And a recent, interesting nonprofit effort has been the "Question Box," which links villagers in Uttar Pradesh to an operator who is connected to the Internet. People ask the operator questions through the box—anything from exam results to the price of tomatoes at the *mandi*—and she gets the answers online and gives them an instant response.

Providing ICT services through kiosks is another mechanism that is proving quite effective in rural India. The National e-Governance Plan (NeGP) launched in 2005 planned 100,000 such kiosks to provide a variety of state services across India, but Indian entrepreneurs are already making waves with their own rural kiosk networks. For instance, Sriram Raghavan's kiosks across

Karnataka are popular for printing out caste certificates and land records. Such networks can be built upon quite easily to support national I.D. schemes. And having an ICT-literate entrepreneur managing a community-based service is often more effective than individual PC ownership, especially in the rural areas—it speeds up the ICT-learning curve, and these entrepreneurs have invested in services tailored to illiterate villagers, such as voice-enabled applications and local-language software. "Our role ends up being something midway between a businessperson and a mentor," Sriram tells me, "but not for very long. Even illiterate villagers learn how to use them very quickly and are never scared of these systems. They want to figure them out."

The access to information that these multiple channels offer in rural India has the potential to trigger a sea change in agricultural productivity. The farmer can, for instance, receive highly localized, relevant and timely information through mobile phones on prices, market trends and weather forecasts. Infosys is doing one such project with ACDI/VOCA, a nonprofit international development organization that is working to make local information available to farmers. Amit Mehra, managing director of Reuters Market Light, which provides such data to thousands of farmers in Maharashtra through mobile phone text messages, tells me that farmers are finding such information very useful, and the illiterate ones get their children to read out the messages to them.

From subsidies to direct benefits

An IT-enabled, accessible national I.D. system would be nothing less than revolutionary in how we distribute state benefits and welfare handouts; I believe it would transform our politics. Right now our elections are virtually defined by subsidy promises, and a whole ecosystem of theft and leakage has emerged around the handling of our public funds. One state chief minister was recently quoted openly telling his party workers to "take one-third of the money, and leave the rest."[4] Across our creaky subsidy distribution systems, leakages average 50 percent and more. The inefficiency of these state schemes has gotten even worse over the last two decades: in the 1980s Rajiv Gandhi had remarked that for every rupee spent on the poor, only 15 paise finally reaches them; in 2007 his son, Rahul, offered his own estimate, saying that now a mere 5 paise of every rupee spent reaches the poor in some districts. Mechanisms to curb corruption can be thwarted if high-level bureaucracy is venal enough, as was seen in the most recent government employment scheme, the NREGA, where more than 30 percent of funds were being siphoned off in some districts in Orissa. "As GDP has surged, corruption across government projects has gone up," Chidambaram tells me. "The widespread leakage of funds mean, for instance, that it costs us anywhere between four to six crore rupees to build one kilometer of road."

A national I.D. system would make these porous distribution mechanisms and our dependence on the moral scruples of our bureaucrats redundant. The state could instead transfer benefits directly in the form of cash to bank accounts of eligible citizens, based on their income returns or assets. Dr. Vijay Kelkar points out that such an approach would not just bring in all citizens within the financial system, but would also give them real financial power. In Dr. Kelkar's conservative estimate, for example, combining the bulk of our subsidies into a cash entitlement could amount to Rs 20,000 per family and make them eligible for loans of up to Rs 100,000.

This would redefine our welfare economy as we know it. The gains in efficiency and transparency would be unprecedented. The additional relief would be of no longer having to endure the harassment of officials for bribes, or being denied benefits that are your right. Such a benefit-linked smart-card model would also make welfare benefits national, allowing citizens who migrate to the city to continue using certain allowances. Essentially it would help our governments adapt to what our country has long been—a nation of migrants, who often cross state and city lines in search of work and opportunity.

Chidambaram tells me that the government is set to implement a direct-benefits model as a pilot project in two states, Punjab and Haryana, for everyone who has a BPL card. "I don't think we have yet fully recognized how politically potent direct benefits could be, compared to indirect subsidies," he says. "The citizen doesn't really know how much benefit he gets from subsidized LPG—he has no idea what the real price is. But a direct cash benefit is a welfare offering whose value is obvious."

Such direct transfers would transform the underlying philosophy of our subsidy systems. Since 1991 Indian governments have implemented reform-oriented policies sweetened with old-style subsidies* directed at various in-

*For example, food and fertilizer subsidies alone have grown at a clip of more than 30 percent. It is estimated that including off-budget items such as oil and electricity subsidies brought India's combined deficit to 9 percent in 2006–7.

terest groups. There is a clear attitude of compensating for something here—of governments trying to cushion the blow of what they see as unpopular, promarket policies. But providing citizens more direct benefits changes these welfare mechanisms from a way of insulating people from the market to a way of empowering them, by giving them capital to access the market. And at the same time, other aspects of the IT infrastructure would connect them to the information and the institutions that they need to participate effectively.

A networked, national I.D. infrastructure would mainstream many localized, pro-poor reforms in our financial systems, pensions, health and so on. For example, the national I.D. when integrated with self-help groups, microfinance and microinsurance institutions, would link financing options for the poor more closely with bank accounts, creating large-scale organized systems that are at the same time accessible and tailored to the local level. "We have to tie in local organizations with banks to make our services truly accessible," Madhabi concurs. "Anything else, considering the small and disparate communities we are targeting, would be too expensive."

Efficient program design

In India IT is flourishing on an infrastructure backbone very different from those in developed countries, and mainly through the low-cost approach of mobile phones and community kiosks. Solutions that take advantage of this infrastructure also ought to similarly prioritize tailoring our existing solutions—in welfare and financial benefits—more effectively for the Indian environment.

"When the most well-intentioned institutions fail," the economist Sendhil Mullainathan tells me, "it is usually because of the mistakes we make in our assumptions about the poor. The challenges of the poor vary considerably across countries, and in India we have to frame Indian solutions to benefit them." Senthil notes, for instance, that many of India's poor are farmers who get paid in bulk every season, postharvest. "But their expenses," he notes, "are on a monthly basis, like the rest of us, of food, school fees, clothes. Everyone knows how difficult it is to plan spending in the long term—weeks and months—with one-time cash in hand, and this is especially a huge struggle." Sendhil suggests that when it comes to loans for farmers, "We should be giving them funds in small amounts, rather than the big bang style handout that banks do now." Small and regular payments compel them to optimize and not make bad choices.

What has also been interesting in our most successful programs is how targeting the community, especially in the poorer, rural areas, seems more effective than targeting individuals. When it comes to the poor, their small assets mean that they rely for support on their families and village communities. Consequently our most successful solutions—whether it has been IT kiosks or microfinance—have been those that targeted groups rather than individuals. India's "traditional" businesses have already tested this, as when HUL created a network of Ashoka Mamis in the late 1990s to teach their communities issues of hygiene and health care; the more promising government programs in rural health and education—such as the volunteer-driven ASHA system and Madhya Pradesh's *guruji* program—also adopted this approach.

Perhaps such approaches succeeded because many of these communities have been isolated for so long, often without roads and power, cut off from governments and entrepreneurs, and are forced to rely on one another. Tapping into the networks of trust and cooperation that these communities have built as a result enables governments, social security systems, banks and entrepreneurs to offer more effective programs.

Other entrepreneurs are also tailoring their business models in rural India toward a more community-based, aggregated perspective. Debasish Mitra describes to me how his company is using technology to manage large "virtual farms" in Karnataka that are in reality several small farms run by individual farmers. "With our databases and mobile communications," he says, "we can send all farmers growing one particular crop a single communication, for instance, on a particular fertilizer that needs to be added on a particular day." It enables them to track origins of the produce across the supply chain. "We have barcodes on all our produce," Debasish says, "and we can track it back to the exact farm it came from."

Focusing on community solutions may in fact be a great fit for the kind of knowledge economy we see evolving in India today. Collaboration and community networks for formal and informal solutions built on ICT infrastructure can reduce information asymmetry in exponential ways, bridging the gaps between urban and rural India and across socioeconomic classes.

Contested lands

A somewhat unexpected place where IT in India has massive potential is in land. Land has never been an easy issue in India—it has been a source of much chest-thumping and of pitched, agitated battles. The crisis of land rights and the abuse many landless workers suffered under the zamindars nearly derailed efforts by Indian leaders preindependence to unite rural communities under the freedom movement. Postindependence, land politics became even more complicated, especially the failed land reform and redistribution efforts of the 1950s and 1960s. Today the politics of land in India still has a deeply adversarial texture—it is seen primarily as a battle between the powerful and the powerless. In the 1960s and 1970s, it was the zamindars on top, but lately it is companies eager to establish special economic zones (SEZs) in partnership with state governments that are seen as new, autocratic overlords. Singur and Nandigram's highly public battles over land reallocation for businesses are only the most visible signs of the continuing ugliness in our land politics.

These disputes stem from the convoluted Indian laws around property. Land laws in India are a bureaucratic sinkhole—registering the sale deed of a property in India, for example, certifies only the transfer of land, and not a change in ownership. Legislation around land titles is also complicated by murky, ancient records that often make it impossible to determine the owner of the land. With 90 percent of land titles in a country of a billion people in dispute and more than 30 percent of pending court cases concerned with land, it is no surprise that this issue has become so emotionally fraught. The confusion and lack of transparency around land rights have created massive opportunities for land sharks looking to make a fast buck. In urban slum areas, for instance, the poor often squat on public land, but slumlords collect either rent or a down payment for a land title. And unlike many countries, India has not recognized the "right to property" as a fundamental one since 1978, which makes it far more difficult for landowners to contest development plans and to ensure that the growth and expansion of markets do not steamroll over their livelihood.

Reforms in land titling and property rights, and linking such titles into the national I.D. system, would be a big step for our land markets. And this would provide powerful momentum toward more inclusive markets—the economist Hernando de Soto noted that the right to property and clear land titles are essential for bringing down poverty.[5] Land is particularly useful for the poor since it is a source of funds, a starting fuel for economic mobility, and instrumental as collateral for obtaining loans from banks.

But bringing IT into India's land markets presents a classic clash of the old and the new. Much of our land legislation and data come from methods used in British India. Considering that land taxes accounted for approximately 40 percent of British India's revenue, land surveys were a big part of the Empire's bureaucratic work. Land mapping for the British was a source of enormous, imperial pride, a way to enumerate the Empire's treasures, its captured territories. In fact the Survey of India covering 2,400 kilometers of the Indian subcontinent that William Lambton began in 1800 and George Everest concluded fifty years later, and which the British undertook with unstinting seriousness, was regarded not only as a unique mathematical and scientific triumph, but also a political one.

But however thorough and detailed for their times, these surveys relied on primitive tools, and very often, as Dr. N. Seshagiri notes, the boundaries defining land ownership "often described a well or a wall that had disappeared for many years, complicating ownership issues even further."

As Abhijit Banerjee points out, land records have also varied from region to region thanks to the differences in how *ryotwari, inamdari* and zamindari systems were surveyed; the princely states too had their own record-keeping and taxation mechanisms. But having seamless information records across states regardless of central versus state jurisdiction, through a national database for land and property records, would still have a dramatic, cleansing effect on land productivity, equity and litigation.

British India's surveys were also largely restricted to "revenue lands"—village lands that collected revenues for the East India Company. As a result we have good maps of rural India, but none for our urban areas. It has not helped that Indian governments did nothing to revise the town and country planning acts that the British had established as early as the 1850s, and also did little to manage expanding urbanization. "Reforming ancient planning laws is not even on the agenda," Swati Ramanathan tells me. "Our urban legislators spend most of their time firefighting, and negotiating between multiple city agencies to get any work done. They have neither the resources nor the energy to take up fundamental reform."

The result is laws that are standing relics and work processes a hundred years old. They are in fact so well preserved that they could be a valuable source of study for Indian historians on the workings of the urban bureaucracy in colonial India. Even now, city maps are hand-drawn sketches—a truly bizarre method to follow, considering the high-resolution digital tools we now have at our disposal for satellite-imagery, aerial and ground surveys. It is only recently that states such as Karnataka have begun to update these records, thanks to the efforts of the eGovernments Foundation and other organizations.

Land boundaries are also very complicated and confused within districts, with different departments—the electricity board, sewage services, the police—defining their own administrative boundaries. If you have had the misfortunate of having to file an FIR in India, you immediately experience the complication that comes from this—police stations across the city have drawn up their own jurisdictions, and there is massive confusion over where one station's authority ends and the other begins. In such cases, a bird's-eye view IT system could streamline information across the various state and local bodies. My experience with the eGovernments Foundation vindicates this; for instance, the foundation's efforts in digitally mapping our cities greatly helped the city's decision making for infrastructure investment and improvements. Global information system (GIS) maps have also enabled us to view ward-wise incomes and expenditure, and these provide a clear picture of where revenues are coming from and where municipalities are spending the money, while tracking citizen complaints highlights where the bottlenecks are.

There have been other remarkable efforts to address the challenge of land reform through IT—such as Rajeev Chawla's Bhoomi project to computerize land-revenue records in rural Karnataka, which he led and implemented almost single-handedly. The central government has taken up Chawla's initiative nationwide, with varying success across states—while Gujarat, Tamil Nadu and Andhra Pradesh have made some progress under the national-level Computerization of Land Records (CLR) scheme, others have lagged. It is difficult and hairy to navigate these reforms through a state's political and bureaucratic maze, and I tell Chawla that what we probably need to expand the scheme nationally is a few cloned copies of himself. But one thing that has changed might explain why implementing the scheme elsewhere is so difficult: before Bhoomi, people were unfamiliar with these IT-based reform initiatives and their potential and power was still unrecognized. As a result bureaucrats could push them through with little resistance. After Bhoomi, this is no longer the case.

These basic building blocks of using IT to identify citizens, and creating accessible electronic channels to reach citizens for financial transactions, classifying land, procuring documents and so on are the key to what I would call "information infrastructure." They are as important as ports, roads, power, water and airports are to physical infrastructure, and without them no larger-level IT project can take off. Once these pieces are in place, there will be huge economic benefits that will cascade to our citizens as well as to our broader economy.

Creating national information utilities

Sure, "national information utilities" sounds a little jargonistic. But it is really the best way to put it. A big way to maximize the impact of a national grid would be by creating a large number of national information utilities (let us call that mouthful of a phrase NIUs from here on). NIUs would be databases that amass information, streamlining it for the government, and also making it more accessible and transparent for citizens. The online depository that NSDL implemented under Bhave was the first hugely successful example of such an NIU in India; it now holds more than $1 trillion of shares in electronic form. The changes it brought about exceeded all expectations—the NSDL enabled the tax authorities to build the Tax Information Network, which in turn contributed to the huge growth in direct-tax collections in India. Now we are poised to build a similar NIU to manage the New Pension System, and the MCA-21 project of the ministry of company affairs is an NIU to record the details of all registered Indian companies. The Supreme Court of India is looking at a national case-management system, an NIU to streamline hearings and unclog the massive backlog of cases across our courts.

NIUs offer us a new kind of governance model—one that is scalable, with a single point of accountability, and where the amount of information available maintains a balance of power between the citizens and the government. Right now India struggles under a governance model where multiple state and central government departments, staffed with differently skilled people, try to accomplish similar goals across Indian states in health care, education and welfare. Repetition, a lack of awareness around best practices and varying degrees of commitment inevitably create different rates of success.

NIUs can make governance across state services both seamless and standardized. For instance, using such a system to handle all fund transfers of government money from the center to the states and local bodies would ensure predictable, efficient and leak-proof cash flows. We could carry this idea into all kinds of services and implement such models for driver licenses and vehicle registrations. This would help in improving traffic compliance, permit dynamic pricing for congested areas and expedite the single market by making interstate borders and toll roads entry–exit quicker. Having a national information system that keeps electronic records of health would change the whole health delivery scenario. And a similar mechanism that keeps track of student loans along with one to create a portable credit system for higher education would greatly improve both access and quality in higher education.

Such an electronification infrastructure would reduce the knowledge asymmetries—and consequently the lopsided power dynamic—that now exists between the citizens and the government. The Right to Information Act 2005 was a direct prod toward changing the balance. But the electronification framework above, if implemented with all the pieces, would go much further in redressing the imbalances in people–state power, by providing the citizens with unfettered access to a broad range of information. Everything from information on state and city budgets, spending details for specific schools, hospitals or a bridge across a river, tax collections and tracking of citizen complaints would be visible to the public.

Such open systems, by reducing intermediaries in funds transfer and benefit allocations, make governments directly responsible to citizens and very much like local governments in their accountability and transparency. The light that we bring to bear on these inner workings of the state will ensure that both the incompetent and the corrupt will have far less chance of escaping undetected. Once the opaque veils on our state are raised, the citizen will be truly in charge.

Anticipating our challenges

For many of us in India, governance has been an intractable problem, one very difficult to change owing to the deep-rooted bureaucracy and opaque lines of power. A senior secretary within the UPA government tells me that one of the biggest challenges for governance reforms in India has been this sense that the old structures are simply untouchable. "Bureaucratic power centers are especially entrenched. The district collectors today, for instance," he tells me, "grew up viewing him as the most powerful man in the region. They are not going to cede that authority without a fight."

This struggle with ancient, draconian systems has long troubled Indian writers and thinkers fighting for fairness and equality, with some calling for nothing less than a revolution. Many believe that only if such structures are completely destroyed can anyone hope to build something better.

But India, a country still caught in a mix of feudalism and a promising market economy, has the advantage of the flattening, transformational power of electronification. Bureaucrats such as Rajiv Chawla, Ravi Narain and Ravi Kumar have already demonstrated the power of information systems in bringing about dramatic, citizen-friendly reforms, and making governance immediately fairer, transparent and more inclusive. The potential of these tools, if taken nationally and implemented with all the parts in place and without compromises, could be huge. But to do this, we have to change the way we think about electronification. First of all, this is too important to leave to the technologists. IT is less of a tool than a strategy for public policy reform—which can be fundamental in making the economy more efficient in addressing concerns of equity and for making public spending more effective. The design and implementation of this information infrastructure is as important to the country's future as the number of power plants and roads that we build.

Secondly, e-governance is not just about hardware and software. Every conversation on using technology ends in a discussion on which server to use, or which ERP (enterprise resource planning) package to deploy. These are the least of our problems and are eventually the easiest things to figure out. Far more critical is the database design, the governance structure and the process reengineering needed to build scalable, replicable and seamless systems that are convenient and practical for citizens.

Finally we must recognize that e-governance projects have been successful when there has been a single owner with a clear, national-level mandate responsible for it. IT transformation projects that span multiple departments or multiple levels of government have fallen short, since these require complex decision-making processes and high levels of collaboration and authority. The inability to manage such interdepartment decision making has been the reason for the plethora of successful pilot projects that can neither be scaled up nor replicated. Tackling this would require national standards that IT projects must follow, so that they can fit in seamlessly with the existing infrastructure. A rare, successful attempt of a broader IT standard demonstrates how this can work—the Comptroller Auditor General (CAG) along with the ministry of urban development put out the National Municipal Accounting Manual (NMAM), which helped dozens of city municipalities across India migrate to a sophisticated double-entry, IT-enabled accrual accounting system. The creation of standards such as the NMAM can enable similarly huge multiplier effects when it comes to improving our governance systems and delivering public services.

A transformational force

They say fortune is all about timing, and India has been incredibly lucky that our growth story is happening at a time when the technological revolution is providing us with a basis for a fundamental transformation in governance, better public services and for creating a targeted safety net for the poor.

Technology is extremely powerful as a liberal force, in its ability to empower citizens and minimize the sway of the state. It would strengthen India's advantages as an open, democratic society and would ensure that information, knowledge and services flow unimpeded. But for much of the 1980s and 1990s, our e-governance projects and technology initiatives tended to flounder, usually derailed by political interference and bureaucratic apathy. Technology itself is not the Midas touch—however, if we are sufficiently able to get the technology foundation up and running, the change it triggers across the government has the capacity to become a juggernaut.

India is particularly well suited to harness the powerful capability of IT just as we are undertaking our biggest development journey. The talent that made India the center of global delivery in IT over the last fifteen years has now developed the skills and experience it needs to apply this learning at home. In the next fifteen years, these skills can help us build the kind of politically and economically inclusive environment that can take India into a second phase of dramatic, technology-aided growth. The acceptance of technology by the common man means that there will be no resistance to its widespread deployment. And the open society that we have created and nourished is the ideal ground for IT-led transparency in governance. But to realize this vision we have to take IT-led transformation from the sidelines of public policy and make it the centerpiece of our development and reform strategy.

When Tom Friedman was in India, he was asked what he thought about China as the emerging superpower of the century. He answered, "I don't think that this century can belong to a country that censors Google." His statement speaks multitudes of how critical information technologies have become to a country's economic strength, and how India's particular advantage—its combination of an open society and its positive attitudes to IT—can transform our country in the coming years. India's potential here to become an open, wired economy, unregulated by any kind of "intellectual license permit raj," can be a strength difficult to beat in today's information age.

CHANGING EPIDEMICS

From Hunger to Heart Disease

A dual challenge

Within the maze of Delhi's government ministry buildings—in that part of the city where the roads are all named after Indian luminaries, from leaders of the freedom movement to Mughal emperors—we can find the ministry of health and family welfare in a surprisingly central location, beside the ministry of industry, on Maulana Azad Marg.

The location is unusual for a department that has played what is likely the smallest possible role in public health, compared with the rest of the world. The health ministry—or Nirman Bhavan, the "house of creation," as it is imaginatively called—has long been tangential to our budgets, debates and policies. "We've had no sense of mission or urgency in health," Jairam Ramesh tells me. "Our funds for public health have stayed far below what we've needed."

The consequences of this are health statistics that cast a long shadow over the growth achievements of the last two decades. India's impressive economic numbers juxtapose themselves next to disease incidence and infant mortality rates that resemble those of a desperately poor country—figures that should be a bucket of cold water in case the growth party gets too raucous. Four years after the 1991 reforms, as the "new" economy was on the rise, India fell victim to a medieval epidemic when the pneumonic plague swept through the ghettos of Surat, a city in Gujarat, one of our richest states. And even our biggest cities have endured spasms of jaundice and dysentery epidemics from contaminated water.

Indian governments have been beaten over the head with the cudgel of our miserable health figures for decades. The first postindependence government had promised "a new era in health," but the state proved immensely fickle in this commitment in the face of budget crunches. As a result state hospitals crumbled, health staff were underpaid and even the most basic services were underfunded.

But the problem now in these postreform years is that our health challenges are no longer as straightforward as they were two decades ago. The big difference today is that India is no longer a desperately poor country. The effects of our growth on our health indicators have been complicated—good, bad and pretty ugly. While life expectancy averages have soared, industrialization is bringing along with it all its positive and negative impacts on wellness with astonishing speed.

The speed of these changes, Dr. Srinath Reddy tells me, has astonished him. Dr. Reddy, president of the Public Health Foundation of India (PHFI) and head of cardiology at AIIMS, is at my house. I am as guilty as the next person in my fondness for both Indian sweets and savory chaat that cannot be limited to a single handful. Dr. Reddy, however, is conspicuously frugal, drinking milkless, sugar-free tea; he does not snack. Such spare eating habits, he notes when I remark on it, are the first things to disappear with economic growth. "India's especially high rate of growth presents a challenge to our health in terms of our risks for diabetes, heart disease and obesity," he says. "In the U.S. and Europe, more moderate growth rates meant that the shift from 'shortage' based sickness such as malnutrition to such 'excess' based illnesses occurred slowly, with enough time for policy to catch up." India however, thanks to its dramatic rise, is facing an unhappy spectacle where health extremes are already beginning to coexist.

We are now increasingly caught between the realities of the developing and the developed worlds—witnessing epidemics of hypertension and diabetes alongside that of malaria. Our malnutrition numbers place us among the world's weakest countries, while our diabetes rates vault us over the United States. And even as one third of our children are severely undernourished, with bowed legs and distended stomachs, a new epidemic of childhood obesity is emerging in our cities. Neighboring communities—rich and painfully poor, rural and urban—are clearly battling with very different health challenges, and so far our policies have failed to deal with either crisis.

The peculiar habits of the people

Shankar Acharya once remarked to me of how, well into our reform decades, "The Indian government has shied away from reforming itself." The state has rarely tried to turn its gaze inward—across sectors where government had a prominent role, we typically saw reform by circuitous routes, as the state allowed private competition in. By offering market alternatives to weak state services, the government sidestepped having to make difficult reform decisions, and public or public-financed organizations in these industries eventually cleaned up their act as a result of competition.

But public services such as health care are a unique challenge, because the typical Indian approach to reform—do it by bringing in private competitors—simply does not work here. The problem is that health is too much of a public good, offering a very limited role for the private sector. When it comes to the health of the public—creating awareness, controlling epidemics and ensuring basic nutrition and vaccination for even the poorest citizens—the government has to play a role, as market solutions for these services are neither effective nor universal. In addition, "catastrophic" health care—when treatment is literally a matter of life and death—is often expensive. This means that private sector health care in the most critical situations becomes unaffordable for the poor.

Private hospitals and clinics in India have not done much to counter ineffective public health care services. The lack of universal health services has come with terrible consequences, especially for the health of the poorest Indians. It is not uncommon to see children with copper-colored hair clinging to exhausted mothers on the sidewalks of even our biggest cities. "Even in our more developed states, we still see large numbers of sick, stunted children, weak mothers and a generally unhealthy working class," Dr. Reddy says.

Our persisting failures here arise in part from our lack of initiative in changing the colonial approach to health care we inherited. The fact that British India bungled health care badly is hardly shocking—even effective, democratic governments around the world have struggled with how to provide better health care. An imperial government unaccountable to Indians ended up, unsurprisingly, with unrelentingly bad figures.

A major problem for the colonial administration in India was that its officials were transplanted here from a country that already had a public health system in place. Thanks to rising incomes, England had come a long way from the decadence of the pre-1800s. The population had languished in filth for much of the time before then—people rarely bathed and considered bathing unhygienic, and communities lived in crowded huts surrounded by sewage. The European writer St. Bernard, noting the common filth the people wallowed in, said, "Where all stink, no one smells."[1]

These attitudes changed only with the hygiene movements and medical advances of the nineteenth century, when European administrations installed more effective sanitation measures and emphasized personal health care, clean water and food to counter the constant outbreaks of cholera and dysentery.

But when they arrived in India, British officials found a state of affairs very like England, pre–health reforms. Much of the discussion on public health as a result was conducted by these fastidious Victorian-era officials in a tone of muted horror. Administrators wrote in traumatized reports of a "shocking indifference" to the basic concerns of hygiene and cleanliness, and near-total ignorance when it came to aspects of preventive health care. They noted, for instance, that Indians would wash their corpses in the same river from which they drank their water, that they were nonchalant about sanitation and incredibly suspicious of medical care, from vaccination to routine examinations. Florence Nightingale termed the Indian bazaars as "simply the first savage stage"[2] in an environment dominated by multiple, germ-strewn ways to contract infection and disease. Across British literature, India was at once mysterious and dreaded for its sicknesses—it was "a land of death and disease, of desolation and deficiency."[3]

A foreign government also found that making strides in preventive health care in an unfamiliar country was complicated. Even in the best of conditions, changing health habits entails a good deal of negotiation and many uncomfortable moments between a government and its citizens. No one after all likes to be told that they are filthy and need to do something about it. A prominent British surgeon general remarked about this problem in the 1880s, "Those who know anything about . . . sanitary reform in England are aware that sanitation was to a great extent forced on the people."[4] At best analysts damned Indian attitudes toward preventive health care with faint praise, noting that Indians "were not uniformly hostile" to the idea.[5] The yawning gaps in India between the rulers and the ruled were not just a conflict on sewage lines and clean water, but also cultural and traditional. For instance, parts of north India had a smallpox deity called Sitala—"the white-bodied one, mounted on an ass"—and vaccinations for the disease were considered a direct insult to the goddess.[6]

Health laws in British India as a result largely gave up on persuading people toward better habits and remained draconian and imperious. Health ordinances such as the Contagious Disease Act in Calcutta and the Plague Prevention Measures in the Bombay Presidency were effective mainly as instruments of harassment in the hands of the police. In 1897, for instance, efforts to control the spread of the plague in Bombay resulted in "house to house searches, and the inspection and detention of railway passengers."[7]

It did not help the floundering administrators that Britain's trade laws contributed to epidemics of hunger—compelling farmers, for instance, to grow crops like indigo and cotton over food crops triggered domestic famines, leaving officials to focus primarily on emergency, Band-Aid health responses rather than long-term health care. In the nineteenth century, for instance, an estimated 20 million people died across British India from famine. Indian mortality rates shot up to twice the rates in Europe and England, and life expectancy actually fell by twenty years between 1872 and 1921. The picture that emerges out of all this is that of local administrations overwhelmed and strained for money, and finally abandoning any pretense of preventive care. One surgeon general complained that British officers in India ended up embracing a very Indian fatalism about health and disease and the idea that sanitation measures and preventive care were an "interference with the laws of nature"—things were better off left to fate, or to a preferred deity.

This attitude is still far from being just a memory. Postindependence, the lackadaisical attitude to our health—in both prevention and cure—got virtually written into the Constitution. India did not have a national health policy till 1982, and the funds the government earmarked for health care have been budget leftovers, hovering around 1 percent of GDP through the postindependence years.

Our lack of focus on health was pretty surprising, considering the eloquence on health care policies from Indian politicians preindependence.

Congress leaders had equated the health "of the Indian people" to the health of the Indian nation and made it central to their nationalist rhetoric.[8]

For a while after independence, our health issues did look as if they were headed in a positive direction. Sir Joseph Bhore, a prominent ICS officer, was appointed the head of a committee on health, which was empowered to put in place the direction of India's public health policy. The Bhore committee aimed at an internationalist, progressive approach, including among its members British and American health advisers such as John Ryle and Henry Sigerist. But the main influence on the committee turned out to be the Soviet health care system, of which Sigerist was a great admirer. Bhore's recommendations eventually suggested a tiered approach to public health care similar to the one in the USSR—of health centers focused on primary, preventive care in India's rural areas, "curative services" at the district level and more sophisticated care at the urban level.[9]

But when it came down to the wire, the health centers were set up incredibly slowly, with limited resources and badly trained workers. The problem, as was often the case in our early years, was of money—India's finances were spread too thin, the budget simply not enough for a broad and intensive health system. The Tamilian minister K. Santhanam noted in 1947 that implementing the Bhore recommendations required Rs 3 billion, which was at the time the "*total* of the provincial and central taxation."[10] By 1950 the MP Brajeshwar Prasad was complaining that things had rapidly taken a turn for the worse in India's hospitals, thanks to tightening budgets. "If you go to a general hospital," he said, "you will see that flies and bugs are multiplying, that the clothes of the nurses are dirty, that phenyl and medicines are not available and the patients are not treated well."[11]

Apparently, then, it was all or nothing. In 1950 the Indian government limited the promise of health in the Constitution, placing it in the "directive principles" rather than the fundamental rights.[12] The best the Constitution could do was offer a vague promise of "free health care," and health policy stuck to the earlier preindependence goal—controlling outbreaks. India pitched what there was of its health budget toward vaccinations and control programs for epidemics such as malaria, where workers would descend on villages with spray guns loaded with DDT.

The MP H. V. Kamath had noted that within the Indian government, public health had become "the Cinderella of portfolios in the Cabinet."[13]

In every central government, the health minister was the position least coveted, and for an ambitious legislator the title was nothing less than a rebuke. But what helped the Indian governments get away with this lackadaisical approach to health was the fatalistic attitude to disease among the Indian poor, who have never experienced anything close to effective health care. In much of India outside our cities, people have few health care options, and when faced with a family member dying from a curable illness—tuberculosis, malaria, dysentery—they can do little more than shrug and point their fingers to the sky. As Sendhil Mullainathan told me, "Health comes pretty low down on the list of popular priorities. Sickness only gets the attention of the poor when it becomes debilitating and makes it impossible to work."

A loss of vision

In 1947 the Congress Planning Committee had tied India's health challenges to its pervasive poverty: "India is a country whose people are poor beyond compare, short lived and incapable of resisting disease and epidemics. The poverty of the people is proverbial."[14] This was a wide vision on India's health care problems, and the Bhore report echoed it, stating that "social, economic and environmental factors . . . play an equally important part in the production of sickness." Consequently, it added, health policies would have to encompass all these issues. But this idea vanished soon after and has not surfaced since.

Even the bare-bones health solutions that Indian governments offered early on soon faltered thanks to drastic underfunding. Tight budgets through the 1960s and 1970s resulted in the central government lobbing the responsibility of health care services to equally cash-strapped states. Such state-level responsibility for health care has resulted in achievements that vary dramatically as we move across the country. While in Kerala popular movements such as the People's Campaign and public pressure led to fairly accessible and quality health care,* the health achievements of Madhya Pradesh, Orissa and Rajasthan are comparable to the poorest countries in the world. "State gov-

*A caveat here is that government health services in Kerala have in recent years declined once again. Less than one third of even the state's poorest citizens now choose to go to a state hospital.

ernments had very little money to spare for health," James Manor tells me. "The challenge for even the most reformist ministers was that they had to carry out these programs on shoestring budgets."

But something else soon interrupted even this plodding progress of India's health sector—or rather, someone, in the person of Indira Gandhi's son Sanjay. By 1961 the government health message had begun to shift toward family planning. By the mid-1970s, the winds of change had become a hurricane, as India's public health sector was co-opted to promote Sanjay's disastrous family-planning agenda. Ashish Bose notes that under this program, the government turned doctors, nurses and health workers into foot soldiers for the sterilization effort, with weekly district- and state-level targets. The walls of primary health centers across the country were papered with posters of families with two children, and the centers became places offering primarily family planning services. "The forced abortions that happened during this time worsened the health of the women, and IUDs inserted without checkups gave them infections," Ashish tells me, "but what mattered was population growth."

India's primary health services never fully recovered from this onslaught. The state admitted as much, declaring in 2002 that "the rural health staff has become a vertical structure exclusively for the implementation of family welfare."[15] In some states such as Uttar Pradesh, the family planning strategy still dominates, ineffective and counterproductive as it is, and it has made the poor suspicious of seeking treatment from government hospitals. "Nurses in these hospitals still speak of 'targets,'" Abhijit Banerjee says. "It's code for the number of people they have to sterilize that month, or in that quarter."

Much worse before it got better

I invite Dr. Abhay Bang, the remarkable physician who has been working on women's health care in tribal Maharashtra, to my house so that I can talk to him about his work. When I enter the living room, I find a thin, intense man, sparely dressed, and remarkably thoughtful about the health problems of India's rural women. He carries a battered briefcase out of which he hands me booklets about his organization, Society for Education, Action and Research in Community Health (SEARCH), and their work with Adivasi women.

Dr. Bang's successes are well-known—SEARCH made headlines when its efforts in Gadchiroli, Maharashtra, brought down maternal and infant morbidity rates at a speed the government has not matched anywhere. The infant mortality rate in the region fell from seventy-six to thirty. His results came from training women and the midwives within the village in the fundamentals of maternal and child health care. His workers went about setting the best practices, educating and recruiting villagers and then identifying and training the best among these women as midwives. This created an adaptive, bottom-up model where already-trained midwives pass off their know-how to younger women, supervise them working on patients, and ensure quality care. Dr. Bang's success also makes the point that health efforts do not have to, and in fact should not, be exclusively carried out by the state, even if it is funded by it. Rather, such bottom-up systems favor local, responsive organizations.

A big part of Dr. Bang's approach has been in educating women and mothers in health care, which he says had a remarkable effect on the overall health of their families and children. This dovetails with my belief that targeting social schemes, benefit payouts, as well as education and health information at women is effective in not just empowering them, but is overall a strong approach to tackling the problems of the poor. Every social scientist and NGO activist I spoke to echoed this sentiment—in the poorest families, the most successful outcomes came from specifically targeting women for education, information and loans.

"It sometimes overwhelms us," Dr. Bang tells me of the struggles the poorest women face when it comes to basic care. "Reform-minded organizations such as ours only had the courage to provide health services because we didn't know what we were getting into, and the scale of the problems we were going to face." He points to just one among several of our disheartening health figures—100,000 Indian women die in childbirth every year, a figure that the government "has barely managed to put a dent in." Today much of rural India still remains completely untouched by any form of health care. Although, as Dr. Bang says, "People in India now have a large number of unmet health needs," the mainstay of government health interventions has continued to be epidemic-related programs, vaccinations and family planning. It is especially telling that it has taken programs by private companies and NGOs to raise basic health awareness around issues such as the use of soap and the boiling of water.

In fact by 2000 the bottom had completely fallen out of India's public health care and what we had on our hands was a system in ruins, broken down, incapable of servicing the ill and with thousands dying on its watch. As one government report's self-flagellating assessment of public health centers reads, "the presence of medical . . . personnel is often much less than that required . . . the availability of essential drugs is minimal; the capacity of the facilities is grossly inadequate."[16]

As a result people across urban and rural India have voted against public health services with their feet, with more than 85 percent of patients choosing private health care, and even the poorest paying for often financially ruinous treatment out of their pocket. "Health costs," Jairam tells me, "is now the second largest reason that people in rural India are in debt." This trend toward private care has made us the only economy in the world where the private sector massively outspends the government on health. Our public–private ratio in health spends is 1:4, even worse than that of Pakistan, which is no overachiever—the ratio there stands at 1:3.

The reluctant state

Abhijit notes that both genuine entrepreneurs and quacks have filled the vacuum left by public health care in India. "Good health care for most of the poor now means a saline drip and a steroid injection," he tells me. "People have got used to the quacks for whom this is the standard one-two treatment for every possible ailment." The steroids give a quick, feel-good rush, and the drip is comforting. "Patients in rural areas are becoming dismissive of effective health treatments that offer anything less," Abhijit says. "It's become the sort of problem that makes your head hurt just to think about it."

The early argument the Indian state made against providing universal health care was that it simply did not have the money, but governments nevertheless continued to give lip service to universal health in policy statements. One of the primary promises—however hollow—of the 1983 policy was that India was committed to attaining the goal of "Health for All by the Year 2000."

Since the 1980s, however, there has been a growing sense among the political class that health care is simply not a priority for voters. Wild horses cannot drag a politician to endorse something he does not find popular support for, and perhaps this goes some way in explaining why the 2001 Health Policy was the meekest in terms of our health goals. It was a step back from the endorsement of the Alma Alta declaration of 1978, which had pledged "Health for All" by the end of the century, and included neither "comprehensive" nor "universal" in its health care promises. "Governments began backtracking in this sector," Yogendra Yadav tells me. "Instead, they envisioned private players filling its role."

Our nonfocus has not only ensured a hobbling public health care system, but also the neglect of an area governments typically dominate—emphasizing preventive health care through awareness drives, education and regulation. As a result, when it comes to their health spends, the share that Indians now spend on curing sicknesses is 92 percent.

A slow recovery

Astonishingly, the 1943 statement on health and the 1983 National Health Policy had the same complaints. The 1983 report noted the lack of "preventive, rehabilitative . . . measures" in our public health care systems; the Bhore Committee emphasized the need for "preventive measures" in health. Four decades in between, but the same challenge.[17]

"We are only now coming out of a long, dark period in health policy," Dr. Reddy says, and turning the lights on has meant battling the cobwebs and dust that have accumulated over the years. For this we must give some credit to the UPA government, which put curative health care prominently on India's policy map. Since launching the National Rural Health Mission (NRHM) in 2005, the government raised targets for public expenditure on health from below 1 percent to 2–3 percent. The government is also, through both NRHM and the urban health initiative, attempting to model health care solutions toward effectiveness and better access. The rural initiative, for instance, has attempted to "communitize" health care efforts across villages through a massive ground force of accredited social health activists (ASHAs), who interface with government health centers and advise people on preventive and basic care.

Lately, we have also seen more ambitious efforts such as the PHFI Dr. Reddy heads, which—in a public–private partnership with the Indian government, the Gates Foundation and Indian philanthropists—is developing seven public institutes of public health. The PHFI is attempting to address manpower shortages in rural areas by training many more health workers.

Our approach to health still has some large blind spots. India has the advantage of having witnessed the massive health impacts of industrialization in both Europe and the United States since the 1950s, and we have a chance to avoid the same booby trap of soaring health costs and lifestyle-disease epidemics. As Dr. Reddy notes, "We don't have to go through the entire cycle of suffering before we look for relief. It would be easier and cheaper for us to head off these health crises before they happen." This aspect is, however, completely missing.

We have to be careful about how our growth is impacting our health as we surge toward higher incomes and rapid urbanization. The condition of our cities, for instance, is affecting physical activity, disease incidence and life expectancy among urban citizens. Infrastructure impacts health when accident rates soar and when ancient sewage lines leak into our water supply. Consumer food standards affect obesity rates as well as pesticide levels in food. People living longer thanks to development means more challenges for social security. And crowded cities mean that epidemics, when they occur—in the form of SARS (severe acute respiratory syndrome) or chikunguniya (a disease spread by mosquitoes)—spread much faster.

The changes are disconcerting—these challenges look like an already unmanageable monster that is growing several new heads. Alongside the persisting crises of malnutrition and child mortality rates, India is now seeing rates of diabetes, heart disease and obesity racking up very quickly. "As present trends go, India is projected to become the largest contributor of heart deaths in the world, at 4 percent," says Vindi Banga, president of foods at Unilever and former Hindustan Unilever Ltd chairman. So while we have managed to bring down death rates, it turns out that this is not the success that it first seemed. Instead, Indians might be seeing the beginnings of an unhappy bargain: of living longer, but of also being sick longer, and from new and frightening illnesses.

A space for inventiveness

Our approaches to health have drawn sharp, constraining lines around what we can and cannot do, and put public services in a box. We have long defined health care extremely narrowly, with the barest minimum in services and standards. As Jeffrey Sachs tells me, "The Indian government has not yet seen health as a horizontal challenge, that moves across its departments and offices." For individual citizens, health encompasses all sorts of lifestyle decisions—where we live and work, what we eat and how educated we are, all determine the quality of our health. This means that health concerns should interlace with our approaches to housing, education, agriculture, industry standards and the environment, and we should be fashioning the kind of regulation that pushes the public and industries into making "health-optimum" decisions.

"We've not yet recognized how people react to incentives within regulations," Dr. Reddy says. He notes as an example that cities can be planned to encourage people to either walk or drive—a dense but well-planned city with wide walkways for pedestrians and safe crossings make citizens more active. Pedestrian-unfriendly cities, on the other hand, force people to retreat into cars and buses, increasing overcrowding, pollution, city sprawl and health risks. But urban planning in India does not consider these trade-offs. "Right now, we are allowing the city to expand on auto-pilot, and even basic services are failing, with sewage systems breaking down, and shrinking water supplies," Dr. Reddy says. Already, badly planned cities have made India the country with the largest number of road fatalities in the world—even with our present low penetration of automobile ownership. Our cities are now magnets for filth and dirt, with garbage piles spilling onto the streets, open drains and groundwater contaminated by environmental pollution and bad drainage systems. Bad urban design is also increasing the chances for epidemics, as people come into closer contact with not just pollutants, but also with animals, as they live next to poultry and piggery farms, and in wet environments that attract rats and infestation.

Our lack of incentives for better health across our policies is pretty apparent in our approach to tobacco consumption. Tobacco, which was scaled up into a major agricultural asset in British India, has long been patronized as a revenue-earning commercial crop by Indian governments postindependence. Dr. Reddy suggests, "Tobacco is probably even more addictive to governments than to individuals!" As a result Indians now consume it in large quantities, not only as cigarettes but in myriad other forms: beedis, cheroots, hookahs, gutkha and so on. About one million Indians die each year from tobacco-related diseases, and our rates of lighting up are second only to China. Similarly, our food policies need to take into account the consumption of foods such as fruits and vegetables. Trade laws that allow cheaper food imports in greens and fruit would bring down their prices and encourage people to buy them more. Right now, however, Indian policies on food remain stuck on the 1960s-era emphasis on food security, and the state has failed to keep up with the changing food habits of Indians, both rich and poor.

In fact our lack of concern for preventive care has made us ignore the big downsides in our present agriculture and retail policies. Our limits on FDI in retail, for example, has constrained the growth of cold chains across the country, and 30 percent of our agri-produce today is damaged in transit due to the lack of such infrastructure. Deeper investments in such supply chains would make fruit and vegetable produce both cheaper and fresher, something that we rarely consider when we discuss retail policy.

Ignoring these health angles has had some terrible side effects. Pesticide subsidies, for example, have led to large-scale overuse of these chemicals in farms, and we now hear horror stories of cancer epidemics sweeping entire villages in Punjab and Haryana. And Harish Hande tells me, "We are facing a lot of hidden dangers in health in rural India that are right now flying under the radar. The dependence of people on wood fuel and charcoal for cooking, for example, is creating widespread, and often fatal, respiratory diseases in women."

These issues of health are popping up in all kinds of unexpected places. Standards in areas such as television advertising (where many developed countries are belatedly introducing restrictions on ads for fatty, salty and sugary foods), agriculture-subsidy structures, auto emission standards and environmental planning—all have to be framed with an awareness of their health impacts. But on issues such as food standards, most governments have been sleeping on the watch. "One of the problems with food standards," Vindi tells me, "is how the processed food industry evolved in the West. Most people perceived that ready-to-eat food tasted bad, and all advertising and much of the research focused on making and promoting such food as tasty." The health impact of these food products, however, was never part of the debate.

"The West made the connection between bad food and bad health pretty late," Vindi says. People turned toward preventive health care only after unforeseen spikes in illness related to diet and lifestyle. For instance, a lack of emphasis in the United States on a good diet has made the country prone to lifestyle diseases such as obesity, cancer and diabetes, with huge amounts spent on treatment and cures, whose costs in turn are not borne by the patients. This approach of enabling bad lifestyles and then turning to expensive solutions to treat the consequences is obviously something India has to avoid.

A focus on preventive health care is critical if we are to avoid the mistakes made by the West in health policy. But instead of broader, preventive solutions, Dr. Bang notes, "We have all kinds of one-point national health programs. They aim at specific diseases, or have extremely narrow-view agendas such as 'postpartum care.'" Most of these programs fail to achieve even their modest goals, and are isolated from one another.

Testing new solutions

The state will have to hunker down and enable universal, basic and effective health care, accompanied by the health insurance to make it affordable. It is quite possible that we will have to go back to basics here, in how we have fundamentally approached health care. From the beginning, the state appointed itself as the sole go-to provider of health care for the poor and tried to deliver it through a top-down, tiered system. What works might be virtually the opposite solution. "Our approach should focus more strongly on bottom-up empowerment which includes the state as well as other health providers," Dr. Bang says.

The more choices patients have between accessible systems, the better. The state should be one provider among many, but concentrate more on funding and regulation for preventive care. A useful way to do this is a publicly financed health system where "money follows the patient," giving patients the right to choose his or her physicians and hospitals. Such a universal but open-choice system would also guarantee everybody, regardless of income, a health voucher that buys a standard plan offering basic insurance coverage for treatments. Such a voucher could also be used as partial payment for a more expensive health policy, making it a magnet not just for the poor but also for the middle class. Such a mixed-care, universal system is in place in France, where health care is packaged within the social security program, and social security payments that individuals and companies make fund a universal health care plan that has both the state and insurance companies participating in it. French citizens also have the option of adding on a "mutuel"—a private health insurance company that pays for additional services beyond the universal cover.

And as Martin Feldstein—former chief economic adviser to Ronald Reagan and pension-policy-expert-extraordinaire—notes, offering incentives such as cheaper health insurance for people who make active and more healthy choices, and linking up health histories with social security costs through unique "health savings accounts" would bring preventive health care into focus within our universal solutions. In India proposals such as the negative income tax could also be tagged for health care, rewarding good health automatically with higher payouts from the state. As Martin points out, "Tying in health care with strong incentives for people to prevent illness is the only way governments can pay for good health policy."

Focusing on preventive care in this way could be dramatic in lowering disease rates. Dr. Reddy points out to me, "If we were to lower the average diastolic blood pressure by just two milliliters across the Indian population, we would have three lakh fewer deaths." A stress on prevention, for that matter, ought to come naturally to us. India's traditionalist approaches to health care, such as Ayurveda and yoga, have long focused on preventing illness by managing diet and lifestyle to avert disease. The elements of the Indian diet—the liberal use of spices and the focus on legumes, vegetables and whole grains—were tailored toward both longevity and the prevention of diseases like cancer. Traditional herbs and spices, such as gotu kola and ashoka as well as turmeric and fenugreek, have been noted in medical studies as powerful anticarcinogens and antioxidants. Such diets and health approaches are now catching on in the United States—yoga in particular has become an enduring and popular exercise, and the West is incorporating Indian spices into their food as people become more aware of their benefits. It would be a pity if Indians meanwhile create the sort of incentives that marginalize such diets and behavior.

Running against a clock

When it comes to health care, we have some deadlines that are ticking away. It is critical that we establish an effective universal system in India now, when we have enough of a young working population to pay for the health costs they will incur as they age.

The one advantage we have is that initiatives such as the NRHM, despite their flaws, are instituting a viable and workable model of basic health care—by training ASHAs for the villages, and USHAs, urban social health activists, for the cities.

But the big missing piece of effective health access continues to be in providing low-cost health options in rural areas outside the government's primary health centers. A model that includes a health voucher is of no real use without treatment alternatives: in rural areas, the number of physicians per thousand people is a miserable 0.6, compared with 3.9 in urban areas. And rural health choices get constrained further by how much a sick person can travel on a bumpy road to a health care center.

Potentially, a model that could provide viable treatment options in rural areas could incorporate IT networks. These are no longer pie-in-the-sky ideas—our existing infrastructure can easily support some very practical, technology-based health care. We can, for instance, leverage telemedicine services quite effectively to bring quality health care to remote parts of the country, and hospitals such as Narayana Hrudayalaya have demonstrated the effectiveness of telemedicine treatments. Countries in Africa have already shown that this can be done on a large scale by using telemedicine systems to connect several hard-to-reach villages to effective health services. Rwanda uses TRACnet, an online information system also accessible through mobile phones, which is meant exclusively for getting AIDS medication and lab results to patients in villages; in Uganda the organization Satellife has been linking rural clinics to city doctors with email-enabled PDAs.

Over the last decade, India has been putting in place IT infrastructure that I think would fit well into telemedicine and remote health services—Internet kiosks and mobile phone networks. Building a telemedicine system on top of this merely needs the right information systems that connect doctors to these unattended corners of the country.

Sameer Sawarkar, CEO of Neurosynaptic Communications, describes such a system his firm has recently developed. "ReMeDi," or Remote Medical Diagnostics, Sameer tells me, "is a low-cost telemedicine solution that has features like low bandwidth video/audio conferencing for live consultations. It can also keep comprehensive patient medical records, so that doctors don't have to start from scratch." The system can network hospitals, clinics, labs and pharmacies with villages, and has been tried out in districts in Tamil Nadu and Maharashtra. But such initiatives, while successful, have so far remained largely pilot projects and NGO-funded schemes. Linking these services with a government-funded health voucher system, and portable electronic records for patients, can go a long way in making them viable and widespread.

Technology innovations that could lower health costs are also now falling into place. BigTec is a biotechnology company in Bangalore, with an office tucked unobtrusively behind a supermarket in one of the city's residential suburbs. The company's directors are an interesting mix of engineers and doctors who are presently developing a remarkable "handheld diagnostic device," that can carry out the kind of blood analysis and disease testing that is usually done through expensive labs. As the BigTec team notes, "A device costing ten thousand rupees can give you results that would have earlier taken two days, in fifteen minutes." The device also has a potentially transformative feature—its accuracy in diagnosing disease from a blood drop. This changes diagnosis from a "skill in guessing" by a physician to a process that is accurate to the decimal point and independent of the physician's talent. Health workers equipped with such devices can carry out work that would have earlier required expert physicians, and this would be invaluable in the hands of health workers such as ASHAs. These various IT efforts, as they begin to come together, can change the face of universal health care in India, bringing in a low-cost health network that reaches India's isolated villages. Village centers equipped with handheld diagnostic tools could vastly reduce the need for doctors. Doctors could be contacted, via tele-infrastructure, on a case by case basis. And thanks to technology that now provides us connectivity as well as inexpensive, point-of-patient diagnostics tools for a variety of ailments, we can create a truly effective "hub and spoke" for curative health. And taken to its logical end, the model could ultimately make diagnosis a self-service that can be done at home.

A chance to redefine our health space

We do not have to lurch from crisis to crisis in our health—from shortage to excess, from starvation to fat. If we are able to foresee our biggest health threats, we can shape dynamic new policies that ensure low-cost, universal care, healthy behavior and remarkably long-lived, productive human capital.

Crises often give countries a chance to innovate and make a fundamental change in our approaches to the economy—resulting in productivity leaps, shorter growth paths and development models that are superior to the existing ones. For India, the coming decades give us an opportunity to shape a truly unique, innovative approach to health, which will address our unfinished goals in basic care while anticipating the challenges that come with growth. This means making health as much about prevention as cure, putting health funds into the hands of citizens and using IT to build a bottom-up, competitive model with multiple options for care.

The twentieth century was a painful one for India, especially in our health struggles under both the British and independent India's straitened governments. Our public health care system has long been on life support. In the early decades, we approached our population as a burden, and our approaches in health, pensions and welfare were focused on handouts, basic care and population control.

But our economy has now fundamentally changed into one that builds its wealth primarily on the skills of its workers, and our people have value both as citizens and as human capital that ought to be protected as much as possible. Yet, as a country, we are still largely oblivious to the signs of ill health that surround us—the rail-thin children across Indian villages, their malnourished mothers, people falling ill from pollution and bad work environments, the growing number of chunky, middle-class children with type 2 diabetes. We accept our padlocked and forgotten primary care centers, our deaths from treatable illnesses and our burgeoning numbers of fast-food joints. For sixty years as an independent nation, we have been fine with being imperfectly healthy and carrying a pallor on our face. But this acceptance is a choice. We have a chance to transform this landscape—to walk a little straighter, with a little more care, and redefine wellness in innovative, astonishing ways.

OUR SOCIAL INSECURITIES

The Missing Demographic

ALL OF US HOPE, without exception, to live forever. Losing jobs, falling ill and in particular getting old—pondering on the inevitable wrinkles and wattles, creaky knees and papery skin—are crises that we do not want to waste our time thinking about, especially when we are young. This, as Dr. Martin Feldstein tells me, is probably the biggest challenge we now have with social insurance in India. The brighter the times and the younger you are, he notes, "the less you want to consider the possibility of crises and ill health." And India right now is demographically an improbably young country, in her mid-twenties, and in the throes of the good times.

Perhaps as a result of this, our government, flush with cash and a burgeoning treasury, has only recently begun to think of social insurance seriously. Even today, our ministers from the most populist to the professor-politicians, have concentrated on social policies aimed at working-age voters. It is job-related and subsidy benefits that now take up the chunk of electoral promises and preelection speeches. Political concern for what I would call our "book-end people"—the children and the aged—is missing.

Of late Indian governments have become aware that they need to build up our human capital, and child-oriented social investments in education and health care have gained some attention and funds. But both our ministers and voters are happy to ignore policies for the old, save for the disproportionate attention given to pension coverage for employees in the government and organized sector. Our ideas of what we owe our elderly have in fact been extremely complicated and are influenced by our notions of family loyalty, and that the responsibility for the elderly lies with the children. As a result, when it comes to the hope for a universal and sustainable pension system, no one yet seems to have the answers.

Our culture of the elders

There is a big element of pride and identity when it comes to our notions about financial and social security for the aged. Indians have long thought of the family as a "self-sufficient unit, center of the universe."[1] For many Indians this dynamic became especially important against the backdrop of colonial rule—the family became a refuge, the primary caretaker.

Within the family, caring for elders has long been an important responsibility. The inability among children or relatives to provide such care was considered to be a source of great shame. As the writer Lawrence Cohen points out, the neglect of parents, of the "old mother" in India was a symbol of decadence, the sign of rotten character—and in films from *Deewar* to *Vaastav*, this elderly parent's role included delivering an eviscerating polemic on the wayward, corrupt son. The actress Nirupa Roy became well-known in the 1970s as a character actor who played such mother roles.

Indian governments and its citizens have long agreed on this idea that services and care for the aged "should be the responsibility of the children." This belief also encouraged that somewhat Asia-specific and hugely India-specific preference for sons, since many families saw male children as necessary for financial, emotional and social support in old age. For these families, sons provided a kind of social security. As one proud Indian patriarch pointed out to a well-meaning but, according to him, clearly misguided sociologist, "You were trying to convince me . . . that I should not have any more sons. Now you see I have six sons and two daughters and I sit at home in leisure . . . because of my large family, I am a rich man."[2]

One Indian ethnographer noted that most respondents to old-age surveys "did not know what a senior citizen is"[3] or that an elderly person outside the government sector could have special rights from the state. Across

Indian budgets, social welfare for the aged typically received somewhere between a doleful 0.1 percent and 0.6 percent of total plan outlays.

This blasé approach to such social protections may have been compounded by how the British approached such policies in India—mostly they ignored it. The reason was probably, as the economist John Williamson has suggested, "the intense labor tensions the British faced in India from the 1920s."[4] Indian labor had identified itself closely with political parties within the independence movement, and British administrators were not inclined to offer these workers protective policies. Instead, the one major act around pensions, the 1925 Provident Fund Act, aimed old-age security squarely at government employees and civil servants.

Nevertheless, we can say that in terms of policy influences, India got lucky. The British colonies including India adopted the provident fund system, as was the trend in Britain, and French colonies adopted the social insurance system that existed in France, which has turned out to be both difficult to sustain financially and politically impossible to get rid of.

But the rules of the provident fund in India generally bowed to the demands of union members and organized labor, who were far more concerned with policies that would benefit themselves than with efforts to help the least well-off. These workers shaped the pension plans for government, civil servants and organized labor into what it still is today—a fairly overprivileged, risk-averse plan that coddled a tiny minority. On the other hand, the rest of India's workers, pitched outside this charmed circle, were in their old age dependent on the mercy of the gods and on family—the latter group somewhat less fickle than the former, but still not entirely reliable.

The great divide: Inside and outside a charmed circle

"One thing I've noticed across many of India's social policies," Kanchan Chandra tells me, "is how benefits for one group have been closely intertwined with exclusion for another." This holds true in our approach to social insurance. Efforts toward social security in India have been limited to the tiny minority of employees in the government and organized industries. In independent India, the first law that provided social security to workers in the private sector was the 1948 Coal Mines Provident Fund and Bonus Scheme Act. It became so popular among workers that other industries demanded similar acts, and the 1952 act extended the benefit to other organized workers.[5] But the large majority of the population remains without financial security.

We have obviously scored big misses in providing financial support on a broad scale. In 1982 the United Nations announced the International Year of the Aged and sent out questionnaires to member countries about which social security policies they had in place. Lawrence Cohen notes, "Again and again, the questionnaire demanded 'Does the Government . . . ,'" to which the Indian ministry officials could only respond in the questionnaire they returned to Vienna: No, No, No."

Governments since have kept up a high fence between these two groups: the government and organized-sector employees, and everyone else. For the uncovered group, the state's approach to social security has mainly been to strengthen punishments for family and children who fail to take care of their elderly parents and relatives. Following the Hindu Adoption and Maintenance Act of 1956, which allowed old people unable to take care of themselves and facing "abandonment and acute neglect" to file cases against their children, similar laws have explicitly stated that the duty to provide for the elderly lies with the family. And in 2007 the Indian Parliament passed a law that allowed the state to put neglectful sons and daughters in jail. The reaction to these laws seems to suggest that people see such legislation as fair. The Himachal Pradesh Maintenance of Parents and Dependants Bill, for instance, was defended strongly in the media, which described it as essential to "help bent, sad people stand up straight with pride."[6]

A well-trodden line of argument is that this system of family support in India worked well in the earlier decades. But economic growth and the rise of "nuclear family values" have created a new despair and helplessness among the old. These black-and-white, then-and-now portrayals evoke a time when filial respect for the elder and his authority was sacrosanct, an aspect of Indian culture driven home in our epics, such as the constant genuflecting to elders that accompanies most of the drama in the Mahabharata.[7] Birthdays of our aging politicians, celebrated with fanfare and weighty twenty-kilo cakes, are notches that mark their rise in authority and political status in the party—as the commentator Amit Verma agonizingly points out, this has made India the youngest country with the oldest politicians.

It seems unlikely, however, that we will return to the good old days, considering the realities of dual-income families, urban migration and the rising cost of space in cities, all of which impact the joint family structure. But this whole pitch of our cultural devotion to the old is also a bit of a whitewash. Plenty of the old, for instance, fell through the cracks between family and state, because of abandonment, the lack of close family or poverty. "For many of the poor," the economist Jean Dreze tells me, "the focus of their lives is from day to day, and sometimes can barely get by. This means that there is little left for taking care of their old, once these family members can no longer work." Even in places such as rural West Bengal in the 1970s, observers remarked on the many old people on the streets, who were either beggars or vagrants. Indian pilgrimage sites also became magnets for the old and the alone, and across Puri, Varanasi and Shirdi they lined the "holy" rivers and slept in rags near the temples.

But our traditional mechanisms of old-age security, while imperfect, still provided some cushion, regardless of how thin it was or how easily the old could feel the ground beneath it. The emerging trends of urbanization and the migration of children from family homes are, however, presenting us with an awful truth: these traditional support systems for the aged will only get weaker, irrespective of the finger-wagging new laws that stress family responsibility.

And since the 1970s, old-age homes, many of them free and run by NGOs and religious organizations, have mushroomed across the country—cold water over our argument that all the old in India ever needed was family. For the aged, it has been the harshest of betrayals by a state that pursued a policy of looking the other way when the working life of its citizens was done.

Change in the air?

"These days, when I ask people, even in the villages, if they expect their families to support them," Gautam Bhardwaj, who heads the Invest India Foundation, says, "they tell me that they don't. Many think that they will be on their own."

It took some time for the government to recognize the changes that have come with India's growth and urbanization, and it had to be prodded into action by social activists and by the work of key state governments. It was the demographically older states—Kerala, Tamil Nadu and Maharashtra—

that first began to respond to the challenges of social security and benefits as their populations began to gray and as urbanization complicated traditional social support systems. In the 1980s these states began to broaden public health access, tentatively implement pension schemes for the elderly and create mechanisms such as the "death benefit," where the state paid out on the death of the earning family member. Largely however, these policies involved token payments, which would at best help the most destitute and miserable. This was not just because of lack of vision—the states had very little money through these years to implement more effective schemes.

One of the more influential state movements toward social security took place through the 1960s and 1970s in Maharashtra's cities—Bombay, Nagpur and Pune—where urban migration and economic shifts had fragmented traditional support systems faster than anywhere else in the country. Here *hamaals*—urban migrants who had taken up jobs carting loads of grain, wood and metal on Bombay's docks—began organizing to demand work benefits such as pensions and provident funds. They courted arrest, struck from work and camped outside the legislature.[8] Even so the law took thirty-five years to pass, entering the books only in 1980.

Baba Adhav, the fascinating, voluble former doctor and social activist who has been fighting for universal social security, points out that efforts to expand social security across India have been blocked time and again by governments at the state and the center. Today, however, government willingness is much less of a question mark. Government finances are healthy and the state treasury is flush with cash. A universal policy as a result looks more possible, and the government has moved in its usual hesitant but steady way toward it. The state started with some early tokenism—in 1999 it announced a National Policy on Older Persons and 2000 was the National Year of Older Persons. By 2003, however, the government had made its commitment explicit: the 2003–4 union budget announced a restructured pension scheme "offering a basket of pension choices . . . to all employers and the self-employed."

The problem India now faces is of policy detail. In the corridors of Delhi's government offices, there have been competing efforts to define a universal social security policy. Besides the National Pensions Scheme (NPS) that Surendra Dave, Gautam Bhardwaj, Ajay Shah and other economists worked on under the NDA and later the UPA governments, the National Commission for Enterprises in the Unorganised Sector (NCEUS) pushed two bills into the 2005 session of parliament for debate: the Unorganised Sector Workers Social Security Bill and the Unorganised Sector Workers (Conditions of Work and Livelihood Promotion) Bill. The living principle behind these bills has been to provide a guaranteed payout from the state for workers' security. The NPS meanwhile focuses on setting aside a part of the income that workers earn. The NCEUS and the NPS are thus contrasting approaches to social security, forks in the road that will have enormously different implications on the kind of protections the government can create for its citizens and their impact on the budget. The champions of these approaches have been actively hostile to one another, having it out in stormy sessions behind closed doors—"stooges of the capitalists," Ajay Shah (a champion for the NPS) says, has been a phrase often thrown in his direction.

Our age-old notions of security

Dr. Feldstein, or Marty, as he likes to be called, explains the state of social security in the West to me with a joke popular among social insurance experts. "A man jumps from a building, and halfway down someone asks him, 'How are you doing?" He answers, 'So far, I'm fine.'"

Marty is nearly seventy, but he presents a truly enviable figure of health—trim, clear-eyed and animated. As we talk over breakfast, he munches over a strip of bacon and consumes a doughnut—a diet that I have to admire from a distance, for the sake of my HDL levels. But Marty is hardly representative of the typical health situation in his age group across much of Europe and the United States. Most of the social security systems in the West are exploding in costs, as a result of soaring costs of care for aging populations, to the point that these schemes are biting big chunks out of budgets and driving high deficits. "The system is in a mess," Marty says, "in part because it's an old framework, from a time when our understanding of our markets was very different."

The social security system in the United States, for instance, came about when marginal tax rates in the country were stratospheric, with the highest rates averaging around 90 percent. "Policy makers at the time didn't really study incentives all that well," Marty says. "For instance, we now know that fully state-funded social security leads to low personal savings, and people retire earlier. Fully paid-for health coverage, where the user doesn't have to contribute, makes users of health care unconcerned about the costs, and generous unemployment insurance makes people slower in retraining themselves and looking for new jobs."

The generous social benefits in the Unites States and countries in Europe were signed into law in the midst of massive economic upheaval, when large numbers of people were unemployed and in financial despair. The Great Depression and the years of runaway inflation following the end of the Second World War were a painful time for the U.S. economy and its citizens—by 1933 the U.S. GDP was half of that in 1929, almost a fifth of the country's workforce was unemployed and more than half of the country's old were below the poverty line. Many former "middle class" workers were living in shantytowns that came to be known as "Hoovervilles," after the U.S. president—the unlucky Herbert Hoover—who had presided over the crash.

It is not surprising that people caught for years in the deep trough of a prolonged recession were concerned with having security, both long-term and short-term, that would enable them to ride through future unemployment and crisis. The Social Security Act that Franklin Roosevelt signed in 1935, and similar acts that countries across Europe introduced around the same time, brought in a range of "defined benefits"—unemployment insurance as well as generous pensions paid by the state that encouraged older workers to retire and make space for younger ones, thus reducing high unemployment rates.

These laws came from governments willing to do anything to reassure hurting workers. But as Marty notes, it is now that the results of European and U.S. legislation of the 1930s and 1940s—policies that at their core established a highly generous "social state"—are coming home to roost. Even as the finances of social security programs in the United States and Europe have grown shaky, it has become clear, as Marty points out, "once you have entitlements, you will never be able to get rid of them." As the demographics in these countries changed and grayed, the people being taxed to fund these social programs have shrunk, while the number of retirees has boomed. Across Western Europe, the proportion of senior citizens in the population is at an all-time high, and even in the United States, the better placed among these countries thanks to immigration, 80 million Americans will enter retirement in the next two decades. And as the West's citizens turn to retirement homes and dip into their pension funds, these countries are beginning to undergo a financing crisis that is stretching their budgets and will tip tax rates over to unacceptable levels. In the United States, for instance, 12 percent of the payroll now goes into retirement benefits, and it will touch 20 percent in the next decade—a level the European Union has already reached. Other social security disasters have also unfolded, such as companies in the United States that had pledged to pay employee pensions in the 1940s and 1950s—General Motors, Ford and steel and airline firms—having paid dearly for their promises, as these payouts send them reeling into financial crises. "There was a familiar tendency among company management to make long-term promises they did not have to fulfill personally," Marty says. "They made these promises without an idea where their revenues would stand. In some ways, these disasters were inevitable."

Our great, big growth advantage

As Surendra Dave notes, one of the first things the Indian economists in the committee working on pension reforms did was study the failure of these social security systems in the West. India, in shaping a universal social insurance scheme so late in the game, had a great opportunity to survey the disasters gone past and frame a better policy.

At the very least, the challenges developed markets are facing around pensions and social security tell us "what not to do"—which mechanisms, for example, trigger health carelessness, low savings and high future taxes. What was clearest to Indian policy makers such as Dave was the impact here of "defined contributions," versus "defined benefits" approach of the United States and Europe. They noted that when governments such as Chile implemented defined contribution systems where citizens contributed to their pension and social security savings from their own incomes, people became more cautious about health expenditures. It gave them, as Marty notes, "a sense of responsibility."

India is fortunately shaping these policies at a time when it is experiencing high growth. It is not handicapped consequently by the populist political compulsions that pushed the United States and Europe into providing social crutches rather than supports. And a diverse market gives our policy makers several options toward effective and sustainable social security.

The urge to make overambitious promises, however, is still pretty strong.

"Our growth and market optimism does give us some elbow room," Ajay tells me, "but there's a flip side to it. Now that the government is flush with cash, there is a tendency to overspend on social security schemes, and promise more than we can do." But India ought to be hyperaware of unmanageable pension costs. India's "implied debt" on civil service pensions alone—relatively a tiny demographic of 24 million—was calculated at more than 55 percent of the country's GDP in 2004. Universal pension access that places even a comparable per-person cost burden on the government is simply unworkable. "When I look at proposals that are both universal and defined benefit," Montek Singh Ahluwalia says, "I question where the money will come from. The numbers don't add up—we cannot afford that kind of scheme."

This means that India will have to inevitably look to a model that is based on "defined contributions," where a share of the money going into social security comes from the worker's income. But what may play spoiler to establishing such a policy are the champions of India's existing, defined-benefit-based pension fund system, who have blocked efforts toward a universal, defined contribution system that would be a signficant departure from what now exists. The challenge we are facing here is of getting old habits out by their roots—of confronting, as Raghuram Rajan notes, "our comfort with the traditional, and our aversion to change."

India's present pension schemes have staggering problems. Government employees in India are all covered under a direct-benefits pensions plan, which sucks deeply from the state exchequer. The Employees' Provident Fund Organization (EPFO) that manages the pensions of organized workers and the private sector is not much better. This fund, which is located deep within the bowels of the government, has avoided too much scrutiny and remains stuck in mainly low-yield government securities. The board of the fund includes union representatives who have been extremely risk-averse to investing in equity, and this has limited even the success of a 1998 amendment, which was a small wedge of change permitting a 10 percent investment into rated private corporate bonds. The attitude within these funds has been so static that, as one commentator noted, "when even the car cleaner knew that IFCI was going bust, the EPFO continued to hold on to its IFCI deposits." The finance ministry has long restricted the ability of the fund to get rid of bad investments. A 2003 "reform," for instance, allowed the EPF to exit failing investments, provided that the instrument "was downgraded by two credit agencies"—not much use for the fund considering that by that point there would not be any takers for the sale. The EPFO board has also taken the sort of decisions that make a bad thing retrograde—even though the EPF was meant to be a defined-contribution fund, the board has insisted on fixing the interest rate for fund investments at the beginning of the year rather than at the end, thus wrangling artificially high rates from the government.

The Employees' Pension Scheme (EPS) that was introduced in 1995 for workers in the private organized sector is—there is a resounding chorus of consensus on this one—especially terrible. "It's a ticking time bomb," one pension expert tells me. The scheme is a fully defined benefit, pay-as-you-go plan. To put it kindly, the scheme has been disastrous, with its finances awash in red and underfunded by more than Rs 250 billion. That's a lot of zeros. What allows this scheme to go on, as Marty points out, is that governments always find it easier to promise retirement money than to provide cash up front. "After all," he notes, "retirement funds will be another government's problem." And perhaps worst of all, these defined-benefit schemes in India are subsidizing the upper and middle classes of employees at the expense of the poor, by taking funds from government budgets that could have been used on more universal social security coverage.

What is especially puzzling is the stubborn hostility we see toward investing savings in our stock markets. Pension assets amount to less than 6 percent of India's GDP, far less than in other countries—in Thailand the share is at 10 percent, Korea 22 percent, Singapore 61 percent and Malaysia 64 percent. Opponents to such investments point to the cycles of boom and bust India's stock markets have gone through, but in the longer term, these cycles do not hurt returns. India's pension regulator chief, D. Swarup, has noted that equities in India have averaged 14 percent in annual returns over fifty years, giving them an enormous advantage over returns from bond and securities, or in fact anything a government could reasonably pay out. And bringing domestic savings into India's stock market would make the swings that have been caused by foreign funds swooping in and out less extreme—the Sensex had zoomed past 20,000 in 2007, thanks to a record $17 billion in FII inflows that year. In September 2008 it fell below 12,000 as $9.5 billion fled the market. More stable investments such as long-term pension funds would be a counterweight to such global storms, and a source for calm. "Our over-reliance on foreign flows holds us hostage to global trends," Dr. Vijay Kelkar points out. "We should instead be making sure that our markets reflect our strong domestic fundamentals, by bringing our domestic savings in them."

But some ministers have taken a monsters-under-the-bed approach when it comes to investing savings into the market. The problem, one senior bureaucrat tells me, is the knee-jerk aversion among India's left to capitalism and private business. "They see the private sector as a group of scheming villains," he says. "It's a black-and-white view, where the market players are a greedy lot out to loot people of their savings."

This completely ignores the fact that equity returns far exceed bond investments in the longer term and that pension funds of other countries now make up for almost 13 percent of the FIIs in India. In fact, even as India's pension funds are locked out of our apparently malevolent equity markets, funds from the United States, Canada, United Kingdom, Malaysia, Australia and South Korea—along with 150 other global pension funds—have all invested in Indian stocks. In 2007 the pension fund for members of the European Parliament also entered India. "We have foreign capital hugely benefiting from our stock market, while Indians are being forced to invest in low-return government bonds," Raghuram says. "The government is actually going out of the way to create unnecessary future liabilities for ourselves, despite India's fast-growing economy."

Risk, sometimes described as the "forgotten factor of production," can be as powerful as capital and labor when it comes to driving growth and investment. Our deliberate channeling of savings into low-yield, low-risk investment has, I believe, been lose-lose for investors as well as for overall development, since businesses—especially in the more innovative and R&D-based industries—suffer when capital unequivocally gravitates toward lower-risk and obviously lower-value investments.

Additionally, the common view of equity-based policies as high risk depends on how we see the options available to such policy holders. On retirement, for instance, policy holders can choose to purchase annuities with their money, which gives them the option to convert to a defined benefit system once they retire. The default option in these plans can also be the safest one, to safeguard against both excessive risks and financial illiteracy. Providing indexing options is also a way to minimize risk within such plans, and make them palatable even to the most anxious. These choices the market offers in terms of social insurance clearly are not just based on risk–reward—they are preferences that can be tweaked to individual taste.

Ignoring the market and focusing on low returns have big downsides—in the long term, as incomes rise, diverting savings into investments with low returns means that people are unable to keep up with changes in their cost of living. The newly retired, for instance, find that a long career with lifetime mid-to-high incomes has ended with a whimper, thanks to the real value of their savings accounts. India's real returns on pension funds between 1980 and 2000, for instance, barely managed 2 percent at a time India was growing at 5–6 percent every year. In 2004 the Indian government, with the Sensex at 5,000 points, proposed that 10 percent of pension funds be pumped into equities. We entered 2008 with the stock market having risen more than three times that, but with the shift yet to be made. Even after its steep falls in September 2008, a fund that had invested money in 2004 would have turned in good returns. The stock market is expected to touch $5 trillion by 2020, and we are still stalling.

A BIG CHALLENGE to pension reforms and a sustainable social security policy is the danger of politics creeping in. What our experiences and those of developed markets make clear is that a universal scheme, to be effective and sustainable, must be insulated from political compulsions as much as possible. Otherwise, long-term funds become easy prey for election-minded governments and end up getting tweaked and changed and overhauled, especially in times of low growth. Privately invested funds from pension accounts, run by state-appointed fund managers or pegged to indexes, do a good job of ensuring such insulation.

But changing our approach to equity investments requires, as Sendhil Mullainathan notes, a decisive step that challenges this bias. "Unless we actively put across policies that take on existing systems and prove themselves to be better, you will have people unwilling to break with tradition, and with what they already believe." And it is here that the NPS holds promise.

A chance to set the bar

When I consider the possibilities that have come with our belated push toward a social security system, I think of the many depressing instances across India where elderly retirees cannot get their pension disbursements started unless they pay the officers a large bribe. We have a chance now to implement a better pensions system as well as much better delivery channels for pension payouts, which can bypass these sleazy middlemen.

"Since 2002," Marty tells me, "India has had some great opportunities to design more effective pensions and investment models." Over the last few decades, social security theory has evolved from the quick fixes of the depression era, and India has become a dream testing ground for talented economists and policy makers to address age-old problems with new ideas.

Information technology, for instance, has become transformational here, and Ajay says that the IT systems implemented in the NSE-50 index he designed has had substantially lower "market impact costs" compared with any other in the world. Using IT intelligently can dramatically lower transaction costs in any social security system we implement. Additionally, now that India has some key institutions in place—in the shape of the NSDL and a strong regulatory system—we can build a pensions model that is unprecedented in efficiency and seamlessness.

On pension approaches, the World Bank had outlined three "pillars" in 1994 that set out choices for a government. One was mandatory, universal basic coverage that the state provided for; the second was voluntary, and depended on the amount of private income; and the third was private contracts from insurance firms. These provide a chocolate box range of choices for Indian policy—mandatory, universal, voluntary or not, hard and soft systems.

Marty, who usually grapples with bringing reform to his country's now politics-soaked social security system, finds India's blue-sky opportunity invigorating, and he is by turns animated and considered while proposing an approach. "Keep the basic, universal offering simple," he says, "such as a compulsory annuity system, which has automatic enrollment starting when the citizen is very young." Marty believes this is necessary to keep healthy people from opting out of social systems and driving the average risk upward. And he is in favor of strong incentives that "make people—and that includes everyone, regardless of individual tendencies—save."

But India faces some unique challenges in savings and social security—it has to provide solutions not just for the middle class, but also for the large numbers of its poor. Our challenges here are on every level, from how to get universal coverage in places with little or no infrastructure to how to tackle the large numbers of self-employed workers, and connect our spread out, disparate communities under a universal system. "We have a large agricultural sector, people miles away from any bank, and a huge unorganized labor market," Gautam points out. "We would have to approach each of these problems differently."

I believe that universal coverage is essential, and that the state cannot renege on it. But how do you create a system that is sustainable financially for the government while offering a sufficient cushion of social insurance for India's poor? Most of the poorest live hand to mouth, where saving for rough times becomes pretty unrealistic. Dr. Kelkar's proposal of the negative income tax, paid directly into the hands of the poor through individual accounts, presents a possible solution. Locking in a portion of this money for pensions and providing an option to subscribers to match this portion with their own savings—money that can then be invested in a range of funds—would go a long way in creating a sustainable and universal social insurance system. And such a system would benefit from our strengths in IT; we could build a national ID system to manage individual accounts and investments.

There are already some interesting social security solutions emerging in India that tap into these features. Dave, Gautam and Ajay were at the forefront of a dramatic new initiative with the NDA government, which in its innovativeness and cost is, as many Indian economists have pointed out with some pride, "among the best in the world." It was taking shape as early as 1998, but the Indian state being what it is, the bill has yet to be passed and we are still referring to it as the "new" pensions scheme in 2009!

A great blueprint

The opportunity for reforms in pensions sneaked up in 1998 in the guise of Project OASIS (Old Age Social and Income Security). The initiative came from the ministry of social justice, which was focusing on pensions for the uncovered, unorganized sector. The supremely elegant system that OASIS, and later a more broad-based expert committee, finally designed was a defined-contribution-based social security scheme that included both the unorganized sector and the civil service. The scheme would allow employees a choice of investments for their pension savings under an independent regulator and included strong IT support to drastically reduce transaction costs.

OASIS, however, quickly found itself tugged in different directions—the ministry of labor eyed the EPFO as the potential designer of the scheme, which was obviously the last thing that the committee, which favored both defined contribution and low transaction costs, wanted. And politics being what it is, each proposal had its chances of succeeding; so Ajay, who was part of the expert committee, tells me that much of the next few months were spent in a blur of talking and persuading people. The reformers got their way. "We were lucky that Jaswant Singh and Vajpayee had a long-term vision on pensions, rather than a next-election time line," he says. "But it still seemed like an endlessly long battle."

The NPS was publicly notified and made applicable to all of India's new central government employees from January 1, 2004, five months before the NDA government fell. And seventeen states across India followed the lead of the center and placed their state government employees within the scheme. The shift to the defined-contribution scheme affected the take-home salaries of civil servants without creating an uproar—an unimaginable political win.

But once the government changed after the unexpected election rout of the NDA government in May, the progress toward the pension reform came to a standstill. While it got Chidambaram's support, he was bent on getting legislation introducing the pension regulator through parliament, which stalled when the left parties opposed it. Chidambaram waited and finally, in exasperation at two and a half years of stalling, decided to start work on the scheme without legislation. The opponents of the bill have been furious with the finance minister ever since and have labeled it "Chidambaram's pension reform," implying that he is working on it without the parliament's aye.

With all the committee meetings and changes in government, Gautam says, "The NPS reforms have got delayed by a decade." But the fact that it may finally arrive in the shape that it was initially conceived is, for the people who navigated it through, a great triumph. The features of the system are cutting-edge—a national low-cost pensions network with distribution and disbursement channels that include banks and post offices, and where the cost for fund managers comes to a maximum of five basis points a year, compared to typical costs for mutual funds of one hundred basis points annually.

A new momentum?

Overall, however, our pensions system, despite the NPS initiative, has stayed untouched and remains largely in a mess. But the good news is that the NPS has entered the system. There is a chance that the results it generates will encourage reform in the rest of our pension systems, and the blueprint can be applied across our other pension structures. The NPS also has promise in providing people security in a country where 16 percent of the population is so poor that it has no savings at all. In fact the committee implementing the NPS is now trying out a series of pilots to tailor the scheme to lower-income sectors. One pilot links the NPS to milk cooperatives buying milk from farmers. Here, instead of getting paid, say, six rupees for a liter of milk, the farmer would be paid five, with the remaining one rupee going into a pension account at the milk cooperative. Gautam hopes to similarly use self-employed women's groups such as SEWA, taxi driver unions, and so on to allow people to access the system.

Expanding access to the NPS can be a win-win situation both for old-age savings and for the dramatic effect it can have in deepening our capital markets. Of course, as Gautam notes, the policy will be ahead of the politics. "Getting the politics and the debates to align with these ideas is the tricky part," he says, "but the NPS is out there, at least with some possibility for success, and it's giving us a foot in the door for the right kind of changes."

The right kind of social insurance plan, built around defined contributions and implemented now, would touch a demographic sweet spot—by being able to take advantage of the growing incomes of a large working class, as well as leveraging the growing value of India's capital markets in the next few decades.

But there are efforts afoot to implement a massive defined-benefit plan—political bait that could be disastrous in fiscal terms. The NCEUS, for instance, offers a byzantine National Security Scheme that would be, unlike the defined-contribution approach of the NPS, a defined-benefit scheme funded by the government. The NCEUS program does make some pertinent points—that a universal social security policy would enable labor reforms and is in fact the only way we can both empower and protect Indian workers within free markets. But in offering universal social insurance to India's

300 million informal workers through a guaranteed defined-benefit plan, the NCEUS makes the same assumptions countries before us did: that taxes will only grow and dependency ratios will not rise, and that governments will not keep raising the benefits. "The scheme," one bureaucrat tells me, "takes us down a social insurance path we should be really wary of."

From one perspective, the NPS, with its principles of defined contributions, may be tapping into a sentiment that is quintessentially Indian. Split as the country is along caste, class, religious and regional lines, India is hardly an ideal setting for mass-based social schemes funded by the state. "We have too many communities in India with conflicting interests, very unlike the socially homogeneous countries that have adopted state-funded, universal programs," one bureaucrat points out. In pre-British India, the independence and assertiveness of its various communities was at the core of the region's identity—Indian rulers held onto their power through negotiations with an intricate network of local, big men, and town and village communities functioned as self-reliant, local economies largely unconstrained by central rule.

In independent India, there have always been strong signs of such assertiveness at the local level when it comes to social protections—in the absence of effective, national-level social insurance, groups such as SEWA and CDF as well as small "thrift and credit" groups and chit systems that provide various kinds of social insurance to their communities have flourished in towns and villages.

The arguments we have for a defined-contribution system of social insurance are overwhelming ones. Generous pensions, unemployment insurance and health benefits can have unintended consequences, like people retiring early, taking longer breaks between jobs and focusing too little on preventive health care. Defined benefits are also fraught with political risk, and once a nation ages it cannot bear the burden of social security. We have already seen the debilitating impact of index-linked pensions in India for a small set of government employees. To extend it to the entire population would cripple a country.

Right now—when the country is buoyant, fast growing and young, with the potential of many decades of positive stock market returns—is the ideal time to make a complete transition to a defined-contribution system for all forms of social insurance. We are lucky to possess the IT tools that can help individuals earmark their savings for the future, and also choose their own risk profiles. And for those who cannot put in a contribution the state can provide a negative income tax.

The choices in our social security schemes present a clear option between a complete change and the status quo. As India transforms, our approaches in dealing with our social challenges must necessarily change. Market economies should frame their social insurance policies around individual choice, allowing people to tailor them to their preferences—whether it is health benefits or provident fund accounts. But the spirit of India's paternalistic state is still very strong in our approach to social benefits. We still attempt to tackle our challenges—in labor, unemployment, old age and health—through suboptimal guarantees, socialist-style state protections and subsidies, all carried out by a creaky bureaucracy.

However, as people individually play a far greater part in the Indian growth story, and as direct taxes dominate government revenues and fund our welfare schemes, we are demanding much more in accountability and results from the state. The push right now is toward results in social investments that are tangible, direct and recognizable, which will replace the fuzzy, indirect subsidy system in place. Such indirect systems have essentially meant that I benefit much more from fuel subsidies than the working class or the poor, and can fill up my Camry with subsidized fuel while my cook walks to work. But with the tools and the skills we have with us today—in low-cost, transparent, direct IT systems, broad-based infrastructure and of course hindsight in what worked and what did not—we now have the chance to build a social system that sets new standards in effectiveness, transparency and cost, as well as provides security that can offer real comfort.

THE FOREST FOR THE TREES

India's Environment Challenge

The gathering clouds

I meet Anantha Padmanabhan, executive director of Greenpeace, on an overcast evening in Bangalore, and I arrive for our meeting just as it is beginning to drizzle. Anantha rides over on his bicycle, which is how he travels everywhere, braving the dangers of the city's messy traffic and its jaywalkers.

Anantha and I have met to chat about the weather, which in the last few years has ceased to be an easy, time-filler topic. "It is quite possible," he tells me, "that everything we've experienced about the world's climate may come tumbling down around our ears in our lifetime." Not so long ago, he would have sounded extreme. Till the 1990s, environment was at best a marginal topic, one tied up with notions of social responsibility and "green" activism. But it has morphed with disconcerting speed into a serious global concern that now draws enormous political heat.

Governments have usually given long-term concerns such as the environment short shrift, focused as they are on monthly polls and quarter to quarter trade and inflation numbers. Clearly, then, for the environment to have gained the level of global political and public attention it now has is a sign of a crisis that looms too large to be ignored.

Even our personal experiences with the climate have changed in disturbing ways. Globally, we are experiencing soaring temperatures, shorter winters and unseasonal rainstorms. Carl Pope, a leader of the environmental movement in the United States and executive director of the Sierra Club, tells me, "Previously, climates were tied to particular places—you had wintry regions and summery towns. Now there is no such thing as a particular climate for a place—it has become completely variable and unpredictable." And at the extremes, climate change is playing a role in war and political unrest. Darfur, for example, is caught in a drought-induced civil war, triggered in part by changing rainfall patterns and competition for the remaining fertile lands. The violence in Somalia and the Ivory Coast has also emerged from a similar oppressive mix of water and food shortages.

There is now a growing consensus for action among the world's scientists that we must tackle these accelerating trends of climate change across the planet. Climate papers and studies betray a rising sense of alarm within their dry paragraphs, and their extrapolations predict natural disasters within this century. "During the Rio and Kyoto discussions, the sense of urgency was less, and the two percent targets for emission reductions in the agreements reflected that," Shiv Someshwar, an environmental research scientist and director of the Asia Pacific program at Columbia's Earth Institute, tells me. "But now, people are worried."

For India, however, the rising global consciousness on the environment comes at a very inconvenient time. India is growing quickly, guzzling coal, gas and oil in large quantities as it plays catch-up with the developed world. Our emissions are rising fast, matching our growth spikes, and the new popularity of emissions curbs in the developed countries seem in direct conflict with India's interests.

Environmental factions

One Indian politician recently offered me an unusual take on the climate change debate. He suggested that the global warming crisis was nothing more than a "Western conspiracy" meant to keep India poor and underdeveloped.

While one hopes this is not the majority view among us on climate change, it signals the wide chasm between our views and those of the developed world. The consensus in India is that the climate change crisis is a marginal concern, and the majority of our politicians and policy makers believe that "our first priority" is economic growth. Our government partners with China in asserting that environmentalism cannot come before growth nor "compromise" India's development.

But the pressures on India to accept emission targets and cuts are only going to increase. The first global climate change agreement had brought the countries from the developed world together on meeting carbon emissions targets to control global warming. However, as the 2012 policy and the successor to Kyoto is being negotiated, developing countries like India, China, Brazil, Mexico and Russia are also under pressure to take on goals in reducing carbon emissions.

Understandably enough, the demands from developed markets to control our emissions have annoyed Indian ministers, who point out both subtly and not so subtly that Western concerns on climate resembles a fat guy going on a diet right after a massive dinner. Politicians across developing countries including India have suggested that the climate change crisis is a problem created by rich nations, and they ought to be the ones taking the steps necessary to solve it. "At the climate negotiations," Shiv says, "what Indians and other developing country participants insisted on was that first and foremost, 'we need to get the U.S. to agree to emission cuts.' They wanted developed markets to take on some responsibility for climate change."

These are legitimate concerns. But unfortunately, the nature of our environmental challenge does not allow us to take such a straightforward stance or shrug off any role in addressing the crisis. Climate after all is mobile, and so are its problems, and India is the afflicted, passive smoker when it comes to the emissions the developed world has created over the last century.

For us the crisis in places like Darfur is a warning, a sign of how natural balances can unravel across India. Global warming will impact sea levels and rain patterns and will consequently affect our agriculture, food supplies and water resources. India may even be disproportionately vulnerable—the immediate catastrophe from climate change, as Kevin Watkins, an economist and lead author of the UNDP's *Human Development Report 2007*, has noted, "won't happen in Manhattan, but in Andhra." India is already feeling the heat of global warming. "The effects of emissions and environmental abuse," Dr. R. K. Pachauri, chairman of the now famous Intergovernmental Panel on Climate Change (IPCC), tells me, "is already quite apparent across India." Environmental degradation is becoming visible here in all its grimy splendor—for example, in the vast bank of "dirty clouds" formed from industrial emissions that hang suspended over the subcontinent, which India sleeps and wakes under. The past years have also seen the country struggle with massively delayed rains and unexpected droughts. The seasons are becoming unpredictable, and the moodiness of our monsoons is worrying.

"India has approached the environmental debate as if it's an external challenge," Dr. Nicholas Stern notes, "but the reality is that it is more immediately an internal crisis." He elaborates: "India's water towers—the Himalayan glaciers—are beginning to melt. For an agricultural country, that is a big red flag." Even as we refuse binding targets on emissions and ambitious pollution control and duke it out at the climate negotiations, our rivers are shrinking and our forests have retreated, leaving behind arid earth on which nothing grows, and the glaciers that feed our rivers are melting away. The reality is that no matter who we believe deserves blame for climate change, or how much we try to explain away the crisis with conspiracy theories, the relationship between our growth and our environment has already become an uneasy one. And by ignoring this, we are allowing a crisis to fester.

A moody kind of weather

Our present apathy around the environment contrasts quite sharply with India's historical reverence for nature; our natural resources have long been at the center of our everyday life and culture. Indian mythologies resonate with the spirit of animism—Hindu gods and heroes resemble Greek and Roman mythology in their evocation of rivers, forests, the sun, seas and rain. The king of gods in Hindu mythology is the god of rain, and most Indians regard the river that irrigates the northern plains, the Ganga, as holy. Major religious festivals in India are associated with the harvesting seasons. The ecologist Madhav Gadgil has even suggested that India's most rooted social structure, the caste system, emerged partly to define control over natural resources, from its land to forests, which in turn may have allowed people to use them sensibly and sustainably.

Our present attitude, however, is the outcome of an entirely different sensibility. Early on in British India, administrators were keen on strengthening its control over Indian agriculture and expanding cropping into India's jungles. These forests were consequently seen as a blight on the land and razing them down was an "unmixed good"[1] for the colonial administration. R. K. Pringle, the collector of Khandesh, said in 1848, "The destruction of the Jungle, far from being looked at as an evil . . . has been considered a benefit, and measures have been proposed to accelerate it." He added that in India, "the jungle would gradually disappear and the country become more healthy."[2]

The dumping of waste, sewage and industrial effluent into rivers bordering Indian cities was also an uncontroversial policy in British India, and independent India uncritically adopted this lack of concern for the environment. Mahesh Rangarajan points out that post-1947, our governments approached these issues with a typically socialist bent, embracing the idea that "the environment, along with agriculture, would gradually become marginal in an industrialized, modern economy." The ideology of the planned economy and its fascination with heavy industry that India favored paid little heed to the environment, as was already obvious in Stalin's vision of "building an iron and cement brotherhood"[3] and Mao's exhortation to "transform and conquer nature . . . move mountains to build farmland."[4]

It may not have helped that India's most prominent environmentalist at this time was Mahatma Gandhi. His concern for sustainability was both visionary and central to his thinking, but his views, when juxtaposed with his village-industry model for the economy, seemed quaint in the eyes of other Indian leaders. Postindependent India as a result took a black-and-white approach toward the environment, sidelining these concerns in its quest for growth.*

An outcast in times of growth

The world's history of industry-led growth has not been a very presentable one. In its approach to development, India has taken the cue from Europe and the United States, which in their years of rapid growth did little to control massive environmental abuse. The persistent London smog during the nineteenth and early twentieth centuries, for instance, was a direct consequence of rampant coal burning in the city. In the United States as well,

*In fact Nehru later had a change of heart about his big industrial projects in the light of the environmental and social displacements that came in their wake, and in 1958 he called them a "disease of giganticism." But by then the path for India's development had been set on its course.

manufacturing-led pollution severely degraded its rivers and land in the 1960s and 1970s. The consequence of such growth in the history of the developed world is that pollution during industrialization is taken for granted.

Every major city in India now fails emission standards. "These laws," the environmentalist Sharad Lele tells me, "are already far more relaxed than global WHO requirements. The fallout of lax standards and minimal enforcement is obvious for us urban residents. I came over to meet you on my bike, and driving just a few kilometers in the city makes me feel like I have a smoker's lungs."

People arguing in favor of the development-before-environment approach hold up the environmental Kuznet's curve as the Holy Grail. This theory has a neat logic that has made it instantly appealing—it suggests that there is a bell-shaped, "inverted U" trend in the relationship between a society's economic growth and environmental degradation. In the early stages of growth, environmental losses go up, but as citizens get richer, people can afford to deal with the problems that have built up. Shorter version: nature can be trussed up and ignored until growth is attended to. "The idea here," Anantha tells me, "is that if we have to tackle climate change, we are better off rich than poor."

The curve has had a "happily ever after" appeal for developing countries, but its logic is both dangerous and incomplete. It does not, for instance, take into account the advantages the Western world had in being able to export industrial pollution elsewhere by shifting their dirtiest industries abroad, first through colonization and later through globalization. In comparison, developing economies today have no untouched lands to exploit—if trees have to be felled and rivers polluted, it will have to be done in the home country. We have no other place to run to.

The unquiet country

The environmentalist Dr. Kamal Bawa is visiting India from the United States, where he teaches. When I meet him, he is in holiday attire, and his outfit, I tell him, is wonderfully apt for our conversation—he is wearing a floral Hawaiian shirt and looks quite festive in it.

Dr. Bawa offers me an interesting perspective on our ongoing environmental losses. "India is very different from the Western world," he says. "Tropical areas like India have highly complex ecosystems and are very difficult to recover once destroyed, compared to the temperate areas of the West." And this, he says, can make investments in dirty industries far more disastrous for us than it was for the West.

Our share in the world's natural resources only confirms our relative vulnerability. India sustains around 17 percent of the world's population, but accounts for only 2.4 percent of the world's surface and 3.5 percent of the world's freshwater resources. And our forest cover averages at one third that of the United States. "India's people pressures on the environment are almost unprecedented," Dr. Bawa admits, "and that makes our relationship with nature very fragile."

India's environment has never been benign—rather, it was stepmotherly, often cruel. In this country of lush fields and tropical forests, climate is often unreliable, even tyrannical, periodically bringing both storms and droughts. When it came to rain, farmers would face a long period of thirst and a fleetingly short reprieve. Turmoil in our climate has consequently played a prominent part in India's upheavals, and people frequently emigrated or became refugees from their areas following the unpredictable ravages of the weather. Nature was second only to wars in its ability to destroy crops and livelihoods. An old saying defined Indian tragedies into two kinds, *asmani rua sultain*, those inflicted by the heavens and by the kings.[5] These struggles with an uncertain climate have continued postindependence, with the cycles of droughts and floods that threatened the country's agriculture through the 1960s, which have since been better managed thanks to the green revolution. Most recently, the ability of nature to wreak havoc was brought home with the tsunami in 2004, and in 2008 when the Kosi river in rural Bihar changed course and displaced millions in floods.

India's political and public opinion, however, does not reflect the realities of our environment, a trend that has gained strength since 1972, when Indira Gandhi used the argument of "development before environment" at the United Nations. That year, Indira was one of exactly two heads of state (including the host Olof Palme, prime minister of Sweden) who attended the United Nations conference on the environment. While defending India's dismal track record in conservation, Indira said that it was all very well for industrial countries to focus on the environment because "they had enough to feed their bellies."

Our early chances

There were a few moments in the 1970s and 1980s, however, when India glimpsed an alternative vision. "The early tone of our environmental movements, especially from the 1970s, was very ambitious," Sharad says. The movement was shaped by the environmentalists and writers Anil Agarwal, Ravi Chopra and Kalpana Sharma, who edited the 1982 Center for Science and Environment (CSE) report titled *The State of India's Environment.* The report marked a radical, innovative shift in environmental thought and offered a new vision for such policy.

In essence, the report provided a roadmap for how environmental policy could be aligned with our efforts toward economic growth. This approach was, as Sharad notes, very different from existing views. "The Western idea of sustainable environment was to keep it behind glass and cage," Sharad tells me. "The assumption was that we *couldn't* coexist with nature."

Instead, the West, due to its abundant natural resources and its advantages, as Carl Pope puts it, of the "frontier commons" in their colonies and global markets, focused on productivity in labor and capital but allowed inefficiencies to soar in terms of land use, air pollution and forest degradation. "This has created a mind-set," Sharad says, "where people will drive several miles in an SUV to camp in a pristine, protected forest. The incentives by default tilt toward hurting the environment, and making it seem irrelevant to our daily life."

The CSE report suggested an alternative vision to this, where the environment existed within the economic framework of consumption and production. Economies, Anil Agarwal wrote, needed to account for environment costs, and growth had to be seen as "a gross nature product rather than a gross national product."

Considering the innovative, path-breaking ideas that these environmentalists as well as other writers such as Ramachandra Guha and Madhav Gadgil shaped, it is surprising how we ended up so conventional and uninspired in our approach to climate change. But our views here were shaped somewhat accidentally—during the global debate around emissions that emerged in 1992.

That year, Anil Agarwal attended the 1992 UN conference at Rio de Janeiro as an adviser to Narasimha Rao and also as a member of the Indian delegation. At the conference, he brought up the question of historical responsibility for emissions and criticized the tendency of some global analysts to place the blame for higher emissions squarely on the shoulders of developing countries such as India, by discussing total emissions rather than per capita numbers. Sharad notes that the argument Anil made for developed countries to take on more responsibility for emissions became a two-edged sword and took a life of its own, much beyond what Anil or other Indian environmentalists had intended. The morality of the 1992 view allowed the Indian government to reject not just making the first move in global environmental policy, but to also dismiss legitimate and growing concerns around India's weakening natural resources.

Economic development thus became the skirt for Indian policy makers to hide behind, an all-or-nothing approach that has consigned environment-friendly policy to the closet. It has in short become a disaster paved with the early good intentions of Indian environmentalists, who responded angrily to these reckless policies by calling the Indian government "among the most incompetent in the world when it comes to the environment." And our early steps toward a different approach—one that Rajiv Gandhi championed in a speech saying, "Development which destroys the environment eventually destroys development itself"—have been forgotten.

Silver linings

"India is unique among nations on the global stage," Sir Nicholas Stern tells me, "in the opportunity it now has to lead the climate change debate." As a young country still early on the development curve, India has a chance to shape an approach to growth that acknowledges the unacceptable costs which accompanied the growth model of industrialized countries. India can potentially shape a low-emission arc toward development that is more efficient in using our natural resources. It has the opportunity to take early moves toward carbon reduction, similar to how we reduced our trade tariffs much earlier than WTO agreements required us to—especially once we recognized that such steps would only work to our advantage. But India has been reluctant to take the lead in environmental policy, preferring instead to be a backbencher who is prominently against signing the climate change treaty or accepting emission curbs. The government refuses to let go of the 1992 argument, of assigning historical responsibility to the developed world and refusing to commit to serious targets for controlling domestic carbon emissions. But Anantha points out that the high road India currently takes based on its position as a low-emission, still-developing country may be the worst possible strategy. "We are acquiring carbon-intensive habits that are difficult to break," he says. "Right now, we are hiding behind the poor in our per capita emission figures, and our businesses and our middle class have already adopted the fuel-intensive habits of the developed world." And as the economist Joseph Stiglitz points out to me, failing to consider such environmental costs while we build up export-oriented, low-cost manufacturing and services sectors means that "India is absorbing the pollution of the developed world, for products and services that developed countries eventually use."

We might, however, have committed ourselves to steeper goals than we now admit to. At the G8 conference in 2007, Manmohan Singh had emphasized a "common but differentiated responsibility" on the environment, and made a commitment to match India's per capita emissions to that of developed countries. The National Climate Action Plan that the UPA government launched in June 2008 also reiterated that goal. "These promises mean really steep cuts," Shiv says, "especially if you take into account our development forecasts, and how much pressure our population is going to bring on our natural resources." India's greenhouse gas (GHG) emissions right now stand at just two tons per capita, as compared to five in China, eleven in Europe and twenty in the United States. However, Europe has committed to emission reductions of potentially 30 percent by 2020, and a 60–80 percent reduction by 2050, on the condition that other developed countries also agree. With the United States now likely to sign on these targets, India will have to develop ambitious strategies if it is to keep its emissions below that of the developed world, even as it grows much faster and increases its consumption of carbon-heavy fuels. This means that even as our per capita income grows by sixteen times by 2050 at our present growth rate, India can only let its per capita emissions grow by two times in the same period.

This is a pretty tall order, and possible only if we incorporate pro-environmental policies right now into our agenda of growth. It is after all much easier to shape behavior before the bad habits of the older industrialization model—with its legacy of "dirty" infrastructure, intensive car ownership and high fuel consumption—catch on. "Unless we take our emission goals into account right now, while building our infrastructure and expanding our cities," Sharad says, "we will soon be stuck in the same dilemma as the developed world." We will have to start here by addressing the potential environmental costs of the $500 billion infrastructure investments that we plan to make over the next five years.

A very local crisis

Suprabha Seshan is the director of the Gurukula Botanical Sanctuary in Wayanad, and she brings me organic, home-grown vegetables and golden-skinned mangoes when she arrives for our meeting. She lives out of the sanctuary, and I ask her about the climate changes she has witnessed on the ground. Environment-driven crises after all tend to grow bottom-up, first affecting those parts of the economy that are most in touch with the country's land, water and air. And in India the impact is now probably strongest in our agriculture sector.

"There is already a clear awareness of global warming among the farmers I work with," Suprabha tells me. "They have noticed it in the changes in local rainfall and monsoon patterns." An early indicator of uncomfortable environmental changes across India has been the stagnation of our agricultural sector, where soil degradation and growing droughts and water shortage have affected farm productivity and income growth. Over the last decade, the growth of India's agriculture has been remarkable only for how low it has been: below 3 percent a year.

This crisis has been amplified by the green revolution. The revolution rescued at least parts of India's rural populations from a life lived at the edge of destitution, turning once barren land into lush, sprawling fields of wheat and paddy and bringing in new wealth into the rural country. But in time its successes have begun to come unstuck. "The government's price guarantees for rice, wheat and sugar cane persuaded Indian farmers to grow these water-intensive crops en masse even in arid regions," Dr. Ashok Gulati, Asia director of the International Food Policy Research Institute, tells me. "We are consequently now wasting enormous quantities of water." He adds, "I met an Israeli scientist recently who told me that they are astonished by how much water we waste. Israel uses far less water than we do per hectare, and still surpasses us in agricultural productivity."

The catastrophic policies around India's water resources bear out how counterintuitive the economic incentives surrounding natural resources are. Electricity subsidies, the absence of pricing for groundwater and badly targeted funds for water management have combined to create both shortage and overuse of water. Tushar Shah, coordinator of the International Water Management Institute, points out that India is just one third canal fed and the rest of India's crops depend primarily on groundwater. "Our groundwater levels have sunk by more than half in many parts of India, thanks to overpumping," he says. "Farmer after farmer across India drills holes in the land and uses free electricity to pump the water out. There is no incentive to save water at all, and no projects for recharging these sources." Free power to farmers has been a vote magnet for governments, and consequently illegal connections in rural and semiurban areas (from which people draw unlimited power) are rarely penalized and usually made legal—in Karnataka, the government called this move to legalize illegal connections *akrama-sakrama,* or "illegal to legal." And the use of subsidized fertilizer and pesticides has desalinated and poisoned the soil, triggering in some cases horror-show consequences in disease and death rates in our villages.

India's governments have yet to fully accept that these weaknesses in our natural resources are slowly becoming an intense part of our local politics. Across the country, the result of decades of environmental abuse shows up in a landscape increasingly of "the dead tree that gives no shelter . . . and the dry stone no sound of water."[6] The Indian countryside is gripped in a crisis of water shortages, parched earth and failing crops, which has driven over half of the country's farmers into debt, and several to suicides. Ironically, the spate of farmer suicides has compelled politicians to continue the policies that have proved so damaging—free electricity to pump out our fast vanishing groundwater and cuts in pesticide and fertilizer prices that will further degrade soil quality.

The degradation of land and soil is now beginning to really pinch and costs India an estimated 20 percent of its agricultural output every year. And as agriculture becomes unviable, Indian cities have seen an influx of "ecological refugees" leaving rural livelihoods that can no longer support them. At this rate, India will have to import forty million tons of food grain by 2030—that would take us back to where we were in the 1960s, a country riven by shortage, driven by the politics of hunger.

One instance of pollution that has had a particularly ruinous impact on India's economy and its politics has been our coal mines. Across central India, the fly ash generated by India's vast, badly regulated coal manufacturing industry turns the sky the color of rust, and the waste is discarded in the open, creating large areas of barren wasteland. The environmental destruction from coal mining has fanned peasant anger across these regions and aided the rise of the Naxalite movement. Their presence is now strongest in Chhattisgarh, Andhra Pradesh, Orissa, Jharkhand and West Bengal—all states with open coal mines and which together account for 85 percent of India's coal reserves.

These losses in our environment are spreading. As a country that was once Asia's sleepy backwater transforms itself, our cities have become sites of fervid crowds, lines of honking and jammed up traffic and widespread pollution. In the next few decades, our urban population alone will equal Europe's entire population. The size of one continent crammed into India's urban spaces will create intense and unprecedented pressure on natural resources. It is pressure that can potentially break the back of our growing economy.

Laws versus realities

"The problem with our environmental regulations so far," Tushar tells me, "is that they are difficult to enforce and trigger a lot of backlash from different groups." It has not helped that India has often taken a fairly crude approach to such regulation. The government has tended to follow the "outlaw and ban" route when it comes to products that pollute, which, as a result of the massive negative impact on business revenues, paints environmental concerns as the nemesis of markets. The ban on plastic bags in Maharashtra in 2005, for instance, immediately raised the specter of lost jobs in the state, with companies estimating that 100,000 workers in the plastic industry would be affected.

Most scientists lump India and China together while discussing the climate change crisis for developing economies. But the drivers of environmental corrosion are very different for the two countries. China's environmental degradation has taken place within a very lax government policy, and government officials have been quite willing to trade pollution for growth. But as China has become a landscape of copper-red and cobalt-blue rivers, unbreathable air and villages literally disappearing under seas of sludge, the Chinese government has begun to enforce stricter regulations and standards.

In India, however, the challenge is different. India has often been hyped as the more "can-do" economy compared with China—highly entrepreneurial, and one where development has been bottom-up rather than China's top-down, state-directed model. But our strengths are also our flaws. Since state control in India is either weak or counterproductive, state-led environmental policy—such as pollution standards—are notoriously difficult to enforce. For instance, as Sharad says, "We may be adopting the best standards in car emissions now, but these cars quickly become less efficient thanks to fuel adulteration and weaknesses in the maintenance, renewal and routine checks of vehicles."

Even government industrial projects rarely follow the pollution guidelines laid out by the states. Dr. Gulati tells me, "I find the indifferent approach toward these guidelines frankly astonishing." He notes, for instance, that some of India's sanctioned SEZs would build industrial units on India's most fertile farming regions—the Ganga and Yamuna basins. In fact, Indian governments have only grown more lenient with such regulations—the government's environmental impact assessments (EIAs) have been widely inaccurate and off-target in evaluating proposed industry projects, and this has allowed several potentially destructive projects near sensitive ecosystems. For instance, in 2006 the ministry of environment and forests released a clearance for a bauxite mining project in Maharashtra. The EIA report accompanying the clearance contained data from a Russian document on bauxite mining, which had nothing to do with the Indian project. The report mentioned "spruce and birch forests"—neither of which exists in the project's site Ratnagiri nor anywhere else in India.[7]

The apathy has been made worse by the government's reluctance to pass better, much needed environmental laws. Indian environmentalists who work on a wide range of concerns—biodiversity, water, agricultural health, forestry—have pointed out to me that we need specific policies to sustain key natural resources. For instance, Suprabha notes that we need biodiversity policies that promote more sensible cutting and help preserve plant diversity, which is "critical to keep tropical ecosystems from collapsing."

Similarly, our water policies require a complete reorientation. Tushar points out, "As our agriculture has started shifting from grain to fruits and vegetables, it's not quantity of water that matters, but quality and timing."

This means that we have to focus less on seasonal monsoon rains and more on year-round water sources such as groundwater. "We need policies for groundwater recharging, since it is our only long-term water source," Tushar says. "But instead, our five-year plans have consistently focused on canal irrigation projects—which isn't sensible, since the canals dry up in the summer." In the 2008–9 budget, while irrigation received funds of Rs 200 billion overall, groundwater projects were lumped under "minor irrigation" schemes, and the whole program has Rs 8.8 billion earmarked for it.

This problem of policy versus reality was in stark evidence when I visited the deserts of western Rajasthan to survey the projects supported by the Arghyam Foundation, an NGO focused on water issues set up by my wife, Rohini. On the one hand, I saw long, expensively funded canals that the government had built, which were completely dry. But the project I visited had managed to restore a traditional water body from which I watched villagers pull water for their goats, sheep, cattle and camels. The village, which made its living from livestock, was managing both its own and its livestock's water needs from this one water source.

Governments, however, have been unwilling to reconsider our policies around land and water, if it threatens an existing political balance. Even as canal irrigation projects have been largely unsuccessful, our budgets have allocated massive amounts to them. The compulsions to give away power and fertilizer freebies have also remained strong in our state and national budgets.

"The political problem is that if we have a water crisis," Montek says, "giving away free water, the most counterintuitive thing, becomes an even more critical subsidy." The tenacious grip of such policies on our politics is worrying in a country in the heat of development, which is now building, consuming and expanding at a breakneck rate.

A new math for the economy

As Manmohan Singh has often remarked, "our advantages lie in our entrepreneurs," and India can approach our environmental crisis with its greatest strength—the deep power of its markets. Integrating our environment into the economy and creating a cost around these resources will be a step in the right direction, a tip of the hat to the strategy that Anil Agarwal championed.

It dramatically shifts our natural resources from being in permanent conflict with our livelihood—where nature "is constantly driven out, with a pitchfork"[8]—to an approach that, as Sharad notes, "makes nature part of our lived environment—part of our production and consumption system."

Till now, the "calculus of the bootlegger" has prevailed in our natural resources—Indian businesses, for instance, do not pay a cost for environmental losses from industrial emissions or penalties for effluents flowing into water bodies. The consequences of this have been horrendous. The banks of the river Damodar, for instance, present a sight that is now true for many of India's numerous lakes and rivers. This river, which flows through Jharkhand and joins the Hooghly in West Bengal, has more than three hundred coal, iron ore, limestone and mica mines dotting its banks, which draw water from the river and release their effluents back into it, turning its water into a dank sludge. And another big river, the iconic Yamuna, has nearly 3 billion liters of waste poured into it every day from small industries and sewage lines, and is now polluted by effluents to a level 100,000 times above which the water would be considered safe for bathing.

We have to account for such costs of pollution, since without this the market stays uncompetitive for green policies and investments in environmental productivity. An effective way to create a market-driven mechanism for environmental costs is through the pricing of carbon, an idea that Dr. Nicholas Stern recently promoted in his *Stern Review on the Economics of Climate Change*. Using carbon as the major currency bill for environmental costs is useful since carbon generation and loss tend to cycle through the entire natural system—through air, trees, soil and water. Such pricing consequently incorporates the impact of direct carbon sources such as coal plants, as well as indirect sources such as the destruction of carbon "sinks" like forests and water bodies.

Such carbon pricing can only be effective if we have the governance to manage it; else it will go the way of our other environmental regulations. An effective, enforceable pricing mechanism would require an independent, institutional carbon regulator. "A carbon regulator like SEBI," Vinod Khosla says, "would bring in both auditing and transparency, and could form a regional exchange in Asia for carbon trading."

In addition, decentralized governance—empowering towns, cities and villages—would be critical in monitoring carbon projects more effectively. "The politics of environmentalism is most powerful at the local level," Sharad says. "So as we strengthen local governments, we are likely to see much more pressure and interest in managing these resources better." Such decentralization of power would be especially important to enable cities and villages to immediately respond to natural crises, such as the seasonal droughts, floods and storms that are becoming commonplace.

Additionally, embracing clear, ambitious environmental goals that include pollution caps would allow India to influence the terms of the global climate change debate more clearly in its favor. By accepting carbon pricing mechanisms, for instance, India gains the bargaining power to negotiate for transfers of technology and funding for emission cuts. Such negotiations are reasonable on the grounds that the rich nations with their emissions have used up a large part of the emissions "reservoir" since 1850, leading to the potentially massive climate adaptation costs for India.

Probably the biggest advantage for the Indian government in taking up a carbon-pricing policy is that it makes environmental policy a "single issue" challenge. Such a pricing approach would be an overarching policy and would spare the government from having to implement piecemeal environmental laws while wrestling each time with different interest groups and lobbyists. It could also impact our approaches in broader policy issues. For example, India would have found it easier to push through the nuclear deal with the United States if it had had a tax on carbon in place—such a tax would have made alternative energy options more important from both an economic and a business perspective.

Nevertheless, we cannot diminish carbon pricing as a political challenge. Carbon pricing and inclusion of resources such as forests and water bodies into markets are massive changes to make. It would bring up difficult questions of water pricing and subsidies for wet agriculture, all extremely touchy topics. It would also mean changes in India's Forest Act to allow planting, cutting and replanting of forests, more assertive community rights and decentralization of governance at multiple levels.

Additionally, even progressive carbon prices will in the short term create economic upheaval and readjustments. After all, there would be a new cost on resources that we have long come to regard as free, and even as entitlements. It will require firms to invest in capital-intensive technologies and alternative energy sources, as well as in processes such as carbon capture and storage to cut their pollutants.

But there is also a lot we can potentially gain from this, in the innovation that new green standards and investment can unleash, particularly in sectors such as agriculture. Farming in India has remained hugely fragmented—Dr. Gulati tells me, "Our average farm-holding size is tiny, less than two hectares for 80 percent of our farmers"—and remains beholden to age-old, outdated agricultural practices and inefficient cropping methods. Allowing private entrepreneurship in agriculture, such as contract-based agricultural and ecosystem services, in parallel with carbon-pricing systems can shift farmers away from destructive agricultural practices and also create a large, new market for green agribusiness. Interlinking farmers more effectively to markets would also help them directly access carbon markets.

Environmental costs will also force businesses to view and treat pollution as a sign of resource inefficiency.[9] For example, as Suprabha points out, "We have so much metal and recyclable material within our consumer goods. Carbon prices could encourage more intensive recycling of this material, and that could give us big productivity gains."

The fact that markets, under the right policies, can be more effective in using India's natural resources is already visible in the impact of global corporations expanding into the country. Foreign investments in India are rapidly emerging as a source of "green IP" and technology. In the IT industry, exposure to global sustainability practices has pushed Indian IT/BPO companies toward environmentally friendly business approaches. Infosys has been at the forefront of this and has rapidly adopted among the most stringent sustainability standards in the country.

Similarly other industries are also seeing how external competition and foreign investment by companies committed to new, global environmental standards can create headway in India toward better green practices. For example, Wal-Mart's policy to source fish in its retail chains only from sustainable fisheries is impacting fisheries across developing markets. Companies such as Toyota and IKEA are implementing environmental audits across their supply chains and are forcing domestic companies linked into their procurement and distribution processes to adopt green strategies.

If carbon pricing was not already complicated enough—economists are still figuring out how to build a coherent pricing mechanism around the various sources and sinks for carbon—the Indian economy's particular characteristics complicate the picture even more.

"One of the challenges for any kind of environmental pricing," Suprabha says, "is deciding how we should include the communities in India that live on our common land and use these resources." India is struggling with large-scale informal systems in the use of our natural resources, which make mechanisms such as carbon pricing both highly complex and a political minefield. But I think that in this informal sector lie the most enormous positives and potential for carbon pricing. It can be the Midas touch in the politics of environment policy, transforming it into a "common man" approach.

The tribal and peasant communities whose very existence depends on the environment are often ready to risk their lives to protect these resources, as seen in the Chipko, Appiko and Jharkhand movements. These communities have built their livelihoods on cutting and selling grass and firewood, as well as gathering and selling jungle fruits, herbs and honey. A broader group of Indians—a staggering 84 percent of India's poor, rural households—also depends on such "common" land resources for firewood, fodder and grazing their animals, and such land contributes 14 to 25 percent of their income.[10]

On the flip side, such use has led to the degradation of more than two thirds of common land in India. The rapid loss that has taken place across these resources has been the "tragedy of the commons"—resources that do not clearly belong to any individual or a group are likely to be overexploited, since conserving them is in no individual's interest. The result is that everyone competes to destroy. As Manoj Dabas, regional director of the Ashoka Trust for Research in Ecology and Environment, tells me, "There is nothing wrong with tribal communities cutting wood from forests and selling it to the market. The key is keeping the forest sustainable." He points out that older forests need to be cut since they become sources of carbon rather than carbon sinks. "When trees stop growing," he says, "they start exhaling carbon like the rest of us." But India's wandering communities of tribals tend to cut wood both young and old, decimating forests to the point of no return.

Effective solutions for the informal economy can have the same philosophy that carbon-pricing mechanisms embrace—tying the use of resources to responsibility. "Our history is full of instances where these communities defended these natural resources in the face of real threats from the state, especially with the colonial government," Ramachandra Guha says. Providing these communities with more unequivocal rights to these resources can help preserve these environments, as communities turn these common lands into sustainable sources of income. India has already carried out some experimentation in providing rights and responsibilities for forest management to tribals in projects in Siwalik and Midnapore, and through *van panchayats.* Such rights can even be extended to the use of common water resources. Giving fishing communities some rights over the span of water that they use, for example, encourages them to implement sustainable practices in fishing and to monitor the diffuse pollution that comes from homes and businesses onto the waterfront.

Resource rights also give us the chance to integrate these communities into the broader market. Once resource rights are established, rural and tribal communities can earn incomes by participating in carbon cap and trading schemes with businesses and industries. For example, a coal refinery that is releasing smokestack emissions might require a few years to phase out polluting infrastructure and can in the meantime purchase carbon credits through investing in a forest renewal project with a tribal group. Connecting these tribal groups to carbon markets through IT and carbon exchanges (in the same way the NCDEX has connected India's farmers to commodity markets) would bring these communities into our markets in a big way.

It is in these areas that environmental policy can gain a potentially powerful political flavor. It is that rare bird, the kind of economic policy that is both effective and would have immense populist appeal. Business opportunities around the ecosystem strongly favor India's rural, poor and marginal communities, whose livelihoods center on natural resources and processing waste. For example, India's recycling and waste management industry is dominated by microenterprises run by poor communities—Bombay's Dharavi slum has a recycling industry worth $1.3 billion annually. Policies such as carbon taxes in the organized sector would enable businesses to build strong linkages with such informal enterprises to manage recycling and waste reuse activities, and at the same time create new sources of income for these communities.

Some of our most powerful grassroots protests, including the Naxalite insurgency, the Narmada Bachao Andolan and most recently the protests in Singur, have been rooted in disputes for natural resources. All of these were also movements that failed in their negotiations with the states. Despite such powerful local activism, these protests saw little success—in fact, as in Singur, it usually resulted in opportunist politicians exploiting the popular anger, rather than working toward results. I believe the failure of these grassroots protests and concerns is in large part due to the lack of powerful local governance.

The absence of such local authority in India—the kind that is directly accountable and face-to-face with its citizens—has especially made concerns around our natural resources harder to address. As a result we have seen people resort to violent and widespread agitation when the government failed to resolve even the most desperate and essential demands, in providing for water and tillable soil, or limit their abuse. Resource rights will clearly be ineffective without the empowerment that comes with strong local governance.

Right now the absence of these two critical reforms—clear rights to natural resources as well as effective local governance—in India is resulting in more than just widespread environmental abuse. It is enabling corporate–government deals on natural resources that lack oversight and are not being assessed for their environmental impact, such as the mining deals in Orissa and Jharkhand, and it offers little chance of redress for the people living around mine excavations, expanding business zones, logged forests or polluted waters.

Our pricing options: Adapting to change

Dr. Stern is well aware that the *Stern Review* has added significantly to the raucous global debate on carbon pricing and the concerns around "effective mitigation." "There are champions for both cap and trade* and carbon taxes when it comes to environmental pricing," he says, "but I prefer a combination." Taxes and cap and trade policies, he points out, fit snugly into different parts of a sensible policy that would emphasize "reduce, recycle and reuse."

Carbon taxes are particularly effective in pricing environmental impacts in sectors that have a "large number of small emission and pollutant sources." This is typical of the transport sector, as well as commercial establishments.

*A cap and trade system first sets limits on pollution (a cap) and then the emissions allowed within the cap are divided into individual permits. Companies can then trade these permits, as polluters buy "pollution credits" from nonpolluters.

Such taxes can, for example, rapidly push our gas-guzzling transport sector toward favoring more low-emission, high-economy vehicles and would also help drive investments toward exploring alternative fuels and the biofuel promise. Similarly, levies on emissions and waste disposal compel commercial establishments to invest in pollution controls, treatment of effluents and waste management systems.

But as Dr. Stern points out, "Carbon taxes are pretty impractical for businesses whose infrastructure is both locked-in and capital-intensive." For instance, 80 percent of carbon emissions come from sectors in energy and heavy industry whose investments cannot be easily replaced, and flat taxes would amount to a padlock on the door. Cap and trade policies would give these sectors the ability to purchase carbon credits, and thus give them flexibility in "what, where and when" to adopt energy-efficient processes and low-carbon infrastructure.

International markets for cap and trade systems are already in place, and these would allow India some level of plug-and-play, by allowing the country to link its internal carbon market to international ones. The European Union carbon market and the Chicago Climate Exchange (CCX) together trade more than $30 billion worth of carbon. Such an approach also allows developed-market businesses to invest in "emission-reducing projects" such as renewable energy projects in developing countries to offset their emission-creating activities.

This market is still young and, as Anantha notes, snags on a range of issues, such as speculative trading, and has developing country green projects garnering developed markets' carbon credits that are far more than they are actually worth. But fixing these flaws needs the active, focused participation of powerful developing countries like India. "Not having a clear carbon-pricing policy is hurting us in all kinds of ways," Sharad says. For example, he tells me the Indian government has already sanctioned close to six hundred Clean Development Mechanism (CDM) projects, the large majority of which do not carry the expected "green" benefits. "We are rapidly selling off our carbon credits rather than holding onto them to negotiate for more effective green projects," Sharad adds. "For us, it's become an easy revenue source rather than a tool for climate mitigation."

And however deep the shades of green with which we paint Indian markets, we must be conscious of its impact on economic competitiveness.

The lack of sensible policy can quickly kill any good feeling on carbon pricing, especially in a high-growth, developing market such as India. For example, expensive green technology alternatives would mean that carbon taxes would simply be transferred by businesses to consumers, driving up prices. "What we ought to be doing," Shiv tells me, "is negotiating hard on low-cost technology transfers to developing countries. This is where the real fight is, not in carbon caps."

And as Nicholas Stern points out, we will also need regulatory policies that complement carbon pricing mechanisms. Here we can start with the easier but big impact regulations that target the surging footprints of our growing middle class, and nip environmentally unfriendly behavior in the bud. We could have, as Dr. Stern suggests, "higher taxes on energy intensive goods such as air conditioners and polluting vehicles, and zero import tariffs on clean technology products."

Our environmental future

I believe that there lurks a new, potentially transformational idea for economic development within our present environmental challenges. Our presence at the head of the curve in terms of a natural crisis means that we can also lead the curve in solutions and build a low-carbon economy that addresses these challenges. "Fundamentally," Jeffrey Sachs says to me, "we have to revise our view of development versus the environment." Our advantage here is that we do not have the developed world's baggage—India, a latecomer to the game and unencumbered by old, polluting industry practices and infrastructure, has the opportunity to build development solutions that are new, innovative and inclusive.

The challenges we face in environment and energy will only become crises if we choose to let them. These have been called the global challenges of our generation, and taking the lead in addressing it—through adaptation, innovation and more sustainable practices—can give us a profound and long-term economic and political advantage.

Whatever our differences of opinion on the issue of climate change, it is in our strategic self-interest to have a proactive environmental strategy, which combines growth with sustainability. The arguments at Kyoto, Bali, Copenhagen and beyond will decide what a just and equitable global arrangement should be. But India has to face up to its own challenges in adapting to global warming, meeting our energy needs, preserving our forests, cleaning up our cities, addressing soil degradation and restoring water resources that have already reached crisis levels. If we ignore these warnings and eventually see our growth rates tumble as our economy becomes unsustainable, we will have no one to blame but ourselves.

POWER PLAYS

In Search of Our Energy Solutions

DESPITE THE grand optimism inspired by our economic growth, most of us in India have a frequent, often daily, reminder of how much ground our country has yet to cover: the power cut. These hours of darkness are for the large majority of us in both villages and cities—farmers, entrepreneurs, office workers—a routine and telling sign that surging GDP or not India remains a "developing economy." Our story of growth still skips a beat on very fundamental questions of energy supply and sustainability.

"Our energy problem," Vinayak Chatterjee tells me, "is the most significant crisis for India's politics right now." Energy has long been a crick in the neck for our economy, and the politics surrounding it has been convoluted. Ever since the topsy-turvy 1970s—when multiple oil crises almost brought the country to a standstill, fueled widespread anger against the government and helped trigger Indira Gandhi's experiments with populism and authoritarianism—energy has played a near-determining role in our elections. State governments are regularly tossed out because of their inability to provide power, and free electricity is the policy cornerstone of every populist politician.

But over the last two decades, our "energy problem" has gained a new dimension—instead of relatively benign, short-term inefficiency and supply concerns, we are now facing larger questions around the sustainability of our current energy strategy. Our economy has developed a ravenous appetite for energy at a time when conventional energy sources, especially oil, are rapidly diminishing. And with temperatures set to move up in a stubborn, inexorable curve and the global environment in upheaval, it has become increasingly difficult for a large, fast-developing economy to justify pursuing a hydrocarbon-based path to growth.

Our legislators have so far shrugged off the recent massive price volatility in energy, especially in oil. After all there have been warnings of energy crises since the 1970s, and the predictions of frightening scarcities inevitably failed to materialize. These early miscalculations have inured us to short-term energy shortages, and we wait in the expectation that this storm of worry too will pass. But this time round, there are other signs. Oil has touched stratospheric peaks of more than $140 a barrel in 2008 before dipping below $100, and some forecasts are predicting price spikes of $200 toward the end of the decade, validating its title of "black gold" more by the day.

India has, ostrichlike, largely ignored these various challenges around energy. Our focus on coal, our search for oil deals and our insistence on a conventional growth model are all signs of an old-style economy refusing to come to terms with new realities. But as Sharad Lele notes, "It would be economically destructive for India to go all the way up in our oil consumption, and then be forced to come down."

In doing this, we are missing the immense opportunities for new ideas and innovations the changing energy environment offers us. "We have shrugged off our domestic energy issues," Shiv Someshwar tells me. "I get the sense that for now we are pretending the crisis is not there." Overcoming this mind-set, entrenched as it is against change, is our single biggest energy challenge.

A changing template

I manage to catch Dr. R. K. Pachauri in Bangalore just before he is to give a speech on India's climate and energy challenges.

Dr. Pachauri is an expansive, genial man, generous in taking time out to speak to me, despite his packed schedule. He speaks plainly of the energy challenges we face. "When it comes to India's fuel needs," he says, "our biggest challenge may be that we do not have an existing template that we can use."

This fact has yet to dawn on many of India's policy makers, and Dr. Pachauri often finds himself a lone voice in the woods in matters of energy. He believes that India, with still low levels of fuel consumption per capita, has the opportunity to emerge as a country at the forefront of a clean energy revolution. But this is a difficult change to make both in mind-set and in policy, especially considering that for the last two hundred years a carbon-intensive growth path is all that we have known. The carbon-based economy has actively enabled industrialization and economic growth across the world, and right now there is no other model that could take us to the levels of growth we have seen today.

Hydrocarbon-based energy has in fact fundamentally reshaped our modern economic and political structures. For much of our premodern history, wood fuel served as the primary energy source, and agriculture—or traditional hunter-gatherer livelihoods—was the major source of sustenance. As civilizations settled, the inevitable decline of both forests and land as populations grew forced kingdoms to capture more territory to feed their citizens, and war became essential to economic wealth. The "military principle" and growth through empire underpinned the very idea of economic growth—economies were fueled through captured land and captured labor in the form of slaves.

It was the rise of coal-based manufacturing in the West and the Industrial Revolution in England that finally enabled a new era of mechanization, industrial cities and smokestack factories. The role of wood fuel and agriculture became peripheral for the first time in history as the industrial culture shifted economies away from farming, and people flowed in from the rural counties into city factories powered by coal. In the United States, it was George Bissell, a fortune hunter and speculator, who in the late nineteenth century discovered the real value of rock oil at a time, as energy writer and economist Daniel Yergin notes, it was being used as folk medicine to heal wounds and for stomach upsets. From that period, oil grew into an indispensable part of the U.S. economy, enabling the oil-led industrial revolution and the economic rise of the United States through the twentieth century.

Between Europe and the United States, we saw economic growth that for the first time enabled countries to progress toward stable nation-states and embrace the democratic ideals that nineteenth-century European thinkers had imagined but found impossible to achieve. From this perspective, it may have actually been the energy revolutions led by oil and coal, this century's dirty, problematic fuels, that enabled the movement from empire to democratic nation-states.

Since then, the model of fossil-fuel-led industrialization has been replicated around the world, in the postwar rebuilding of Japan, the rise of the East Asian economies and in the emergence of China and India. The oil and coal economy has made industrialization sustainable and has raised our per capita energy consumption to once unimaginable levels, from 20,000 kcal a day preindustrialization to more than 230,000 kcal a day in the industrialized world by the end of the twentieth century. It has driven the increase in world GDP, which has grown to more than fifty times its level in 1900. GDP growth now moves in lockstep with energy use, to the point that "the second law of thermodynamics now trumps the laws of economics." Even our ability to achieve social goals and to effectively create jobs and provide food, health services, housing, education, transportation, communication services and security depends on the availability of energy.* "Energy access now makes all the difference," Shiv points out. "It determines who is poor and who isn't."

Perhaps this is why we have been so reluctant to accept the rapidly changing paradigm of energy. In 150 years—which in history is really nothing more than a blink of an eye, about two human lifetimes—we have seen the ideas of human comfort, economic growth and political institutions radically transformed by fossil-fuel-led industrialization and growth. The price trends around coal and oil are now threatening this setup for the first time in nearly three centuries. And India is facing a challenge that the developed world never did—of driving our growth around an entirely new energy model.

*This relationship is startlingly direct: countries with a human development index (HDI) of above 0.8 use at least 1,000 kgoe (kilogram of oil equivalent; one kgoe approximates 10,000 kcal) in energy per capita, and to reach an HDI of above 0.9, energy use must rise above 2,000 kgoe per capita. India currently uses approximately 520 kgoe per person.

An early search for alternatives

India's venture into coal and oil began early, when exploration for energy started under British rule; generals such as Lord Lansdowne discovered oil in Burma and coal in India's Central Provinces in the late nineteenth century. Most of the well-known British-run trading houses owned collieries in India by 1947, and British India was the major exporter of Indian coal to East Asia and China through the first half of the twentieth century.

India's energy strategy post-1947, however, was complicated by the Indian government linking energy independence with independence from foreign influence and participation in energy policy. Nehru, for instance, was critical of the role of foreign capital in energy policy and wrote of oil's significance in how it "grows and affects imperialist policies." Coal post-independence became fully owned by Indian interests, and the government was remarkably cool in responding to any interests U.S. or British companies expressed in oil exploration.

When independent India imported its oil, it was from Iran's Abadan fields, as the government sought out non-American and non-British energy sources. But with the nationalization of Iran's oil from the 1950s India faced the rising threat of shortages, and the government was forced to invite foreign oil companies such as the U.S. firms Standard-Vacuum Oil and Caltex and Britain's Burmah-Shell to open refineries in India. Many Indian ministers regarded this as a humiliating, crow-eating moment, and the minister of works, mines and production N. V. Gadgil went out of his way to try to soothe ruffled feathers, and promised some distance during the negotiations. "Let us," he said, "use a long spoon while discussing the matter."[1]

For the government, the lack of energy independence was a big blow, and the state, through the 1950s and 1960s, focused more and more on alternative solutions for energy. India approved of and funded ideas such as solar heaters, along with other large-scale energy projects such as hydroelectric dams. In fact the now infamous Narmada project was endorsed by the government as early as the 1940s, but the project got mired in delays thanks to a string of legal disputes within the states. India also focused on nuclear energy projects spearheaded by the charismatic and ebullient physicist Homi

Bhabha, whose efforts resulted in the atomic power plant in Maharashtra in 1969 and a plutonium plant two years later.

But as much of 85 percent of India's energy needs during this period came from "informal sources" such as wood and biogas. The widespread reliance of the Indian poor on collecting wood from forests for fuel meant that India could still get by without massive energy imports. For industrial uses, India primarily depended on its existing collieries. Oil and gas exploration was beyond the Indian government's means, and Nehru had to time and again deny his energy ministers money for exploration.

Overall, India's energy use has been deeply constrained by both costs and resources, and we have followed a highly orthodox policy, trying to get by with what we had. India's primary energy sources were the deep veins of coal across its central states—Bihar, Madhya Pradesh, Orissa and West Bengal. But India's coal strategy in particular was cursed by bad approaches. The government had not interfered with the industry through the 1950s and 1960s, allowing private firms to run the collieries. Nehru had remarked that the government had enough on its hands when it came to public sector responsibilities, and the minister for mines K. D. Malaviya said in 1963, "We want coal, we badly want coal . . . whosoever produces it is most welcome to do it."[2]

But in the 1970s, the industry attracted the attention of ministers in search of a political cause. Mohan Kumaramangalam, the then minister of steel and mines, suggested that the mines were treating workers unfairly, and cited reports from 1937 that profit mining had led to a form of "slaughter mining," where workers were killed in mine accidents across collieries. Critics pointed out that these reports were from a time when the mines were under British control, but nationalization went ahead anyway.

Since then, India's coal industry has been plagued by falling production, low investments and large-scale inefficiencies. Price controls that do not cover the cost of production have given rise to a sizeable mafia in coal, and an intricate, illegal mining and distribution network, where coal is cut by machines and crude pickaxes by the mafiosi and tribals and transported on trucks and bicycles. The large-scale wastage in this sector has also been quite appalling—some mine fires in Bihar have been burning since 1916, and have consumed some thirty-seven million tons of coal while making another two billion tons inaccessible.

Even as inefficiencies pile up, our energy needs are changing fast. More than half of our energy consumption is still powered through domestically produced coal and one third by oil, 70 percent of which is imported.* Since 1991 our thirst for energy has grown relentlessly—our oil consumption has doubled, and our coal intake has surged by more than 75 percent. We have begun to import coal to support our domestic supplies, and by the best guess we will import 95 percent of our oil by 2030. This level of external reliance is especially bad at a time when the world is facing enormous stresses in its oil fields, and some even suggest that owing to the escalating battle for global oil resources, India might actually import less oil in 2012 than it does today. "Our world is becoming more unsettled," Sunil Khilnani tells me, "and with India and China's growing hunger for energy, a lot of the global equations around these resources are being tossed out of the window."

In the heart of the theater for oil

"The Indian government," Dr. James Manor says, "has been terribly unresponsive about addressing growing energy shortages." So far, our politicians have resisted revising utterly counterintuitive energy policies, including fuel subsidies when oil is prohibitively expensive and fertilizer and electricity subsidies that encourage vast energy inefficiencies across our rural sector.

Faced with hugely subsidized domestic prices in conventional energy, our efforts in alternative energy—led by Indian entrepreneurs who are building clean energy technologies, such as Suzlon in wind and Praj in ethanol—are finding their biggest markets abroad. In addition, our lack of standards for clean energy technology in imports, Harish Hande points out, "means that India has become a dumping ground for dirty technology, low-quality LEDs and substandard CFLs."

The trends in the global energy market do not bear out the cheerful optimism of India's energy approach. As oil prices soar, it has become increasingly difficult to access key oil fields, and major oil and gas fields—especially in Latin America and Russia—are facing risks of being nationalized. The Middle East, from which we obtain 50 percent of our oil, is in a state of political uncertainty.

*India spends 46 percent of its export earnings on oil imports.

The crisis has forced both China and India to diversify supply sources, a move complicated in an already locked-in energy market where major oil sources are with the first movers, the United States and Europe. This search for new energy sources is exposing India to political risks from unstable nations, and competition with China is limiting our successes among the suppliers that remain—as when PetroChina signed a deal with Burma in late 2005 to build a gas pipeline, interrupting a long-negotiated Burma–Bangladesh–India pipeline project.

This scramble for energy is having wide-ranging repercussions on India's foreign policy overall. Our energy concerns now deeply influence our positions toward Burma and Iran, with India taking stances that essentially condone human rights violations, such as the atrocities against the Burmese monks. Fraternizing with these countries can undermine India's broader geopolitical ties and its record as a democratic nation, and potentially hurt our efforts to become a "bridge nation" between countries in the West and the East.*

Mainstreaming our energy policy

"Countries like India," Daniel says, "are still building new infrastructure and expanding their industries and have the chance to shape new models of energy use. But it's not an easy challenge."

Currently there is little clarity in India's ideas for energy, outside the somewhat sketchy statements made by our ministers in favor of being "economical" in our energy consumption. But we have not yet heard specifics on how we will manage consumption growth while balancing our environmental commitments, as well as the problem of tightening supply.

Even our long-term policy plans around energy—such as our Integrated Energy Policy—have not tackled these fundamental issues head-on. Instead, our energy approach remains complicated by interest groups—such as unions in the energy sector, who have pretty much defined policies in the sector. Our domestic energy industry is dominated by inefficient, entrenched

*Economists have pointed out the link between the presence of huge energy reserves in a country and political instability and human rights abuse. The reason many suggest for this is that countries rich in energy reserves do not need the efforts of its citizens to raise revenue, and consequently such states usually become (and can afford to be) undemocratic.

government-owned monopolies. "The state of India's energy sectors, such as power and coal," Shankar Acharya tells me, "is very similar to our telecom sector in the mid-1980s—plodding, entrenched, highly resistant to reform." It took visionaries such as Sam Pitroda and A. B. Vajpayee to transform telecom, but our energy sector has yet to see its reformers.

This sector also has another weakness, which for Indian reformers is our most intractable policy knot—our massive subsidy economy. Energy subsidies are a big obstacle to efficiency gains as well as to changing energy behavior and popularizing clean energy solutions. They have only worsened what they were meant to solve—widespread energy shortages. In fact the more the shortage, the less successful the subsidy usually is, thanks to the massive "leakages" that occur across our supply chain.

But to be elected, politicians in India must genuflect to the subsidy economy, and the tradition of freebies surrounding energy is a gold standard as a vote-getting campaign promise. While the central government keeps oil and kerosene prices low and the energy sector bleeds under price controls, state governments across India incorporate free power to farmers into their election promises. The BJP in Karnataka, having won the 2008 state elections on a promise of free power, is going to drive the utilities here into even more desperate straits. It is what I would call "run it into the ground, and then stomp on it." The problem is that Karnataka has 1.6 million irrigation pumpsets mainly used by farmers, which account for more than one fourth of the state's electricity consumption. This is a big chunk of lost revenues for the state's electricity companies, which are already, owing to subsidized power, Rs 20 billion in the red.

Finally, in the midst of all our challenges in fuel supply and new environmental standards, we cannot overlook one fact: in a year an Indian on average consumes about one fifteenth the energy the typical American consumes. Thanks to our surging growth, we have nowhere to go but up in our consumption of energy.

Few economies have successfully and rapidly industrialized on a low-carbon energy path. But Dr. Pachauri tells me that this is well within the realm of the possible. "The real challenge," he says, "is being open to exploring new energy solutions."

The entrepreneur in energy: Pushing for cleaner, cheaper, better solutions

In my view one big advantage India has is momentum—in its growth and its inventive private sector—and this can play a critical role in the search for new energy ideas. As Daniel points out, "Businesses are the most responsive in adapting to changing energy markets."

In fact we should not underestimate the ability of industry to respond quickly and effectively to new energy standards and efficiency needs—businesses have done it before. The 1973 oil embargo triggered significant energy efficiencies through new technology across the developed markets, and technological advances enabled dramatic efficiencies in business processes. Energy intensity fell more than 2.5 percent a year between 1972 and 1985.*

The 1973 oil crisis seriously crippled the industries in the United States that were built on cheap oil—chemical, steel, heavy machinery and textile—and sent the world economy careening into a decade of inflation and recession. But it also enabled the rise of new industries in IT, biotechnology and electronics that used a fraction of the energy consumed by old-style, fuel-guzzling businesses.

The crisis clearly had disastrous short-term effects, but it eventually unleashed a level of innovation and new industry forces that transformed the core technologies of our lives. The capabilities of businesses and entrepreneurs to adapt, even in crisis, gives me hope in what energy efficiency standards and a new approach to carbon pricing can trigger among industry—both in short-term savings and in the drive toward energy innovation and change.

In India the trend toward energy efficiency in the private sector has not really been helped by explicit energy incentives and has taken place indirectly and in small steps. Nevertheless, the growing trade linkages between India and the world are compelling Indian companies to adapt to global efficiency and emission standards.

---

*This has also been visible when energy efficiency standards have been imposed on particular industry sectors. For instance, refrigerator efficiency standards imposed in 2002 created models that were 15 to 20 percent more efficient than average, and surplus energy savings allowed manufacturers to introduce additional feature offerings in newer models.

The Indian private sector has already played a prominent role in the search for new energy sources. Montek Singh Ahluwalia tells me, "India's private companies have discovered more gas in the last decade than the government did in the past sixty years." Globally the scent of market opportunity in the low-carbon energy sector is attracting private investment and talent.

Encouraging entrepreneurs to offer energy solutions would also tap into the entrepreneurial capabilities that now exist across India. Roopa Purushothaman tells me that infrastructure, particularly in roads and power, has been the major bottleneck to growth, and it is the momentum of the private sector that is now compensating for it. For example, retail entrepreneurs are moving into both urban and rural markets in a big way, reaching some places before roads and power lines. "You see a mall come up," Roopa says, "before there is a road that leads to it." These retail companies will need energy investments to support their rural supply and cold chains. Private setups for decentralized solar and biofuel-based energy could hotwire the growth of these rural businesses, address energy shortages and accelerate our shift to alternative, long-term energy solutions.

Firms in India are already demonstrating inventiveness in alternative energy solutions. For instance, the company Acme Tele Power has developed a low-cost cooling solution—chemical-gel cooling packs—that replaces air-conditioning for cellular towers in India. Tata BP Solar has implemented solar projects that can power irrigation and lighting systems in rural areas. Harish Hande's SELCO provides small-scale photovoltaic systems such as solar headlamps to the poor, which are funded by microfinance loans. Harish tells me that his solar lamps have greatly helped small markets in rural areas. "A big part of my sales comes from small rural stores that want to stay open after dark," he says. "Night workers such as sewing cooperatives, rose-pickers are all my customers."

It is not just alternative energy that is seeing the benefits of innovation and private investment. Tapping conventional energy sources is quickly growing more efficient and less polluting, thanks to gains made in material sciences and process technologies. Even coal, considered the fuel that "darkens everything it touches," has seen a variety of recent "cleaner coal" technologies that gives hope for reducing the pollution from its use. Plans are already afoot in India for more efficient coal plants funded in part by private enterprise—a coal-gasification plant is being set up in Orissa through a joint venture between Gas Authority of India Ltd (GAIL), Oil and Natural Gas Corporation and Reliance Industries.

Besides coal, our reserves in natural gas—India's most benign hydrocarbon—have been expanding rapidly, and a cleaner energy strategy can in part adopt natural gas as feedstock in the power sector. Krishna Kumar, CEO of Turbo Tech, believes that the role of natural gas is vastly underestimated in India. "If we can build the right infrastructure within the country," Krishna says, "we can leverage the world's global gas resources pretty effectively." Here India has a unique advantage. Carl Pope notes that India sits in the middle of a natural gas triangle, with Iran in the west, Russia in the north and the Indonesian gas fields in the east. In India itself new gas discoveries in the Krishna Godavari basin and in Cochin are quickly driving up our total reserves—Reliance Industries' oil and gas discoveries in parts of the Krishna Godavari basin, it estimates, could supply 40 percent of our domestic production.

Dr. Nicholas Stern thinks that these finds make an ambitious nationally networked gas infrastructure viable. "Encouraging LNG terminals and pipelines on both sides of India and extending the country's gas pipeline should be a core energy strategy," he says. In fact a complex, intricate grid for piped gas is emerging across the country. And once there is a gas grid in place, we will see economies of scale taking over, with CNG networks into homes and into outlets for buses and cars, and more gas-powered plants.

Counting pennies and cents

A huge challenge for India has been our inability to think small-bore in energy, to look at the unfashionable yet highly effective reforms in improving our energy efficiency. "Our ministers are constantly looking for that 'bang' in their energy policies," the CLSA analyst Aniruddha Datta tells me. "So you never see the much-needed plumbing work take place." Efficiency is not a compelling notion politically; it does not induce grand visions of exploration and discovery that are immensely appealing to citizens, or provide fodder to governments for dramatic political rhetoric.

But it is no small spike that India needs in terms of new energy supplies—our power and upstream energy sectors need $766 billion in investment to meet energy demands over the next twenty-five years. For such investment to make sense, we have to tackle the inefficiencies that are now reducing current energy consumption by as much as 60 percent. "Getting more value for every unit of fuel is critical," Daniel says. "If India can build habits of efficiency into the fabric of the economy, and into consumer behavior even as it develops, it can see massive savings."

But negotiating a tough international energy deal is probably a lot easier for the Indian government than implementing efficiency reforms. We recently witnessed how the UPA government managed to push through and sign the India–U.S. nuclear deal, despite the loss of political support from allies and a topsy-turvy period when it seemed that the government would fall. And yet, implementing efficiency reforms is something this government and the previous ones have studiously avoided.

The landscape of India's Coketown* is dominated by the pits of blue-black rubble of India's open-cast coal mines and smoke-belching factories of power stations that consume nearly 80 percent of the mined coal. This is literally the mother lode of India's crisis with energy, and its inefficiencies run wide and deep.

Both the coal mining and power industry in India have illegal groups as major players in the sector who are often well connected with mine managers and state electricity board bureaucrats. Money is skimmed off from state-owned coal companies as well as from power transmission and distribution, where electricity theft is rampant. As a result India's coal excavation, power generation and transmission are almost unique in the world in their inefficiencies. More than 75 percent of the coal is excavated by miners from open-cast mines, which creates coal with high ash content, and productivity in the industry is abysmal, at 20 percent of global averages. The inefficient exploitation of coal reserves and the lack of regulation or standards in mining practices are also sterilizing a part of the existing coal reserves. "Our regulations here are invisible," Suprabha Seshan says, "and it's resulting in resource devastation on a large scale." Additionally, the losses and theft in the adjacent power sector are so vast that more than 40 percent of the energy that finally enters the power grid is lost during transmission and distribution.

The fallout of the crisis in mining and power is that Indians end up paying the highest rate in terms of PPP for energy in the world, and power in

*As Charles Dickens called the polluting, coal-based economy in his novel *Hard Times*.

India costs 40 percent more than global averages. The power that comes at such a steep price is often unreliable—nothing is more familiar to an Indian than a blackout, and what varies across India is only the length of these power outages. In the cities, the usual range of a power outage is one to three hours—the time it takes for your kid, depending on his competency and enthusiasm, to play a neighborhood cricket game while waiting for the electricity (and the television) to return. But in India's small towns and rural areas, outages last as long as eighteen hours at a stretch—we can say that the status quo is power outage interrupted by occasional supply.

Energy efficiencies in power transmission and distribution improve 10 percent simply with better energy auditing and new information systems. But this is chump change next to what can be achieved with broader reforms. India's Electricity Act in 2003 did bring in limited reforms and opened up the power grid to private players. But we desperately need further tough-love policies that address the entire legacy of bad power generation policies—our lumbering, financially sick state boards, the incomplete metering at the end-user level, electricity leakage and unchecked theft.

Importing inefficiencies

People have made much of India's and China's ability to leapfrog in technologies and operational models, which enabled young, emerging economies to adopt the latest models of growth from the developed world. These "late bloomer" economies can choose the shortest paths to development, with the kinks already ironed out. As a consequence the GDP growth of U.S. and European economies during the industrial revolutions of the nineteenth and twentieth centuries fades in comparison with the growth of India and China in the last couple of decades.* The growth of India's software industry is a microcosm of these broader patterns of economic growth. Through the 1990s, India's IT/ITES industry adopted new technologies, work-flow processes and operational standards at an astonishing pace. Within a few years, Indian IT firms had in place the infrastructure that had taken American companies decades to develop. This leapfrogging over older and less efficient

*Britain, for example, led the Industrial Revolution with growth in GDP per head at 1.2 percent a year between 1830 and 1910, which was hailed as "miraculous" at the time.

technology, manufacturing models, infrastructure and regulation has taken place across our industry and has enabled rapid gains in productivity and economic growth.

However, we do have an unfortunate habit of importing *existing* developed market inefficiencies wholesale—by adopting, for instance, energy-intensive manufacturing and operational processes that have persisted since the 1950s and 1960s, when fuel was cheap, reliable and plentiful. The replication of the American highway culture* of "long cars in long lines and great big signs" (with a lot more potholes and other "inefficiencies" thrown in) is just one instance of our adopting an inefficient energy model that in the United States costs an estimated $300 billion every year in energy losses.

Here, as Anantha notes, "We have taken the path of least resistance." Such 1960s-style fuel guzzling has also left its mark on business process and IP transfers into India. Energy savings are not a core focus across Indian businesses. An Indian business—even one with an expensive power generator—is often apathetic toward investments for heat and power recovery in machinery, low-cost electric equipment for consumers and heat-saving materials.

If we have been able to leapfrog inefficient technologies and infrastructure, we ought to do the same with inefficient behaviors. "When tough energy standards have been introduced, they have caught on without much trouble," Albert Hieronimus, head of Robert Bosch in India, tells me. He points out the success of Indian automobiles such as Tata Nano in developing new small-car technologies that meet strict emission standards. "I tell my European counterparts that the next stage of energy efficiency technologies will come from India," he says.

A rule of thumb for efficiency standards is that they should be "tough, but not panic-inducing." Efficiency initiatives should give businesses space and time to react with new products and services. For example, it is well and good to suggest an immediate shift in lighting systems to low-energy compact fluorescent lamps (CFLs), but today these account for less than 30 percent of all bulbs produced. Lighting standards would, therefore, need to be

*The emphasis on private transport was helped by U.S. military policy, and also by the actions of three major energy companies, who created a shell company, the National City Lines, in the 1940s and 1950s. The firm bought up the local mass-transit systems in the United States and tore up the tracks so that no one else could use them. They were later found guilty and fined, but the damage they caused was significant.

phased in to allow the market to shift to low-energy lighting systems. By providing enough time for the market to react to efficiency requirements, businesses also have the opportunity to innovate and experiment toward low-energy technologies.

India has already moved faster than many European and U.S. markets in adopting low-emission fuel standards for transport. Europe and the United States took twenty years to remove lead from gasoline; India did it in four. India is also experimenting with zero-emission technologies and with electric cars such as the Reva. But even with moves toward fuel-efficient, low-emission vehicles, the rate of automobile growth and expansion of road infrastructure in a country of more than a billion people is simply unsustainable.

"The mind-set favoring car ownership," Sharad tells me, "is something we have to limit. But to do that, we have to offer good alternatives." The majority of Indian cities lack mass-transit systems, the most energy-efficient form of travel. This could be a major aspect of our efficiency effort. "Mass transit would suit our cities quite well," Shiv points out. "We have high urban densities, and people in India are extremely sensitive to fuel costs."

Renewing our energy strategy: Renewable energy

"The renewable energy sector is set to have a great time," one analyst tells me. I think this industry is, as I write this, having its very last quiet moments before it takes off and expands into a powerful sector in the next few years. Across global markets, there is a buzz around renewable energy initiatives, and it is attracting significant business interest and investment. But while renewable energy sources have become cheaper and more viable globally, in India they continue to languish in the backroom closet of our energy policy, and these sources—wind, solar and biofuels—account for less than 8 percent of our energy generation.

When I ask Shiv about our alternative energy initiatives, he concurs that India is not even close to realizing its potential. "We have several options in alternative energy," he says, "and these can provide 50 percent of our energy requirements by 2050. Nuclear, solar, wind, hydrogen, biofuels—we should have a multipronged strategy around these."

It is important above all else to keep our options open around energy sources, especially in the light of the various strides made by companies in the field. Nuclear energy, for instance, has gained some much-needed respectability as an alternative source and has lost much of its Chernobyl-era taint. Improved safety technologies and disposal methods have helped revive it as a part of our energy solution. Emerging global deals in nuclear power with France and the United States can increase the share of nuclear energy in India's energy consumption from 3 percent to approximately 9 percent. But again, our debates here have indicated that we have not become serious about our energy alternatives. For instance, while the nuclear deal will allow India to import nuclear fuel at a time when our sole uranium mine is in decline, domestic opposition from India's left parties and the BJP had brought India's international negotiations to a standstill for a long period.

Other renewable energy technologies are quickly ramping up in both cost-effectiveness and energy output. The costs of wind-generated and solar energy, for example, have fallen rapidly in the last five years, to less than Rs 5 per kilowatt-hour (kWh). Moser Baer in India is setting up the world's largest fabrication lab for thin film solar, which would significantly bring down the costs for solar power. The rise of concentrating solar power (CSP) technologies is also creating new potential for electricity generation with both solar photovoltaic and thermal power. As Anantha points out, "The advantages of solar right now are both in the limited space it needs and in its falling costs." A field of 3,600 square kilometers would be enough, for instance, to power India's entire energy requirement, and costs for solar power are coming down rapidly; it is now only 40 percent more expensive than fossil fuel per kWh.

When I meet the venture capitalist Vinod Khosla about the future of such fuels, he tells me that it is just a matter of a decade before alternative sources are competitively priced in comparison to fossil fuel. In India, considering the soaring domestic prices for traditional energy, this time line could be much shorter. Yet, as he notes, "India and China are making very short-term cost–profit decisions when they expand their coal plants at present rates. One coal plant is coming up every three days in China. That's quite staggering."

Vinod notes that carbon pricing would also be a big disincentive for coal and make alternative fuels much more attractive. "The price of one ton of coal is right now less than ten dollars," he says. "CO_2 emissions however will end up costing twenty U.S. dollars a ton, and since one ton of coal generates three tons of CO_2, coal will cost sixty dollars more."

He adds, "My pick for the future is solar thermal."* And he has put his money where his mouth is. Vinod has invested in Ausra, a Silicon Valley solar company that is betting big on solar thermal technologies and is already setting up agreements with U.S. power utilities—including in California—to supply their power. And in the more up-in-the-air group of renewable energy options is hydrogen—the "forever fuel" and the energy revolution's great big hope. This is already being employed in fuel cells as stationary sources of energy, and in an experimental way in cars.

"But a major problem with alternative energy in India," Shiv tells me, "is the reams of red tape around these initiatives." Government regulation has seriously hamstrung the growth of alternative energy. Subsidies toward solar energy have actually served to limit the growth of the market in India, by directing subsidy assistance to the production of solar panels, rather than enabling market entry and investment. Consequently, while India produces large numbers of solar panels with a capacity of 100 megawatts (MW) a year, most of this is exported to Europe, the United States and Japan. In addition, fuel subsidies make hydrocarbon fuels far less expensive than they should be. Only when they are priced properly—and, if required, topped with a carbon tax—will the price of renewable energy look more attractive.

From India's perspective, biofuel remains one of our most promising alternative energy sources, especially for India's rural sector. Besides the rise of second-generation bioenergy crops such as jatropha, switchgrass, sorghum and pongamia, new process technologies have also made it possible to use wood and crop waste for producing ethanol fuel. The current manufacturing cost of ethanol in India is roughly the same as that of petrol and diesel—and this cost can fall further with new technologies. Indian businesses already have the capability for low-cost ethanol production, and companies such as Praj Industries are marketing ethanol technologies in global markets, including Brazil and Europe.

But regulatory constraints are limiting the growth of biofuel, because of the enormous red tape around the transportation of ethanol. Some Indian legislators have objected to removing these restrictions on the argument that bootlegging activities—and the population of wandering drunks—would

*Solar thermal energy (STE) differs from solar photovoltaic in that it converts solar energy first to heat and then to electricity rather than converting it directly. The advantage is that heat can be stored and then used to generate electricity throughout the day.

spiral up. This has significantly limited the growth of a market that could be India's new big growth story.

Our regulations around biofuel are dealing a death blow to a potentially huge market for India. Cultivating biofuel crops presents us with a rare opportunity to not just build a sustainable, more equitable energy strategy, but also create a new momentum in agricultural growth.

A big advantage that India has in biofuels is in land. Recently, new doubts have come up around the carbon friendly nature of biofuel, since clearing land—of forests or scrubs—to plant biofuel crops releases a large number of GHGs into the air and makes them hugely unfriendly in terms of emissions in the overall carbon cycle. In India, however, biofuels can leverage large tracts of wasteland in our central regions, making India's biofuel strategy both low cost and low emissions. In addition, India's focus on second-generation biofuels does not compromise food availability the same way ethanol derived from corn and sugar cane does. But the real potential of biofuels in India emerges when we look at the big picture of India's growth. We can sum up India's economic rise since independence into three growth "revolutions." The first of course was the extraordinary green revolution of the 1960s and 1970s, which drove up agriculture productivity across India's irrigated, river-fed areas. This led to a rapid rise in income predominantly in Punjab, Haryana, Jammu and Kashmir and western Uttar Pradesh.

The second revolution, India's "white revolution," centered on the dairy industry, with the Operation Flood initiative that V. Kurien spearheaded in the 1970s. This triggered a wave of economic growth in Gujarat, Maharashtra, Andhra Pradesh and parts of Uttar Pradesh and made India independent of dairy imports. The third wave of growth that came with India's IT revolution in the postreform period dramatically raised the incomes of India's English-speaking areas—the southern and western states.

But India's economically "sick" central states—eastern Uttar Pradesh, Bihar, Madhya Pradesh and Rajasthan—have remained in the deep pit of poverty precisely because they failed to participate in any of the earlier growth paths, and missed out on all three revolutions.

Dr. Ashok Gulati points out, for instance, that while Bihar has what is probably among the most fertile land in India, "the green revolution petered out before it reached the state." The main concern of the green revolution was food security, and India achieved this once the movement took root in north India. Once India reached that goal and recurrent famine was no longer a threat, state enthusiasm for the initiative waned. As a result the crop technologies and the procurement agencies that had driven the movement did not reach these states. "The Food Corporation of India doesn't even exist in these central states," Ravi Kumar of NCDEX told me. "Our commodity exchange warehouses are the first procurement systems to enter the region."

Renewable energy solutions, however, could be the source of a new economic renaissance for these Indian states. A renewable energy approach turns the weaknesses of these states into strengths—their hot, arid climates are uniquely suitable for wind and solar projects. Their rural economies and vast tracts of land are suited to the large-scale growth of bioenergy crops. As bioenergy crops such as jatropha and switchgrass need very little water and fertilizer and are drought resistant, they are perfect for growing in the arid land of these states. With 7 million hectares of land across the central region, we can realize a potential biofuel production of 7 million tons, which is more than 5 percent of India's total energy needs. The large-scale production of bioenergy crops could also cater to the surging global market for biofuels.

A fairer, better answer

"The big danger," Aniruddha tells me, "is that the Indian economy is coasting on the reforms that we passed years ago." India's economic rise over the last twenty-five years has been remarkable, but our economic success is potentially dangerous in its ability to lull us into a sense of complacency around our more challenging issues.

Beneath the ugly politics that we witness today around energy—both in the global market and domestically—lies a stark rationale: access to energy means access to economic power. In the modern economy, energy has been the currency underlining every economic process and is one of the biggest sources of income inequities. Access to energy services draws a dark line between the people who can participate in economic growth and those who cannot; consequently our unreliable energy services do not just hurt growth, but have intensive, damaging effects on people's lives. "Your life choices change remarkably when that happens," Harish says. "Families in villages, for example, don't send their daughters to school because they have to go out to collect wood for fuel during the day. And as the forest has retreated, what took the grandmother two hours to collect, takes the mother four hours, and the daughter six." This is true for more than two thirds of India's households who still depend entirely on wood fuel—they walk a few miles a day to collect wood for a fire and burn cakes of cow dung in polluting, open stoves. The lack of energy thus entrenches these households further into their poverty and loads the dice against them in accessing economic opportunity. Without electricity and better fuel sources, it becomes near impossible for these people to start a business, access information, or educate and feed their children well.

A shift to diverse energy sources can potentially help us build a more equitable energy model, one far superior to our inefficient, centralized and sparsely connected power grid. Our existing energy infrastructure is something akin to a giant mainframe with dumb terminals. The alternative could be something built on the model of the Internet—a network of energy sources that is democratically decentralized, and where entrepreneurs using their own energy sources can sell surplus energy back to the grid.* Such a grid is particularly suited to the dispersed communities across rural India. As Carl Pope notes, "India is a country tailored for a variety of players rather than a single monopoly." A modular grid would accommodate innovative energy solutions in villages—such as a two-megawatt biofuel plant in a village that supplies local power and also generates revenues by selling surplus power to the grid.† Such a structure offers massive opportunities for entrepreneurship across rural India and would encourage plants powered by biofuel, solar or wind.

But these will not be easy adjustments. Making the Indian economy self-reliant and increasingly carbon neutral in its energy needs will require massive political will. The biggest challenge here, however, is changing our mind-set toward energy and ensuring openness toward new ideas in energy sustainability. For too long, our policies have been hamstrung by a paternalistic approach focused on price controls and energy monopolies that the government sees as essential to its survival. And yet, as Ajay Shah says, "The

*This vision of decentralized energy is hardly a radical one and goes all the way back to Thomas Edison, who strongly favored electricity supply through a decentralized DC network. His DC "micropower" systems failed because the technology was unreliable and expensive. Edison had to watch a couple of his DC plants literally go up in flames before he gave up on the idea.

†I have chaired two committees on IT in the power sector, and the second one recommended having such "Smart Grids" that can deal with distributed generation and multiple renewable sources.

big advantage we have is, ironically, our big gaps in energy supply—our energy infrastructure is not yet fully in place, and this gives us numerous options to explore."

Flipping our weaknesses over

The history of development over the last two hundred years and the rise of industry-led growth across the world were closely entwined with carbon. Energy graphs have shown us how disconcertingly linear the relationship has been between carbon-based energy consumption and economic growth. But this well-worn, reliable model of development now faces the triple challenge of global warming, rising costs and insecure energy supplies.

This means that India has to urgently shift toward a low-carbon energy strategy. Fortunately, the country is blessed with plenty of sun, wind, land and natural gas resources. The economy is at a stage in development where the big investments in energy infrastructure are yet to happen, and the emerging possibilities for distributed green power and for IT-enabled grid intelligence means that we can create a whole new sustainable paradigm of energy generation, distribution and consumption. We have an opportunity here to transform from an energy approach dominated by handouts and shortages to a postcarbon, energy-rich economy. We can move to empowerment and decentralization, from monopolistic, inefficient systems to a market governed by both efficiency standards and carbon pricing, and from subsidies to funds for new technologies and R&D in energy. It is a chance to choose a solution that is not "dirty, insecure and unsafe," but one that is far more democratic and equitable, and which leverages India's greatest strength—the momentum of our human capital and our capacity for bottom-up growth.

THE NETWORK EFFECT

OUR ANSWERS TO our emerging challenges—in technology, health, pensions, environment and energy—depend very much on decentralized approaches, and these will have to come, in part, from the same people who built the *jugaad. Jugaad*, which means "everything put together," quick-fix and improvised, is the name of the vehicle that people in many parts of rural north India use to travel. This "car" is a brilliant improvisation, nailed together from whatever parts rural mechanics can get their hands on. Its bottom is a floor made out of waste wood pieces, built over four wheels and a chassis, and over which, if you are lucky, you will have benches. The small engine that runs it is usually cranked up by hand, and a gear box keeps it from careening off the road. They are illegal, of course, and so they tend to ply far from the cities. And for its cost—averaging less than Rs 20,000—the vehicle is a steal.

Effective, innovative policies will depend on harnessing this ability of people at the local level to take charge and innovate. Our health approach will need hub-and-spoke models that empower workers down to the village level; our pensions systems will need local networks to reach unorganized and casual labor; our environment and energy solutions will have to rope in our tribal and village communities to be truly effective. I believe such approaches are uniquely suited to India, with its untapped pool of local, entrepreneurial and innovative talent. But implementing these solutions will put to test our ability to effectively balance our short-term, populist demands, our growing civil society concerns and the state's capacity to frame a long-term, regulatory vision for growth.

Implementing the right kind of policies here would also give us an enormous advantage over economies that are still working with more inefficient legacy models. But if we fail to anticipate and address these challenges, our present impressive growth will turn out to be a pyrrhic victory, as our prosperity comes with environmental and human capital costs that are too high to bear. Our answers here will determine whether in the long run the Indian economy turns out to be a comet in the sky, or a star.

CONCLUSION

The Awakened Country

IN THE 1960S an Indian bureaucrat put the blame for the country's economic failures on our climate, which he said exhausted us and made us incapable of working. "Our people are frail," he lamented. As it turned out, nothing could have been further from the truth. It is precisely India's strength in human capital that has spurred our economic transformation since the 1980s, even as we battled daunting infrastructure challenges, capital inefficiencies and land shortages.

I remember Sam Pitroda telling me that between the time he left India and came back, thirteen years later, in 2004, it had turned into a different country. "I left a little after Rajiv Gandhi was killed," he said. "I had liked him a great deal, and I lost heart when it happened." When he returned, he was astonished. In the decade that he had missed, entrepreneurs, civil activists and reformists in the government had remade India's identity. "So much had changed, especially our sense of confidence," said Sam. "There was this new belief among people that they could be successful and that there were opportunities here for the taking."

Freed from the oppressive weight of the control raj, India has revealed itself to be a keen, chaotic and incredibly entrepreneurial economy. And entrepreneurship here has been as much about Tata, Reliance Industries and Ranbaxy, with their global focus and markets, as about the small businessperson setting up her vegetable stall in a street corner, all her savings invested in her dream of achieving success. This is what is unique about the Indian growth story. A people-driven transformation of a country holds a particular power; it is irreversible. As Shankar Acharya said to me, "You can't bottle up India's economy again. No matter the uncertainties and challenges of our growth, the Indian people are not going to cede the economic ground they have gained back to the state."

Where the power lies

During my research for this book, I would occasionally run into economists or analysts who argued that India, in retrospect, had not done all that badly even in the first decades after independence. They pointed to the early growth numbers of the 1950s as proof and to our healthy GDP in the non-crisis years. But looking back, it is clear that the difference between the periods before and after the mid-1980s is not about the average GDP. The problems of our past lay in the sudden, sharp slide in our growth rates every time the country faced a crisis—the death of a political leader, for instance, or a spike in oil prices. Each such slump was a failure of our state-controlled economy, which tried to direct the traffic of capital and labor into areas that our governments and planners judged essential.

No plan in India, however visionary, was able to achieve what bottom-up economic power and initiative have enabled in the last two decades. Instead, it was Indian citizens who embraced new ideas for development and became the main impetus of our trajectory toward sustained growth. Since the time people were allowed to make the majority of decisions on investment and enterprise, India's markets have followed economic demand quite naturally, encouraging innovation and diversity and limiting the kind of bad decisions that dominated our first forty years and led to chronic shortages and emergency aid.

Indian firms, big and small, are innovating in business models and in products in a way that will have a greater impact on economic growth than routine increases in capital and labor utilization. For instance, the inexpensive solar lamps SELCO offers people in villages without electricity help shops to stay open longer and children to study after sundown. The community

IT kiosks that businesses have opened in villages are becoming a way for people in the countryside to connect to India's urban markets. The manner in which businesses are targeting consumers—with the Tata Nano car as well as the Honda City and Blackberrys and hundred-rupee mobile phones, one-rupee shampoo packets as well as high-end consumer products—points to a market that is expanding and touching an incredibly broad base of Indians.

The diversity in our markets has spilled over into the realm of ideas. V. S. Naipaul once described Indians as "a people grown barbarous, indifferent and self-wounding." We appalled him. Today, even that famously provocative, curmudgeonly uncle has revised his opinion. Ordinary people now have more influence than ever before in shaping Indian attitudes toward a variety of issues—from infrastructure and the nature of our cities to our education system and the role of the English language. In this sense, the impact of India's reforms process has not been limited to the economic sphere alone. Its language has been a much broader one, of empowerment.

Indians are now keenly following and participating in a variety of debates, and we are arguing about markets, politics and governance in a manner I have never seen before. Our discussions have become not just spontaneous but—and there is no other word for it—raucous. An explosion of new media has accompanied this urge for public analysis and debate, and we now have more than two hundred television channels, with more than forty channels for news alone. We are a country with a vibrant public square lit up by camera flashbulbs, our chatter caught by a blur of microphones.

The most encouraging fact is that change is spreading across the country and reaching villages and small towns. Sriram Raghavan and Debashish Mitra describe their encounters in rural India with parents who encourage their daughters to learn English and farmers who have linked up with export markets. Such villages may for now still be in a minority, but it marks a remarkable shift from the Indian village of the past, a place that was allowed to wallow in a timeless, romanticized poverty. As Jaideep Sahni tells me, many of our most talented youngsters are now coming from these once-forgotten parts of India. "These people are more ambitious and willing to work very hard to get where they want to be." Drawing a cricket parallel—which any two Indians engaged in a long conversation are eventually likely to do—he says, "These places have brought us players like Mahendra Singh Dhoni and

Irfan Pathan, who are far more aggressive and competitive compared to the old guard. They are hungrier for success."

The rise of the middle class is driving a demand for transparency in local administration, rule of law and better infrastructure. It has also triggered the growth of a vibrant NGO sector concerned with issues ranging from health and literacy to human rights and rural employment. Since the mid-1980s, this group has become a powerful voice that serves as an effective counterpoint for both business and government. Madhav Chavan of Pratham, for instance, has drawn attention to India's problems with its schools and triggered shifts in public policy toward education. Vijay Mahajan and Al Fernandez helped bring microfinance to the attention of our governments and big banks. Ramesh Ramanathan of Janaagraha has highlighted the flaws in our urban planning and policy. The reports of these organizations—such as the State of the Environment report of the Center for Science and Environment and Pratham's Annual Survey of Education Report—have greater credibility than government reports.

Individual activists have also become influential, thanks to media coverage and their efforts to enforce citizen rights through the courts. Medha Patkar's protests against large dam projects have helped raise awareness around the displacement and environmental damage they cause. Aruna Roy's efforts were key to the passing of the revolutionary Right to Information Act. And Jean Dreze has helped empower people in our villages through the National Rural Employment Guarantee Act.

We are closer today than we have ever been to a truly effective "deliberative democracy," where individuals and groups across the country are chipping away at the once absolute power of the state. We are shifting away from the "cathedral model" of growth, with its closed, top-down influence, to the "bazaar model"—an open-source model of development.

The transformation in people's outlook and expectations is most evident in how quickly the trend of anti-incumbency has caught on in India since 1980. "Eighty percent of our elected, incumbent governments," Yogendra Yadav tells me, "now get voted out of power." This anti-incumbency trend is a sign that people are ahead of their leaders in demanding a better pace of change. They expect their governments to provide answers to the daily economic challenges they face, and though the old compulsions of caste and region still inform our politics an increasing number of people are voting for material improvement, for better lives.

Safeguarding our future

Many with whom I have shared my thoughts on India's future are skeptical about the promise of our new ideas. They believe that politics will derail these positive shifts and that things are just as likely to get worse in the coming years. They tell me my optimism ignores the numerous risks and pitfalls on the road ahead. But my own experience at Infosys has been that when we start thinking of solutions in terms of the future, rather than just the present or our past, it unlocks the imagination and energizes people. So far, we have limited our arguments and debates to day-to-day agendas. But if we look at the Indian promise today—the combination of universal suffrage, rapid economic growth and a new politics defined by historically oppressed groups—it is clear that we are in the throes of a heady, uplifting opportunity. It offers us a real chance to address our massive income inequalities and challenges in job creation within the next few decades. But to get there, we will require the courage and optimism to embrace good ideas and not remain imprisoned by bad ones.

Of course, winning people over to an idea and making it popular is only half the battle. Over the last few decades, Indians embraced the ideas of education, entrepreneurship, globalization and urbanization because they saw them as keys to a better life. But eventually—once the rhetoric is done, the policy analysts have wrapped up their blueprints and the politicians have finished their pitches—people will continue to embrace certain ideas and policies only if, as Isaiah Berlin wrote so clearly and simply, "they believe that these will bring them happiness." If these ideas fail to deliver what they promise, they will just as quickly lose favor.

For instance, if the fruits of globalization do not reach a vast number of our people, the political backlash will overrule its intellectually argued benefits. It is not enough to enact reforms; we must implement them well, or else India's time as a dynamic, growing economy will pass quickly, as more and more people are shut out of the dream and promise of growth.

Implementation, sadly, has long been India's weak spot, especially where government responsibility is divided and where issues end up orphaned, owned by no one. Primary education, where the onus is shared by the central, state and local governments, has been a regular victim of budget cuts thanks to straitened funds on every side and a refusal by any of the governments to take complete charge and responsibility. Infrastructure, spread across multiple ministries at the center, has long lacked a cohesive vision, as well as budget priority. And when new ideas have challenged existing political equations, such as efforts aimed at empowering local government, it has led to the ouster of reformist ministers and bureaucrats.

India has at various times shown remarkable courage in implementing reform policies, biting the bullet when it had to. Most of our prime ministers have backed policies that transcended opinion polls and immediate electoral benefits. But we have also turned the shades down, ignoring flaws in some of our most critical issues—such as in our education systems, land and labor regulations, and in the quality of our welfare systems and delivery models. These concerns now loom large over us, affecting our ability to execute new ideas effectively, challenging the long-term success of our reforms.

Our prereform, but still persistent, perception of the state as the "giver and taker of all" has doomed many of our most urgent policy proposals. I think that the single reform that will change this is bringing direct benefits into our welfare system. With health and education vouchers, citizens can choose between private- and public-sector alternatives. These and similar vouchers for essential commodities will free the poor of the middleman in India's public distribution system and from the tyranny of the bureaucracy. Putting benefits such as cash in the hands of the poor, which would in turn allow them to participate in markets more effectively, can also rid us of the confrontational relationship that now exists between the government and our markets.

An equally urgent and far-reaching reform is that of decentralizing our governance. The difference between the Indian state in imagination and in action has been enormous, and a big reason for this is that an impenetrable bureaucracy protects the elected minister from the often spiky concerns of citizens. Strong and vibrant local governments are the only effective way to address citizens' concerns directly and effectively, and to give them access to the benefits of technology, the market and globalization. Powerful local governments become especially crucial in the light of our challenges in environmental and natural disasters. If local governments have the authority to take immediate action—evacuating people from flooded areas, providing food and medical care—it can make all the difference between a crisis and a calamity.

Ensuring growth in today's competitive, interactive dynamic also requires us all—our governments and big business, most of all—to commit to transparency and efficiency like never before. This has become particularly critical after we linked ourselves closely with the global market. We need economic and fiscal discipline to manage the trinity of exchange rates, interest rates and free capital movements. And as the private sector expands as the key economic player, the government needs to engage with it more thoroughly in policy making and welfare, instead of building parallel systems—through subsidies, pensions and financial systems—that shut the private sector out.

Our entrepreneurs too have to realize that their role in nation-building and public welfare is critical. Our reforms have distributed not just economic power and the burdens of growth, but also the burdens of equity and development. This is a contract that entrepreneurs have taken up across the world. In the early twentieth century, for example, America's wealthiest entrepreneur and oil tycoon, John Rockefeller, set up the Rockefeller Foundation with more than $235 million in funds, and his charity activities funded schools and hospitals throughout the American South. Together with the Ford Foundation, set up by yet another American entrepreneur, Henry Ford, it also played a significant role in India's green revolution by funding new farming ideas as well as the high-yielding dwarf varieties of wheat and rice. This culture of philanthropy still holds strong in the United States and Europe—the Gates Foundation, funded by Bill and Melinda Gates, has worked toward better health care and school education for the poor around the world. If our entrepreneurs do not similarly put their newfound wealth to socially productive use, their permission to make money can quickly be withdrawn.

It is not as if the idea is entirely new to India. Some of our entrepreneurs have had a rich history of philanthropy, and their contributions have built some of India's most iconic institutions—the Indian Institute of Science, funded by Jamsetji Tata; the Birla Institute of Technology and Science, founded by G. D. Birla; the Mahim Causeway, linking Mahim to Salsette, funded by a donation from Lady Avia Jejeebhoy. These early examples ought to serve as guiding lights for today's Indian entrepreneurs. In a country with vast numbers of poor, this is a necessary investment for sustaining India's growth. It is also, of course, crucial for the widespread acceptance of our reforms.

Running out of time

It is time to recognize that the opening up of India, and granting people economic opportunity and freedom, has been a vital turning point in our history. A mercurial, fast-growing economy such as India's has a very short window for implementing reforms that broaden access to a large group of people—countries grow fastest in these early years and newly opened markets are a source of enormous opportunity. But such expansionary reforms have come to a grinding halt in India, as people stall and question the effectiveness of these policies.

Politicians and economists who opposed reforms first argued that it did not lead to growth or reduce poverty—an argument that could have been made in the jittery early 1990s. But when growth took off and poverty rates fell, it was alleged that much of this growth has been jobless growth. Over the last few years, however, it has become clear that the economy has created millions of jobs, accommodating the many job seekers coming into the city from smaller towns and villages. Job creation has in fact reached the point that it allows economists such as Dr. C. Rangarajan to postulate that "we'll reach full employment by the end of this decade." This for India would be a landmark never seen before—although in the light of the number of India's self-employed, it is also a muted success.

Most recently, the charge of the antireformers has been that with economic growth we are now facing rising inequality. This argument does give me pause. There is no doubt that both liberalization and globalization load the dice in favor of people who are better placed to take advantage of the new opportunities and who have easier access to markets. But this is also a rationale for making the economy *more* open, not less.

Emerging inequalities have been especially evident in India from a regional perspective; even as most of India has taken off with growth, middle India—the BIMARU states—languishes. Here, the emerging demographic dividend comes with a largely illiterate population. The green revolution, the white revolution and the IT revolution have, to a great extent, passed them by. And the politics of revenge has obscured development.

Addressing these rising inequalities in class and region means opening the doors wider and empowering more people to enter the market and benefit from it—this will entail ensuring full literacy, creating a common market so that people can get the best price for their wares, and building better cities and infrastructure to access markets. It will also mean removing the shackles on higher education, which is one of the most potent means of social mobility; enacting the labor reform laws necessary to create large-scale jobs in the industrial sector; and opening up organized retail and revamping supply-chain infrastructure so that farmers have access to better, freer markets.

The challenge now is that many voters, or rather interest groups within our electorate, view the solution to such inequalities as the problem. The policies that would address our challenges in inequality and emancipate our farmers, our illiterate and our rural poor are precisely the ones that are now politically volatile and locked in debate or lost in committee. But without these reforms in place, we will again have a system that promotes the sharing of elite power between a strong state and a dominant business sector at the expense of the large majority. As before, the elite will "close themselves in . . . and close others out."

We are in a new era of speed. Montek Singh Ahluwalia has pointed out that India has moved from a time "when growth was at 3.5 percent every year, while population grew at 2 percent, which meant per capita income doubled every forty-five years." But now, he notes, "a growth of 8 to 9 percent and population growth at less than 1.5 percent means that our per capita incomes are doubling every nine years." Such growth is coupled with rising aspirations and is fueled by media in a country where television sets are quickly becoming ubiquitous. We only have a dim comprehension of what this pace of change means in terms of how we will cope with challenges in our environment, energy, health and infrastructure sectors.

This is why I believe that the only way to push changes through and safeguard our economic future is to create a safety net of ideas. It is imperative to ensure that our ideas transcend political agendas and are endorsed and demanded by a large number of people. If we can do this, we will insure our future against instability, slow growth and inequality.

A politics of hope

India has never been short on dreams. A century ago, Tagore talked about the kind of nation that India should awake to, free of divisions, shaking off its discontents and forever looking outward. Nehru spoke passionately about

India's tryst with destiny. But as an independent country, we have in many ways been through a trial by fire—we have been an unquiet country, prone to demonstrations, rebellions and governments upended by economic woes and assassination. We went through a period in the 1970s when our civil rights were taken away. We struggled through long periods of shortage and crisis, when our economy survived only thanks to emergency shifts in policy and the kindness of others.

We had to ask for aid too many times, and it wounded us, a country that had hoped for so much in 1947 and saw far too little in the ensuing years to sustain hope. This hopelessness tainted our politics, as governments made the same basic promises again and again—food, clothes, shelter—and always failed to deliver. We became a country that to many people seemed apathetic, resigned, our anger at our governments a constant, unchanging factor.

India has always had its share of Cassandras, pessimists who point to the country's deep divides, the feudal nature of our politics and our slowness in reforms to suggest that the country's success remains improbable, difficult to sustain. Time and again India has endured massive turmoil—the wave of bomb blasts across the country in 2008 was only the most recent of terrorist attacks. Our religious divisions have often exploded in violence. The hold of caste over our politics has allowed corrupt legislators to amass power and distribute influence within their own families and community, and the weakness of our coalition governments drives ordinary citizens to despair.

But I still think that after a long and convoluted path, after many a stumble and wrong turn, a different kind of moment seems to be upon us. For the first time, there is a sense of hope across the country, which I believe is universal. There is a momentum for change, evident in the enthusiasm of our younger legislators, the mushrooming of civil society organizations, and activists fighting in the courts for reforms in governance and for the protection of fundamental rights. I agree with Jaideep Sahni that a majority of Indians now believe they can leave their village behind, and there will be something better waiting for them, round the corner, in the next town, in the big city—perhaps even in their village should they return.

As I traveled around India, I realized that this feeling, this intense belief in the future, has not yet infiltrated our governments, and our ministers still talk about the people as masses to be taken care of, as one would tend an ailing patient, rather than as fellow citizens to empower. In our politics, we have yet to tap into our new language of hope. For this to be mirrored in our political institutions it requires us to imagine an India that rests not on the struggles of our past but on the promise and challenges of the future. It requires us to shape systems and policies that give people the ability to travel in search of work, to educate their children and to tap into economic growth, to recognize how fully India is transforming itself. Nehru, in a moment of despair, had once worried, "Are we Indians . . . just carrying on after the manner of the aged, quiescent, devitalised, uncreative, desiring peace and sleep above all else?" India, rediscovered, has proved to be the opposite. It is young, impatient, vital, awake—a country that may finally be coming close to its early promise.

ACKNOWLEDGMENTS

THIS BOOK REALLY BEGAN on a wintry evening in Coonoor, in the Nilgiris in December 2006. Ramachandra Guha, Rohini and I were chatting over hot coffee when Rohini mentioned that I was thinking, very cautiously, about writing a book. Ram, who had been following my various opinion pieces, endorsed the idea and gave me encouragement.

Coincidentally enough, a couple of weeks later I ran into Chiki Sarkar, from one of India's publishing houses, who was generous enough to introduce me to the legendary agent Andrew Wylie. He offered to take me on as a client, and that turned out to be one of the best decisions I made as I began to navigate through the strange new world of book publishing. I eventually decided on Penguin.

As I was contemplating what to do next, I had a serendipitous meeting with the very talented Devi Yesodharan, and over the course of our conversation I asked her to be my research associate on the book. She threw caution to the winds and agreed. Devi is not only enormously gifted, she is a meticulous researcher and a perfectionist. I could not have asked for a better aide and am convinced the book would have been a far inferior product but for her.

Now that I had an agent, a researcher and a publisher, the full enormity of my task dawned on me. My plan of covering eighteen ideas in the book—from entrepreneurship to energy, from schools to single markets and population to pensions—was daunting indeed. In an era when writers were getting more specialized, I was going the other way. I realize now that it was the happy ignorance of an amateur.

I decided that to make up for my inadequacies, I would use my Rolodex to talk to the experts and participants in the great journey of India's transformation. And they were without fail generous with their time, while discussing their work with me and directing me to the right texts. My engineering education had little time for sociology, and I am especially grateful to the wise André Béteille, who explained the intricacies of India's castes and the dramatic changes happening there. I got excellent insights from Atul Kohli at Princeton, Kanchan Chandra at Columbia, Ashutosh Varshney at Michigan, Sunil Khilnani at John Hopkins, James Manor in London, Yogendra Yadav and Pratap Bhanu Mehta in Delhi, and my old Dharwad neighbor Girish Karnad. And Chandrabhan Prasad helped me enormously with his take on our ongoing caste politics.

My knowledge of economics, urbanization and demographics was a little better, but I still needed help. Here my years of attending Davos and other events paid off—I knew people in varied fields, who were very gracious and did not raise their eyebrows at this software entrepreneur on his quixotic mission. Joseph Stiglitz and Jeff Sachs at Columbia were thoughtful and made time for me during their short trips to India; I got wonderful inputs from Douglass North at Washington University, David Bloom and Senthil Mullainathan at Harvard, Kaushik Basu at Cornell, Lord Nicholas Stern at the LSE, Abhijit Banerjee at MIT, Raghuram Rajan at UChicago, Arvind Subramaniam at the Peterson Institute, Dr. Martin Feldstein at NBER, C. Rangarajan, Shankar Acharya, Omkar Goswami, Ashish Bose, O. P. Mathur, Mahesh Rangarajan and Roopa Purushothaman.

It was also important for me to get a global perspective on what was happening in India. Here I am extremely grateful to Ruchir Sharma, as well as Ernesto Zedillo and Nayan Chanda at the Yale Center for the Study of Globalization.

I had gained some understanding of India's challenges in education through my stint on the National Knowledge Commission. Nevertheless I was greatly helped by my NKC colleagues Sam Pitroda and Deepak Nayyar, James Tooley in Hyderabad, Ateeq Ahmed here in Bangalore and Madhav

Chavan and Rukmini Banerjee of Pratham. Govinda Rao helped me enormously with his expert take on single markets, as did Vineet Agarwal with his discussion on the bumps on the way.

Understanding agriculture was another challenge. I am grateful to Ashok Gulati and Tushar Shah for explaining the nuances of agripolicy to me, and Debashish Mitra for throwing light on its promise. As I delved into the complexities of our energy and environment issues, I met and spoke to many people committed to dealing with this enormous challenge—R. K. Pachauri of TERI, Daniel Yergin of CERA, Vinayak Chaterjee of Feedback, the venture capitalist Vinod Khosla and the passionate environmentalists Suprabha Seshan, Carl Pope, Anantha Padmanabhan of Greenpeace, Sharad Lele, Kamal Bawa, Manoj Dabas and Shiv Someshwar.

The story of India is also the tale of talented and committed individuals who have worked behind the scenes as administrators and bureaucrats to create new institutions and solutions. Some of those whom I met in the course of this book and who helped a great deal—C. B. Bhave of NSDL and now at SEBI, Ravi Narain at NSE, the team at NCDEX, Rajiv Chawla, N. Sheshagiri, K. C. Sivaramakrishnan, Parthasarathi Shome, Sudhir Kumar and N. Gopalaswami, the Chief Election Commissioner.

The rise of NGOs has been one of the most exciting features of modern-day India. Some very idealistic people have given their entire lives to make a difference. I am very grateful to Sanjay Bapat for a bird's-eye view, Jean Dreze who was kind enough to talk to me, even though he was as usual doing his work quietly in UP villages, Swati and Ramesh Ramanathan who have been decade-old partners in various kinds of reform initiatives, Trilochan Shastry for letting me have a glimpse into his wonderful efforts on government transparency, and Anil Gupta on his grassroots innovation effort. Srikanth Nadhamuni has been another ally. Gautam Bhardwaj talked to me about our social security challenges, and Vijay Mahajan and Al Fernandez helped me get a handle on microfinance. Dr. Srinath Reddy, Dr. Abhay Bang and Vindi Banga of Unilever were very helpful in explaining the health challenges of India.

This is also a story of first-generation entrepreneurs—Sriram Raghavan of Comat, Harish Hande of SELCO, Captain Gopinath of Air Deccan and Jignesh Shah of Financial Technologies. Manish Sabharwal of Teamlease, Sanjeev Bikhchandani of Naukri.com, Rajendra Hinduja and Rajeev Chandrasekhar. Bhavtosh Vajpayee and Aniruddha Datta of CLSA helped me to get an investment analyst's perspective. Jaideep Sahni and Rama Bijapurkar were perceptive insiders when it came to the aspirations of India's post-1991 generation.

My understanding of the political dimension was considerably enhanced by P. Chidambaram, Yashwant Sinha, Chandrababu Naidu, Praful Patel, Jay Panda and my IIT contemporaries Jairam Ramesh and Sudheendra Kulkarni. The ever courteous L. C. Jain spoke to me about the early idealism of independence.

A lunch meeting at Infosys is as much about the state of the planet and India as about business. The emotional fuel here from day one has been the prospect of changing the world. I am grateful to Narayana Murthy and Mohandas Pai for their insights as they have been at the forefront of so many missions to make a difference. The Infosys directors Kris Gopalakrishnan, S. D. Shibulal, K. Dinesh and Srinath Batni were enormously supportive of my project, as were my other colleagues in the company. They probably view this book as the most benign manifestation of a midlife crisis in the post-CEO phase of my life!

Most of all I want to thank my mentors on this book—Ramachandra Guha, who stayed the course with me and was extraordinarily helpful in spite of violent disagreements on whether it was IIT Bombay or St. Stephen's that won the quiz in Mood Indigo in 1976. Vijay Kelkar, with whom I could bounce around so many ideas, Montek Singh Ahluwalia, who was always gracious with feedback, insights and anecdotes of the Rajiv years. Ajay Shah, another irrepressible reformer, was also very helpful.

I have also had the good fortune of having two of the finest editors in India, Vir Sanghvi and Ram Manohar Reddy, take a look at my manuscript and give me some valuable inputs.

In all I would have talked to more than a hundred people from very different backgrounds. My deep apologies to anyone whose name I may have omitted.

There are also the people who I did not meet at all, but whose work I read during the course of writing this book. Francine Frankel, Baldev Raj Nayar, Zoya Hasan, Shashi Joshi, Paul Brass, Christophe Jaffrelot, Morris Jones and Myron Weiner kept me awake late into the night with their illuminating, beautifully rendered studies on Indian politics. Robert King was a marvel to read on language policy, as was Partha Chatterjee on nationalism and Krishna Kumar and Amrik Singh on education. There are many more to thank, that I wish I had the space for.

Sujata Keshavan of Ray & Keshavan was gracious enough to design the book cover in spite of her really crowded schedule. As usual, her class has come through.

The book has been considerably enhanced by a stellar team of editors around the globe. John Makinson, chairman of Penguin, has been a terrific support. David Davidar in Canada found time for me in spite of his day job at Penguin Canada and his other job of writing novels, the conscientious Vanessa Mobley in Penguin Press USA helped me shape the manuscript for the U.S. reader, William Goodlad in Penguin UK caught what I had missed, and Ravi Singh and Jaishree Ram Mohan at Penguin India burned the midnight oil and never lost their good humor despite all the provocation.

I am very grateful to my mother who at eighty-three is as solicitous about my well-being as when I was a child. My mother-in-law, Mrs. Yamutai Soman, has been a cheerleader for me, and I do hope this book lives up to her expectations.

My boundless thanks to my wife, Rohini. She was unfazed by the chaos of this last year and traveled with me, read my drafts and pointed out the missing links. Her compassion and her work in the social sector made a stunted IIT nerd into a more rounded human being. She and her friends and associates in India's NGOs gave me insights that are usually inaccessible to those of us cocooned in the corporate sector. And my thanks to my children, Janhavi and Nihar, who, despite their skepticism at my forays into different worlds, have been unstinting in their support and love.

NOTES

INTRODUCTION: NOTES FROM AN ACCIDENTAL ENTREPRENEUR

1. Ved Mehta, *Walking the Indian Streets,* Little Brown & Co., 1961.
2. Partha Chatterjee, *The Nation and Its Fragments: Colonial and Post-colonial Histories,* Princeton University Press, 1995.
3. C. A. Bayly, *Indian Society and Remaking of the British Empire,* Cambridge University Press, 1990.
4. Simon Schama, *Citizens,* Knopf, 1989.
5. Arvind Rajagopal, *Politics after Television: Hindu Nationalism and the Reshaping of the Public in India,* Cambridge University Press, 2001.
6. Paul Brass, *Language, Religion and Politics in North India,* Blackpress, 2005.
7. Steven I. Wilkinson, "India: Consociational Theory and Ethnic Violence," in *India and the Politics of Developing Countries: Essays in Memory of Myron Weiner,* edited by Ashutosh Varshney, Sage Publications, 2004.
8. Isaiah Berlin, Henry Hardy and Joshua L. Cherniss, *Political Ideas in the Romantic Age: Their Rise and Influence on Modern Thought,* Princeton University Press, 2006.
9. Bill Gates, Harvard Commencement Speech, June 2007.
10. Claudia Rosett, "The Big Bailout: A Taxpayer Does the Math and Writes a Letter," The Rosett Report, September 2008.
11. "The Sleepy Country," *Time,* September 18, 1964.
12. George C. Marshall, Harvard Commencement Speech, June 1947.

INDIA, BY ITS PEOPLE

1. B. M. Bhatia, *Famines in India,* Konark Publishers, 1985.
2. Asoka Bandarage, *Women, Population and Global Crisis,* Zed Books, 1997.
3. Savitri Thapar, "Family Planning in India," *Population Studies* 17(1), 1963.
4. Ashish Bose, "The Population Puzzle in India," *Economic Development and Cultural Change* 7(3), 1959.
5. Clark D. Moore and David Eldridge, *India: Yesterday and Today,* Bantam Books, 1970.
6. S. Chandrasekhar, "How India Is Tackling Her Population Problem," *Foreign Affairs* 5(2), 1968.
7. Indu Agnihotri, "Endurance of a Malthusian Discourse," Review of *From Population Control to Reproductive Health: Malthusian Arithmetic* by Mohan Rao, *Economic and Political Weekly,* December 2005.
8. Clark D. Moore and David Eldridge, *India: Yesterday and Today,* Bantam Books, 1970.
9. P. N. Dhar, *Indira Gandhi, the "Emergency" and Indian Democracy,* Oxford University Press, 2001.

10. Kai Bird, "Sterilisation in India: Indira Gandhi Uses Force," *The Nation,* June 1976.
11. P. N. Dhar, *Indira Gandhi, the "Emergency" and Indian Democracy,* Oxford University Press, 2001.
12. Margaret Sanger and H. G. Wells, *The Pivot of Civilization in Historical Perspective,* edited by Michael Perry, Inkling Books, 2001.
13. Ibid.
14. Steven Mosher, "China's 25 Year One-child Policy," *The Human Life Review,* Winter, 2006.
15. Ibid.
16. Asoka Bandarage, *Women, Population and Global Crisis,* Zed Books, 1997.
17. Ibid.
18. Julian Simon, *The Ultimate Resource* 2, Princeton University Press, 1998.
19. Charles Dickens, *Sketches by Boz,* Penguin Classics, 1995.
20. S. Pollard, *The Genesis of Modern Management,* 1965, cited in Keith Grint, *The Sociology of Work,* Polity Publishers, 2005.
21. Sunil Amrith, "Political Culture of Health in India: A Historical Perspective," *Economic and Political Weekly,* January 2007.
22. Helen (Hong) Qiao, "Will China Grow Old Before Getting Rich?," in *Goldman Sachs BRICs Report,* 2006.
23. Valerie Hudson and Andrea den Boer, *Bare Branches: The Security Implications of Asia's Surplus Male Population.* BCSIA Studies in International Security, MIT Press, 2004.
24. Myron Weiner and Michael S. Teitelbaum, *Political Demography, Demographic Engineering,* Berghahn Books, 2001.
25. Ibid.
26. Dominic Wilson and Roopa Purushothaman, "Dreaming with BRICs: The Path to 2050," Global Economics Paper No. 99, Goldman Sachs, October 2003.
27. P. N. Mari Bhat, "Demographic Scenario, 2025," Study #S-15, Research Projects on India—2025 conducted by Centre for Policy Research, New Delhi, July 2003.
28. Tim Dyson, "India's Population: The Future," in *Twenty-First Century India: Population, Economy, Human Development, and the Environment,* edited by Tim Dyson, Robert Cassen and Leela Visaria, Oxford University Press, 2004.
29. P. N. Mari Bhat, "Demographic Scenario, 2025," Study #S-15, Research Projects on India—2025 conducted by Centre for Policy Research, New Delhi, July 2003.
30. Dr. R. A. Mashelkar, "Opening Avenues for Growth of IT, i.e. Indian Talent," *Indian Express,* September 2005.

FROM REJECTION TO OPEN ARMS: THE ENTREPRENEUR IN INDIA

1. B. Zachariah, *Nehru,* Routledge Historical Biographies, Routledge, 2004.
2. David C. Engerman, "Modernization from the Other Shore: American Observers and the Costs of Soviet Economic Development," *The American Historical Review,* April 2000.
3. Adam Smith, *An Inquiry into the Nature and Causes of the Wealth of Nations,* Random House, 2003.
4. Tariq Ali, *The Nehrus and the Gandhis,* Pan Books, 1985.
5. Vivek Chibber, *Locked in Place: State-Building and Late Industrialization in India,* Princeton University Press, 1965.
6. Ibid.
7. Ibid.
8. Ibid.
9. Ramachandra Guha, *India after Gandhi,* Picador India, 2007.
10. Baldev Raj Nayar, *India's Mixed Economy: The Role of Ideology and Interest in Its Development,* Popular Prakashan Books, 1989.
11. Ibid.
12. Ibid.
13. Ibid.
14. Sudipta Kaviraj, "A Critique of the Passive Revolution," *Economic and Political Weekly,* November 1988.
15. Baldev Raj Nayar, *India's Mixed Economy: The Role of Ideology and Interest in Its Development,* Popular Prakashan Books, 1989.

16. Rahul Mukherji, "India's Aborted Liberation," Pacific Affairs 73, 2000.
17. Ramachandra Guha, *India after Gandhi*, Picador India, 2007.
18. Balraj Puri, "A Fuller View of the Emergency," *Economic and Political Weekly,* July 1995.
19. "Clamor against Liberalisation," *Economic and Political Weekly,* July 1982.
20. Madhu Kishwar, "Extortion Rackets Find Easy Prey among Street Vendors," *India Together,* 2001.

THE PHOENIX TONGUE: THE RISE, FALL AND RISE OF ENGLISH

1. Probal Dasgupta, *The Otherness of English: India's Auntie Tongue Syndrome,* Sage Publications, 1993.
2. Nicholas Ostler, *Empires of the Word: A Language History of the World,* HarperCollins, 2005.
3. Ibid.
4. Ibid.
5. Lawrence James, *Raj: The Making of British India,* Abacus Books, 1997.
6. Stephen Evans, "Macaulay's Minute Revisited: Colonial Language Policy in Nineteenth Century India," *Journal of Multilingual and Multicultural Development,* 23(4) 1997.
7. Ibid.
8. Ibid.
9. Ibid.
10. Robert King, *Nehru and the Language Politics of India,* Oxford University Press, 1998.
11. Badri Raina, "A Note on Language, and the Politics of English in India," in *Rethinking English: Essays in Literature, Language and History,* edited by Swati Joshi, Trianka Books, 1991.
12. Lawrence James, *Raj: The Making of British India,* Abacus Books, 1997.
13. Braj B. Kachru, *Asian Englishes: Beyond the Canon,* University of Washington Press, 2005.
14. Lawrence James, *Raj: The Making of British India,* Abacus Books, 1997.
15. N. Krishnaswamy and Lalitha Krishnaswamy, *The Story of English in India,* Foundation Books, 2006.
16. Percival Spear, *History of India,* Vol. 2, Penguin Books India, 1990.
17. N. Krishnaswamy and Lalitha Krishnaswamy, *The Story of English in India,* Foundation Books, 2006.
18. Aijaz Ahmad, *Theory: Classes, Nations, Literature,* Oxford University Press, 1993.
19. N. Krishnaswamy and Lalitha Krishnaswamy, *The Story of English in India,* Foundation Books, 2006.
20. Robert King, *Nehru and the Language Politics of India,* Oxford University Press, 1998.
21. Ibid.
22. "Out of Babel," *Time,* September 26, 1949.
23. Robert King, *Nehru and the Language of Politics,* Oxford University Press, 1998.
24. Robert L. Hadgrave, Jr, "The Riots in Tamilnad: Problems and Prospects of India's Language Crisis," *Asian Survey,* August 1965.
25. N. Krishnaswamy and Lalitha Krishnaswamy, *The Story of English in India,* Foundation Books, 2006.
26. Vaidehi Ramanathan, *The English–Vernacular Divide: Postcolonial Language Politics and Practice,* Multilingual Matters, 2005.
27. Sunil Raghu, "Gujarat Fuels English Hopes of Many," *Mint,* July 2, 2007.
28. James Tooley and Pauline Dixon, "Private Schools Serving the Poor: A Case Study from India," Reading, CfBT Report, 2003.
29. Braj B. Kachru, *Asian Englishes: Beyond the Canon,* University of Washington Press, 2005.
30. Robet King, *Nehru and the Language of Politics,* Oxford University Press, 1998.
31. Ibid.
32. Robert McCrum, William Cran and Robert MacNeil, *The Story of English,* Penguin Press, 1986.

FROM MANEATERS TO ENABLERS

1. Steven R. Weisman, "The Rajiv Generation," *The New York Times*, 1986.
2. Kenneth Keniston and Deepak Kumar, *IT Experience in India,* Sage Publications, 2004.
3. R. Mukherji, "India's Aborted Liberalization: 1966," *Pacific Affairs,* September 2000.
4. Ibid.
5. Bruce Nussbaum, *The World after Oil: The Shifting Axis of Power and Wealth,* Simon and Schuster, 1983.
6. Balaji Parthasarathy, "Globalizing Information Technology: The Domestic Policy Context for India's Software Production and Exports," *Iterations,* May 2004.

7. Dani Rodrik, Arvind Subramanian and Francesco Trebbi, "Institutions Rule: The Primacy of Institutions over Geography and Integration in Economic Development," National Bureau of Economic Research, Working Papers 9305, 2002.
8. "Leveraging IT Assets," *Economic and Political Weekly,* April 2003.

HOME AND THE WORLD: OUR CHANGING SEASONS

1. E. J. Kahn, Jr, "The Wayward Press," *The New Yorker,* January 1952.
2. Nayan Chanda, *Bound Together: How Traders, Preachers, Adventurers and Warriors Shaped Globalization,* Penguin Books India, 2007.
3. Andre Gunder Frank, *ReOrient: Global Economy in the Asian Age,* University of California Press, 1998.
4. Constituent Assembly Debates, December 11, 1946.
5. Harold Robert Isaacs, *Scratches on Our Minds: American Views of China and India,* M. E. Sharpe Publishers, 1997.
6. "Schoolboys Come of Age," *Time,* April 1966.

THE DEEPENING OF OUR DEMOCRACY

1. Partha Chatterjee, *The Nation and Its Fragments: Colonial and Post-colonial Histories,* Princeton University Press, 1995.
2. Ibid.
3. Ramachandra Guha, *India after Gandhi*, Picador, 2007.
4. R.C. Dutt, *State Enterprises in a Developing Country,* Abhinav Publishers, 1990.
5. Partha Chatterjee, *The Nation and Its Fragments: Colonial and Post-colonial Histories,* Princeton University Press, 1995.
6. Thomas Metcalf, *Ideologies of the Raj,* Cambridge University Press, 1997.
7. James Chiriyankandath, "Democracy under the Raj: Elections and Separate Representation in British India," *Commonwealth and Comparative Politics* 30(1), 1992.
8. James Chiriyankandath, "Democracy under the Raj: Elections and Separate Representation in British India," *Commonwealth and Comparative Politics* 30(1), 1992; Thomas Metcalf, *Ideologies of the Raj,* Cambridge University Press, 1997.
9. Ibid.; David Washbrook, "The Rhetoric of Democracy and Development in Late Colonial India," in *Nationalism, Democracy and Development,* edited by S. Bose and A. Jalal, Oxford University Press, 1998.
10. Shashi Joshi and Bhagwan Josh, *Struggle for Hegemony in India, 1920–1947,* Sage Publications, 1994.
11. James Chiriyankandath, "Democracy under the Raj: Elections and Separate Representation in British India," *Commonwealth and Comparative Politics* 30(1), 1992.
12. Ibid.
13. Ibid.
14. Siba Prasad Nanda, *Economic and Social History of Modern India,* Anmol Publications, 1999.
15. Shashi Joshi and Bhagwan Josh, *Struggle for Hegemony in India, 1920–1947,* Sage Publications, 1994.
16. William Gould, *Hindu Nationalism and the Language of Politics in Late Colonial India,* Cambridge University Press, 2004.
17. Ibid.
18. Shashi Joshi and Bhagwan Josh, *Struggle for Hegemony in India, 1920–1947,* Sage Publications, 1994.
19. Ibid.
20. Gyanendra Pandey, "The Construction of Communalism," cited in Shashi Joshi and Bhagwan Josh, *Struggle for Hegemony in India,* 1920–1947, Sage Publications, 1994.
21. B. D. Dua, "The Prime Minister and the Federal System," in *Nehru to the Nineties,* edited by James Manor, C. Hurst & Co., 1994.
22. Ibid.
23. Atul Kohli, *The Success of India's Democracy,* Cambridge University Press, 2001.
24. Christophe Jaffrelot, "The Politics of OBCs," *Seminar* 549, May 2005.
25. Francine Frankel, *India's Political Economy 1947–77,* Princeton University Press, 1979.
26. Ibid.
27. Baldev Raj Nayar, *Minority Politics in the Punjab,* Princeton University Press, 1966.

28. Sujata Patel and Alice Thorner, *Bombay: Metaphor for Modern India,* Oxford University Press, 1995.
29. Lloyd Rudolph and Susanne Rudolph, *In Pursuit of Lakshmi: The Political Economy of the Indian State,* Chicago University Press, 1987.
30. M. N. Srinivas, "Caste in Modern India," *The Journal of Asian Studies,* August 1957.
31. Baldev Raj Nayar, *India's Mixed Economy: The Role of Ideology and Interest in Its Development,* Popular Prakashan Books, 1989.
32. Mary Katzenstein and Raka Ray, *From State to Market,* Rowman and Littlefield, 2005.
33. Yogendra Yadav, *Understanding the Second Democratic Upsurge,* Oxford University Press, 2000.
34. James Manor, "Making Federalism Work," *Journal of Democracy,* 9(3), July 1998.
35. Sanjaya Baru, "Economic Policy and the Development of Capitalism in India: The Role of Regional Capitalists and Political Parties," in *Transforming India: Social and Political Dynamics of Democracy,* edited by Francine Frankel, Zoya Hasan, Rajeev Bhargava and Balveer Arora, Oxford University Press, 2002.
36. Ibid.
37. Sudipta Kaviraj, "The Imaginary Institution of India," in *Subaltern Studies,* Vol. 7, edited by Partha Chatterjee and Gyanendra Pandey, Oxford University Press, 1992.
38. James Chiriyankandath, "Democracy under the Raj: Elections and Separate Representation in British India," *Commonwealth and Comparative Politics* 30 (1), 1992.
39. Francine Frankel, "Introduction," in *Transforming India: Social and Political Dynamics of Democracy,* edited by Francine Frankel, Zoya Hasan, Rajeev Bhargava and Balveer Arora, Oxford University Press, 2002.
40. M. N. Srinivas, "An Obituary on Caste as a System," *Economic and Political Weekly,* February 2003.

S IS FOR SCHOOLS: THE CHALLENGES IN INDIA'S CLASSROOMS

1. Balachandra Rajan, *Under Western Eyes: India from Milton to Macaulay,* Duke University Press, 1999.
2. Ibid.
3. Krishna Kumar, *Political Agenda of Education,* Sage Publications, 2005.
4. Ibid.
5. Ibid.
6. Ibid.
7. Poromesh Acharya, "Education, Politics and Social Structure," in *Education and the Process of Change,* edited by R. Ghosh and M. Zachariah, Sage Publications, 1987.
8. Constituent Assembly of India, Vol. 7, November 23, 1954.
9. Poromesh Acharya, "Education, Politics and Social Structure," in *Education and the Process of Change,* edited by R. Ghosh and M. Zachariah, Sage Publications, 1987.
10. V. S. Naipaul, *India: A Wounded Civilization,* Penguin Books Ltd, 1979.
11. Amit Varma, "Fund Schooling, Not Schools," *Mint,* September 20, 2007.
12. Krishna Kumar, "Education and Elites in India," in *Education and the Process of Change,* edited by R. Ghosh and M. Zachariah, Sage Publications, 1987.
13. Barbara Harriss, *Child Nutrition and Poverty in South India: Noon Meals in Tamil Nadu,* Sage Publications, 1986.
14. P. R. Panchamukhi, "Universalising Elementary Education in Madhya Pradesh," in *The Economics of Elementary Education in India,* edited by Santosh Mehrotra, Sage Publications and UNICEF, 2006.
15. Geetha Gandhi Kingdon and Mohd Muzammil, "A Political Economy of Education in India," *Economic and Political Weekly,* August 2001.

OUR CHANGING FACES: INDIA IN THE CITY

1. Ajay Mehra, *The Politics of Urban Redevelopment,* Sage Publications, 1991.
2. Ibid.
3. A. N. Murthy Rao, *Bengaluru,* Sangra Lalitha Prabandhagulu, 1999.
4. Jan Morris and Simon Winchester, *Stones of Empire: The Buildings of the Raj,* Oxford University Press, 1986.
5. Ibid.
6. Janaki Nair, *The Promise of Metropolis: Bangalore's Twentieth Century,* Oxford University Press, 2005.
7. Awadhendra Sharan, "In the City, out of Place," *Economic and Political Weekly,* November 2006.

8. Michael Foss, *Out of India: A Raj Childhood,* Michael O'Mara Books, 2001.
9. A. K. Dutt, A. G. Noble, G. Venugopal and S. Subbiah, eds, *Challenges to Asian Urbanization in the 21st Century,* GeoJournal Library Series, Springer, 2003.
10. Ramesh Arora, Rajni Goyal, *Indian Public Administration,* Wishwa Prakashan, 1996.
11. Stuart Corbridge, Glyn Williams, Manoj Srivastava and René Véron, *Seeing the State: Governance and Governmentality in India,* Cambridge University Press, 2005.
12. Ramachandra Guha, *India after Gandhi*, Picador India, 2007.
13. Ibid.
14. Ravi Kalia, *Gandhinagar: Building National Identity in Postcolonial India,* Oxford University Press, 2004.
15. Ravi Kalia, "Modernism, Modernization and Post-colonial India: A Reflective Essay," *Planning Perspectives,* April 2006.
16. Ibid.
17. Ashish Bose, *India's Urbanization: 1901–2001,* Institute of Economic Growth, Tata McGraw Hill, 1978.
18. Ananya Roy, *City Requiem, Calcutta: Gender and the Politics of Poverty,* Globalization and Community, Vol. 10, University of Minnesota Press, 2003.
19. Suketu Mehta, *Maximum City: Bombay Lost and Found,* Penguin Books India, 2004.
20. Ramesh Ramanathan, "The Urban Inflection Point," *Janaagraha Times,* May 2007.

THE LONG ROADS HOME

1. Ian J. Kerr, *Railways in Modern India,* Oxford University Press, 2001.
2. Balachandra Rajan, *Under Western Eyes: India from Milton to Macaulay,* Duke University Press, 1999.
3. David Smith, *Hinduism and Modernity,* Wiley-Blackwell Publishers, 2003.
4. Ashish Bose, *India's Urbanization: 1901–2001,* Institute of Economic Growth, Tata McGraw Hill, 1978.
5. Atul Kohli, *State-directed Development,* Cambridge University Press, 2004.
6. Ibid.
7. Kanchan Chandra, "Elections as Auctions," *Seminar* 539, July 2004.
8. Baldev Raj Nayar, *India's Mixed Economy: The Role of Ideology and Interest in Its Development,* Popular Prakashan Books, 1989.
9. Satyanarayana N. Kaladindi and Koshy Varghese, *Project Procurement for Infrastructure Construction,* Morgan and Claypool, 2004.
10. José A. Gómez-Ibáñez, *Regulating Infrastructure: Monopoly, Contracts, and Discretion,* Harvard University Press, 2006.
11. Ibid.
12. Ibid.
13. Steven Wilkinson, "The Politics of Infrastructural Spending in India," University of Chicago, July 2006.
14. "A Long and Winding Road," *Business Week,* March 2007.

ERASING LINES: OUR EMERGING SINGLE MARKET

1. Harish Bhattacharyya, "Federalism and Regionalism in India," Working Paper 27, South Asia Institute, Heidelberg University, 2005.
2. Ibid.
3. Ibid.
4. Paul Brass, "The Strong State and the Fear of Disorder," in *Transforming India: Social and Political Dynamics of Democracy,* edited by Francine Frankel, Zoya Hasan, Rajeev Bhargava and Balveer Arora, Oxford University Press, 2002.
5. Ibid.
6. Harish Bhattacharyya, "Federalism and Regionalism in India," Working Paper 27, South Asia Institute, Heidelberg University, 2005.
7. M. Govinda Rao and Nirvikar Singh, *The Political Economy of Federalism in India,* Oxford University Press, 2005.
8. Ibid.

9. Ibid.
10. Nirvikar Singh and T. N. Srinivasan, "Federalism and Economic Development in India: An Assessment," UCSC Economics Department Working Paper, October 2006.
11. Ibid.
12. Shankar Acharya, "Thirty Years of Tax Reform in India," *Economic and Political Weekly,* May 2005.
13. M. Govinda Rao and Nirvikar Singh, *The Political Economy of Federalism in India,* Oxford University Press, 2005; Devesh Kapur and Pratap Bhanu Mehta, "The Indian Parliament as an Institution of Accountability," UNRISD Program Paper no. 23, January 2006.
14. Aseema Sinha, *The Regional Roots of Developmental Politics in India,* Indiana University Press, 2005.
15. Paul Brass, "The Strong State and the Fear of Disorder," in *Transforming India: Social and Political Dynamics of Democracy,* edited by Francine Frankel, Zoya Hasan, Rajeev Bhargava and Balveer Arora, Oxford University Press, 2002.
16. Jeanie J. Bukowski and Swarna Rajagopalan, *Redistribution of Authority: A Cross-regional Perspective,* Praeger Publishers, 2000.

THE SOUND AND THE FURY: OUR BIGGEST FIGHTS

1. Rajat Ray, "Two Decades of Left Rule," *Seminar,* January 2001.
2. Sukanya Banerjee, "Mercury Rising: India's Looming Red Corridor," *South Asia Monitor,* CSIS, October 2008.
3. Atul Kohli, *Democracy and Discontent,* Cambridge University Press, 1990.
4. Christophe Jaffrelot and Thomas Blom Hansen, *BJP and the Compulsions of Politics in India,* Oxford University Press, 1998.
5. Partha Chatterjee, *The Nation and Its Fragments,* Princeton University Press, 1993.
6. C. A. Bayly, *Indian Society and the Making of the British Empire,* Cambridge University Press, 1990.
7. Shashi Joshi and Bhagwan Josh, *Struggle for Hegemony in India 1920–47,* Sage Publications, 1992.
8. Francine Frankel, "Caste, Land and Dominance in Bihar," in *Dominance and State Power in Modern India,* Vol. 1, edited by Francine Frankel and M.S.A. Rao, Oxford University Press, 1989.
9. Zoya Hasan, "Patterns of Resilience and Change in Uttar Pradesh," in *Dominance and State Power in Modern India,* Vol. 1, edited by Francine Frankel and M.S.A. Rao, Oxford University Press, 1989.
10. Myron Weiner and Ergun Ozbudun, *Competitive Elections in Developing Countries,* Duke University Press, 1987.
11. Zoya Hasan, "Patterns of Resilience and Change in Uttar Pradesh," in *Dominance and State Power in Modern India,* Vol. 1, edited by Francine Frankel and M.S.A. Rao, Oxford University Press, 1989.
12. Francine Frankel, "Caste, Land and Dominance in Bihar," in *Dominance and State Power in Modern India,* Vol. 1, edited by Francine Frankel and M.S.A. Rao, Oxford University Press, 1989.
13. Harish Damodaran, *India's New Capitalists: Castes, Business and Industry in a Modern Nation,* Permanent Black and New India Foundation, 2008.
14. Christophe Jaffrelot and Thomas Blom Hansen, *BJP and the Compulsions of Politics in India,* Oxford University Press, 1998.
15. Surinder S. Jodhka, "Marginalisation of Punjab," *Seminar* 497, January 2001.
16. Morris Jones, *The Government and Politics in India,* Hutchinson University Library, 1967.

JOSTLING FOR JOBS

1. Aaron S. Klieman, "Indira's India: Democracy and Crisis Government," *Political Science Quarterly* 9(2), 1981.
2. Rajnarayan Chandavarkar, *Imperial Power and Popular Politics,* Cambridge University Press, 1998.
3. G. D. Birla, "Industrialization in India," *Annals of the American Academy of Political and Social Science,* May 1944.
4. Moni Ghosh, *Our Struggle: A Short History of Trade Union Movement in TISCO Industry at Jamshedpur,* Das Gupta, 1959.
5. Ranajit Guha and Gayatri Chakravorty Spivak, eds, *Selected Subaltern Studies,* Oxford University Press, 1988.
6. Rajnarayan Chandavarkar, *Imperial Power and Popular Politics,* Cambridge University Press, 1998.
7. Ibid.

8. Bhagwan Josh, *Struggle for Hegemony in India 1920–47,* Sage Publications, 1994.
9. Lloyd Rudolph and Susanne Rudolph, *In Pursuit of Lakshmi: The Political Economy of the Indian State,* Chicago University Press, 1987.
10. Mark Holmstrom, *South Indian Factory Workers,* Cambridge University Press, 1976.
11. Lloyd Rudolph and Susanne Rudolph, *In Pursuit of Lakshmi: The Political Economy of the Indian State,* Chicago University Press, 1987.
12. Rajnarayan Chandavarkar, *Imperial Power and Popular Politics,* Cambridge University Press, 1998.
13. Lloyd Rudolph and Susanne Rudolph, *In Pursuit of Lakshmi: The Political Economy of the Indian State,* Chicago University Press, 1987.
14. Mark Holmstrom, *South Indian Factory Workers,* Cambridge University Press, 1976.
15. Amandeep Sandhu, "Why Unions Fail in Organising India's BPO-ITES Industry," *Economic and Political Weekly,* October 2006.
16. Mark Jacobson, "Mumbai's Shadow City," *National Geographic,* May 2007.

INSTITUTIONS OF SAND: OUR UNIVERSITIES

1. Ritty Lukose, "Private–Public Divides," *Seminar* 494, October 2000.
2. M.V. Mathur, R. K. Arora and M. Sogani, eds, *Indian University System: Revitalization and Reform,* Wiley Eastern Ltd, 1994.
3. André Béteille, "Universities at the Crossroads," Lecture delivered at the Annual Meeting of the Indian Academy of Sciences, Indore, February 2007.
4. Lawrence James, *Raj: The Making of British India,* Abacus Books, 1997.
5. Mia Carter and Barbara Harlow, eds, *Archives of Empire,* Vol. 1, Duke University Press, 2003.
6. Lawrence James, *Raj: The Making of British India,* Abacus Books, 1997.
7. Philip Altbach and Jorge Balan, *World Class Worldwide: Transforming Research Universities in Asia,* JHU Press, 2007.
8. Anu Kumar, "New Lamps for Old Colonial Experiments with Vernacular Education, Pre- and Post-1857," *Economic and Political Weekly,* May 2007.
9. Amrik Singh, *Fifty Years of Higher Education in India,* Sage Publications, 2004.
10. Amrik Singh, *Asking for Trouble: What It Means to Be a Vice-chancellor Today,* Advent Books, 1984
11. P. V. Indiresan, "W(h)ither IITs?," *Seminar* 494, October 2000.
12. Amrik Singh, *Asking for Trouble: What It Means to Be a Vice-chancellor Today,* Advent Books, 1984.
13. Ibid.
14. T. N. Srinivasan, "Information Technology Enabled Services and India's Growth Prospects," *Brookings Trade Forum,* Yale University, 2005.
15. Devesh Kapur and Pratap Bhanu Mehta, "Indian Higher Education Reform: From Half-Baked Socialism to Half-Baked Capitalism," Center for International Development Working Paper No. 108, September 2004.
16. André Béteille, "Universities at the Crossroads," Lecture delivered at the Annual Meeting of the Indian Academy of Sciences, Indore, February 2007.

ICT IN INDIA: FROM BANGALORE ONE TO COUNTRY ONE

1. Sugata Mitra, "Self-Organising Systems in Education," *International Journal of Development Issues* 4, 2005.
2. C. K. Prahalad, *The Fortune at the Bottom of the Period,* Wharton School Publishing, 2004.
3. Simon Szreter, "The Right of Registration: Development, Identity Registration, and Social Security, A Historical Perspective," *World Development* 35, 2007.
4. Jos Mooij, "Smart Governance? Politics in the Policy Process in Andhra Pradesh, India," Working Paper 228, Overseas Development Institute, October 2003.
5. Hernando de Soto, *The Mystery of Capital: Why Capitalism Triumphs in the West and Fails Everywhere Else,* Basic Books, 2003.

CHANGING EPIDEMICS: FROM HUNGER TO HEART DISEASE

1. Katherine Ashenburg, *The Dirt on Clean: An Unsanitized History,* North Point Press, 2007.
2. Mark Harrison, *Public Health in British India,* Cambridge University Press, 1994.

3. David Arnold, *The Tropics and the Traveling Gaze: India, Landscape, and Science, 1800–1856,* University of Washington Press, 2006.
4. Ghanshyam Shah, *Public Health and Urban Development: The Plague in Surat,* Sage Publications, 1997.
5. Mark Harrison, *Public Health in British India,* Cambridge University Press, 1994.
6. Ira Klein, "Plague, Policy and Popular Unrest in British India," *Modern Asian Studies,* November 1988.
7. Mark Harrison, *Public Health in British India,* Cambridge University Press, 1994.
8. A. K. Shiva Kumar, "Poverty and Human Development in India: Getting Priorities Right," in *Human Development Report,* UNDP, 1996.
9. Sunil Amrith, "Rockefeller Foundation and Postwar Public Health in India," Rockefeller Archives.
10. Sunil Amrith, "Political Culture of Health in India," *Economic and Political Weekly,* January 2007.
11. Constituent Assembly Debates, Vol. 9, September 1949.
12. Sunil Amrith, "Political Culture of Health in India," *Economic and Political Weekly,* January 2007.
13. Constituent Assembly Debates, Vol. 9, September 1949.
14. A. K. Shiva Kumar, "Poverty and Human Development in India: Getting Priorities Right," in *Human Development Report,* UNDP, 1996.
15. National Health Policy, GOI 2002, cited in Mohan Rao, *From Population Control to Reproductive Health,* Sage Publications, 2004.
16. Sunil Amrith, "Political Culture of Health in India," *Economic and Political Weekly,* January 2007.
17. Ibid.

OUR SOCIAL INSECURITIES: THE MISSING DEMOGRAPHIC

1. Lawrence Cohen, *No Aging in India: Alzheimer's, the Bad Family, and Other Modern Things,* University of California Press, 1998.
2. Sarah Lamb, *White Saris and Sweet Mangoes: Aging, Gender and Body in North India,* University of California Press, 2000.
3. Lawrence Cohen, *No Aging in India: Alzheimer's, the Bad Family, and Other Modern Things,* University of California Press, 1998.
4. Fred Pampel and John Williamson, *Old Age Security in Comparative Perspective,* Oxford University Press, 1993.
5. Ibid.
6. Sarita Ravindranath, "Sans Everything . . . but Not sans Rights," *Statesman,* 1997, cited in Sarah Lamb, *White Saris and Sweet Mangoes: Aging, Gender and Body in North India,* University of California Press, 2000.
7. Lawrence Cohen, *No Aging in India: Alzheimer's, the Bad Family, and Other Modern Things,* University of California Press, 1998.
8. Baba Adhav, "Some Reflections," *Seminar* 568, December 2006.

THE FOREST FOR THE TREES: INDIA'S ENVIRONMENT CHALLENGE

1. Sumit Guha, *Environment and Ethnicity in India, 1200–1991,* Cambridge Studies in Indian History and Society, Cambridge University Press, 2006.
2. Ibid.
3. F. R. Shtil'mark, "The Evolution of Concepts about the Preservation of Nature in Soviet Literature," *Journal of the History of Biology,* September 1992.
4. Judith Shapiro, *Mao's War against Nature: Politics and the Environment in Revolutionary China,* Cambridge University Press, 2001.
5. Sumit Guha, *Environment and Ethnicity in India, 1200–1991,* Cambridge Studies in Indian History and Society, Cambridge University Press, 2006.
6. T. S. Eliot, *The Waste Land,* Penguin Classics, 1998.
7. Padmaparna Ghosh, "Are the Govt's Green Clearances a Farce?," *Mint,* December 27, 2007.
8. Mahesh Rangarajan, *Out in the Wild: Environmental Issues in India,* Pearson Longman, 2007.
9. Stephan Schmidheiny, *Changing Course: A Global Business Perspective on Development and the Environment,* MIT Press, 1992.

10. N. S. Jodha, "Rural Common Property Resources: Contributions and Crisis," *Economic and Political Weekly*, June 1990.

POWER PLAYS: IN SEARCH OF OUR ENERGY SOLUTIONS

1. Hriday Nath Kaul, *K. D. Malaviya and the Evolution of India's Oil Policy*, Allied Publishers, 1991.
2. Baldev Raj Nayar, *India's Mixed Economy: The Role of Ideology and Interest in Its Development*, Popular Prakashan Books, 1989.

A TIME LINE OF KEY EVENTS

The seeds

1757—The Battle of Plassey, where Robert Clive, commander of the East India Company's army and renegade (he would later be tried in Britain for looting the Bengal treasury) overthrows the Nawab of Bengal. It is a battle won through both money—bribing the Nawab's loyalists—and the military.

1833—In an effort to cut costs, the East India Company's Governor General William Bentick decides to outsource work in the civil service and amends the Charter act to open up posts to Indians.

1835—Macaulay delivers a paint-peeling "Minute" on Indian education, while defending the English-language bill.

1857—Small, dirty piles of chappatis begin to pass from hand to hand at the beginning of the year across British towns and cantonments—a form of chain letter among the Indians, accompanied by a demand to remove the British. Later that year, the army mutiny breaks out against British rule, triggered in part by the British capture of Oudh, a wealthy Mughal kingdom, and by a rumor within the army that the cartridges for the Pattern 1853 Enfield rifle have been coated in animal fat (a notion that was repulsive to both Hindu and Muslim soldiers).

—The British also start their first foray into education in India, opening three large universities. This would have a marked impact—far more than the mutiny—on their ability to maintain hold over the Indian colony.

Baby steps

1885—The Indian National Congress is founded by Allan O. Hume, a British political reformer and avid bird watcher, who had sided with the Indian soldiers during the army mutiny.

—The Bengal Tenancy Act comes into force—the first law that is a wedge into India's feudal system and which gives some rights to the Bengali peasants tilling the land.

1906—The All-India Muslim League is formed, a party that will soon have immense influence on India's path to independence, as the key group favoring partition.

—Morley is appointed Liberal Secretary of State for India. He will push Governor General Minto into providing Indians with their first chance to vote, through a minor elected role in the legislature. But this annoys the Congress party as there is a provision to give reserved seats to Muslims.

1911—Gopal Krishna Gokhale introduces a universal education bill to the imperial council, which fails to pass. The goal of universal education is destined to languish without attention for more than seventy years.

1914—The First World War breaks out and Indian soldiers are sent to fight on the British side.

—M. K. Gandhi, an idealist young lawyer, regarded as eccentric by some and a visionary by others, returns to India from South Africa.

A fresh wave of anger

1919—One step forward for democracy and two steps back:

—The British pass the Montagu-Chelmsford reforms, giving Indians limited self-rule. Also passed is the Rowlatt Act, which gags the Indian media and allows political trials without juries and the holding of suspects without a trial.

—A massacre of ten thousand civilians who had assembled in a peaceful protest against the Rowlatt Act at the Jallianwala Bagh, Amritsar, infuriates Indians, and Congress leaders begin to demand complete independence from British rule. In the years that follow, Jawaharlal Nehru becomes a familiar face as he travels through India recruiting volunteers for the movement.

1920—Gandhi, who until 1919 had supported the British in India and even helped recruit Indian soldiers for the British army, now heads the independence effort. He bursts into the limelight with his quirky yet visionary approaches to protest. Gandhi had read Henry Thoreau's essay on civil disobedience (which Martin Luther King would also study) and he launches the Civil Disobedience Movement in 1920, where civilians defy British laws, court arrest and are led to jails. The jails fill up.

1922—Gandhi calls the movement off when violence breaks out among his protestors, which disappoints many of his supporters as well as Congress party members.

1926—The Trade Union Act gives Indian workers the right to form unions. Strikes grow more intense and more frequent over the next decade.

1929—The Congress declares independence, and raises the tricolor flag in Lahore.

1930—To protest against the extortionary British Salt Act, Gandhi initiates the Salt March to the village of Dandi, which sits on the Gujarat coast. Once at the seashore, he leads protestors in making salt. Sixty thousand protestors are arrested in the following weeks.

1931—Gandhi is invited to the roundtable conference, and he attends in his usual outfit, a loincloth. The British press remark on his "odd appearance, his strange and ascetic ways." The seemingly placatory invitation, however, is a red herring and Viceroy Lord Willingdon unleashes a wave of arrests and repressive measures in India.

But even as Britain strengthens its hold on its Empire, Hitler is on the ascent in Germany, triggering a series of events that leave Europe deeply scarred and Britain weakened.

1935—The British pass the Government of India Act, giving India its first steps toward independence, creating a constitution and elected governments in the provinces. Indian leaders assert that the law does not go far enough. Nehru thunders, "The basic policy of this Congress is to combat the Government of India Act—the new Constitution—and destroy it!"

1937—Congress sweeps most of the province elections.

1939—The British impose war controls, regulating pricing, imports and the use of foreign exchange. Inflation and a black economy explode.

1944—Six prominent Indian businessmen release the Bombay Plan, which endorses a massive role for the state in the Indian economy.

1946—Exhausted by war and its restive colony, Britain offers India independence.

A hopeful but tenuous country

1947—India gains independence after prolonged negotiations involving Hindu and Muslim leaders. The region is partitioned, after widespread violence, into Pakistan, a Muslim majority country, and India.

Independent India is poor and illiterate but led by leaders from its educated, upper middle class.

1948—Gandhi is assassinated. In a key 1948 meeting, in the wake of riots and the assassination, Congress leaders emphasize a centralized government.

1950—India adopts its new Constitution. Despite the determination to start afresh, many ties, its leaders find, cannot be fully severed, starting from the Constitution, which owes a lot to the 1935 Government of India Act.

—Caught in an argument between the north and the south around the proposal to make Hindi the national language, Nehru declares a temporary compromise: English will be used as a co-official language till 1965.

1951—India's first five-year plan begins, prioritizing agriculture and water and power projects. Many war-era economic protections stay on the books.

The Bharatiya Jana Sangh (Indian People's Alliance), the predecessor to the modern-day Bharatiya Janata Party (BJP), forms as the political arm of the Hindu nationalist Rashtriya Swayamsevak Sangh (National Volunteers Organization).

1952—Potti Sriramulu's fast unto death while demanding a separate state for Telugu-speaking people is only the beginning of Delhi's arguments with the states on language boundaries.

1953—A process of land reforms begins, with mixed results—the state laws passed typically have too many loopholes. Eventually only 0.7 percent of land across sixteen states is declared surplus and redistributed.

The government gains new authority to impose interstate taxes, setting off a chain of new regulation that will quickly turn into a snarl.

1957—A decade into independence, things are not as calm as would be hoped. The Bombay riots a year earlier have simmered down, but the country is generally restive. The first opposition government wins—a communist one—in Kerala. India faces its first financial crisis and goes to the United States for a loan.

Simmering tensions notwithstanding, India's budding film industry sees a major hit with the nationalist film *Mother India.*

1962—India loses a border skirmish with China, and China occupies the strategically valuable Aksai Chin. The Chinese attack had coincided with the Cuban missile crisis and the United States suspects a coordinated communist attack. When the United States prepares to intervene, China declares a ceasefire.

The locusts decades

1964—For the government, the crises seem to have arrived all at once. Nehru dies. Crop failure and drought trigger spreading food shortages and rioting threatens to paralyze the country.

1965—Drawing lines in gunpowder: The Indo-Pakistan war to defend Jammu and Kashmir territory against Pakistani troops.

—With the help of the American agronomist Norman Borlaug, Indian scientists develop a crop hybrid that triggers the green revolution and a new era of self-sufficiency.

1966—Indira Gandhi becomes prime minister, primarily because powerful Congress leaders (The Syndicate) want a placeholder on the highest seat while they fight it out for prime minister among themselves.

—Indira proves more difficult to manage than party leaders had hoped. She introduces some reforms, in return for aid promised by the World Bank.

1967—Aid fails to arrive. Opposition politicians sharply criticize government policies. "You sold the country and have not even got the price," a parliamentarian accused the government. Indira Gandhi rolls back reforms.

—The Language Act is amended to make English an associate official language.

—A non-Congress government wins for the first time in Tamil Nadu on an anti–Hindi language wave.

—The government proposes the first of many new restrictions on Indian markets. The Monopolies and Restrictive Trade Practices Act is meant to "keep the concentration of wealth down" by limiting the size of big business.

1969—Indira Gandhi opposes bank nationalization in April, but supports it in July in an early repackaging of herself as a more populist political leader. Her strategy will turn her into a political force to reckon with.

—In an effort to tap into diverse energy sources, India opens its first atomic power plant in Maharashtra.

1971—India's third major skirmish with Pakistan, which results in the independence of East Pakistan.

Uprisings

1973—The global oil crisis. International headlines predict an imminent worldwide famine from overpopulation. In India a drought brings it once again to the brink of famine. Rioting engulfs the country once more.

—The Foreign Exchange Regulation Act is passed by the government, imposing massive restrictions on foreign currency and investment.

1975—The socialist leader Jayaprakash Narayan comes out of retirement to protest against Indira Gandhi's government. Indira announces the Emergency, suspending elections, curbing civil rights, gagging the media and introducing a hugely unpopular sterilization program.

—The movie *Sholay* releases, a rebellious, irreverent film that astonishes its audiences—the halls are entirely silent and no one laughs at the jokes. The young director of the film, Ramesh Sippy, is certain it is a clunker, but *Sholay* goes on to break box-office records.

1976—Indira introduces the Urban Land Ceiling Act, placing a ceiling of five hundred to two thousand square meters on land ownership in urban areas. The government also toughens labor regulations, requiring factories with more than three hundred employees to take government permission before firing anyone.

The crumbling of the old order

1977—The Congress party led by Indira loses the elections for the first time since 1947, and it is a landslide defeat. The prime minister of the Janata coalition government, Morarji Desai, who had been arrested along with other opposition leaders during the Emergency, has Indira Gandhi and her son Sanjay arrested.

—The government asks IBM and Coca-Cola to pack their bags and leave. The industry minister George Fernandes later explains why he threw them out: "Coke had reached India's villages, even those that didn't have drinking water."

1980—The Janata coalition falls apart. A landslide election results, this time in favor of the Congress party.

1983—India wins the Cricket World Cup, turning its team into superstars within the country.

—India adopts a "Health for all" goal by 2000, a date that it will not keep. The date will be notable, however, for the beginning of a growing concern around India's dismal health indicators.

1984—In Punjab, militancy reaches a head. Indira orders Operation Blue Star and troops storm a hideout of militants in the Golden Temple in Amritsar. Several civilians are caught in the crossfire. Four months after the operation, Indira's Sikh bodyguards assassinate her.

—Indira's son Rajiv Gandhi becomes prime minister in the new Congress government. He announces a computer policy that creates incentives for the Indian information technology industry. The government also loosens state controls on Indian business.

—The government announces a National Policy on Education, an early but unsuccessful effort to reform crumbling state schools.

1985—Sam Pitroda's telecom policy gives unprecedented access to telephones in a country with a teledensity well below one.

—India establishes a ministry for urban development. Over the next two decades, this ministry will focus mainly on house allotments for Members of Parliament in Delhi.

—India is anything but peaceful. Sikh militants blow up Air India flight 182 over the Atlantic, killing all passengers. The Indian Parliament passes a controversial new law, the Terrorist and Disruptive Activities (Prevention) Act (TADA).

1986—For the first time, the government attempts to bring in some tax reform and simplifies excise taxes through the MODVAT.

1987—India conducts military exercises along its China and Pakistan borders, and sends forty thousand peacekeeping troops to Sri Lanka to disarm Tamil rebels.

1989—Rajiv Gandhi and the Congress party lose the elections, and the National Front coalition comes to power.

1990—The government gets sandwiched between two major caste/religious flare-ups:

—Large-scale protests erupt, after Prime Minister V. P. Singh pledges to implement the 1980 Mandal Commission report bringing in reservations in colleges and central government jobs.

—Two months later, Hindu nationalist thugs shouting "Hail to Lord Ram!" target the small sixteenth-century Babri Masjid in Ayodhya, which they claim sits on the site of a temple dedicated to Lord Ram. They plant a saffron flag on top of the mosque.

The National Front government falls, after the BJP withdraws support.

The ceding of power: New opportunities and fractures

1991—While campaigning for general elections, Rajiv Gandhi is assassinated by a female suicide bomber linked to Sri Lankan Tamil rebels.

—The Congress wins the election in a sympathy wave, similar to the one that helped Rajiv win in 1984.

To fill the leadership gap, P. V. Narasimha Rao, a seventy-something former minister with a heart problem, is brought out of retirement and becomes the new prime minister.

—Almost immediately, the government faces a foreign-exchange crisis. To bail out the economy, the government pawns twenty tons of its gold for $200 million and sends the rest as collateral for a loan with the Bank of England and the Bank of Japan.

—Finance Minister Manmohan Singh introduces the New Economic Policy, a comprehensive reform plan.

1992—Hindu extremists again target the Babri Masjid. This time they demolish it, as police watch. In the ensuing riots, 1,700 people are killed.

—A $1.6 billion bank securities scam crashes India's Bombay Stock Exchange.

—The government passes the Seventy-second and Seventy-third Amendments to give more power to local governments in cities and villages.

1993—The National Stock Exchange, India's second national exchange, is established.

—The Reserve Bank of India, the central bank, allows private banks into the banking sector for the first time since 1969 and more reforms in the sector will follow through 2000.

—The threat of large-scale Hindu demonstrations forces the Congress government to barricade its ministers behind barbed wire, and arrest 100,000 people.

—Thirteen bomb blasts in India's commercial capital, Bombay, carried out by Muslim mafia, kill more than two hundred people.

1995—India joins the World Trade Organization.

—Mayawati, a Dalit leader, becomes chief minister of Uttar Pradesh.

1996—The Congress party is thumped in the elections, and the BJP attempts to form a government. A. B. Vajpayee becomes prime minister for thirteen days. He loses the House vote, and the United Front (UF), a clunky coalition, comes into power.

1998—The UF government falls after the Congress withdraws its outside support. The BJP and its allies form a government. This time, it lasts a little longer, for seven months. During this period, the government successfully conducts nuclear tests in Pokaran for its bomb.

—Gloom descends: sanctions are imposed on India and a growth slowdown pushes the country close to a second fiscal crisis.

1999—Third-time lucky, the BJP and its thirteen-party coalition come to power without a definite majority of seats, but maintain control. Vajpayee is prime minister once again.

—Vajpayee announces the Golden Quadrilateral project, a cross-country highway to connect India.

—The New Telecom Policy frees up the telecom sector to competition and establishes an independent regulator for the sector.

A new impatience

2000—Vajpayee announces his education-for-all scheme, the Sarva Shiksha Abhiyan.

2001—For the first time in an Indian election, the Election Commission successfully uses electronic voting machines (EVMs) across its voting centers.

2002—Riots in Gujarat lead to widespread killing largely targeted at the Muslim population. It is triggered by the burning of the Sabarmati Express train returning from Ayodhya; the fire kills fifty-eight people.

—Finance Minister Yashwant Sinha sets up an Empowered Committee of Chief Ministers toward implementing a value added tax (VAT) system. State governments regard the idea coolly—there is no consensus and everyone is certain it will fail.

2003—The government passes the Fiscal Responsibility Act, to curb soaring deficits.

2004—The NDA government notifies central government employees on including them in the National Pensions Scheme, which brings new reforms into social security.

—The Congress comes back to power while expecting to lose. The United Progressive Alliance (UPA) coalition they lead is one of unexpected bedfellows and includes outside support from the communists.

—West Bengal reverses its twenty-seven-year-old stance against using English as the language of instruction in primary schools.

2005—The government launches the Jawaharlal Nehru Urban Renewal Mission (JNNURM) to address the infrastructure and governance crisis of India's cities.

2006—The government passes the National Rural Employment Guarantee Act (NREGA).

—The government also passes the Other Backward Castes (OBC) quota bill, which provides 27 percent reservation of seats for these castes in center-aided institutes.

—India and the United States sign a nuclear deal for civilian fuel supply, with India opening its nuclear sites to inspection.

2007—At the G8 meeting, Manmohan Singh emphasizes "common but differentiated responsibility" for India when it comes to controlling carbon emissions.

2008—The first state elections are held after the Delimitation Commission gives a greater share of legislative seats to the cities, on the basis of shifting demographics.

—The UPA coalition teeters, but does not fall. The government swaps support from the left with Uttar Pradesh's Samajwadi Party as the proposed India–U.S. nuclear deal becomes a deal-breaker for the former.

INDEX